MAL COUCH, GEN. ED.

THE GATHERING STORM

UNDERSTANDING PROPHECY IN CRITICAL TIMES

Kerby Anderson • Paul N. Benware • Mal Couch • Arnold Fruchtenbaum
Steven Charles Ger • George Gunn • Dave Hunt • Thomas Ice
Manfred Kober • Mark Hitchcock • Tom McCall • Mike Stallard
Robert Thomas • Stanley Toussaint • Elmer Towns • Andy Woods

21ST CENTURY PRESS
PUBLISHING WITH PURPOSE
WWW.21STCENTURYPRESS.COM

The Gathering Storm

General Editor Mal Couch
Fort Worth, Texas

Published by 21st Century Press
2131 W. Republic Rd.
PMB 41
Springfield, MO 65807

For more information about 21st Century Press visit our web site: www.21stcenturypress.com

ISBN 0-9749811-7-6

Cover Design: Keith Locke
Book Design: Terry White

About the Authors

Kerby Anderson, MA, M.F.S., is president of Probe Ministries, based in Richardson, TX. He is an author, lecturer, and radio commentator.

Paul N. Benware, Th.M., Th.D., is professor of Theology at Philadelphia College of Bible, Langhorne, PA.

Mal Couch, MA, Th.M, Ph.D., Th.D., D.D., is founder and president of Tyndale Seminary in Ft. Worth, TX. He is professor of languages and Theology, an author, lecturer in hermeneutics, and is also a radio teacher. He is a Silver Medallion award-winning author.

Arnold Fruchtenbaum, Th.M., Ph.D., is founder and director of Ariel Ministries, Tustin, CA. He is an author and conference speaker.

Steven Charles Ger, Th.M, is founder and director of Sojourner Ministries. He is an author and lecturer in Old Testament studies. He lives in Garland, TX.

George Gunn, M.Div., is the chairman of the Department of Bible and Theology at Shasta Bible College in Reading, CA.

Dave Hunt, is a lecturer and author, and is the founder of The Berean Call Ministry in Bend, OR.

Thomas Ice, Th.M., Ph.D., is the Director of the PreTrib Research Center. He is an author and lecturer in prophecy, and lives in Arlington, TX.

Manfred Kober, Th.M, Th.D., is a missionary to Germany, and teaches at Faith Baptist Bible College. He lives in Bondurant, IA.

Mark Hitchcock, Th.M, J.D., and Ph.D. candidate. He is an author and pastor of the Faith Bible Church in Edmond, OK.

Tom McCall, Th.M., Th.D., is the founder of the School of Tyrannus in Tyler, TX. He is an author, lecturer, and teacher on satellite television.

Mike Stallard, STM, Ph.D., is an author and professor of Systematic Theology at Baptist Bible College and Seminary, Clarks Summit, PA.

Robert Thomas, Th.M., Th.D., is an author and professor at Masters Seminary. He lives in Santon, CA.

Stanley Toussaint, Th.M., Th.D., teaches worldwide, lecturing in many foreign countries. As well, he is an author and lives in Dallas, TX.

Elmer Towns, MA, M.R.E., Th.M., D.Min., is an author and teaches Theology at Liberty Baptist University in Lynchburg, VR. He is a Gold Medallion award-winning author.

Andy Woods, Th.M., J.D., is a Ph.D. candidate and is an author and lecturer. He lives in Dallas, TX.

About the Authors

[illegible] Anderson, MA, [illegible] director [illegible] based in [illegible] is [illegible] communication.

[illegible] M. Berwald [illegible] professor [illegible] Philadelphia College [illegible] CA.

[illegible] McCann [illegible] M. [illegible] Ph.D. [illegible] Department of [illegible] National [illegible] Ministries [illegible] and [illegible] ministry [illegible] director [illegible] Madison [illegible] and [illegible].

Arnold Fruchtenbaum, Th.M., Ph.D., is founder and director of Ariel Ministries [illegible] CA. He is [illegible].

[illegible] Charlie [illegible] Bible [illegible] and director [illegible] in [illegible] TX.

George Gunn, M.Div. [illegible] of the Department of Bible and Theology [illegible] University [illegible] MA [illegible].

[illegible] and [illegible] of the [illegible] CO.

Thomas Ice, Th.M., Ph.D., is the executive director of the Pre-Trib Research Center. He [illegible] prophecy [illegible].

Manfred Kober, Th.M., Th.D., is a [illegible] Faith Baptist Bible College [illegible].

[illegible], Ph.M., D.D. [illegible] Ph.D. [illegible] Bible [illegible].

[illegible] McCall, Th.D. [illegible] is the founder of the School of [illegible] and [illegible] as [illegible] speaker, and [illegible].

Mike Stallard, Ph.D. [illegible] is [illegible] professor of Systematic Theology at Baptist Bible [illegible] Seminary [illegible].

Robert [illegible] Th.M., [illegible] is an author and [illegible] professor [illegible] Seminary [illegible].

Stanley [illegible] Th.M., Th.D. [illegible] teaching at [illegible] in [illegible] TX.

[illegible] Tuma [illegible] MA [illegible] and teaches [illegible] University [illegible].

[illegible] Th.M., Ph.D. [illegible] and [illegible] in [illegible].

A Dedication to Dr. John F. Walvoord
May 1910 – December 2002

As so many men up to the 1970s, I was privileged to have studied doctrine and Bible prophecy in the early 1960s under Dr. Walvoord while a student at Dallas Theological Seminary. My course with him on eschatology was profound yet simple, and to the point with logical and biblical arguments. He loved Bible prophecy and had more of a grasp on the issues of Christ's Second Coming than any scholar of his day.

However, my most appreciative times with him were in his twilight years. In his nineties I hosted him on a Bible study program on Christian radio. And then I had the opportunity to write his official biography (in autobiographic form), and his obituary that was later published at the time of his death.

Dr. Walvoord had given his life studying the great biblical fact, the doctrine of the rapture of the church. While interviewing him for writing his biography, I realized that to him this was not a theoretical subject, a sidebar to the study of biblical prophecy. In a pensive moment Dr. Walvoord looked out his office window and with meaningful emotion said, "Maybe today! Maybe He will come today!" However it was not to be. Within a few months he would face death and was quietly called home to glory before hearing the trumpet that would announce the Lord's return for His church.

The larger Evangelical church will never fully realize how blessed it was to have Dr. Walvoord in its service. He labored for Christ from the early 1930s, right up until the time of his going home. Few bond-servants of Christ have worked so long, and so faithfully and consistently as Dr. Walvoord. While he often appeared somewhat stoic and without humor, just the opposite was true. He loved a joke, and he was warm and personable in private conversations or in a small group. And more than anything, he loved teaching God's Word, whether the audience was large or small. He traveled as long as he could from pulpit to pulpit almost to the very end.

This book is also dedicated to prophecy Bible teachers who, for the most part, have been taught by Dr. Walvoord, either in person in a classroom setting, or by textbook. None of them are simply mimics of this great man. He imparted the biblical interpretative hammers, drills, and saws, that made it possible for each of these men to understand the issues of prophecy on their own. Each writer on these pages would echo the heartfelt thanks for the lasting influence of Dr. Walvoord.

Here are exerts in his own words from his biography, *Blessed Hope* (AMG Publishers, 2001).

Although people and institutions come and go, the same problems exist today as always. Having said that, I am concerned about the growing lack of emphasis on the fundamentals of the faith—salvation, sanctification, and the teaching of prophecy. There's silence, too, on eschatology and the blessed hope of the coming of the Lord. Prophecy conferences are no longer popular. All of this may not mean a change in doctrine, but a shift in emphasis certainly has occurred.And that shift can soon lead to a downgrading of doctrinal truth.

The rapid strides toward a more secular world indicates that we're approaching the time of the Rapture. Some people are hoping for a spiritual revival, but the Bible doesn't indicate this will occur. Instead, the Bible indicates an increase of apostasy. And, in fact, many seminaries and churches are departing from the faith. The majority of seminaries in America neither accept the inerrancy of the Bible nor hold to the literal interpretation of prophecy. ... If one believes that prophecy is to be understood consistently and literally, one will not hold to a wrong view. ... Theological brush fires won't stop, however, until the Lord Jesus returns.

Thank you for such wise counsel, Dr. Walvoord!
General Editor, Mal Couch, MA, Ph.D., Th.D.

Forward

Why This Book?

As the November election of 2004 neared, America awakened and found itself split down the middle between two ideologies, between liberal and conservative, but more, between moral Christian values, and between humanistic and secular values. Never before has the nation been so divided in such a deep and devious way. Events that unfold and transpire past 2004 will tell us just how deep the split is in the psyche of the nation. But while America is coming to terms with a liberal agenda that is without doubt destructive, in Europe and Asia there is no division because Christian mores have nothing to do with what is taking place in those cultural and religious climates.

Europe long ago repudiated the spiritual heritage left over from the Reformation. And it can be fair to say that the tombstone is about to be placed over the Christian influences that have so led this nation in the past. The changes are now coming so fast spiritually and morally that the entire social fabric of the country is about to tear and fragment. Here are some examples:

- In 1993 63% of Americans claimed to be Protestant, but unfortunately in that survey, Mormons and Jehovah Witnesses were included in the count. In 2002 the number saying they are Protestant Christians had dropped to 52%. Within a few years Protestants will be a minority in America!
- In 2003 14% percent of Americans claimed to have no religion.
- Up to 1993 Protestant denominations retained 90% of their congregants. The number now is 80%.
- It is admitted that because the mainline denominations are turning so quickly to liberalism, they are shrinking rapidly and may soon disappear altogether.

The signs that the nation, and the world, is rapidly moving quickly to social and moral humanism are seen in the issues listed below on which Christian values no longer have an influence:

- Abortion
- Stem-cell research using aborted baby tissue
- Homosexual agendas
- Same-sex marriage
- Galloping socialism
- Euthanasia

While some argue that these issues are simply social shifts that will not sap the strength of the western nations, such rapid changes point to an outright repudiation of biblical morality.

Then there is the Middle East and Israel.

Evangelicals who hold strongly to what the Bible teaches about the end times, see prophetic patterns in the establishment of the nation of Israel along with the return of the Jewish people to the promised land, and the rise of militant Islam. The Middle East is a powder keg that could explode and draw into that area the entire world. Changes in Europe also point to prophetic signposts. Europe is now virtually a united one nation! It now uses a Euro-dollar, and has a sitting parliament with an elected president. It also is rapidly moving to a total economic inter-dependence. Many of these changes point clearly to the prophesied one-world government that will dominate the globe during the great seven-year tribulation period.

I have assembled some close friends and outstanding spiritual scholars to write about the deepening moral darkness looming on the horizon of our world. I trust that what they have written will help believers in Christ to understand the times we live in, but too, to become more diligent about sharing the good news of salvation found only in the Lord Jesus Christ.

The apostle Paul warns that a time will come when segment of Christians will not want to hear the truth. There will be a turning away from what the Bible teaches. However he adds that there is a special crown awaiting those who look for the day of Christ's appearing. The apostle writes:

> *For the time will come when they will not endure sound doctrine; but wanting to have their ears tickled, they will accumulate for themselves teachers in accordance to their own desires [lusts]; and will turn away their ears from the truth, and will turn aside to myths. …[But] in the*

future there is laid up for me the crown of righteousness, which the Lord, the righteous Judge will award to me on that day; and not only to me, but also to all who have loved His appearing (2 Timothy 4:3-4, 8).

--Mal Couch, MA, Ph.D., Th.D.

About the Title:

THE GATHERING STORM*

*Following World War II, Winston Churchill wrote the history of that horrible conflict but also the history of the buildup leading to its beginning. One of the volumes he authored is entitle, The Gathering Storm. In it he attempts to document the social and geo-political factors that were put into place in the 1930s.

The purpose of this book is to signal the warning that the storm is on the horizon. Events are leading us closer to the prophesied apostasy and the rapture of the church. In the growing darkened social and spiritual climate, Christians may face a deepening isolation and an outright denial of the opportunity to witness the saving grace of Christ Jesus. Churches may also begin to feel a sharp curtailment of ministry, especially in speaking against the moral evils of the culture.

Not all of the chapters in this book are warning chapters, but together they are meant to lay out a mosaic of things to come. Some of those things have to do with what is taking place in the world, but other issues also point to drastic changes within the larger Evangelical culture.

Meanwhile, taking a cue from the apostle Jude, believers are urged to "contend earnestly for the faith which was once delivered to the saints" (Jude 3).

Table of Contents

PART THREE
GOD'S PRESENT AND FUTURE PROGRAM FOR THE CHURCH

PART FOUR
TO GOD BE THE GLORY!

PART ONE

GROWING CONFUSION ABOUT BIBLICAL PROPHECY

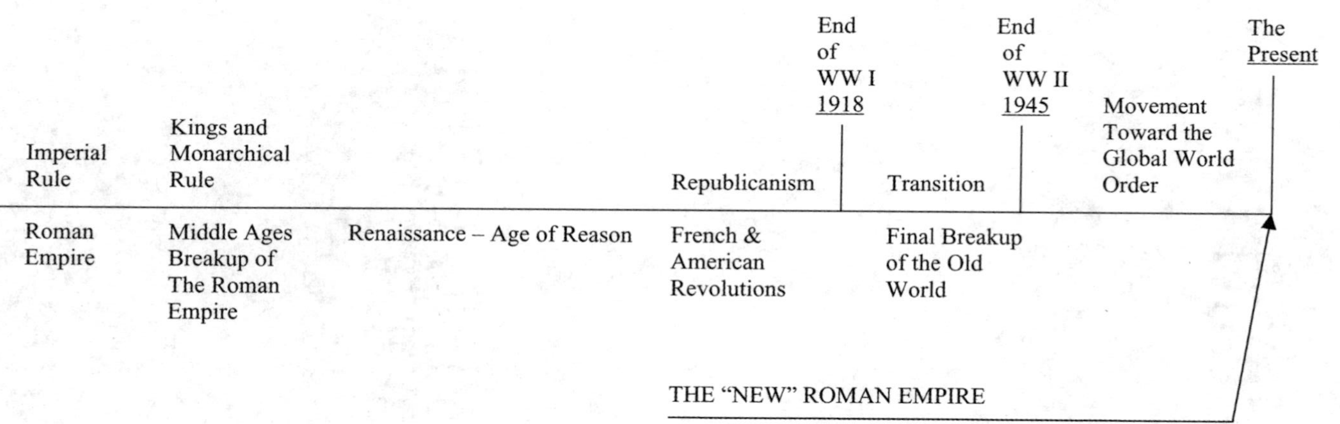
STEPS TOWARD GLOBALISM
Imperial Rule
Kings and Monarchical Rule
Republicanism
End of WW I 1918
Transition
End of WW II 1945
Movement Toward the Global World Order
The Present
Roman Empire
Middle Ages Breakup of The Roman Empire
Renaissance – Age of Reason
French & American Revolutions
Final Breakup of the Old World
THE "NEW" ROMAN EMPIRE
• Elimination of European Wars
• Euro-dollar
• President of the United States of Europe
• Parliament of the United States of Europe
• European Free Trade

CHAPTER 1

GLOBALISM AND THE NEW WORLD ORDER

Kerby Anderson

The desire to control world events and to bring all the nations of the world together is not a new idea. Dictators, military leaders, and internationalists have tried to do this for centuries. But events in this first decade of the 21st century are making these dreams reality.

Globalism is the belief that events in one country cannot be separated from another and that the world is moving toward a form of government and economics that transcends traditional nation-states. A small but powerful group of internationalists have been working for decades to bring various aspects of our society under one, universal system. Although they are quite diverse with differing opinions and agendas, they are nevertheless unified in their belief that the problems of the world can be better solved under world government and a unified economic system. These globalists are convinced that they will bring about a global network that will save mankind from its current problems.

The forums for these discussions have usually been at United Nations conferences or UN-related events. Some of the most prominent UN conferences have taken place in such places as Cairo, Egypt; Istanbul, Turkey; or Beijing, China.

Another important venue for these discussions has been the Group of Eight Summit meetings. The Group of Eight began as the Group of Six in 1973 (U.S., Japan, Germany, France, Britain, and Italy). They became the Group of Seven-G7 when Canada joined several years later. Now they are called the Group of Eight-G8 when Russia became a partner in 2002.

NEW WORLD ORDER

The term "new world order" has been used by leading establishment media and think tanks for decades. These groups advocate a world government, a merging of national entities into an international organization that centralizes political, economic, and cultural spheres into a global network.

Those promoting this idea of a new world order are a diverse group. They include various political groups, such as the Club of Rome, the Council on Foreign Relations, and the Trilateral Commission. Foreign policy groups, secret societies, and international bankers have also promoted the concept.

Historically, internationalists have used the term to describe their desire to unite the world politically, economically, and culturally, and it is hardly a recent phenomenon. After World War I, President Woodrow Wilson pushed for the world's first international governmental agency: the League of Nations. Yet despite his vigorous attempt to win approval, he failed to get the United States to join the League of Nations.

But by the end of World War II, the world seemed much more willing to experiment with at least a limited form of world government through the United Nations. President Harry Truman signed the United Nations Charter in 1945, and a year later John D. Rockefeller, Jr., gave the U.N. the money to purchase the eighteen acres along the East River in New York City where the U.N. building sits today.

For the last fifty-plus years, globalists have tried to use the U.N. and other international organizations to birth this new world order. Yet most of their actions have been to no avail. Except for its peacekeeping action during the Korean War, most of the time the U.N. has been nothing more than an international debate society.

Although the U.N. has not provided internationalists with much of a forum for international change, that does not mean they have not been making progress in their desire to unite the world. Through political deals and treaties of economic cooperation, internationalists have been able to achieve many of their goals.

How these goals fit within the current political context is unclear. But we already have an emerging world order in Europe through the European Union. Europeans are beginning to speak of themselves as Europeans rather than as Germans or as English. They have developed various cooperative arrangements including a common European currency.

The term "new world order" gained common prominence when former President George H.W. Bush delivered his September 1990 speech to a joint session of Congress when he referred four times to a new world order.

At the time, *Newsweek* magazine described the genesis of President Bush's vision of the new world order: "As George Bush fished, golfed and pondered the post cold-war world in Maine last month, his aides say that he began to imagine a new world order." It went on to say that "It is a vision that would have chilled John Foster Dulles to the marrow: the United States and the Soviet Union, united for crisis management around the globe."[1] Perhaps it would have surprised former government leaders, but it is noteworthy that nearly all secular media and most politicians seem ready to embrace the concept of a new world order.

Former President Bill Clinton proposed a variation of this idea. He described it as global multilateralism. When the Clinton foreign policy team took office, they wanted to extend President Bush's ideal of a new world order. Dedicated to the rapid expansion of U.N.-sponsored "peace keeping operations," the Clinton team began developing agreements to deploy American troops to hot spots around the globe. The goal was to upgrade the professionalism of the U.N. troops and placement of American troops under U.N. commanders using U.N. rules of engagement.

The Clinton policy of global multilateralism attempted to honor the U.N. request for a standing rapid deployment force under the secretary-general's command. But what it ended up doing is calling for American servicemen to risk life and limb for ill-defined causes in remote places under foreign leaders with constrained rules of engagement. The loss of American sovereignty and the undermining of strategic interests of the United States is significant.

SUSTAINABLE DEVELOPMENT

Although United Nations conferences have been taking place frequently over the last three decades, most Americans have ignored the proceedings and their ominous implications. Conferences in Cairo, Beijing, and Istanbul have been a vivid reminder of the radical ideology of the UN and the threat it poses to our faith, family, and freedom.

The direction of the last few conferences illustrates this point. The 1992 Earth Summit in Rio de Janeiro established an environmental foundation for all the UN's radical social and economic agendas. The 1994 Cairo Conference focused on population control and attempted to push abortion and contraception as solutions to the perceived "problem" of overpopulation. The 1995 Women's Conference in Beijing, China, proved to be the most radical of all. It continued to push abortion as a human right and attempted to make sexual orientation a human right by promoting the idea that genders are not clearly defined but are socially constructed. The White House has already created an Inter-Agency Council to implement the Beijing platform in the private sector and every executive agency.

The UN conference in Istanbul, Turkey, built upon the foundation of the other conferences and was the culmination of the conferences. Wally N'Dow, Secretary General of Habitat II, predicted that the conference would be a "new beginning that will reflect and implement the actions called for at the unprecedented continuum of global conferences that have marked this closing decade of the century." He said, "a new global social contract for building sustainable human settlements must be forged" for the "new global urban world order." Mindful of the controversy surrounding the other conferences, he declared, "There will be no roll-back of any of the conferences, including Beijing."

A key concept of these conferences was the idea of "sustainable development." In the school curriculum developed by the UN, sustainable development was defined as "meeting the needs of the present generation without damaging the Earth's resources in such a way that would prevent future generations from meeting [their needs]."[2] It includes "changing wasteful consumption patterns" and "emphasizing equitable development" in order to "bridge the gap between rich and poor countries." In practice, sustainable development is a radical concept that will limit the amount of food, energy, or general resources that citizens of a nation can consume. Rather than consuming what they can afford, "rich" nations (like the U.S.) might only be allowed to consume what they need to stay alive.

One UN publication declares that we "must learn to live differently" and calls for this international agency to "ensure that the benefits of development are distributed equally." To achieve this so-called "equal distribution," there must be a redistribution of wealth throughout the planet. The UN has already drafted specific plans for implementing sustainable development in the U.S. In spite of the frightening implications of these conferences, U.S. taxpayers have been footing the bill for them and their radical agendas.

GLOBAL TAXES AND NATIONAL SOVEREIGNTY

The Habitat II conference called for national governments to manage economic systems. These include public and private investment practices, consumption patterns, and public policy. UN Secretary Boutros Boutros Ghali told the first plenary session that he wanted the conference to be a "Conference of Partners."

Another section was devoted to the international community and its involvement with national governments. The Global Plan of Action calls for the international community to force changes in the world's economic structures.

The UN also intends to reach sustainable development by changing the structure of national governments. The agenda from the Habitat II conference depends upon UN oversight of national, regional, state, and local governments. The document asks city administrators to re-design their regulations, political systems, and judicial and legislative procedures. It was no accident that the conference was filled with mayors from many U.S. cities as well as from cities around the world.

One topic that has surfaced both in UN conferences and at the G8 summit meetings is the idea of a global tax. It has often been called the Tobin tax in honor of the late Yale University economist James Tobin. The target is the more than one trillion dollars per day being exchanged as currencies around the world. Revenue from even a small Tobin tax is estimated to be in the trillions of dollars per year.

Proponents of the tax warn others not to call it a "global tax" for fear that will adversely affect its likelihood of being implemented. Many UN leaders hope that in the next few years they will be able to implement this global tax so they can free the UN of U.S. influence and enact their radical global agenda.

The tax would also remove the UN's dependence on sovereign nations.

No longer would the United States or other countries have a check and balance against an international organization. The UN could pay for its activities, fund UN peacekeeping forces, and conduct many of its affairs independently of the United States.

There has also been discussion at the 2000 UN Millennium Summit and at the recent G8 summit of creating a "global rapid deployment force." Current plans are for the creation and equipping of 42,000 soldiers to provide a peacekeeping force in Africa.

This global vision coupled with an independent military force and an independent funding proposal should concern Christians mindful of end-times prophecy. At the time when the world seems to be moving swiftly towards global government, the prospects of a stronger United Nations (autonomous of sovereign nations) is a scary scenario. This bolder and stronger United Nations would further erode U.S. sovereignty and strengthen the hand of world leaders who are promoting globalist visions of a one-world government.

UN CONFERENCES: FOUR AREAS OF CONCERN

What are the possible effects of the UN conferences on our families and communities? I see several issues of great concern to Christians.

The first issue is education. Many of the concepts like "sustainable development," have already infiltrated America's schools. Textbooks promote global citizenship and minimize national sovereignty. Other textbooks blame rich northern countries (like the U.S.) for retarding the growth and development in lesser-developed countries. "Tolerance" and "global peace" are emphasized as the ultimate aims of society.

A second issue is the impact on families. UN conferences continue the UN attempt to redefine the family. Many UN leaders see the traditional family as an obstacle to UN dominance.

The Habitat II platform stated, "in different cultural, political and social systems, various forms of the family exist."[3] Many participants asked that "sexual orientation" be included as a civil rights category. In many ways, this merely extended the concept promoted during the Beijing Women's Conference that gender be defined not as male and female, but as one of five genders that are socially constructed. Habitat II also promoted "gendered cities" which are to be organized in terms of "gender roles."[4] The third issue has to do with population. The UN Population Fund says that population growth is a key inhibitor of sustainable growth. UN recommendations of population control are based upon the faulty premise that the world is in the midst of a population explosion that cannot be controlled. Participants raised the fear of losing resources even though there is empirical evidence to the contrary.

Because of the UN's anti-population bias, the Habitat II document emphasizes "sustainable development" as the mechanism for population control. Thus, "family planning" is a key concept, and the document therefore emphasizes surgical abortions and chemical abortions (RU-486). The Habitat platform specifically mentions "reproductive health services" for women in human settlements and calls for government management of economic and population growth.

A final issue concerns the area of ecology and pollution. At the 1992 UN Earth Summit, Canadian developer Maurice Strong stated, "It is clear that current lifestyles and consumption of large amounts of frozen convenience foods, use of fossil fuels, appliances, home and workplace air conditioners and suburban housing are not sustainable."[5] Many believe Maurice Strong may someday become the UN Secretary General and are rightly concerned about his New Age views on ecology.

GOALS OF GLOBALISM AND THEIR OBSTACLES

What are the goals of the globalists? Though they are a diverse and eclectic group of international bankers, politicians, futurists, religious leaders, and economic planners, they are unified in their desire to unite the planet under a one-world government, a single economic system, and a one-world religion. Through various governmental programs, international conferences, and religious meetings, they desire to unite the various governments of this globe into one single network.

Although this can be achieved in a variety of ways, the primary focus of globalists is on the next generation of young people. By pushing global education in the schools, they believe they can indoctrinate them to accept the basic foundations of globalism. According to one globalist, global education seeks to "prepare students for citizenship in the global age." Globalists believe that this new form of education will enable future generations to deal effectively with population growth, environmental problems, international tensions, and terrorism

But several obstacles stand in the way of the globalists' goals. Consequently, they have targeted three major institutions for elimination because their continued existence impedes their designs to unite the world under a single economic, political, and social global network.

The three institutions under attack by globalists today are: the traditional family, the Christian church, and the national government. Each institution espouses doctrines antithetical to the globalist vision. Therefore, globalists argue, these institutions must be substantially modified or replaced.

The traditional family poses a threat to globalism for two reasons. First, it is still the primary socializing unit in our society. Parents pass on social, cultural, and spiritual values to their children. Many of these values such as faith, hard work, and independence collide with the designs of globalists who envision a world in which tolerance for religion, dependence on a one-world global community, and international cooperation are the norm. These values are not taught in traditional American families; therefore globalists seek to change the family.

Second, parental authority in a traditional family clearly supersedes international authority. Children are taught to obey their parents in such families. Parents have authority over their children, not a national or international governmental entity. Globalists, therefore, see the traditional, American family as an enemy, not as a friend.

Well-known humanist and globalist Ashley Montagu speaking to a group of educators declared that, "The American family structure produces mentally ill children."[6] From his perspective, the traditional family that teaches such things as loyalty to God and to country is not producing children mentally fit for the global world of the twenty-first century.

One of the reasons globalist educators advocate that childhood education begin at earlier and earlier ages is so that young children can be indoctrinated into globalism. The earlier they can communicate their themes to children, the more likely their success in breaking the influence of the family.

Not only do globalists oppose the traditional family, but they also believe that the Christian church and a sense of national identity are contrary to their vision.

Globalists feel that the Christian church threatens their global program because of its belief in the authority of the Bible. Most other religious systems (as well as liberal Christianity) pose little threat. But Christians who believe in God, in sin, in salvation through faith in Jesus Christ alone, stand in the way of the globalist vision for a one-world government and a one-world religion.

The coming world religion will merge all religions and faiths into one big spiritual amalgam. Hinduism and Buddhism are syncretistic religions and can easily be merged into this one-world religion. But orthodox Christianity cannot.

Jesus taught that "I am the way, and the truth, and the life; no one comes to the Father, but through Me" (John 14:6). Globalists, therefore, see Christianity as narrow, exclusive, and intolerant. Paul Brandwein even went so far as to say that, "Any child who believes in God is mentally ill."[7] Belief in a personal God to which we owe allegiance and obedience cannot remain if globalists are to achieve their ultimate vision.

National governments also threaten globalism. If the goal is to unite all peoples under one international banner, any nationalism or patriotism blocks the progress of that vision. Globalist and architect Buckminster Fuller once said that, "Nationalism is the blood clot in the world's circulatory system."[8]

Among nations, the United States stands as one of the greatest obstacles to globalism. The European community has already acquiesced to regional and international plans, and other emerging nations are willingly joining the international community. By contrast, the United States remains independent in its national fervor and general unwillingness to cooperate with international standards. Until recently, Americans rejected nearly everything international, be it an international system of measurements (metric system) or an international agency (such as the United Nations or the World Court).

The globalist solution is to promote global ideas in the schools. Dr.

Pierce of Harvard University speaking to educators in Denver, Colorado, said, "Every child in America who enters schools at the age of five is mentally ill, because he comes to school with allegiance toward our elected officials, toward our founding fathers, toward our institutions, toward the preservation of this form of government."[9] Their solution, therefore, is to purge these nationalistic beliefs from school children so they will come to embrace the goals of globalism.

All over the country programs on Global Education, Global History, and Global Citizenship are springing up. Children are being indoctrinated into a global way of thinking. Frequently these programs masquerade as drug awareness programs, civics programs, or environmental programs. But their goal is just the same: to break down a child's allegiance to family, church, and country, and to replace this allegiance with the globalists' vision for a one-world government, a one-world economic system, and a one-world religion. These then are three institutions the globalists believe must be modified or destroyed if they are to achieve their globalist vision. Christians must, therefore, be diligent to defend their family, their church, and their country.

PRACTICAL SUGGESTIONS

Christians must challenge the goals and vision of globalists. In an effort to unite all peoples under a one-world government, one-world economic system, and one-world religion, globalists will attack the traditional family, the Christian church, and the American government. We, therefore, must be willing and able to meet the challenge. Here are some important action steps we must take to prevent the advance of globalism in our communities.

First, we must become informed. Fortunately a number of books have been written which provide accurate information about the goals and strategy of globalism.

Second, find out if globalism is already being taught in your school system. Materials from groups like the Center for Teaching International Relations at the University of Denver are already being used in many school districts. Look for key words and names that may indicate that global education is being used in your district.

Other names for global education are: International Studies,

Multicultural International Education, Global R.E.A.C.H. (Respecting our Ethnic and Cultural Heritage), Project 2000, Welcome to Planet Earth, and World Core Curriculum. Key buzzwords for globalists include: global consciousness, interdependence, and new world order.

Third, express your concerns to educators and leaders in your community. Often educators teaching globalism are unaware of the implications of their teaching. Globalism, in attempting to unite nations and peoples, will have to break down families, churches, and governments. Educate them about the dangers of globalism and its threat to the foundations upon which your community rests. Encourage them to be better informed about the true goals of globalists and the danger they pose to our society.

Fourth, Christians should be in prayer for those in government. We are admonished in 1 Timothy 2 to pray for leaders and others in authority. Pray that they will have discernment and not be lead astray by the designs of globalists.

Finally, I believe Christians should question the current interest many of our leaders have in developing a new world order. What are our leaders calling for us to do? Are they proposing that the United States give up its national sovereignty? Will we soon be following the dictates of the U.N. Charter rather than the U.S. Constitution?

These are questions we should all be asking our leaders. What role will the United States play? Aren't we merely being moved towards the globalists' goal of a one-world government, a one-world economy, and a one-world religion? Congress and the President need to know that you have questions about current attempts to move us into a new world order.

<table>
<tr><th colspan="3">THE COMING APOSTASY AND THE DEATH OF LITERAL INTERPRETATION AMONG EVANGELICALS</th></tr>
<tr><td>1923 – 1993
Old Dallas Seminary</td><td>1993 – On
New Dallas Seminary</td><td>The Coming Death of Normal and Literal Interpretation</td></tr>
<tr><td>Normal Hermeneutics applied to Bible Prophecy:</td><td>Beginning of Progressive Dispensationalism:</td><td rowspan="2">• Imposing on the biblical text current sociopolitical thinking
• Interpreting the biblical text with subjective attitudes
• Hybrid interpretations imposed on the book of Revelation
• Re-interpreting OT prophecy in light of later events
• Postmodern thinking: “Everyone is right, no one is wrong”
• Fascination with nonliteral interpretations
• Fascination with “a new scholarly sophistication”
• “Academia” vs. academics</td></tr>
<tr><td>Lewis S. Chafer
John F. Walvoord
Charles C. Ryrie
J. Dwight Pentecost
Merrill F. Unger</td><td>Darrell L. Bock
Craig A. Blaising</td></tr>
<tr><td>Consistent Interpretation</td><td>Compromised Interpretation</td><td>Return to liberalism and allegorical interpretation</td></tr>
</table>

CHAPTER 2

THE *NEW* INTERPRETATION OF BIBLE PROPHECY

Robert Thomas

It is a privilege to have a part in this work honoring the memory of John F. Walvoord. Dr. Walvoord had a vital interest in biblical prophecy and toward the end of his life especially in the impact of hermeneutics on biblical prophecy.[1] The following discussion of *New Evangelical Hermeneutics and Eschatology* is dedicated to the memory of this faithful expositor of Scripture.

RECENT TRENDS IN EVANGELICALISM AND EVANGELICAL HERMENEUTICS

Since the 1970's, evangelicalism and evangelical hermeneutics have undergone radical changes, changes that have affected interpretation of the Bible's prophetic teachings. I have elaborated on the changes in *Evangelical Hermeneutics: The New Versus the Old.*[2] Here we can only offer a sample of some of the changes.

David F. Wells has written,

> It was clear to us, even in 1975, that Evangelicalism was about to change, the core consensus was beginning to weaken, strategic coherence was beginning to disappear, and that in the absence of these things we could anticipate seeing many new ad hoc definitions as to what Evangelicalism was and many new and ad hoc silences when it was not what it was supposed to be.[3]

Iain Murray specifies the general time period of evangelicalism's slippage: "We have seen that the new evangelicalism, launched with such promise, had lost its way in the United States by the late 1960's."[4] Later he notes regarding evangelicalism's attempt to attain academic respectability,

> The academic approach to Scripture treats the divine element – for all practical purposes – as non-existent. History shows that when evangelicals allow that approach their teaching will sooner or later begin to look little different from that of liberals.[5]

What Wells and Murray have observed was substantiated just last month on November 19th when the Evangelical Theological Society membership refused to dismiss two leading open theists from its membership. That Society is rapidly returning to the theological stance of the nonevangelical society from which it separated in 1949. Evangelicalism is rapidly losing its distinctiveness.

Also, note the following: On November 23, 2003 the *Los Angeles Times Magazine* carried a feature article entitled "The New Believers." The article carried the abstract that read as follows: "The 'Post-Evangelicals' embrace both science and the Bible, oppose war and abortion, and believe Right can meet Left. Their inspiration: Fuller Theological Seminary. Are they dangerously deluded, or scary smart?"[6] If you are wondering what post-evangelicals believe about the Bible, they believe that "biblical inerrancy ... is not so much right or wrong as a divine waste of time."[7]

The front page of the November 30, 2003 *Los Angeles Times* carried an article entitled "Evangelical Colleges Make Marks in a Secular World." An excerpt from that article read, "In California and nationally, evangelical colleges and universities are gaining broader acceptance and moving closer to the academic mainstream."[8] Does this mean that the mainstream is becoming more evangelical or evangelicalism is becoming more mainstream?

The December 6, 2003, *Los Angeles Times* carried a column entitled "Evangelical Seminary Reaches Out to Muslims."[9] It told of a $1-million project by Fuller Theological Seminary, funded by a grant from the U.S. Department of Justice. The project purposes to relieve tensions between Muslims and evangelical Christians, particularly those evangelical Christians whose view of Islam is rooted in a commitment to Israel and a belief that the physical presence of the state of Israel is required for Christ's return. Sherwood Lingenfelter, Fuller's provost and senior vice president, says that many at Fuller do no believe Israel will play any special role in the second coming. He favors a code which agrees that Muslims and Christians worship the same God and which prohibits the two religions from proselytizing each other.[10]

The cover story in the *US News and World Report* which is dated December 8, 2003 carries the title "The New Old-Time Religion" and the abstract "Evangelicals defy easy labels. Here's why–and why their numbers are growing."[11] Among other interesting facets of this lengthy column is the following:

> Today, according to a Gallup survey, roughly 4 out of 10 Americans identify themselves as evangelical or born-again Christians. And, as Boston College sociologist Alan Wolfe argues in his book *The Transformation of American Religion*, many characteristics of the evangelical style—its strongly personalist and therapeutic tendencies, its market-savvy approaches to expanding the flock, and *even a certain theological fuzziness*—have permeated other faith traditions in America, including Roman Catholicism and Judaism. Wolfe, says, only half facetiously, "We are all evangelicals now."[12]

The editor of the *Journal of the Evangelical Theological Society* stated the following in his March 2004 "Editorial":

> The difficulty seems to be that "inerrancy" had a fairly well understood meaning (and implications) for the founders of ETS. In crafting the ETS doctrinal basis, they assumed things that, two generations later, can no longer be taken for granted. The battle they thought they won by defining and affirming inerrancy has been eroded through hermeneutics.[13]

In other words, changes in hermeneutics have created widely divergent definitions of biblical inerrancy.

Radical changes in evangelicalism have gone hand-in-hand with radical changes in evangelical hermeneutics. After reading recent evangelical works on hermeneutics, one of my students was puzzled over the definition of the word *meaning*. His puzzlement was no mystery because recent evangelical writers have offered at least eight definitions of *meaning* when it comes to explaining what the Bible means.[14]

Probably the single most devastating change in hermeneutics has been a widespread endorsement of the step of *preunderstanding* at the beginning of the exegetical process. It has dispensed with the goal of a traditional grammatical-historical approach for achieving objectivity in letting the text speak for itself, and substituted in its place a goal of defending what an interpreter thinks a passage should mean. Such a marked shift toward subjectivity has had dramatic effects on traditional principles of literal interpretation and has opened the door for the birth of a number of new sub-"isms" under the umbrella of evangelicalism.[15] So radical has been the effects of preunderstanding that a well-known evangelical scholar, who must remain unnamed, has left his prestigious position at an evangelical seminary and turned in his ministerial credentials because he could no longer embrace traditional evangelical propositional truths exegetically derived from Scripture.[16]

The flippant way many evangelicals have forsaken the traditional principle of single meaning illustrates the impact of incorporating preunderstanding into the exegetical process. In the nineteenth century, Terry wrote, "A fundamental principle in grammatico-historical exposition is that the words and sentences can have but one significance in one and the same connection. The moment we neglect this principle we drift out upon a sea of uncertainty and conjecture."[17] In contrast, evangelical Grant Osborne in his recent work on hermeneutics advocates double meanings in cases of single words.[18] In fact, he cites the Gospel of John as famous "for its widespread use of double meaning."[19] Such a shift in principles of interpretation has had a huge impact on evangelical interpretation and its impact will continue to grow if allowed to continue.

An illustration of how preunderstanding has begotten a number of new "isms" within evangelicalism is the existence of the movement of Progressive Dispensationalism [PD]. Blaising and Bock affirm that PD has resulted from the hermeneutical shift among evangelicals:

> Evangelical grammatical-historical interpretation was … broadening in the mid-twentieth century to include the field of biblical theology. Grammatical analysis expanded to include developments in literary study, particularly in the study of genre, or literary form, and rhetorical structure. Historical interpretation came to include a reference to the historical and cultural context of individual literary pieces for their overall interpretation. And *by the late 1980s, evangelicals became more aware of the problem of the interpreter's historical context and traditional preunderstanding of the text being interpreted.* These developments … have opened up new vistas for discussion which were not considered by earlier interpreters, including classical and many revised dispensationalists. *These are developments which have led to what is now called "progressive dispensationalism."*[20]

One of the areas in which PD has departed from traditional grammatical-historical principles lies in its notoriety for violating the traditional hermeneutical principle of single meaning. Its preunderstanding that it has to find a midpoint between dispensationalism and covenant theology, causes its advocates to find multiple fulfillments of a single Old Testament passage. They propose that not only national Israel of the future will fulfill her Old Testament prophecies, but also the church is currently fulfilling those same prophecies. What PD calls "complementary hermeneutics" clearly violates traditional principles of literal interpretation.[21]

Time forbids that we dwell further on recent general trends in evangelical hermeneutics. The temptation to delve into how the new hermeneutics have furnished opportunities for Open Theism, evangelical feminism, the new perspective on Paul, and other recently developed movements within the evangelical camp is great. Suffice it to say that each one stems from a preunderstanding that in most cases is a response to current developments in the secular culture of which Christians are a part. In other words, evangelicals are now practicing a type of hermeneutics that has been common among nonevangelicals for over a half century, a type called reader-response criticism.

We must turn now to the other part of our assigned topic of relating the new evangelical hermeneutics to eschatology.

NEW EVANGELICAL HERMENEUTICS AND ESCHATOLOGY

A consideration of the impact of recent hermeneutical trends on eschatology should cover several areas: the book of Revelation must, of course, come first, and then PD, theonomy, and the New Testament use of the Old Testament.

THE BOOK OF REVELATION AND APOCALYPTIC GENRE

The genre of Revelation. Genre analysis divide the Bible books into groups based on comparisons with extra-biblical literature from the periods immediately before, during, and after the composition of the New Testament. Literary features such as structure, style, content, and function are included in these comparisons.[22] Blomberg identifies the categories of general style to which Revelation has been compared as prophecy, apocalyptic, and epistle.[23] To these may be added edict, to which Aune has recently likened the messages of Revelation 2–3,[24] and drama, for which Blevins has argued.[25]

No consensus exists as to a precise definition of "genre,"[26] so discussions attempting to classify portions of the New Testament, including Revelation, are at best vague. A few general observations regarding proposed answers to the question of "which genre?" are in order, however. The epistolary element is clearly present at certain points of the Apocalypse, such as in Rev 1:4-5a which has a customary epistolary salutation and in Rev 22:21 with its normal epistolary benediction. Yet so much of the book is clearly of another character that this hardly suffices as an overall category. Aune's case for likening chapters 2–3 to a royal or imperial edict has merit too, but he nowhere claims that this applies to the whole book. Blevins' argument for seeing Revelation as a form of Greek tragic drama provides interesting historical background derived from the Greek theater at Ephesus, but hardly qualifies as an overall literary type.

A recent trend among some scholars has been to view Revelation as primarily apocalyptic genre. This complicates the problem of definition even further because, in addition to disagreement about what constitutes genre, uncertainty prevails regarding a definition of "apocalyptic."[27] Aune launches an effort to solve this problem by formulating a definition based on the book of Revelation.[28] This is appropriate because the term "apocalyptic" arose from the first word of the Greek text of Revelation, *apokalypsis* ("revelation").[29] Yet such an effort prejudices the case in favor of categorizing Revelation in a certain way by assuming an answer to the question under investigation and not allowing for the book's uniqueness. Revelation certainly has features in common with the *Shepherd of Hermas* and other works of this type, including its extensive use of symbolism, vision as the major means of revelation, focus on the end of the current age and the inauguration of the age to come, a dualism with God and Satan as leaders, a spiritual order determining the course of history, and pessimism about man's ability to change the progress of events.[30]

But it also differs distinctly from everything else in this class. Other apocalypses are generally pseudonymous, but Revelation is not. The epistolary framework of Revelation also sets it apart from the works that are similar in other respects. Other writings lack the repeated admonitions for moral compliance that Revelation has (2:5, 16, 21, 22; 3:3, 19). Revelation is not as pessimistic about the present as other works in this category. In others, the coming of the Messiah is exclusively future, but in Revelation He has already come and laid the groundwork for His future victory through His redemptive death.[31]

Most distinctive of all, however, is the fact that this book calls itself a prophecy (1:3; 22:7, 10, 18, 19). Its contents fully justify this self-claim.[32] Of the thirty-one characteristics that have been cited in attempts to define apocalyptic,[33] all when properly understood could apply to prophecy as well, with the possible exception of pseudonymity (which does not apply to Revelation). Alleged differences between the Apocalypse and generally accepted works of prophecy often rest upon inadequate interpretations of the former.

Craig Blaising commits a classic blunder in reviewing my comments about the genre of Revelation. In referring to my words in *Revelation 1–7* (Moody Press, 1992), he writes, "He [Thomas] observes John's own indication that the work is prophecy (Rev. 1:3; 22:7, 10, 18, 19) and concludes that the genre should be classified as prophetic, not apocalyptic (or some combination genre in which apocalyptic is included) since 'it does not allow for the preeminence of the book's prophetic character' (p. 28). But this is contradicted by his earlier statement, 'Of the thirty-one characteristics that have been cited in attempts to define apocalyptic, all when properly understood could apply to prophecy as well, with the possible exception of pseudonymity ...' (p. 25)."[34] Blaising has dreamed up a contradiction. He has failed to notice or chosen to omit several items in the context of the latter quoted statement. First, he fails to note that the sentence he quotes comes from a paragraph that is *denying* Revelation's apocalyptic genre, but he uses the quote to *prove* apocalyptic genre.[35] Second, he fails to notice or chooses to omit any reference to the immediately preceding paragraph which points out further distinctions between Revelation and nonbiblical apocalyptic works besides the thirty-one mentioned in the quote.[36] Third, he fails to notice or chooses to omit my conclusion in the larger section from which he extracts the quote. My conclusion is this: "It may be concluded . . . that the literary genre of inspired writings was not the choice of the human author, but was an inevitable result of the manner in which God chose to reveal His message to the prophet. This, of course, distinguishes them from uninspired but similar works whose writers did, in fact, choose a particular genre."[37]

Without pursuing details of that discussion further, I have concluded that "apocalyptic" does not pertain to the type of literature in Revelation. Instead, it describes the direct-revelatory manner in which God gave the book to John. He inspired writers of the Gospels and Acts in one way, the epistle writers in another way, and the writer of Revelation in still another way. In general, when it comes to books of the Bible, *genre* applies most specifically to the manner of direct revelation, not to a type of literature. Writers of secular works chose the literary style that best suited their purpose, but biblical writers had no choice but to write in the manner in which God revealed data to them. Like all inspired writings, the spiritual gift of prophecy was the medium through which the message came to the prophet and through him to his readers. We therefore conclude that Revelation belongs to a prophetic, not an apocalyptic, genre.

Genre's effect on interpretation. Hermeneutical guidelines for interpreting Revelation correspond at least partially to an interpreter's decision about the book's literary genre. To be sure, various interpretive approaches to the book existed long before the recent attention to apocalyptic genre, but most of the theories have adopted that genre to promote human agendas more formally.

In promoting the preterist approach (i.e., the bulk of John's prophecies were fulfilled in the first century, shortly after he wrote them), Gentry writes, "*Revelation is a highly figurative book that we cannot approach with a simple straightforward literalism.*"[38] To be sure, one must interpret Revelation in light of its historical setting, but to justify a nonliteral interpretation, one must assume an apocalyptic genre in which the language only faintly reflects actual events. Specifically, to see words about Christ's second coming in Revelation 1:7 as fulfilled in A.D. 70 when the temple was destroyed[39] necessitates allowing a particular genre to override normal rules of interpretation. In seeking to justify his postmillennial approach to the book, Gentry characterizes Revelation as "apocalyptic drama" clothed in "poetic hyperbole."[40] On the other hand, understanding Revelation to be primarily a prophecy allows for a literal interpretation of 1:7 as well as the rest of the book. If Revelation is primarily a prophecy, it can be interpreted like prophecies throughout the rest of the Bible, that is, according to grammatical-historical principles.

The timeless-symbolic or idealist approach to Revelation, most commonly associated with amillennialism, has the book representing the eternal conflict of good and evil in every age, usually in reference to the particular age in which the interpreter lives.[41] It sees the book as not referring to specific events but expressing the basic principles according to which God acts throughout history.[42] Sam Hamstra represents the idealist view as follows:

> The message carried by these visions is simple: While at this moment the children of God suffer in the world where evil appears to have the upper hand, God is sovereign and Jesus Christ has won the victory. Yes, you suffer as a resident of this world that bears the imprint of Adam's sin. Yes, you experience persecution as a light-bearer of the gospel, but God the Father will preserve and protect you as well as each one of his children so not one will be lost. …
>
> Scholars describe this pictorial presentation of truth as characterized by bold colors, vivid images, unique symbols,

> a simple story line, a hero and a happy ending. ...You approach apocalyptic literature differently than you would a letter or one of the Gospels.[43]

The idealist view is correct in attributing to God certain principles of action that govern His dealings with the world in every era, but it is blatantly inadequate in denying the prophetic genre of Revelation. Fulfillment of the events predicted in the book, most notably the personal return of Jesus Christ to earth, is not found in a repetitive cycle that marks each generation, but will at some future point be *historical* events in the fullest sense of the word.

The idealist approach relates closely to a proclivity of recent evangelical hermeneutics toward contextualizing in interpretation. *Contextualization* is a term coined in a 1972 publication of the World Council of Churches.[44] It advocates assigning meaning to the text of Scripture based on cultural and sociopolitical factors in contemporary society rather than on the grammatical-historical method of exegesis. It inevitably leads to substituting one or more of many suggested applications for the one correct interpretation of Scripture.[45] Such a practice advocates translating the first-century rhetorical situation into contemporary meanings that may be diametrically opposed to the original meaning.

That, of course, violates traditional principles of literal interpretation, which dictate that "meaning" in the original setting (i.e., interpretation) and "significance" for the present situation (i.e., application) must be kept separate if literature is to have any coherence. To apply Scripture carelessly, without regard for its meaning, is to abuse it for the sake of self-generated crusades. Without a well-defined interpretation in the setting of the author, control of application vanishes and the significance for any given situation becomes a matter of individual whim.[46]

Only the futurist approach to Revelation accepts the book's self-claim of being a prophecy and interprets it literally. In embracing the premillennial return of Christ, it utilizes a normal hermeneutical pattern of interpretation based on the prophetic style, views the book as focusing on the last period(s) of world history, and outlines the various events and their relationships to one another. Blomberg's opinion that an "exclusively prophetic interpretation usually insists on an impossibly literal hermeneutic which is therefore inevitably applied inconsistently"[47] is to be expected from one whose preunderstanding in approaching the book does not align with the consistent futurism espoused in the book itself.

Most preterists and idealists interpret Revelation literally at times and see some futurist aspects in Revelation, but at the same time create hermeneutical confusion. Such "eclectic" hermeneutical approaches to Revelation abound. A combination of idealist and futurist schemes is one example. Such a concept proposes that apocalypses spoke of the historical context in which they were written and can be transferred to new situations of later generations time after time, with one final reference to real end-time tribulation. Idealist Beale typifies this hybrid approach to the book:

> A more viable, modified version of the idealist perspective would acknowledge a final consummation in salvation and judgment. Perhaps it would be best to call this view "eclecticism." Accordingly, no specific prophesied historical events are discerned in the book, except for the final coming of Christ to deliver and judge and to establish the final form of the kingdom in a consummated new creation—though there are a few exceptions to this rule.[48]

This type of analysis satisfies itself with general conclusions and makes details of the text almost useless, since they are nonhistorical.[49]

Beale is not alone in his use of eclectic hermeneutics. Others who do the same include G. R. Beasley-Murray, Robert H. Mounce, Leon Morris, and G. Eldon Ladd.[50] Leland Ryken's eclecticism causes him to combine four approaches to Revelation—the preterist, the continuous historical, the futurist, and the idealist.[51] C. Marvin Pate combines preterism, idealism, and futurism because of his "already/not yet" preunderstanding of the text.[52] All those men would insist that exclusive literal interpretation in Revelation is impossible because of its apocalyptic genre. They would claim that eclectic hermeneutics are necessary because the text of Revelation demands it.

At a meeting of the Whitefield Fraternal in San Jose, California in January of 2002, I was privileged to engage in a dialogue with idealist Dennis E. Johnson of Westminster Seminary California, whose commentary on Revelation was released recently.[53] In defending a literal hermeneutical approach to the book, I called attention to his eclectic approach, which he admitted. His response was the usual: at times the text makes literalism impossible. He called attention to several passages in the book that could not be literal. He pointed to several interpretations in my commentary that were allegedly nonliteral.

(1) In my commentary I interpret "the seven spirits which are before the throne" to be the Holy Spirit. He asked how that could be literal. I responded by referring him to Zechariah 4:1-10, on which I feel that terminology is based. Since Revelation contains so many Old Testament allusions (278 verses out of Revelation's 404 verses have such), a literal interpretation of Revelation must take into account figures of speech derived from the Old Testament.[54] Literal interpretation, of course, allows for figures of speech when the biblical text makes figurative language a clear option.

(2) He also asked how the description of Christ as having a sword proceeding from His mouth could be literal (cf. Rev. 1:16; 2:16; 19:15, 21). Again, Revelation's heavy dependence on the Old Testament is the answer. In one of his Servant Songs, Isaiah wrote, "And He has made My mouth like a sharp sword; in the shadow of His hand He has concealed Me" (Isa. 49:2a). Psalm 57:4b reads, "Even the sons of men, whose teeth are spears and arrows, and their tongue a sharp sword." Similarly, 64:3 says, "Who have sharpened their tongue like a sword. They aimed bitter speech as their arrow." Obvious figures of speech in the Old Testament to depict words spoken with the tongue as a sharp sword carry over into the language of Revelation as figurative language that is commonly recognized in literal interpretation.

(3) Then Professor Johnson brought up the fire that proceeds from the mouths of the two witnesses (Rev. 11:5) as a situation that defied literal interpretation. Speaking of his deliverance by the LORD, David said, "Smoke went up out of His nostrils, and fire from His mouth devoured; coals were kindled by it" (2 Sam. 22:9; cf. also Psa. 18:8). God's promise to Jeremiah was, "Because you have spoken this word, behold, I am making My words in your mouth fire and this people wood, and it will consume them" (Jer. 5:14). Because of Old Testament usage, language of this sort in Revelation falls easily into the realm of figures of speech that are readily recognized by literal interpretation.

It is true that allegorical interpretations were assigned to Revelation long before the invention of terms such as "apocalyptic" and "genre," but new evangelical hermeneutics have put those relatively new terms to use in affording their nonliteral interpretations a new scholarly sophistication.

PROGRESSIVE DISPENSATIONALISM

New evangelical hermeneutics have opened wide doors for PD in implementing its preunderstanding and its quest to find a midpoint between Covenant Theology and Dispensationalism. Already we have cited PD's general endorsement of new hermeneutical principles that automatically separate the movement from traditional literal interpretation. Now it is appropriate to compare the hermeneutics of PD with specific traditional principles.

The principle of objectivity. In the nineteenth century Milton Terry's time-honored work on grammatical-historical hermeneutics said, "We must not study them [i.e., the Scriptures] in the light of modern systems of divinity, but should aim rather to place ourselves in the position of the sacred writers, and study to obtain the impression their words would naturally have made upon the minds of the first readers. ...[55] Traditional principles strongly emphasize the importance of letting the text speak for itself without imposing on it preconceived ideas of what it ought to teach.

Leaders in the PD movement pointedly advocate the opposite. For them one's biblical theology and other elements of preunderstanding become the first step of interpretation.[56] If one approaches a passage knowing what he wants to find, he arms himself to defend his preconception against anything in the text that might change that preconception. An interpretative method that must defend a preunderstanding yields results far different from one that impartially approaches Scripture with the question, "What does this passage teach?"

Blaising and Bock write, "Each of us has our own way of seeing, a grid for understanding, that impacts what we expect to see in the text, the questions we ask of it, and thus the answer we get."[57] They apparently agree with Dan McCartney and Charles Clayton—and they are correct—that preunderstanding, not interpretive methodology, determines the result of interpretation when following new evangelical principles of interpretation.[58]

Such prominence given to preunderstanding by PD is obviously diametrically opposed to principles of traditional grammatical-historical interpretation.

The principle of historical interpretation. Traditionally, the historical dimension in interpretation has referred to the historical setting of the text's origin. As Terry expresses it, "The interpreter should, therefore, endeavor to take himself from the present and to transport himself into the historical position of an author, look through his eyes, note his surroundings, feel with his heart, and catch his emotion. Herein we note the import of the term grammatico-*historical* interpretation."[59]

In contrast, Bock advocates a multilayered reading of the text that results in a "complementary" reading (or meaning) that adds to the original meaning determined by the text's original setting. The "complementary" perspective views the text from the standpoint of later events, not events connected with the text's origin.[60] He also proposes a third layer of reading, that of the entire biblical canon.[61] In other words, he sees three possible interpretations of a single text, only one of which pertains to the text's original historical setting. He calls this a historical-grammatical-literary reading of the text.[62] He notes that "such a hermeneutic produces layers of sense and specificity for a text, as the interpreter moves from considering the near context to more distant ones."[63]

By thus ignoring the way the original historical setting "freezes" the meaning of a text, Bock concludes that textual meaning is dynamic, not static—ever changing through the addition of new meanings.[64] For PD, "historical" has apparently come to incorporate not just the situation of the original text but also ongoing conditions throughout the history of the text's interpretation.[65]

According to traditional hermeneutical principles, such "bending" of a text by PD is impossible to justify because the historical dimension fixes the meaning of a given passage and does not allow it to keep gaining new senses as interpretation of the passage comes into new settings.

The principle of single meaning. Single meaning is a principle that, when violated, brings evangelicals very close to deconstructionism and postmodernism. To restate the principle in the words of Ramm, "But here we must remember the old adage: 'Interpretation is one, application is many.'

This means that there is only one meaning to a passage of Scripture which is determined by careful study."[66] Deconstructionism and Postmodernism allow for multiple interpretations of a single passage, as many interpretations as there are interpreters. Everyone is right, and nobody wrong. PD has not gone that far yet, but with its allowance for multiple meanings of a single passage, it is well on its way.

PD does not limit a passage to a single meaning when it allows for later complementary additions in meaning, which additions of necessity alter the original sense conveyed by a passage.[67] Such later additions are in view when Blaising and Bock write, "There also is such a thing as complementary aspects of meaning, where an additional angle on the text reveals an additional element of its message or a fresh way of relating the parts of a text's message."[68] In part, Bock admits this characteristic of his hermeneutics:

> Does the expansion of meaning entail a change of meaning? ... This is an important question for those concerned about consistency within interpretation. The answer is both yes and no. On the one hand, to add to the revelation of a promise is to introduce "change" to it through addition.[69]

He tries to justify this change by calling it revelatory progress,[70] but revelatory progress speaks of new passages with new meanings, not new passages that change meanings of older passages. Progress in divine revelation is quite apparent in tracing chronologically through the books of the Old and New Testaments, but "progress" only in the sense of adding to what has already been revealed, not in the sense of changing the meaning of previous revelation. To change the substance of something already written is not "progress"; it is "alteration" that raises questions about the credibility of a text's original meaning.

All in all, PD's complementary hermeneutics clash sharply with traditional grammatical-historical principles that deny the possibility of a passage having multiple meanings. It is an example of anachronistic hermeneutics to read New Testament revelation back into the context of the Old Testament under the banner of grammatical-historical methodology.

The principle of *sensus plenior* ("fuller meaning"). Violation of the single-meaning principle leads easily to PD's violation of the *sensus plenior* (i.e., "fuller sense") principle. To find a sense fuller than the grammatical-historical meaning of a passage clearly enters the realm of allegorical interpretation. Terry strongly repudiated that principle when he wrote that the expounder of Scripture "must not import into the text of Scripture the ideas of later times, or build upon any words or passages a dogma which they do not legitimately teach."[71] Yet recent evangelical interpreters have advocated such "fuller meanings."[72] Such a practice is in total disharmony with traditional literal interpretation.

On this issue that has split evangelicals, PD has come down solidly on the side of incorporating fuller meanings into hermeneutical methodology. Its delineation of "complementary hermeneutics," as already described, falls clearly into this category. Blaising and Bock explicitly refuse to limit textual meaning to a reproduction of what the author meant when they write, "These texts have a message that extends beyond the original setting in which they were given. Something about what they say lives on."[73] In essence, they view later applications of the text's one meaning as additional meanings that accrue over a period of time.[74]

That policy is none other than an advocacy of *sensus plenior*, because it refers to a meaning beyond what is determined by the historical circumstances of the text's origin.[75] By basing their methodology on this assumption, Blaising and Bock can interpret Babylon in Revelation 17–18 as both Rome and rebuilt Babylon on the Euphrates, and in addition, in "the sweep of history" it could represent any city, since the world empire's center is always shifting.[76] Using the same complementary hermeneutics, PD advocate Pate expands the meaning of Babylon to include Jerusalem as well.[77] This can be nothing other than adding meanings beyond the literal meaning of the text, in other words, *sensus plenior* interpretation.

In Genesis 12:7 Saucy does the same thing with the meaning of "seed," which in its historical context refers to Abraham's physical descendants.[78] Because of Peter's sermon in Acts 2, he finds an additional meaning for Psalm 110.[79] Such practices follow a historical-grammatical-literary-theological hermeneutics, not historical-grammatical principles. On the other hand, to his credit, Saucy calls Matthew 2:15 an *application* rather than an *interpretation* of Hosea 11:1.[80] The principle of seeing the New Testament use of the Old Testament as applications rather than interpretations is more in accord with grammatical-historical techniques. The fact that added interpretive applications supplied in the New Testament did not become discernible until provided by inspired New Testament writings means that the authority for such interpretations derives from the New Testament citations, not from the Old Testament passages themselves. This being the case, the support for PD vanishes when evaluated by grammatical and historical criteria. Of course, God knew from eternity past that fuller inspired applications would eventually emerge, but so far as human beings were concerned, such applicatory connotations were nonexistent until the time that New Testament apostles and prophets disclosed them.

THEONOMY

Kenneth L. Gentry, Jr., is a leading theonomist whose work on the book of Revelation is typical of Theonomy's approach to eschatology. Behind Gentry's exegetical methodology lies a preunderstanding that controls his interpretation of the book. According to new evangelical hermeneutics, that is a fashionable approach. Gentry's particular preunderstanding is this: a desire for an undiluted rationale to support Christian social and political involvement leading to long-term Christian cultural progress and dominion.[81] Since Revelation's prophecies about a decaying society render impossible long-term cultural progress and dominion, he must find fulfillment of the book's prophecies in the era leading up to and including the fall of Jerusalem in A.D. 70. How preunderstanding distorts certain hermeneutical principles is a matter for consideration.

Eclectic Hermeneutics. A dominion-theological presupposition forces an interpreter into a pattern of picking and choosing hermeneutical principles as he moves from text to text. Not only is the approach eclectic; it is outright inconsistent with itself.

Gentry exemplifies this in several ways in his work, *Before Jerusalem Fell: Dating the Book of Revelation.* He does not interpret the same passage in the same way from place to place, or within the same discussion differing principles take him in differing interpretive directions.

For instance, he accepts the principle of the symbolic use of numbers, but only for large, rounded numbers such as 1,000, 144,000, and 200 million. Smaller numbers, such as seven, are literal for him.[82]

Also, he rejects the equation of *kings* = *kingdoms* in Revelation 17:10, but later in discussing the "Nero Redividus Myth" in 17:11, he identifies one of the kings or heads of the Beast in 17:10 as the Roman Empire revived under Vespacion.[83] The latter is part of his strained attempt to explain the healing of the Beast's death wound.

When discussing the 144,000, Gentry at one time is uncertain whether they represent the saved of Jewish lineage or the church as a whole. Yet just ten pages later the same group is definitely Christians of Jewish extraction, because the author needs evidence to tie the fulfillment of Revelation to the land of Judea.[84] Here is another instance of his lack of objectivism and fixed hermeneutical principles to guide interpretation.

According to Gentry, the forty-two months of Revelation 11:2 is the period of the Roman siege of Jerusalem from early spring 67 to September 70.[85] A bit earlier he finds John, even while he is writing Revelation, already enmeshed in great tribulation (1:9; 2:22), a period of equal length and apparently simultaneous with the Roman siege.[86] In discussing 13:5-7, however, Gentry separates the Neronic persecution of Christians that constituted "the great tribulation" (vv. 5-7) from the Roman siege of Jerusalem in both time and place, dating it from 64 to 68 and locating it in the Roman province of Asia.[87] Such locations and dates are impossible to reconcile with each other. Does the great tribulation take place in Jerusalem or in the Roman province of Asia. Is John writing during "the great tribulation" of 64-68 or the one of 67-70? Later, Gentry assigns 65 or early 66 as the date of writing,[88] so John predicted a forty-two month period of persecution (13:5) that was already partially in the past when he wrote. Such reasoning is incoherent, because the pattern of hermeneutics is utterly inconsistent.

The ends to which new evangelical hermeneutics will go to support its preunderstanding of what the interpreter wants Scripture to teach is nothing short of amazing.

Revelation's Theme Verse. Gentry and fellow theonomist David Chilton agree with most that Revelation 1:7 is the theme verse of the book of Revelation,[89] but they do not refer this to the second coming of Christ. The text reads, "Behold, He comes with clouds, and every eye will see Him, even those who pierced Him, and all the families of the earth will mourn over Him." Theonomists refer the verse to the coming judgment on Israel—for them fulfilled in A.D. 70—which resulted in the church becoming the new kingdom.[90] To interpret the verse in that way, they must implement a strange combination of proposals regarding three phrases in the verse.

(1) For Gentry, "those who pierced Him" were the Jews.[91] From the verse, he sees God's wrath against Israel as the book's theme.[92] In taking such a view, Gentry excludes any reference to the Romans in the theme verse. Yet elsewhere he acknowledges that in Revelation, Romans were the chief persecutors of Christians,[93] and they were objects of the "cloud coming" of Christ.[94] Justification for such inconsistency is impossible to come by.

(2) Without evaluating another plausible option, Gentry sees "the tribes of the earth" as a plural reference to the tribes of Israel[95] as it is in Zechariah 12:10-14, the Old Testament passage alluded to, and in John 19:37, another New Testament citation (Zech. 12:10-14).[96] At the same time, he understands the mourning to be a mourning of despair rather than a mourning of repentance as it is in Zechariah. Yet for this to be a mourning of despair as the context of Revelation requires (cf. Rev. 9:20-21; 16:9, 11, 21), *phylai* must carry the sense of "families" and must refer to peoples of all nations as it does so often in Revelation (cf. 5:9; 7:9; 11:9; 13:7; 14:6).[97] That is the only way to do justice to the worldwide scope of the book, as required by such verses as 3:10. Even Gentry admits that 3:10 refers to the entire Roman world.[98] The sense of a mourning of despair throughout the earth is the meaning Jesus attached to the words in His use of Zechariah 12:10 (Matt. 24:30).[99]

Theonomists actually understand "the tribes of the earth" to mean "the tribes of the land," that is, the land of Palestine.[100] The Greek word "*ge*" can convey such a restricted meaning of "land" if special contextual support necessitates it. Gentry's acknowledged worldwide scope of Revelation already cited rules out a localized meaning of the term in 1:7, however.

Thus Gentry's three supports for his interpretation of 1:7 falter even without a consideration of unanswered questions about the alleged "cloud coming" in the A.D. 60s. At one point he identifies the cloud coming with the judgment against Judea in 67-70.[101] At another point he sees it as a coming against the church through the persecution by the Romans from 64 to 68.[102] Still elsewhere the cloud coming for Rome was her internal strife in 68-69.[103] He identifies the cloud coming in three different ways, but nowhere does he tell how the cloud coming relates to the promised deliverance of the church (e.g., Rev. 3:11). He finds covenantal and redemptive implications for Christianity in the collapse of the Jewish order,[104] but this falls far short of a personal appearance of Christ to take faithful believers away from their persecution.

Is there no limit to what recent evangelicals will do by bringing their preunderstanding into the interpretive process?

The Sixth King. According to Gentry, one of the two strongest internal indicators of a writing date for Revelation in the A.D. 60s is the identity of the sixth king in Revelation 17:9-11.[105] He uses the "seven hills" of v. 9 to conclude that Rome or the Roman Empire is in view,[106] and then identifies the seven kings of v. 10 (English text; v. 9 in Greek) as seven consecutive Roman emperors.[107] He lists ten kings, beginning with Julius Caesar (49-44 B.C.) and comes up with Nero (A.D. 54-68) as the sixth emperor. Since 17:10 says "one is," he concludes that John must have written Revelation during Nero's reign.

In responding to four objections to his theory that the sixth king is Nero, the first three of which responses bypass the exegetical crux of the issue,[108] he assumes that the seven hills tie the Beast to the city of Rome. Contrary evidence against his assumption is plentiful. John's formula introducing the explanation of 17:9-11, "Here is the mind that has wisdom" (Rev. 17:9a), indicates a need for special theological and symbolic discernment to comprehend the explanation. Gentry's proposal requires no such; it only requires a basic knowledge of geography and numbers, not a special God-given wisdom as 17:9a indicates.[109]

Besides this, what could be a connection between the topography of Rome and seven of the empire's emperors?[110] Verses 9-10 refer to the scope and nature of the Beast's power, not to the physical layout of a city.[111] After the reference to the seven hills, the added expression, "they are seven kings," requires that the mountains or hills be seen in a political rather than geographical light. Strangest of all, though, is Gentry's failure to fulfill his obligation to explain what a reference to Rome is doing in the middle of a chapter dealing with Babylon, which he takes to represent Jerusalem.[112] The best he can do is to theorize that the harlot riding on the Beast refers to an alliance between Jerusalem and Rome against Christianity.[113] Rome's prolonged siege and destruction of Jerusalem from the late 60s to 70 hardly gives the impression of any alliance between the Jews and the Romans, however.

In addition to the tenuous nature of Gentry's use of the seven hills, his conclusion that Nero is the sixth or "the one [who] is" faces serious obstacles. The greatest obstacle is his need to begin counting "kings" with Julius Caesar who was never a king. Rome was a republic in Caesar's day, and a thirteen-year gap separated his rule from that of Augustus, who according to Gentry's scheme was the second consecutive king.

Gentry's theory is full of hermeneutical difficulties, as is any theory that begins interpretation of the text with a preunderstanding of what will result from the investigation.

Contemporary integrity of the Temple. Gentry's second principal internal indicator of Revelation's early date is his alleged "indisputable" evidence in Revelation 11:1-2 that the temple was still standing and that Jerusalem's destruction was still future when John wrote the book.[114] His extensive discussion of this point attempts to prove that the Herodian temple of Jesus' day is what 11:1-2 refers to by locating the temple in Jerusalem and showing that it is not a symbol for the church.[115] Yet he gives no attention to the possibility that it may be a *future* literal temple.

He defensively handles the two verses with a mixture of figurative-symbolic and literal-historical hermeneutics.[116] He interprets *ton naon tou theou* ("the temple of God") and *to thysiastērion* ("the altar") in v. 1 as symbolic and *tōn aulēn tōn extōthen tou naou* ("the court which is outside the temple") in verse 2 as literal. He justifies this radical switch in hermeneutics by saying that John Walvoord and Robert H. Mounce likewise combine literal and figurative in their interpretation of this passage.[117] What Gentry does is radically different from these two, however. He uses figurative and literal meanings for what are essentially the same terms in consecutive verses. *Naos*, for example, is symbolic and literal (vv. 1-2). The temple and altar are literal structures earlier[118] and then the spiritual temple of the church a few pages later.[119] In an athletic contest, changing the rules of the game in the middle of a contest can make anyone a winner. So its is with hermeneutics.

Gentry does not explain how John, isolated as a prisoner on the Island of Patmos so many miles from Jerusalem, can visit the literal city to carry out his symbolical task of measuring the temple. He seems oblivious to language indicating that John was in a prophetic trance to receive revelation in the visional portion of the book (Rev. 4:2). He was not to transport himself physically across the Mediterranean Sea to Judea, but "in spirit" he was already there. One cannot quarrel with the conclusion that John's visional responsibility of measuring points in its fulfillment to a literal temple, but it is not the Herodian temple of Jesus' day. It is a future temple to be rebuilt just before Christ's second advent (cf. Dan. 9:27; 12:11; Matt. 24:15; 2 Thess. 2:4). It will indeed be a literal temple, but without a symbolic reference to the church.

Gentry's use of symbolism is inconsistent and self-contradictory. A factoring of preunderstanding into the interpretive process inevitably leads to unimaginable extremes in hermeneutical abuse.

THE NEW TESTAMENT USE OF THE OLD TESTAMENT

Various preunderstandings of the New Testament's use of the Old Testament have clouded present-day explanations of how New Testament writers used the Old Testament, largely because of the neglect of traditional hermeneutical principles, such as the principle of single meaning. The principle of single meaning requires that every Old Testament passage receive its own grammatical-historical interpretation, regardless of how a New Testament writer uses it.[120] An Old Testament Scripture itself must not receive multiple meanings by being read through the eyes of the New Testament. When the single-meaning principle is applied consistently, two kinds of New Testament usage of the Old Testament become evident. On the one hand, sometimes New Testament writers abide by the grammatical-historical sense of the Old Testament. On the other hand, in some cases New Testament writers go beyond the grammatical-historical meaning to apply an Old Testament passage in its New Testament context so as to give it an additional sense. In the former case a New Testament writer adopts the Old Testament's literal sense. In the latter case he adopts a nonliteral use of the Old Testament. We may call this nonliteral use an "inspired *sensus plenior* application" (hereafter ISPA) of the Old Testament passage to a new situation. Such a usage is "inspired" because the New Testament writing in which it appears is inspired by God. It is "*sensus plenior*" in that it gives an additional or fuller sense than the passage had in its Old Testament setting. It is an application because it does not eradicate the literal meaning of the Old Testament passage, but simply applies the Old Testament wording to a new setting.

Examples of the literal use of the Old Testament in the New Testament. In Isaiah 7:10-11 God through Isaiah offered King Ahaz a sign, but Ahaz in feigned humility refused the offer (7:12). Since Ahaz refused that sign, the LORD chose another, described in 7:14, the miraculous birth of a son to a virgin. The Hebrew word for "virgin" refers to an unmarried woman (Gen. 24:43; Prov. 30:19; Song of Songs 1:3; 6:8), indicating that the birth of Isaiah's own son in Isaiah 8:3 could not have fulfilled this prophecy. Besides, birth of a son to Isaiah's wife would hardly have satisfied the promise of a "sign" and the son's name of "Immanuel" in 7:14. Matthew noted the fulfillment of this prophecy in the birth of Israel's Messiah in Matthew 1:23 and applied the name "Immanuel" (i.e., "God with us") from Isaiah 7:14 to Him. That was a literal fulfillment of Isaiah's Old Testament prophecy.

Isaiah 28:16 predicts the coming of the chief corner stone,[121] and Psalm 118:22 foresees the stone which the builders rejected.[122] Combined, these two prophecies found their literal fulfillment in the incarnation and death of Jesus Christ, according to Matthew 21:42[123] along with Mark 12:10; Luke 20:17; Acts 4:11; Romans 9:33; Ephesians 2:20; and 1 Peter 2:6-8. Christ provided the only sure refuge for Israel, who had made the mistake of relying on foreigners instead. At Jesus' first coming, Israel rejected Him, thereby stumbling in literal fulfillment of this prophecy.

Looking ahead prophetically, Isaiah 50:6[124] saw the cruel treatment of Jesus by the soldiers during and after His trial. Matthew 26:67 and 27:26, 30 record His being struck, slapped, scourged, and spat upon[125] as do Mark, Luke, and John also (cf. Mark 14:65; 15:19; Luke 22:63; John 18:22). The Old Testament anticipated that abusive treatment, and the New Testament recorded the prophecy's literal fulfillment.

Fulfillments such as those listed above had great apologetic value in proving to Jewish readers of the Old Testament and others that Jesus was the Messiah promised in the Old Testament. What Isaiah and other Old Testament writers predicted would happen when the Messiah came happened in letter-perfect manner.

Examples of nonliteral uses of the Old Testament in the New Testament. As stated before, the nonliteral uses of the Old Testament in the New Testament are of the ISPA type. In such uses, New Testament writers applied Old Testament texts to situations entirely different from what the corresponding Old Testament contexts entailed. The New Testament writers disregarded the main thrust of grammatical-historical meaning of the Old Testament passages and applied those passages in different ways to suit different points they wanted to make. They may have maintained some connecting link in thought with the Old Testament passages, but the literal meanings are absent from the citations. Several passages will illustrate the ISPA usage.

Luke 20:17-18[126] cites Isaiah 8:14-15.[127] Isaiah's historical context refers the words to Israel's stumbling and consequent captivity in Babylon because they opposed Isaiah's message. Luke applies the same words to the stumbling of the generation of Israelites that rejected Jesus as the Messiah and their consequent eternal judgment. Paul and Peter use the Isaiah passage in the same way (Rom. 9:32-33; 1 Peter 2:8). Note the change of reference. In the Old Testament instance, the words referred to personal enemies of Isaiah and the *temporal* judgment inflicted on them; in the New Testament the generation of Israel that rejected Jesus at His first coming and *eternal* judgment against them are in view.

Isaiah 9:1-2 speaks of the gloom at the northern border of northeast Galilee when the Assyrian king invaded Israel,[128] because that area was the first to suffer from the invasion as the Assyrians entered the land. The verses then speak of the coming of a great light by way of the transformation of that gloom at the end of Israel's captivity to foreign invaders, which will come at the second advent of Jesus Christ. In an ISPA of the words, Matthew 4:12-16[129] applies the two Isaianic verses to the time of Christ's first advent and the honor received by Galilee when He launched His Galilean ministry in that territory. That, of course, is not a literal fulfillment of Isaiah's prophecy.

Isaiah 28:11 foresees the Lord's prediction of subservience of the drunkards of Ephraim and Jerusalem to Assyrian taskmasters, who instruct them in a foreign language.[130] This was God's punishment for not listening to His prophets speaking their own language. In his application of the same words, Paul in 1 Corinthians 14:21-22[131] refers to God's use of the miraculous gift of tongues as a credential to identify those who conveyed new revelation immediately following the first coming of Christ. The meaning in Corinthians is quite different from that in Isaiah.

Isaiah 49:6b contains God's promise that His Servant, the Messiah, will be a light to the Gentiles in providing salvation to the ends of the earth.[132] That will happen during the future kingdom after His return. But in Acts 13:47 Paul uses Isaiah's words in an entirely different way.[133] He applies them to his own ministry among the Gentiles during the present age, not to the LORD's Servant during the future age of the kingdom. Here again is a clearly nonliteral meaning that allows for a New Testament application of the prophet's words.

Without a doubt, the New Testament sometimes applies Old Testament passages in a way that gives an additional dimension beyond their grammatical-historical meaning.[134] This does not cancel the grammatical-historical meaning of the Old Testament; it is simply an application of the passage beyond its original meaning, the authority for which applicatory connotation is the New Testament passage. Such an application is an ISPA.

Questions raised by ISPA-type citations. ISPA-type citations of the biblical writers raise several questions, whose answers serve to clarify the implications of such usages.

First, can today's interpreter imitate what New Testament writers did in assigning additional and different, inspired meanings in applying Old Testament passages? The answers is no, they cannot, because such a practice would violate the important principle of single meaning for the Old Testament passages. Current interpreters and preachers may apply the Old Testament passages to different situations, but their applications are not inspired as are those of New Testament writers. But someone may say, "Don't we learn our hermeneutics from the New Testament writings?" If we learned our hermeneutical principles from New Testament writers, that would imply that we possess the gift of apostleship and/or the gift of prophecy that enabled those writers to receive and transmit direct revelation from God. No contemporary interpreter possesses either of those gifts, which enabled men so gifted to practice what some have called "charismatic exegesis" of the Old Testament.[135] That ability entailed finding hidden or symbolic meanings that could be revealed through an interpreter possessing divine insight.[136] Another way of expressing the difference is to point out that NT writers were directly inspired by God, but today's interpreters are not. Such a difference rules out ISPA of Old Testament texts to new situations other than those applications that appear in the New

Testament.

A second question relates to the principle of single meaning. Does not the New Testament's assigning of an application based on a second meaning for an Old Testament passage violate that principle? That the Old Testament passage has two meanings is obvious, but only one of those meanings derives from a grammatical-historical interpretation of the Old Testament itself. The other comes from a literal analysis of the New Testament passage that cites the Old Testament passage. The authority for the second meaning is in the *New*, not the *Old*. The Old Testament produces only one meaning, the literal one. The *sensus plenior* meaning emerges only after an ISPA of the Old Testament wording to a new situation.

A third question is, "Didn't God know from the beginning that the Old Testament passage had two meanings?" Obviously He did, but until the New Testament citation of that passage, the second or *sensus plenior* applicational connotation did not exist as far as humans were concerned. Since hermeneutics is a strictly human discipline, gleaning that second sense is an impossibility in an examination of the Old Testament source of the citation. The additional meaning is, therefore, not a grammatical-historical interpretation of the Old Testa,emt passage. The Old Testament passage has only one meaning.

Fourthly, someone might ask, "Why did the New Testament writers attach these *sensus plenior* meanings to Old Testament passages?" In most instances, if not every instance, the new meaning given to an Old Testament passage relates to Israel's rejection of her Messiah at His first advent and the consequent opening of the door of salvation to a new people, the church (see Romans 9–11). The new people consist of both Jews and Gentiles as fellow members of the body of Christ, a mystery not revealed in the pages of the Old Testament (cf. Eph. 3:1-7). New meanings through special divine revelation were necessary to relate this new program to what God had been doing throughout the Old Testament period.

Further details regarding ISPA are spelled out in *Evangelical Hermeneutics* (see note 2).

Summary of how New Testament writers use the Old Testament. A summary of how the literal and ISPA uses of the Old Testament in the New Testament should be helpful. A comparison with other explanations of the

New Testament's use of the Old should clarify. The following chart summarizes the comparisons.

IMPACT OF NEW EVANGELICAL HERMENEUTICS ON ESCHATOLOGY SUMMARIZED

We have noticed the part of these eschatological changes in interpreting Revelation, in the origination of new movements such as PD and theonomical postmillennialism, and in the New Testament use of the Old Testament. If the current direction of evangelicalism continues, the movement will eventually reach the status of postmodernist and deconstructionist approaches to the Bible. The only remedy for this sickness will be a return to traditional grammatical-historical principles of interpretation.

NT Use of OT Advocates	*Principles Advocated*	*ISPA Response*
S. Lewis Johnson and J. I. Packer	_ *sensus plenior* in addition to the literal meaning of the OT _ *sensus plenior* an extrapolation on the plane of the literal meaning _ modern interpreters reproduce exegetical methodology of the NT writers	_ agrees _ disagrees _ disagrees
Elliott E. Johnson	_ two meanings discoverable in the OT _ the text has a stable meaning, unchanged with passing of time _ stable meaning is generic or many-faceted	_ disagrees _ agrees _ disagrees
Bruce K. Waltke	_ OT always read in light of the NT _ fuller sense of OT texts always there, their changed intention deeper and clearer with canon's expansion _ original writers and readers were shut out from the text's meaning	_ disagrees _ disagrees _ disagrees
Walter C. Kaiser, Jr.	_ rejects NT assignment of *sensus plenior* meanings to OT _ rejects *sensus plenior* meanings discoverable by modern interpreters _ generic meanings in OT allow for several fulfillments of single passage _ human author was aware of the series of fulfillments	_ disagrees _ agrees _ disagress _ disagrees
Richard N. Longenecker and Douglas J. Moo	_ *sensus plenior* meanings attached to OT passages by NT writers _ methods of Jewish exegesis by NT writers produced *sensus plenior* meanings for OT _ contemporary interpreters can't produce NT methods of handling the OT	_ agrees _ disagrees _ agrees
Darrell L. Bock	_ eclecticism drawing on other approaches _ God sometimes intended more than the human author _ NT events changing the way the church understood the OT _ interpreter's preunderstanding a major factor in interpretation _ allows later complementary additions in meaning	_ disagrees _ agrees _ disagrees _ disagrees _ disagrees
John H. Walton	_ objectivity in interpretation an important goal _ intrusion of the analogy of faith not allowed _ subjectivity allowable only with inspiration _ contemporary interpreter cannot claim inspiration _ Matt 2:15 a *fulfillment* of Hos 11:1 _ objective interpretation determines only one meaning for OT passages	_ agrees _ agrees _ agrees _ agrees _ disagrees _ agrees
Klein, Blomberg, and Hubbard	_ biblical authors intended only one meaning, but the Spirit encoded additional meanings for modern interpreters _ biblical authors intended only one meaning, but modern interpreters may uncover additional senses	_ disagrees _ disagrees

PART TWO

THE ROLE OF ISRAEL IN THE PLAN OF GOD

LITERAL INTERPRETATION AND THE JEWISHNESS OF THE MESSIANIC PROPHECIES						
The Earliest Church Fathers	Second & Third Century Fathers	Origen (d. 254)	Augustine (d. 430) and the Middle Ages	Emile Guers (circa. 1856)	Arno C. Gaebelein (1861-1945)	C. I. Scofield (1843-1921)
Millennial and Premillennial	Began assimilating Israel into Christian Millennialism	Significantly allegorized Bible prophecy	Church equals Kingdom	Affirmed literal grammatical interpretation Saw a clear distinction between Israel and the Church	Replaced spiritualized (allegorical) interpretation of the OT prophecies with literal/historical method	Systematized literal interpretation resulting in biblical dispensationalism, restoring a love for Israel and an understanding of messianic prophecy

CHAPTER 3

THE REDISCOVERY OF THE JEWISH PERSPECTIVE OF THE BIBLE

Mike Stallard

At the outset, the title of this chapter lends itself to questions. When one talks about the "Jewish" perspective of the Bible, what does one mean? The term *Jewish* is perhaps anachronistic to some extent with the more appropriate term being the *Hebrew* nature of the Bible if one intends to communicate that the human authors were Hebrews or almost all Hebrews. The term is used here, however, as a modern accommodation that especially takes notes of how the term *Jewish* was used in this connection among the first modern dispensationalists in the nineteenth century.

The idea of "rediscovery" refers to the rise in the Church of modern dispensationalism in the nineteenth century as, at least partly, a return to a reading of the biblical text, especially the Old Testament prophecies, from the vantage point of grammatical-historical interpretation which places the text in its overwhelmingly Jewish framework.[1] This is contrary to the practice of allegorical interpretation, especially in prophecy, which began to rise to prominence in the Church during the third century. As a result the chiliasm or premillennialism of the early Church was displaced by amillennialism which dominated the Christian landscape for at least thirteen centuries. This amillennial perspective did not read the Old Testament promises in a Jewish way, but presented a kind of replacement theology (the Church for Israel) which abandoned any future for national Israel or any future earthly and concrete kingdom. From a dispensational point of view, such a position owes more to platonic, abstract thought than it does to exegesis of a Bible that is mostly Jewish.

The idea that the debate between classic amillennialism and dispensational premillennialism involves a rejection versus acceptance of a

Jewish perspective of the Bible is illustrated by the well-known words of Oswald T. Allis:

> Literal interpretation has always been a marked feature of Premillennialism; in Dispensationalism it has been carried to an extreme. We have seen that this literalism found its most thoroughgoing expression in the claim that Israel must mean Israel, and that the Church was a mystery, unknown to the prophets and first made known to the apostle Paul. Now if the principle of interpretation is adopted that Israel always means Israel, that it does not mean the Church, then it follows of necessity that practically all of our information regarding the millennium will concern a Jewish or Israelitish age.[2]

Allis, while being critical of dispensationalism, is still largely correct in his understanding of the issue. A literal, grammatical-historical interpretation of the many prophecies of the Bible goes hand in hand with a Jewish perspective of God's coming kingdom.

This is why a dispensational scholar such as Arnold Fruchtenbaum talks of the study of Israel in Scripture (Israelology) as the "missing link" in systematic theology.[3] Little attention has been given to a full orbed systematic understanding of the past, present, and future of Israel as presented in the Bible. As a result, a skewed understanding of Israel has prevented a clear reading of the Bible from the Jewish perspective that it deserves. While it is impossible to trace the historical developments in all their fullness in this present article, we will present some case studies that frame the issue of Christians reading the Bible as a Jewish book.

THE LOSS OF JEWISH PERSPECTIVE

BEGINNING OF THE DECLINE

Few scholars dispute the evidence that the earliest Church Fathers were mostly chiliasts (premillennialists in modern terminology). However, Berkhof rejects the claim by premillennialists that chiliasm was the prominent view in the first three centuries, although he cites Papias, Irenaeues, Barnabas, Hermas, Justin, Tertullian, Cerinthus, the Ebionites, and the

Montanists as adherents.[4] Nonetheless, the better statement comes from Schaff who notes that

> The most striking point in the eschatology of the ante-Nicene age is the prominent chiliasm, or millennarianism, that is the belief of a visible reign of Christ in glory on earth with the risen saints for a thousands years, before the general resurrection and judgment. It was indeed not the doctrine of the church embodied in any creed or form of devotion, but a widely current opinion of distinguished teachers.[5]

Schaff describes Christian chiliasm as a spiritualized version of Jewish chiliasm that fixed its gaze upon the Second Coming.[6]

Diprose argues that the prevalence of millennarianism or chiliasm lasted longer in the early Church and was more widespread than some have suggested: "millenarianism remained a normative doctrine during the first four centuries of the Christian era. It was not overthrown until Augustine brought together the concepts of the Church and the kingdom of Christ in such a way as to identify the two."[7] Diprose cites Methodius, Lactantius, the *Apostolic Constitutions*, and the rise of the school at Antioch to rival Alexandria as proof for his assertion.[8]

What is important for our understanding of the Jewish perspective of the Scriptures during this primacy of chiliasm is the fact that even within chiliasm itself changes were taking place that worked against any Jewish understanding.[9] "Since the time of Justin," writes Diprose, "the prospect of an earthly messianic kingdom had become an altogether *Christian hope*, to the exclusion of *ethnic Israel's eschatological hope*."[10] Justin (d. 165), in *Dialogue with Trypho* (a Jew), presents what Peterson calls an "incipient covenantalism."[11] Diprose notes that in Justin the "eschatological hope of Israel is fully assimilated" into Christian millenarianism.[12] In addition, Barnabas (A.D. 130) teaches that the Jews "lost the covenantal promises to the better understanding of the Christians."[13] Apparently at this early date the Old Testament is more Christian than Jewish.

ORIGEN AND THE RISE OF AMILLENNIALISM

The church father Origen (d. 254) was perhaps the top scholar in Christendom in his own day. As part of the Alexandrian School he imbibed deeply of a wide range of influences including the revival of Greek philosophy from the previous century. While Origen often made use of the plain or historical sense of a passage, when it came to prophecy, he was hesitant to see ultimate meaning in either the Old or New Testaments from the vantage point of a Jewish perspective.[14] Origen made this clear when he commented on chiliasts, which he considered Christian but wrong-headed concerning prophetic passages.[15] He begins a lengthy passage by criticizing their superficial thinking:

> Certain persons, then, refusing the labour of thinking, and adopting a superficial view of the letter of the law, and yielding rather in some measure to the indulgence of their own desires and lusts, being disciples of the letter alone, are of [the] opinion that the fulfillment of the promises of the future are to be looked for in bodily pleasure and luxury; and therefore they especially desire to have again, after the resurrection, such bodily structures as may never be without the power of eating, drinking, and performing all the functions of flesh and blood, not following the opinion of the Apostle Paul regarding the resurrection of a spiritual body.[16]

Notice that Origen views the pursuit of the "letter of the law" in Bible study as shallow intellectually. To be sure, many premillennialists of today would agree with that assessment if given as a general statement. However, notice the content of this wrong-headed pursuit according to Origen. It is the following of such literalism for the purpose of fulfilling lusts and desires as they are expressed in the chiliast understanding of the coming earthly kingdom. Apparently, Origen viewed a carnal understanding of the future as the major culprit that led chiliasts to practice an unnecessary literalism in prophecy (rather than the text leading to the chiliast stance). Part of Origen's justification for rejecting a literal approach is Paul's teaching in I Corinthians 15 that there is discontinuity between the dead body and the resurrected body which is called a "spiritual" body.

Origen adds in the next section his rejection of the chiliast belief that marriage and childbearing will take place after the resurrection,[17] that an earthly Jerusalem is to be rebuilt in literal detail (based on Rev. 21), and that Christians will be ministered to by others from various countries ("they will have control over all their riches").[18] He believes that chiliasts misuse the Bible in several ways in forming their arguments for their literalist positions including the following:

> "And these views they think to establish on the authority of the prophets by those promises which are written regarding Jerusalem" – a reference to use of the Old Testament;
>
> "And by those passages also where it is said, that they who serve the Lord shall eat and drink, but that sinners shall hunger and thirst; that the righteous shall be joyful, but that sorrow shall possess the wicked;"
>
> "And from the New Testament also they quote the saying of the Saviour, in which He makes a promise to His disciples concerning the joy of wine, saying, 'Henceforth I shall not drink of this cup, until I drink it with you new in My Father's kingdom'" – a reference to the use of the New Testament;
>
> "And from the New Testament also they quote the saying of the Saviour, in which He makes a promise to His disciples concerning the joy of wine, saying, 'Henceforth I shall not drink of this cup, until I drink it with you new in My Father's kingdom'" – a reference to the use of the New Testament.

The first two points above are primarily based upon Old Testament texts while the latter two clearly refer to arguments from the New Testament. So Origen is not merely dealing with a debate about the nature of the Old Testament promises for Israel.

In addition, Origen goes on to say that chiliasts are unaware of how many scriptural illustrations "are to be taken figuratively" and they make the error of looking for the future kingdom to be like the present time, with earthly rank and order.[19] On this score he singles out Jesus' parable in the Gospel of Luke which affirms rewards for Christians in the coming kingdom when it says "Have thou power over five cities."[20] In his estimation, this passage has been abused by the chiliasts through their literal rendering.

What is especially intriguing is the summation statement of this lengthy section in Origen. He refers to the literal renderings of the chiliasts with the words, "Such are the views of those who, while believing in Christ, understand the divine Scriptures in a sort of *Jewish sense*, drawing from them nothing worthy of the divine promises" (italics added).[21] Coming from the idealistic and platonic approach of the Alexandrian School, Origen here equates a grammatical-historical sense used by chiliasts in prophecy as a Jewish sense in interpretation. His rejection of this chiliastic approach illustrates a loss of the Jewish perspective of the Bible as Origen's own allegorical approach was gaining supremacy at that time in history.

Origen was not alone in these tendencies, but served as a leader in them for his day. His example served to solidify the move away from chiliasm in the East. In the West, it is the example of Augustine (d. 430), which confirmed and strengthened the anti-chiliastic tradition. After *The City of God,* Church and kingdom are so thoroughly united that almost all hope of seeing a Jewish perspective of the Bible is lost.[22] The Church becomes engrossed with itself, believing that it had already entered its glorious kingdom.

THE REDISCOVERY OF JEWISH PERSPECTIVE

THE SETTING OF THE STAGE

The rise of challenges to Roman Catholic authority that came to a head in the Reformation led to new directions in Bible interpretation that even the Reformers did not envision. Both Luther and Calvin maintained the teaching of amillennialism although Luther dipped more frequently into the prophetic details offered by the early chiliastic Church Fathers such as Irenaeus. However, in spite of fanciful interpretations on occasion, the Reformers were moving toward a grammatical-historical interpretation. Luther commented:

> When I was a monk I was a master in the use of allegories. I allegorized everything. Afterward through the Epistle to the Romans I came to some knowledge of Christ. I recognized then that allegories are nothing, that it's not what Christ signifies but what Christ is that counts. Before I allegorized everything, even a chamber pot, but afterward I reflected on the histories and thought how difficult it must have been for Gideon to fight with his enemies in the manner reported ... It was not allegory, but it was the Spirit and faith that inflicted such havoc on the enemy with only three hundred men. Jerome and Origen contributed to the practice of searching only for allegories. God forgive them. In all of Origen there is not one word about Christ.[23]

Luther is no doubt exaggerating his complaints about Origen, especially in light of his own adoption of the same basic eschatological position. Nonetheless, the comment reflects the move toward a more realistic reading of the Bible via grammatical-historical interpretation that was the growing tendency.

Ironically, the move toward a realistic and more literal rendering of the biblical text that engulfed the sixteenth century led to discussions of eschatological details that early on pushed the envelope in a direction counter to the Reformers themselves. The biblical Anabaptists in the Radical Reformation were already entertaining premillennial thoughts as early as the 1520s, although ethnic Israel does not seem to be on the radar.[24] What develops over the next century is the advance of modern postmillennialism along with the rise of modern premillennialism to challenge the dominant amillennial tradition of the Church. What is pertinent for this study is the role that Israel or the Jews play in the developments.

One instructive example is Daniel Whitby, a Unitarian postmillennialist who is sometimes called the father of modern postmillennialism because of his systematic presentation and popularization of the view. Chapter two of Whitby's *A Treatise of the True Millennium* (1703) begins with the introductory heading, "How far I differ from the ancient and modern Millenaries, and in what I agree with them."[25] This statement shows the probability of a strong current of premillennialism in his day (which he was opposing) as well as his assessment of the chiliasm of the ancient church fathers.

Whitby's sums up his postmillennial faith in the following words:

> I believe then, that after the Fall of Antichrist, there shall be such a glorious state of the Church, by the conversion of the Jews to the Christian faith, as shall be to it life from the dead; that it shall then flourish in peace and plenty, in righteousness and holiness, and in a pious offspring; that then shall begin a glorious and undisturbed reign of Christ over both Jew and Gentile, to continue a thousand years, during the time of Satan's binding.

Notice that there is no picture of a future national Israel associated with the coming postmillennial kingdom of God. However, the future of the Jews is taken seriously, their conversion being perhaps the main factor bringing about the kingdom of God on earth. But their conversion is seen as "to the Christian faith," not in the context of any national restoration.

Whitby goes on to assert his agreement with the chiliasts of his day and in ancient times that the kingdom will be characterized by "great measures of knowledge and righteousness in the whole Church of God." Again this shows the centrality of the Church and a unity in the people of God. There is no doctrine of two peoples of God or even two programs of God. Everything is subsumed under the one category of the Church. Interestingly, that Whitby declares the chiliasts of his day to agree with him points strongly to the conclusion that he was characterizing Christian chiliasm as opposed to any form of Jewish chiliasm. In other words, even among the chiliasts of that day there was little hint of a Jewish perspective of the Bible.

Yet Whitby does show evidence that he carefully wrestles with the literal details of the text without usually appealing to allegory. This is even true of matters that would be discussed by those interested in the Jewish nature of many of the kingdom promises. Whitby says that he cannot deny the possibility that the city of Jerusalem was going to be rebuilt because 1) Jesus taught that "Jerusalem shall be trodden down till the time of the

Gentiles is come in" (Luke 21:24), and 2) the Old Testament prophets "seem to declare the Jews will return to their own land." Thus, there are some slender yet tentative hints of Jewish perspective even within this classical postmillennial position.

Nonetheless, Whitby rejects other elements that are often taught from the vantage point of Jewish perspective as found in modern dispensationalism. For example, Whitby rejects the idea of any Jewish temple being rebuilt relative to the coming kingdom largely due to the fact that there is to be no temple in the New Jerusalem (Rev. 21:22). He continues by declaring his disagreement with chiliasm's belief (as he understood it) that the reign of Christ in the millennium is "only a reign of the converted Jews and of the Gentiles then flowing in to them." While earlier statements showed a chiliasm without any Jewish centrality, here Whitby seems to react to a kind of Jewish perspective of the coming kingdom. However, he does characterize this state of affairs as "uniting into one Church with them" probably using the term *Church* as a soteriological category.

In the post-Reformation development of premillennialism, one can also see similar traits as those cited above for postmillennialism. Proponents are wrestling with the details of the text, in many cases and certain passages trying to implement a grammatical-historical interpretation. In addition, there is usually a historicist mindset when approaching Scripture rather than a futurist approach.[26]

One interesting example is John Wesley (1703-91) and his use of the work of the German pietist John Bengel (1687-1752). While there is evidence that later in life, Wesley opted clearly for a premillennial approach to Scripture, at one point he slavishly follows the double millennium views of Bengel.[27] Bengel taught that the final rage of Antichrist would be a three and one-half year period from 1832 to 1836. Christ would appear to overthrow him on June 18, 1836. Satan would be bound for one thousand years from 1836 to 2836 but then be released for a time from 2836 to 2947. However, from 2836 to 3836 the saints reign for a second millennium in heaven. The year 3836 marks the end of the world.[28]

This double-millennium position reflects the ongoing discussions of Christians wrestling with various texts, especially the book of Revelation chapter 20. Wesley, in his commentary on the book of Revelation, clearly taught Bengel's approach to the passage:

> The thousand years in which Satan is bound, both begin and end much sooner.
>
> The small time [2836 to 2947], and the second thousand years, begin at the same point, immediately after the first thousand. But neither the beginning of the first, nor of the second thousand, will be known to the men upon earth, as both the imprisonment of Satan and his loosing are transacted in the invisible world.
>
> By observing these two distinct thousand years, many difficulties are avoided. There is room enough for the fulfilling of all the prophecies, and those which before seemed to clash are reconciled: particularly those which speak on the one hand, of a most flourishing state of the Church as yet to come; and on the other, of the fatal security of men in the last days of the world.[29]

Wesley demonstrates in this comment the struggle of students of the Bible in those days to handle textual details that had been ignored in the abstract approach of amillennialism. In this case, Wesley (following Bengel) seemed to suggest that the Bible presents elements that support both a postmillennial and a premillennial vision of the coming world. Thus, in some way it might be possible to view these developments as preparing the way for later discussion of literal details concerning the national restoration of Israel.

Is there any hint of a future for national Israel in Wesley's understanding? His comments on the 144,000 in Revelation chapter 7 are enlightening.[30] He believes the 144,000 to be a literal reference to Jews: "To these afterward will be joined a multitude of all nations." These are the Israelites, to use Wesley's term, that are alive and about to encounter the future plagues which are to fall upon the earth. Concerning the book of Revelation he writes, "It seems as if this book had, in many places, a special view to the people of Israel." To this statement a modern dispensationalist would heartily concur, although there is still no hint of a national restoration.

In addition, Wesley's presentation is historicist at many points as he maps church history to various texts within the book of Revelation. He relates elements of Revelation chapter 13 and 17 to the history of the papacy from

A.D. 1033 to 1721.[31] He also maps individual verses scattered throughout the book of Revelation to world events such as the Arian controversy, the tormenting of Jews in Persia, the Saracen cavalry, and the Reformation.[32] Consequently, one can safely say that Wesley was eclectic in his handling of prophecy and is probably emblematic of the spirit of the times. Although the stage is being set for a more complete understanding of the Bible from a Jewish perspective, the full recovery of that outlook is still over the horizon.

THE RISE OF MODERN DISPENSATIONALISM

John Nelson Darby is sometimes referred to as the father of modern dispensationalism due to his systematization and popularization of a futuristic and literalistic approach to eschatology in the early nineteenth century. While the movement sometimes dipped into allegorical and typological extremes, especially in historical narratives in the Bible, prophetic teachings concerning the future of ethnic, national Israel were taken literally at face value. A couple of illustrations will be given to show that this movement constituted a rediscovery of the Jewish perspective of the biblical record.

At almost the opposite methodological pole from Origen, we find the nineteenth century Genevan pastor Émile Guers, who was a contemporary of John Nelson Darby. We know that Darby spent time in 1837 ministering in Guers' church during Darby's continental travels[33] although Guers insisted that many other teachers had influenced him.[34] In 1856 Guers wrote *The Future of Israel*, a large book-length treatise on prophecies related to the nation of Israel.[35] In the book Guers' presentation of the doctrine of the rapture of the Church is not as clear as Darby's outline of the end times, although that could be due to the fact that the Church is a secondary topic in the book.[36] However, Guers' statements affirming a literal, grammatical-historical interpretation of the Bible and a distinction between Israel and the Church foreshadow the later hermeneutical and doctrinal affirmations of a developing American dispensationalism.[37]

What is intriguing about Guers' work is his discussion of the importance of the Jewish nature of the Bible. To Guers the Jewish perspective of the Bible, at least the Old Testament, could simply not be overlooked:

> let us leave to prophetical terms their natural meaning,
> and also to each one the position which belongs to him,

> to the Jew in particular, that which God has given to the Jew; let us not spoil him to enrich the believing Gentile, already so rich in Christ, with all spiritual blessings in heavenly places; let us not expel in a manner the people of the Old Testament from their own book, the Old Testament, to put the Church everywhere in their place; it would be too derisive to make a nonentity of the Jew, to whom the prophets must have addressed words that did not concern him.[38]

In this statement, Guers equates a plain or natural rendering of Scripture with keeping a Jewish perspective of the Old Testament. The Old Testament is a Jewish book. Its prophecies and promises to the Jews must be read in that way. A failure to do so would be to rip the Jew out of the Old Testament text and read it from the perspective of only the Church.

The clarity of Guers' ongoing discussion is striking. He comments, "When we read a prophecy of the Old Testament, let us commence by establishing its first direct *literal Jewish sense*" (italics added).[39] Seemingly, the literal sense of the Old Testament is equated with its *Jewish* sense. Guers allows for secondary allegorical or applicatory meaning, but only if interpretation as cited above precedes application. He has some strong words for those who do not practice this approach.

> But on the principle of interpretation, which sees a metaphor everywhere, in every part a mystical meaning, always substituting the secondary application for the original signification, prophecy assumes a false colour, it becomes perverted, forcibly nullified by being allegorized; a veil is put before our eyes, the facts do not correspond with the words, the sacred text must be twisted, and put in a straight waistcoat to conform it to our traditional systems, and to make it say what it does not say, what it refuses to say.[40]

Thus, to allegorize Scripture as Origen did would be to Guers an abandonment of the text itself. When prophecy in the Old Testament concerning Israel is in view, such an approach is the loss of the Jewish nature of the text. This is apparent when Guers once again brings together the concept of literal interpretation and a Jewish approach to the text: "prophecy becomes diminished, impoverished, it sickens in *de-literalizing, in de-judaizing* it, it loses its amplitude, its beauty, its fullness; its moral applications have neither the same life, nor the same interest, nor the same variety, nor the same savour" (italics original).[41] In other words, to remove literal interpretation of the Old Testament is tantamount to removing the Jewish perspective of the text, which in turn prevents one from grasping the textual message in all its fullness.[42]

Guers did not teach and write in a vacuum. Many students of Scripture were reevaluating the old approaches to Bible interpretation in a post-Reformation and then post-Enlightenment context. In his case, he seems to be part of a movement which restores in some measure a positive understanding of what it means to read the biblical text in its Jewish or literal sense. There is no use here for Origen's belief that a Jewish reading gives "nothing worthy of the divine promises."

Echoes of Guers' language can be found in later dispensational writers. One of note is Arno C. Gaebelein, one of the associate editors of the *Scofield Reference Bible* in the early twentieth century. One would expect hints of Guers' language in Gaebelein because Gaebelein's conversion from postmillennialism to premillennialism was partly due to his reading of *The Future of Israel.*[43] In particular, Gaebelein argued that he gave up his spiritualization method (allegory), in which statements about Israel now refer to the Church. His more literal acceptance of Old Testament prophecies about the future national restoration of Israel was, in his view, in harmony with the Messianic expectations among the orthodox Jews to which he was ministering as a Methodist missionary.[44]

In fact, Gaebelein strongly asserted that "Old Testament prophecy has been much better understood by the old synagogue than by most Christian commentators."[45] Furthermore, he connects this Jewish understanding or approach to the Bible to literal interpretation: "Many a Christian Doctor of Divinity has with a few sentences dismissed the 'carnal' expectations of the Jews and the literal interpretations of the Rabbis, and erected his own phantom, but nevertheless, the Jew with his 'carnal' expectations and literal interpretations holds the truth."[46] In light of this truth, Gaebelein urges Christians to see the connection between literal interpretation and a Jewish perspective of specific passages concerning that nation:

> So let us understand that Israel *is* Israel, namely, the descendants of Abraham, God's ancient people, the earthly people of God. When we speak therefore of the restoration of Israel, and cite from the Scriptures prophecy after prophecy, we mean that which God the Holy Spirit meant, the literal fulfillment of all these prophecies in the literal Israel to whom their own prophets transmitted these oracles of God.[47]

Thus, Gaebelein would agree with the sentiment that there is a literal Jewish sense in which the prophecies about the future of Israel should be taken.

However, Gaebelein goes beyond the hermeneutical question to suggest that Israel is at the center of the plot line of the entire Bible, that is, God's redemption plan as spelled out in Scripture:

> All God's redemption purposes center in Israel, the seed of Abraham, the descendants of the twelve sons of Jacob; all His purposes are linked with that nation. The land He bestowed upon them, called "the Holy land," also "Immanuel's Land," became the theatre of God's manifestations. It was so in the past and it will be so again in the not very distant future. Yet the greater part of Christendom, by far the greatest, gives no heed to this important fact, and knows nothing of the place which Israel holds in the redemption plan and purpose of God.[48]

In Gaebelein's understanding, the redemptive purposes of God were tied, not just to Israel (i.e., the Jews), but to their land which "became the theatre of God's manifestations." Once again Gaebelein laments the fact that most of Christendom in his day had forgotten the Jewish perspective of the Bible. However, he could take heart that the growing influence of the Scofield Reference Bible would be one of many factors which increased the Christian recognition of a Jewish perspective of the Scriptures.

CONCLUDING REMARKS

This chapter has attempted to survey developments within the history of the Church from the vantage point of a Jewish perspective of the Bible. Descriptive language such as *the Jewish sense of Scripture* was used by early Church Fathers such as Origen to describe a wrong approach to Scripture. An early Jewish chiliasm had given way to a Christian chiliasm and finally to an abandonment of chiliasm altogether and the embracing instead of amillennialism. However, the Reformation prompts discussions of the details of prophecy that led to the rise of systematic presentations of both postmillennialism and premillennialism. Eventually, modern dispensationalists reasserted the Jewish perspective of the Bible through a literal interpretation of the hopes promised to Israel concerning national restoration. This welcome recovery allows the Bible to be what it is, a mostly Jewish book highlighting a Jewish hope for the entire world.[49] To abandon such Jewish expectations is to abandon the Bible itself.

SUMMARY OF MESSIANIC PROPHECIES	
• **Gen. 3:15** "… between your seed and her seed; He shall bruise you on the head, and you shall bruise him on the heel."	• **Isa. 7:14** "… Behold, a virgin will be with child and bear a son, and she will call His name Immanuel."
• **Gen. 49:10** "The scepter shall not depart from Judah, nor the ruler's staff from between his feet, until Shiloh comes, and to him shall be the obedience of the peoples."	• **Isa. 9:6-7** "…a child will be born to us … the government will rest on His shoulders … His name will be … Mighty God … There will be no end to the increase of His government or peace, …"
• **Num. 24:17** "…A star shall come forth from Jacob, and a scepter shall rise from Israel …"	• **Isa. 11:1-10** "… a shoot will spring from the stem of Jesse …the Spirit of the Lord will rest on Him … He will strike the earth with the rod of His mouth, …"
• **Deut. 18:15-19** "I will raise up a prophet from among their countrymen like you … I will put My words in his mouth, and he shall speak to them all that I command Him. …"	• **Isa 52:13-53:12** "Behold, My servant will prosper, He will be high and lifted up, and greatly exalted … He has no stately form … He was despised and forsaken of men … He was pierced through for our transgressions, …"
• **1 Chron. 17:10-14** "… I will set up one of your descendents after you, who shall be of your sons; and I will establish his kingdom. He shall build for Me a house, and I will establish his throne forever. …"	• **Dan. 7:13-14** "… One like a Son of Man was coming … And to Him was given dominion, glory and a kingdom … His dominion is an everlasting dominion … And His kingdom is one which will no be destroyed."
• **Psa. 2:1-12** "… Against the LORD and against His Anointed … I have installed My King upon Zion … Do homage to the Son, lest He become angry, …"	• **Micah 5:2** "But as for you, Bethlehem Ephrathah … From you One will go forth for Me to be ruler in Israel … His goings forth are from … the days of eternity."
• **Psa. 16:1-11** "… For Thou wilt not abandon my soul to Sheol; Neither wilt Thou allow Thy Holy One to undergo decay. …"	• **Zech. 9:9-10** "Rejoice … O daughter of Zion … Behold your king is coming to you … And his dominion will be from sea to sea … from the River to the ends of the earth."
• **Psa. 110:1-4** "The LORD said to my Lord: 'Sit at My right hand,' … Thou are a priest forever according to the order of Melchizedek."	• **Zech. 12:10** "…they will look on Me whom they have pierced; and they will mourn for Him, as one mourns for an only son …"

CHAPTER 4

THE JEWISH LONGING FOR THE MESSIAH

Steven Charles Ger

There is a great theme that flows from one extremity of the Hebrew Scriptures to the other, that of the messianic promise. The messianic hope has left an indelible impression on the Jewish people throughout their history and in particular for over the past two thousand years. The cry of a people for King Messiah to finally arrive has been as heartfelt and as heartrending as their nineteen century-long hope of eventual return to the holy city of Jerusalem. The plea for a God-sent deliverer to ease their national pain, to relieve their suffering, to restore justice to a morally and ethically upside down world, to once again restore the Jewish people to their homeland, to grant peace and security, to punish evildoers, to answer all the unanswered questions that have accumulated over two millennia famously awaits fulfillment only "when Messiah comes."

Messianic prophecy is a fundamental area of study for the committed student of Scripture. Jesus made His entry into human history at a moment when the Jewish community's messianic expectations were vigorous and messianic concepts robust. The Roman occupation of Israel, following immediately upon a century of self-government under the Hellenized Hasmonean priest-kings, had galvanized the Jewish imagination and the messianic flame blazed brightly. It is only within this theological, historical, sociological and cultural context that one can fully appreciate the New Testament accounts of Jesus' entrance onto the Jewish stage. The testimony of the New Testament is vividly clear that Jesus is the fulfillment of Jewish messianic expectation, and then some! Although He shattered the confines of pre-existing descriptive categories, the Messiah whom God sent to His people turned out to be a much more spectacular figure than anyone had previously imagined.

Messiah is a transliteration of the Hebrew word, "*mashiach*," which means "*anointed one*." A word with the identical meaning is *Christ*, which is likewise a transliteration of the Greek word, "*christos*." In the Hebrew Scripture, *messiah* generally signifies one who, upon assumption of a sacred office, is specially consecrated (set apart for God) by anointing with oil. This was performed, for example, upon installation of prophets, priests and kings (Exod.28:41; 1 Sam.9:15–16; 10:1; 16:3, 12–13; 1 Chron. 29:22).

Over time, this concept came to be applied to an idealized representative prophet/priest/king figure; an ultimate Moses, ultimate Aaron and principally, an ultimate David. This redemptive figure developed within Israel's collective consciousness alongside an accompanying idealized age of peace and prosperity. These messianic ideas freely percolated throughout the eras of united and divided kingdoms, the exile, diaspora and return, gaining momentum under the Hasmonean dynasty and heating the imaginations of the Jewish populace under Roman domination until finally, Israel began erupting with one charismatic figure's messianic claim after another.[1]

What was the Jewish expectation of the Messiah? Contrary to what many understand, throughout Jewish history there has always been a variety of messianic expectation. In particular, at the time of Jesus, the period of Second Temple Judaism, there was no monolithic perception concerning the coming Messiah. The Messianic ideal in the first century was be no means static and was still very much in development. The anticipated messianic figures run the gamut from king to priest to prophet and back again, and include multiple combinations of the three. Within this state of flux, the scope of messianic expectation stretched over a broad range of possibilities.

Indeed, Judaism itself as a faith system during the time of Jesus existed not as one mighty current of doctrine and belief but as diverse faith streams, dependent upon the influence and authority of various sects, parties, rabbis and traditions. Neusner argues that it is accurate to think not in terms of one single Judaism, but rather, various "Judaisms" being in existence at the time of Jesus.

These faith streams of Judaism converged with the emergent dominance of Pharisaic, rabbinic Judaism by the beginning of the second century AD. Following the obliteration of all other Jewish sects (with the exception of the Jewish Christians) as a result of the Roman destruction of the Temple in AD 70, Pharisaic, rabbinic Judaism quickly evolved into mainstream, normative Judaism. The process of redefining the essentials of

Jewish faith within a post-Temple world began in earnest. This included the compiling, recording and formalizing of rabbinic oral traditions into the vast corpus of literature eventually known as the Talmud.

Yet Judaism, although having successfully transitioned from a Levitically-oriented to a rabbinically-oriented faith system, within a few centuries soon found itself devolving yet again into a fractured, diverse set of parties, sects, faith traditions, propositions and beliefs. As the old expression goes, where there are two Jews, there are three opinions! Contemporary Judaism is the poster child of religions in its ability to illustrate the Second Law of Thermodynamics, entropy. Today, two thousand years after the visitation of the Messiah, Jesus, to Israel and the subsequent destruction of the Temple, Judaism finds itself more fractured and divided than ever. Nowhere is that more clearly illustrated than in the diversity of messianic expectation of the Jewish people.

Even so, self-correcting measures have occasionally been attempted. The great twelfth century philosopher-rabbi, Moses ben Maimon, Maimonides, attempting to unify all Jews around what were commonly considered the essentials of the faith, compiled the *Shloshah-Asar Ikkarim*, a formal, thirteen-point Jewish doctrinal statement in his voluminous opus of Jewish traditions and practices, *Mishnah Torah*. These fundamentals are still recited daily in the traditional synagogue service. The twelfth article of his *Thirteen Principles of Faith*, recognizes the foundational nature of the messianic hope within Judaism, stating,

> *I believe with perfect faith in the coming of the Messiah,*
> *and, though he tarries, I will wait daily for his coming.*

Although it is only today's orthodox Jewish practitioners who still faithfully recite this affirmation, the somewhat diminished messianic flame still flickers, however dimly, through glass however darkly, throughout most of the remainder of Jewry. It is not easy to quench a concept that is rooted so thoroughly within the warp and woof of the Hebrew Scripture and entrenched so deeply within the Jewish imagination.

THE MESSIANIC HOPE IN THE OLD TESTAMENT

The messianic concept finds its basis and origin in the Bible. Based on the

Hebrew Scriptures, what manner of messianic expectation might the careful Jewish student be expected to possess? The following are essential criteria, key streams of data, regarding the messianic hope derived from a limited, non-exhaustive examination of central passages within the Hebrew Scriptures.

THE CRUCIAL FACET OF THE MESSIAH'S GENEOLOGY: DETERMINED NOT BY THE IDENTITY OF HIS FATHER BUT BY HIS MOTHER

Genesis 3:15. The earliest and foundational messianic prophecy is found a mere three chapters into the Bible. Following the fall of Adam and Eve, the Lord declares war on the serpent, i.e. Satan, the motivating cause of Edenic sin. Although both holy warrior and evil adversary will sustain punishing injury in the conflict, the damage dealt to Satan will prove fatal. Although God's vague avowal shrouds the identity of His chosen warrior in mystery, it is clear that the key to this individual has to do with his being the offspring of a woman.

THE MESSIAH WILL BE A JEWISH KING FROM THE TRIBE OF JUDAH

Genesis 49:10. Within Jacob's prophetic blessings of his twelve sons is the promise that Judah's tribe will rightfully rule (possess the "scepter," the symbol of royalty) over the rest of their brethren until a particular moment in history, the coming of "shiloh." The mysterious term, *shiloh*, can be translated as "to whom it belongs,"[2] and has traditionally been understood as a messianic title, a pseudonym for *Messiah*. The first century Aramaic paraphrases of the Scripture, the Targums, consistently treat this as messianic prophecy. Targum Onkelos reads,

> Kings shall not cease from the house of Judah … until Messiah come, whose is the kingdom …[3]

The Palestinian Targum likewise reads,

> Kings shall not cease from the house of Judah … until the time that is King Messiah shall come, whose is the Kingdom … [4]

In addition, the *Midrash*,[5] the vast corpus of homiletical commentary and the Talmud,[6] the oral law, as well as Rashi, the eleventh century rabbinic "Goliath," all take Shiloh with reference to "King Messiah."[7]

The point is clear by the genealogies recorded within the gospels, whether through His adopted father (Matt. 1:1-17) or His mother (Luke 3:23-38), that Jesus belongs to the tribe of Judah. Interestingly, if Jesus had not come prior to the destruction of the Temple and the accompanying loss of all its stored genealogical records that would occur a mere seventy-five years hence, any claims that He had to tribal descent from Judah would have been hopelessly unverifiable. God's timing was impeccable.

THE COMING OF MESSIAH: HERALDED BY THE ASTRONOMICAL SIGN OF A STAR

Numbers 24:17. This prophecy, given by the Gentile seer, Balaam, aligns well with Gen. 49:10, further solidifying the messiah's identity as the Jewish king, whose coming would be heralded by the astronomical sign of a star. This has also traditionally been seen by the Jewish people as messianic prophecy. Targum Onkelos reads, "a king shall arise out of Jacob and be anointed the Messiah out of Israel."[8] Maimonides saw here two "anointed ones:" in the first part of this passage a foretelling of King David and in the second half, the future Messiah.

> "I see him but not now" - this is David; "I behold him but not near" — this is the Anointed King. "A star has shot forth from Jacob" — this is David; "And a brand will rise up from Israel" — this is the Anointed King.[9]

This prophecy was infamously ascribed in the second century AD to the disastrously failed messiah, *Bar Kokhba* by Rabbi Akiva. The revered rabbi set alight the hopes of millions as well as the second Jewish rebellion against Rome when he renamed Simon Bar Kosiba with the messianic assignation, *Bar Kokhba,* the "son of a star." Unfortunately, the great rabbi recognized only the victorious, royal half of Scripture's prophetic messianic portrait and consequently backed the wrong horse, resulting in his own death, the death and enslavement of countless fellow Jews and dispossession of Jerusalem and the land of Israel.

This prophecy should be indelibly inscribed in each believer's heart in association with the familiar story, told and retold annually, of wise men from the east following the star and seeking to find the one "born king of the Jews" (Matt: 2:1-2).

THE MESSIAH WOULD BE A JEWISH PROPHET UNIQUELY SIMILAR TO MOSES

Deuteronomy 18:15-19. In this significant prophecy, it is seen that, in addition to being a Jewish king, the Messiah would also be a Jewish prophet. In fact, he will be the greatest of Jewish prophets. Moses promised that the Lord would elevate a prophet like himself from among the people of Israel. The quality that made Moses distinct from all other Jewish prophets was his intimate relationship with the Lord, speaking together with Him "face to face" (Deut. 34:10) and "mouth to mouth" (Num. 12:8). Moses' relationship with the Jewish people was also unique for a prophet. He was both their deliverer (Exod. 3:10) and an intercessor between them and God (Exod. 20:19).

The passage goes on to stress that obedience to the prophet like Moses would be so crucial, of such utmost importance to God, that those who neither recognize this prophet nor obey him will suffer the severest penalty. God's harshest judgment will fall upon those who willingly disregard this singular prophet.

The nascent church viewed the identification with Moses as a key messianic provision. Jesus' fulfillment of this prophecy was an established association that had been made by the Jewish people throughout Jesus' ministry (John 6:14; 7:40) and in the early days of the church (Acts 3:22-23).

Jesus' ministry shared certain unique features with Moses. Jesus exhibited similar intimacy with the One He called "My Father." Not only did Jesus' intimate relationship with God reflect Moses' prophetic ministry, Jesus also represented God to the people of Israel with an authority unmatched since Moses originally cradled the two stone tablets in his arms. Jesus is the embodiment, the fulfillment, the essence and the application of every regulation, statute and commandment recorded by Moses. Jesus is the living, breathing, resurrected embodiment of God's Word (John 1:1).

The common twenty-first century contemporary Jewish interpretation of these verses is that the prophet like Moses referred to the successive line of prophets in Israel who followed Moses. Yet this is not what the passage plainly teaches, and it is not the interpretation that was held in the first century. This is an unacceptable, modern explanation that fails to realize that no other man or woman in the history of Israel functioned either with God or the people of Israel in a fashion similar to Moses, with the notable exception of Jesus.

THE MESSIAH WOULD BE BORN OF A VIRGIN

Isaiah 7:14. The crux of this messianic prophecy involved the decline of the Lord's offer to King Ahaz of a miraculous sign of divine favor. The Lord responds to the king's refusal by offering His sign to the entire House of David. The miraculous sign will be the birth to a virgin of a child whose name is to be *Immanuel*, God with us.

This prophecy is famously controversial. Discussion has raged for centuries over Isaiah's use of the Hebrew word, *almah* and not *betulah* to mean virgin. However, as Fruchtenbaum capably demonstrates, while *betulah* is commonly but not exclusively used in Scripture in reference to "virgin," the use of *almah* in Scripture is never in reference to anything other than an unmarried woman of marriageable age, i.e., a virgin.[10]

That this was the accepted Jewish interpretation of this verse is clearly seen by the Septuagint's translators who, translating the Hebrew into Greek some two centuries before Christ, chose to render *almah* with *parthenos*, the incontestable Greek word for virgin.

THE IDENTITY OF MESSIAH: BOTH HUMAN AND DIVINE

THE RULE OF MESSIAH: ESTABLISHED BY GOD HIMSELF FOR ETERNITY

Isaiah 9:6-7. The prophet foretells a Davidic son to be born to the Jewish people. That this builds on the virgin-born, Immanuel, *God with us*, is clear by the fact that the son is given four remarkable, characteristic designations. He is called Wonderful Counselor, *Pele Yoeitz*, Mighty God, *El Gibbor*, Father of Eternity, *Avi Ad*, and Prince of Peace, *Sar Shalom*. At least two of these names can only be ascribed to God Himself (in fact, the exact phrase, *El Gibbor*, is used of God a few sections later, in 10:24!) Following these descriptions, Isaiah affirms that God Himself will establish that this royal child will sit on the throne of David and exercise just and righteous rule over the Jewish people for *eternity*.

The Jewish opinion on these has always been diverse. The Isaiah Targum futilely attempts a way around recognizing the divine nature of the Messiah by reconfiguring the verse to ascribe the names not to the child but to God:

> *A boy has been born unto us, a son has been given unto us, who has taken the Torah upon himself to guard it; and his name has been called by the One who gives wonderful counsel, the Mighty God, He who lives forever; Messiah …*

An alternate attempt around the prophecy, without however, truly wrestling with the divine assignations is identifying the child with Isaiah's contemporary, King Hezekiah.[11]

It is curious that the New Testament authors do not make greater use of this passage in their apologetic approach to Israel. Other passages take pride of place in their evangelistic presentations. Nonetheless, this is a potent passage that powerfully demonstrates the mysterious union of two natures, human and divine, within one individual messiah.

THE MESSIAH AS A DESCENDENT OF DAVID: BORN IN HUMBLE CIRCUMSTANCES, LED BY GOD'S SPIRIT, RULING OVER BOTH ISRAEL AND THE GENTILE NATIONS

Isaiah 11:1-10. Isaiah pictures the tree of the House of David as being chopped down to the stump, in other words, having fallen on hard times. In fact, David's royal name isn't even used here; rather, it is that of his father, Jesse. Yet, this humble stump of the Davidic line, no matter how modest in appearance, is described as still possessing life-force and brings forth a fresh new shoot, indeed, a fruit-bearing branch, the messianic descendant of David.

Isaiah then describes the dominant characteristic of *the Branch.* He will be completely and totally dominated by the leading of God's Spirit. This will empower the Messiah's rule to be one of extreme righteousness and acute judgment. Furthermore, his rule extends not only over Israel, but over the nations, the Gentiles, as well. This will not be gratuitous dominance, but rather, the reign of the Messiah will be welcomed by both Jews and Gentiles.

Finally, this passage describes the time of the messianic reign to be characterized by ultimate, perfect peace. This will be a period of worldwide spiritual awareness as well as extraordinary changes within the animal kingdom concerning the abrogation of predatory instincts.

The Branch is a well-worn messianic term which finds its initial usage here. This passage, so vividly portraying both figure and era, has long been acknowledged in Jewish thought as messianic. It is translated in the Septuagint as, "and there shall be in that day the root of Jesse, even he who arises to rule over nations," and paraphrased in the Isaiah Targum as, "and a king shall come forth from the sons of Jesse, and the Messiah shall be exalted from the sons of his sons." [12]

Jesus arrived at a select period in history when Israel dwelt in the land without being ruled by a scion of David, but under the domination of a Gentile power. By that time, the House of David had been reduced to an inglorious stump. The gospels reveal how in Jesus, the Davidic house was to be restored to holy grandeur.

THE MESSIAH WOULD HAVE AN ORDINARY APPEARANCE. HE WOULD SUFFER, BE REJECTED AND ALTHOUGH INNOCENT, BE EXECUTED AS THE MEANS OF ATONEMENT FOR ISRAEL'S SIN. HE WOULD THEN BE RESURRECTED FROM THE DEAD

Isaiah 52:13-53:12. In the passage, by far and away the richest treasury of messianic data in the prophetic corpus, Isaiah described the Messiah as despised and rejected, forsaken of men, a man of sorrows, without esteem (Isa. 53:3). This servant of the Lord was to be rejected by the people of the Lord. Through the suffering of this Messiah, intercession would be made on behalf of all people. This passage stands as a Scriptural monument to Messianic suffering.

The Messiah would have no attractiveness or impressive appearance

(Isa. 53:2), and Israel would believe that His sufferings were brought on as a consequence of His own sin (Isa. 53:4-5). The Messiah would be cruelly pierced through and crushed, chastened and scourged. Yet through His suffering, He paradoxically heals them, bearing Israel's sorrows (Isa. 53:5-6). It is for their transgressions and iniquities that He willingly will suffer, not for His own (Isa. 53:4).

Isa. 53:5 discloses that the Messiah would not merely suffer, but would die. Despite Israel's sin and disobedience, God would divert the just punishment for the nation's iniquity toward the Messiah (Isa. 53:5-6). Although innocent of any violence, rebellion or sin, the Messiah would be killed in the prime of life. Like a perfect, unblemished lamb slain at Passover, He would shed His blood for the redemption of the chosen nation. The ultimate personification of goodness would bear the ultimate punishment, His sacrifice to go largely unrecognized by His own people.

This sacrifice, however, would be central to the divine master plan. It would be the Lord's sovereign aim for His Messiah to be crushed. This was to enable the Servant to do the unprecedented - render Himself as the ultimate and final guilt offering (Isa. 53:10). The Messiah would die, yet through His sacrifice make perfect intercession for all sinners by carrying their sins (Isa. 53:12). He is called the Righteous One who, by bearing the penalty for the sins of others, has justified His people. As the reward for His suffering and death, His self-sacrifice, He will be exalted and glorified. The murdered Messiah must be raised up (Isa. 53:10-12).

The ancient rabbinic literature strongly attests that it was the overwhelming consensus of the Jewish rabbis that Isaiah's suffering servant passage spoke of the Messiah. The first century AD Targum Jonathan translates Isaiah 52:13-53:12 as,

> *Behold, My servant the Messiah shall prosper; he shall be exalted and great and very powerful...It is the will of the Lord to purify and to acquit as innocent the remnant of his people, to cleanse their souls of sin, so that they may see the kingdom of their Messiah ...*

Fruchtenbaum demonstrates this was also the position of the majority of the authors of the *Midrash*.[13] He adds that is also the interpretation of the *Zohar*, the central text of Jewish kabalistic mysticism.[14] Furthermore, this position is upheld in the Babylonian Talmud, which labels the Messiah as "the sick one," and the "leper scholar."[15]

However, in taking this passage at face value, the question eventually arose as to how to square this suffering, rejected and executed Messiah with the supernaturally endowed, victorious conquering hero of other messianic texts. It was at this point that the rabbis devised the ingenious solution of dividing the messianic figure into two separate messiahs. One messiah, ben Joseph would die, the other, ben David, would reign. Conveniently, Messiah ben David would then resurrect Messiah ben Joseph from the dead.[16]

Regardless of the volume of rabbinic opinion, it is incontestable that one particular rabbi, Jesus, explicitly identified Himself as the prophetic fulfillment of the Isaiah 53 passage, the one who would suffer, be treated with contempt and be "numbered with the transgressors" (Mark 9:12; Luke 22:37). His identification with the suffering servant is also implicit in foretelling His death and resurrection (Matt. 26:2; Mark 9:31; 10:33; Luke 24:7)), and in his silence before Pilate (Mark 15:5).

THE MESSIAH WOULD BE DIVINE, CAPABLE OF STANDING IN THE VERY PRESENCE OF GOD HIMSELF IN THE HEAVENS, AND WOULD BE GRANTED ETERNAL DOMINION OVER THE ENTIRE WORLD.

Daniel 7:13-14. In this passage we find the presentation of the preeminent eschatological, supernatural and majestic messianic figure, the "son of man." Daniel envisions within the clouds of heaven an exalted figure who is presented before the enthroned Lord (the "Ancient of Days"). God gives this figure dominion and glory over the entire earth. His reign is described as eternal and his kingdom is characterized as unshakable. Daniel's brief yet potent portrait of this messianic figure captured the countless imaginations. Intertestamental apocalyptic literature is studded through with references to the "star" of this passage, none more so than the second century BC text of 1 Enoch, which, in reference to the preexistence of this figure, states,

> It is for this that he has been chosen and hidden before Him, even before the creation of the world and evermore.[17]

In a following passage, the text elaborates on the absolute dominion of the god-like messiah and his subjects' worshipful relationship toward him, recording,

> And all the kings and the mighty and the exalted and the rulers of the earth shall fall down before him on their faces, and worship and set their hope upon the son of man, and petition him and ask for mercy at his hands.[18]

This enigmatic title of "son of man," the Aramaic *bar enash*, was Jesus' preferred messianic self-designation. His use of this term for Himself is studded throughout the gospels. Although the phrase is often used in the Hebrew Scripture as an alternate means to simply indicate a human being, someone in possession of the character of humanity, "son of man" was not universally used in this fashion. Jesus did not wish to merely indicate that he was a human being, a "regular Joe." Jesus used this phrase as an allusion to the vision of the Hebrew prophet, Daniel, of a divinely exalted figure, "one like a son of man," coming with "the clouds of heaven" (Dan. 7:13-14). This mysterious figure receives authority over God's kingdom from the "Ancient of Days," God Himself.

Interestingly, as frequently as Jesus employed this term, He is the only one in the entire New Testament who does so with the exception of this singular use by Stephen (Acts 7:56). As the church expanded beyond a specifically Jewish context, where familiarity with Daniel's vision of the "son of man" and "Ancient of Days" could be assumed, various alternative messianic titles rapidly came into vogue. Nonetheless, this passage still proves a formidable stumbling block to those who would deny the divinity of the Messiah.

THE MESSIAH WOULD BE BORN IN BETHLEHEM. DESPITE EXPERIENCING BIRTH, THE MESSIAH IS ALSO A DIVINE, ETERNAL BEING.

Micah 5:2. This passage provides the location of the Messiah's birth. Yet, although he is to come forth from the town of Bethlehem, Micah elaborates by revealing that his true origins are to be found from the days of eternity. Messiah is a divine, preexistent, eternal being who will be born to rule Israel.

That this passage was understood to refer to Messiah can be vividly seen in the familiar gospel passage where Herod inquired of the scribes and chief priests as to the location of the Messiah's birth. Basing their answer on this passage, they confidently answered, "Bethlehem" (Matthew 2:4-6).

RIDING INTO JERUSALEM ON A DONKEY, MESSIAH HUMBLY PRESENTS HIMSELF AND HIS KINGDOM OF PEACE TO THE JEWISH PEOPLE

Zechariah 9:9-10. The prophet Zechariah reveals the arrival of the Messiah to Jerusalem, presented here as the Lord's representative agent, ruling for the Lord as the righteous and victorious King of Israel. The Lord Himself performs the introduction of the Deliverer to His people. He describes the Messiah as humble, just, bearing salvation and conveying a kingdom of peace, designated by King Messiah's entrance into the holy city riding not on a war horse, but rather, a donkey. Under Messiah's righteous and peaceful reign, not only will the Kingdom of Israel's national borders expand in all directions to their divinely promised extent by way of the Abrahamic Covenant (Gen. 15:18-21) but the King of Israel will also reign over the whole earth.

Considering the duality of the messianic presentation inherent within Zechariah's prophecy, it is understandable how some considerable interpretive confusion could arise among the rabbis as to how to systematize these seemingly contradictory messianic images *within the same passage*, not to mention the contrasting imagery of "suffering servant" and "son of man." One may even somewhat sympathize with those charged with this task! The most popular solution, as previously mentioned, was the proposal of two messiahs, one who would be humble and one who would serve as conquering champion.

There are numerous examples within rabbinic literature of the messianic interpretation of this passage. Maimonides wrote, "This is the Anointed King, of whom it is stated: 'And his reign shall be from sea to sea.'"[19] There is even the creative example within the Talmud of the rabbi who simply refused to collate the two contrasting messianic portraits within this passage and others, proposing that God would choose between them as to the sort of messiah that Israel would receive, dependent upon the nation's level of righteousness.

> Rabbi Joseph the son of Levi objects that it is written in one place, "Behold one like the son of man comes with the clouds of heaven," but in another place it is written "lowly and riding upon an ass." The solution is, if they be righteous he shall come with the clouds of heaven, but if they not be righteous he shall come lowly riding upon an ass.[20]

Jesus fulfilled the first half of Zechariah's prophecy (v. 9) when he unambiguously presented Himself to His people as the Messiah by riding into Jerusalem on a donkey during the week of Passover (Matt. 21:1-11; Mark 11:1-10; Luke 19:30-38; John 12:14-15). With His subsequent death and resurrection, there is a hiatus in the messianic program, known as the church age. However, this lull in messianic proceedings is only temporary. The second half of the prophecy (Zech. 9:10) will assuredly be fulfilled when Jesus returns to His people as a conquering warrior.

FOLLOWING HIS REJECTION AND VIOLENT EXECUTION, THE HUMAN/DIVINE MESSIAH WOULD SUPERNATURALLY MANIFEST HIMSELF TO ISRAEL AND FINALLY WIN THEIR WHOLEHEARTED ACCEPTANCE

Zechariah 12:10. During the last days of the Tribulation, following the gathering of every nation to make war against the Jewish people and the besieging on every side of their holy capital, Jerusalem, the Lord will intervene on behalf of His people. When the threat posed by Israel's national enemies is finally defused upon their comprehensive defeat, the Lord will infuse the Jewish people with spiritual conviction and contrition. He will enable the Jewish people to perceive their need for divine forgiveness and the entire nation will repent. The reason for their repentance will be their prior rejection of the Messiah, the representative agent of the Lord's loving leadership.

It is unmistakable in this passage that Zechariah is depicting the Lord's identity as being integrated with the Messiah's. He declares that when the Jewish people see the Lord they will suddenly comprehend that in mortally wounding the Messiah it was as if they had physically pierced the Lord Himself ("they will look upon Me whom they have pierced.") Upon this realization, their sorrow will be so enormous that it must be compared to a parent's bitter grief at the death of an only child and the consequent termination of family lineage. In Zechariah's further description of this anguish in the following verses, he reveals that the mourning for this messianic Jewish King will not only yield public national anguish, but private, intense, individual grief, led by the Jewish political and spiritual leadership (12:11-14).

The Talmud records an example of a rabbinic difference of opinion concerning the reason for the intensity of Jewish mourning described within this potent passage.

> Why is this mourning in messianic times? There is a difference of interpretation between Rabbi Dosa and the Rabanan. One opinion is that they mourn for Messiah Ben Joseph who is killed, and another explanation is that they mourn for the slaying of the evil inclination. It is well according to him who explains that the cause is the slaying of the Messiah since that well agrees with this verse. If it refers to the slaying of the evil inclination, it must be asked, is this an occasion for mourning? Is it not rather an occasion for rejoicing? Why then should they weep?[21]

THE MESSIAH WOULD BE THE ULTIMATE SON OF DAVID

I Chronicles 17:10-14. This is one of the two passages (the other being 2 Sam. 7:11-16) in which we find the establishment of the Davidic Covenant, the unconditional set of promises that God made to David of a perpetual dynasty, an unshakable kingdom, and an eternal throne. An additional component of the Davidic covenant not enumerated only in the Chronicles account is the promise of a unique future descendant, an undying son ("settled forever," v. 14) to permanently guarantee the previous promises.

In first century Israel, the title "son of David" conveyed a potent political charge. It was widely understood to refer to an idealized political revolutionary who would cast off the shackles of Roman oppression, judge the wicked and purge evil from the midst of Israel. Israel enthusiastically anticipated that the dynasty of David would be restored and the kingdom of Israel made glorious. This expectation, based on the Hebrew prophets (Jer. 23:5-8; Isa. 11:1-16), is widely espoused throughout first century Jewish literature, including the Dead Sea Scrolls.

Jesus conducted His ministry amidst this whirlwind of amplified Davidic anticipation. In fact, one of the foremost messianic titles ascribed to Jesus in the New Testament is "Son of David." This designates Jesus as the recipient of all the promises God had made to David concerning the future and eternal government of one of his descendants. It specifies Jesus to be a royal, majestic messiah who is entitled by birthright to rule and reign over all Israel.

During Jesus' earthly ministry, while He certainly accepted this title as applicable to Himself (Matt. 9:28; 20:32; Mark 10:49), He abjectly refused to be drawn into either political intrigue or revolutionary activity. While Herod the Great feared the one who was born "king of the Jews" (Matt. 2:2), and although He was crucified as "king of the Jews" (Luke 23:38), Jesus forcefully proclaimed that His kingdom, at least for the present time, was "not of this world" (John 18:36).

According to the teaching of the apostles, the Son of David concept is primarily applicable to Jesus' future function as king of the earth, as He reigns from His father David's throne in Jerusalem. The "Son of David" concept is specifically linked to Jesus by both Peter (Acts 2:30) and Paul (Acts 13:23) and was an important theological component within the presentations of both apostles when addressing a Jewish audience.

THE MESSIAH WOULD BE THE SON OF GOD

Psalm 2:1-12. This is the first of several messianic psalms written by David, both king and prophet. The psalm opens with a description of worldwide opposition to both God and "His Anointed," the Messiah. This is followed by a depiction of the Lord's wrath being unleashed upon all those who contest the Jewish King whom He has installed to rule Israel.

David's poetry then shifts from third person narrative to the first person voice of the Messiah. The text affirms that the Messiah is the Lord's Son, endowed with the very authority of God Almighty Himself, not only over Israel, but over all nations of the earth. The passage then shifts back to the third person with a warning of the unqualified severity of the Son of God's judgment and wrath to be directed toward all those who do not worship the Lord by showing due reverence toward His Son ("kiss the Son," v. 12).

Without question, this passage has traditionally been recognized as messianic. As the revered eleventh century rabbi Rashi (who always stood ready with an alternative interpretation to various pesky messianic prophecies that did not fit his theological grid – see Isa. 52:13-53:12, above) acknowledges, "Our rabbis relate it as relating to King Messiah."[22] The gospel of John, in addition to the rest of the New Testament, comfortably rests on the foundation of the prophetic truths contained within this psalm.

THE MESSIAH WOULD BE RESURRECTED FROM THE DEAD

Psalm 16:1-11. This is another messianic psalm of David, again written in the first person voice of the Messiah, his descendant. The specific circumstances attending David's composition of this psalm are unknown. However, it begins with David's plea for God's preservation of his life. It continues with praise of God's mercy and goodness and comments on the hopelessness of others foolish enough to worship other gods instead of the one true God. David concludes the psalm with a confirmation of confidence in the Lord's sustenance of his flesh and his soul, both in the present and beyond death.

In the book of Acts, Peter interprets this passage to argue the point that David, writing one thousand years earlier, was consciously aware that his subject was the Messiah's resurrection (Acts 2:25-32). Peter boldly and confidently argued that David could not possibly have been writing about himself. David died, was buried, and most assuredly had not been resurrected.

However, God had established an indissoluble covenant with David in which David was promised that one of his descendants would forever rule over Israel (2 Sam.7:12-13; Psa.132:11; 89:3–4). The Holy Spirit enabled

David to look ahead into the future and understand precisely how God's Davidic Covenant promise of an eternal throne was to be fulfilled. God showed David that an eternal throne and an unending dynasty required an immortal descendant. David had been allowed to see the future Anointed One, the Messiah, the One who would neither decompose nor be abandoned to the abode of the dead (Greek *Hades*, Hebrew *Sheol*). After resting in the grave and abiding in Paradise, the Messiah, paradoxically, would still live forever. In order to fulfill the Davidic Covenant, this Son of David would of necessity need to be resurrected.

THE MESSIAH WOULD BE A DIVINE KING/PRIEST OF THE ORDER OF MELCHIZEDEK

Psalm 110:1-4. This is another prophetic psalm of David. There are three individuals referred to within the first verse of the psalm. There are the two individuals who are called "Lord," and there is the author, David. In English translation it is more difficult to perceive the messianic dynamic of the psalm than in Hebrew, primarily because David, in reference to these two individuals, used two different words, both of which are translated as "lord." The first "Lord," is the name YHWH and refers to the covenant making God of Abraham, Isaac and Jacob. The second "Lord" is the Hebrew, *Adonai*. This second "lord," Adonai, is the individual whom David called "my Lord."

If the first "Lord" refers to God and the second "Lord" is David's lord, then, obviously, neither of these "lordly" individuals could have been David. Indeed, it was universally accepted that David had neither been resurrected nor had he ascended into heaven. This raises the question, if God is the first Lord, and David is the "my" of "my Lord," then just who is David's Lord? Jesus Himself had vexed the Pharisees by posing this perplexing issue (Matt. 22:44-45). Certainly, while he lived, David had no mortal lord. As the undisputed sovereign of all Israel, his only Lord was God Himself.

Of course, the answer to this prophetic riddle, Peter reveals in the book of Acts (2:34-35), is Jesus. He announced to the "whole house of Israel," that through God's exaltation of Jesus they might be supremely confident that "this Jesus," whom the Jewish nation had crucified, had been exalted by God and proclaimed to be "both Lord and Christ."

Psalm 110:1 is the most frequently cited messianic prophecy in the New Testament. Peter stands firmly within Jewish tradition in interpreting this passage as referring to the messiah. It has a long pedigree of being so interpreted within rabbinic literature (albeit, never with reference to Jesus). Peter demonstrated, however, that Jesus' exaltation fulfilled this prophecy. Our Messiah is currently sitting as an equal to God at His right hand, until such time as Jesus' enemies are made His "footstool."

Psalm 110:4 builds upon this with an extraordinary statement declaring that the Messiah would not only be a king but also a priest. However, he would not be a Levitical priest, as he is David's son, descended from Judah. His priesthood would necessarily need to go around the Law of Moses and find its basis in that of the inscrutable figure of Genesis 14, the righteous king, Melchizedek, priest of the Most High. The book of Hebrews affirms in great detail that Jesus is, indeed, both eternal priest and king.

CONTEMPORARY JEWISH VIEWS OF THE MESSIANIC HOPE

There is an old Jewish story that illustrates the present status of messianic hope among the Jewish people.

> Many years ago in Russia, a rabbi is approached by a man in need of employment. The rabbi instructs him to stand each morning at the village gate and wait in place to greet the Messiah when he comes. The man inquires as to the salary. The rabbi offers him one ruble per month. "Only one ruble? This pay is very low," the man protests. "True," replies the rabbi, "but you can't beat the job security."

In regard to messianic beliefs, contemporary twenty-first century Judaism is perhaps less diverse today than at any other point in two millennia. The feeling is expressed among many Jews, whether in pulpit or pew, academic ivory tower and local marketplace alike, that contemporary Judaism has theologically evolved, progressing beyond and jettisoning old, antiquated, and unnecessary messianic beliefs. "These earlier systems (of Judaism) resorted to the myth of the Messiah as savior and redeemer of Israel, a supernatural figure engaged in political-historical tasks as king of the Jews, even a God-man facing the crucial historical questions of Israel's life and resolving them: the Christ as king of the world, of the ages, of death itself."[23]

The beliefs among the major denominations, with one exception (discussed below) fall within fairly rigid boundaries. Progressing denominationally from most theologically secular to most traditional, one generally discovers the following beliefs. Among *Reconstructionist* Jews, the concept of a personal messiah is rejected outright. The traditional liturgy has been scrubbed free of all reference to a personal messiah. They do believe that man through his efforts has the capability to bring about some sort of loosely defined messianic age, however. *Reform* Jews similarly reject the concept of a personal messiah and believe that all Jews are obligated to work towards a messianic age, with the possibility that God may assist in the success of their effort.

Conservative Jews believe that all messianic expectations arise from unverifiable, personal speculation, allowing for the possibility of a personal messiah or messianic age, with the caveat that Scripture's teaching on the subject may simply be well-meaning, elaborate metaphor or symbolism, not to be taken literally.[24] Nonetheless, as with Reform Judaism, the Conservative movement holds Jews responsible to strive toward bringing about a messianic age (with the added incentive that there may really be a personal messiah, after all!)

Orthodox Judaism, the standard-bearer for traditional Judaism, mostly holds fast to the messianic teaching and code of the eleventh century rabbi, Maimonides (see above.) In his fourteen volume commentary, *Mishneh Torah*, Maimonides taught the expectation of both a personal messiah and messianic age, although he believed that most biblical messianic prophecies were allegorical. In this, the great philosopher rabbi was able to maintain the appearance of a high regard for Scripture.

With the exception of one infamous group. A large percentage of members belonging to a major ultra-Orthodox Chasidic sect, the *Chabad-Lubavitch*, are a significant anomaly within the contemporary Jewish world. Many, perhaps most, in this group believe that the leader of their sect, the revered Rebbe (rabbi) Menachem Mendel Schneerson, is the Messiah. One problem with this scenario—the Rebbe has been dead since 1994. Even so, thousands of Jewish children in Lubavitch schools are still being taught the chant, *"May our Master, Teacher, and Rabbi, the King Messiah, live forever."*[25] This mantra is fervently sung by the Rebbe's followers in faith that he will return to them through rising from the dead.[26]

As we consider the multitudes of Abraham, Isaac and Jacob's children who are altogether bereft of their messianic hope, misguided in that hope or have misdirected it toward a man whose tomb is still occupied, let us join together with Paul in his heartfelt prayer for his Jewish brethren to, at long last, recognize the identity of God's true Messiah (Rom. 10:1).

GENTILES ARE BLESSED BECAUSE OF ISRAEL
From the standpoint of the gospel [the Jews] are enemies for your sake, but from the standpoint of God's election they are beloved [to Him] for the sake of the [promises] to the fathers [of the Jewish people], for the gifts and the calling of God cannot be revoked (Rom. 11:28-29).
• Israel's transgressions bring forth riches for the world (Rom. 11:12). • Israel's failures bring forth riches for the Gentiles (Rom. 11:12). • God will graft the Jews into a place of blessing again (Rom. 11:23). • Gentiles have been shown mercy because of their disobedience (Rom. 11:30).

CHAPTER 5

A HISTORY OF CHRISTIAN ZIONISM

Thomas Ice

In the last couple of years the secular community and some in the religious community have woken up to the fact that much of the American Evangelical community is very supportive of the modern state of Israel. Guess what? They do not like it one bit! They see an ever increasing danger and even the possibility that Christian Zionism could bring about World War III.

Genesis 12:3 records God's promise to bless those who bless Abraham and his descendants (i.e., Israel). The Abrahamic covenant is directed to Abraham, Isaac, Jacob, and their descendants. It is repeated to them about twenty times in Genesis (12:1–3, 7–9; 13:14–18; 15:1–18; 17:1–27; 22:15–19; 26:2–6, 24–25; 27:28–29, 38–40; 28:1–4, 10–22; 31:3, 11–13; 32:22–32; 35:9–15; 48:3–4, 10–20; 49:1–28; 50:23–25). Although there are multiple features to the Abrahamic Covenant, it always includes the land promises to Israel. Does this promise still stand or has it been changed? If these biblical promises are to be taken literally and still apply to Israel, and not the church, it should not be surprising to anyone that such a view leads one, such as myself, to Christian Zionism. Zionism is simply the belief that the Jewish people have been given the land of Israel by covenant promise from God and have a current right to occupy that land. Christian Zionists are Christians who agree with this belief.

CHRISTIAN ZIONISM UNDER ATTACK

Back in the spring of 1992, *Christianity Today* did a cover story on Christian Zionism. The article "For the Love of Zion" (March 9, 1992; pp. 46-50) reflected a generally negative tone toward Christian Zionists, which is normal for *Christianity Today*. They made the case that evangelical support for Israel is still strong but it has peaked and is declining. Yet, today, over a decade later the consensus appears to be that Christian Zionism is getting stronger, but so are those Christians who oppose it.

In February 2003, the Zionist Organization of America released extensive polling results from the polling firm of John McLaughlin and Associates indicating rising support by Americans of the modern state of Israel as against the Arab Palestinian state. 71% of Americans were opposed to creating a Palestinian state and by almost the same margin Americans oppose any support to the Palestinian Arabs. Much of this current support is surely generated by those who are classified as Christian Zionists.

There have been a number of articles in the media about the alleged dangers of the Christian support for Israel. A widely noted article appeared in the May 23, 2002 issue of the *Wall Street Journal* entitled, "How Israel Became a Favorite Cause of Christian Right." For some, this is horrifying. Jane Lampman of the *Christian Science Monitor* has written "Mixing Prophecy and Politics," an article about the dangers of Christian Zionism.[1] Evangelical historian Timothy Weber has just released a book entitled *On The Road to Armageddon: How Evangelicals Became Israel's Best Friend.*[2] He believes our support for Israel is potentially dangerous.[3] The Presbyterian Church, USA, passed a resolution in the Summer of 2004 in which they "officially disavow Christian Zionism as a legitimate theological stance."[4]

Over the last few years there have been a number of books and articles that chide those of us who believe that the nation and people of Israel have a positive future detailed in Bible prophecy.[5] They think that evangelical support for Israel is a bad thing, because, the modern state of Israel is viewed by them as a bad thing, totally unrelated in any way to Bible prophecy. These naysayers often like to blame J. N. Darby and dispensationalism as the modern source of evangelical views. The truth of the matter is that love for Israel was well entrenched by Bible-believing Christians long before 1830. What is the history of Christian Zionism or the Restorationist movement (as it was known in earlier times) during two thousand years of church history?

THE EARLY CHURCH

While there is some evidence that a few ante-Nicene fathers envisioned the Jews back in the land of Israel, by and large, they did not really look for a restoration of the Jews to the land of Israel, even though premillennialism was widespread. There was a statement or two by some of these early believers that implied a Jewish return to Israel. For example, Irenaeus writing about A.D. 185 expressed this view in the following way:

> But when this Antichrist shall have devastated all things in this world, he will reign for three years and six months, and sit in the Temple at Jerusalem; and then the Lord will come from heaven in the clouds, in the glory of the Father, sending this man and those who follow him into the lake of fire; but bringing in for the righteous the times of the kingdom.[6]

Carl Ehle has summarized the views on the early church as follows: "What is singularly absent from early millenarian schemes is the motif of the Restoration of Israel, ... the Church Fathers from the second century on did not encourage any notion of a revival of national Israel."[7]

Even though the ante-Nicene fathers were predominately premillennial in their understanding of future things, they laid a groundwork that would not only oppose Christian Zionism, but eventually premillennialism as well. Premillennialist Justin Martyr was the first to view "the Christian church as 'the true spiritual Israel' (*Dial. 11*)"[8] around A.D. 160. Justin's views laid the groundwork for the growing belief that the church had superseded or replaced Israel. "Misunderstanding of it colours the Church's attitude to Judaism and contributes to anti-Semitism," notes Peter Richardson.[9] Further, by the time of Irenaeus, it becomes entrenched in Christian theology that "the bulk of Israel's Scriptures [are] indecisive for the formation of Christian doctrine."[10] The details about Israel's future, especially in the Old Testament are simply not a part of the development of Christian theology. Jeffrey Siker cites this issue as the primary reason for the disinheriting of the Jews within the early Christian church. "The first factor is the diminishing emphasis upon the eschatological dimensions of the Christian faith."[11] Lacking an emphasis upon Israel's future, it is not surprising that belief in a future restoration of the Jews to their homeland is sparse in the early and medieval church.

THE MEDIEVAL CHURCH

Apart from a few sporadic medieval statements, Christian belief in the restoration of Israel to her land would not surface until "the second generation Protestant reformers."[12] Normally, support for Christian Zionism appears to go hand-and-hand with belief in millennialism. Some forms of postmillennialism and all kinds of premillennialism make it conducive for its advocates to look for a return of the Jews to Israel. "Inhibitions about millennialism were so pronounced that for the entire time between about 400 and 1050 there is no surviving written product that displays an independent Western millenarian imagination."[13] Since millennialism was absent from the church for about a thousand years it is not surprising that Christian Zionism was not a topic of concern during this time. It should also be remembered that these issues be viewed within the backdrop of a vicious anti-Semitism that governed the thought of the Medieval Church.

Joachim of Fiore (c. 1135–1202) dominated the eschatological beliefs of the middle ages. Even though some think that Joachim could have been of Jewish decent,[14] his thought is typical of the non-Zionist views of the time. "The final conversion of the Jews was a common medieval theme but one of peculiar significance to Joachim,"[15] notes Joachimist scholar Marjorie Reeves. It was popular in medieval eschatology to see a future time in which "Rome was to be the temporal capital of the world, Jerusalem the spiritual."[16] "The great rulers of Jewish history—Joseph, David, Solomon, Zorobabel—were interpreted in a priestly rather than an imperial sense,"[17] notes Reeves. Thus, while medieval eschatology saw a role for the Jews in the future, it was one of subservience, having been absorbed into the Gentile church. Medieval prophetic thought provided no real distinct future for the Jews as a regathered nation of Israel; certainly little that could be labeled as Zionism.

In spite of the overall trend to the contrary, there is some evidence that a few stray late-medieval voices did see some kind of a future for Israel. An example of one who held to a Jewish restoration is Gerard of Borgo San Donnino (around 1255). He taught that some Jews would be blessed as Jews in the end time and would return to their ancient homeland.[18] John of Rupescissa (ca. 1310–1366) could most likely be viewed as a Christian Zionist. "For him the converted Jews would become God's new imperial nation and Jerusalem would be completely rebuilt to become the center of the purified faith. For proof he drew on a literal exposition of the Old Testament prophecies which until then had been read by Christian exegetes to apply either to the time of the incarnation or to the heavenly Jerusalem in the beyond."[19] For the most part, medieval European Christendom remained overwhelmingly anti-Semitic in thought, word and deed, which would not lend itself to seeing a future for the Jews in Israel.

THE REFORMATION

As I have noted, the flourishing of millennialism and a belief in a future return of the Jews to their land often go hand-and-hand. This is evident as the second generation Reformers begin to fade. Thus, to date, I have not been able to find any reformers who supported the restoration of the Jews back to their land in Israel. Such views must await the post-reformation era. However, the Reformation in many ways prepared the way for the later rise of Christian Zionist views. "It marked the end of the medieval era and the beginning of the modern time."[20] The main gift of the Reformation was that of the Bible in the language of the people.

"Since Wyclif's time," notes Barbara Tuchman, "the New Learning had revived the study of Greek and Hebrew, so long ignored in the Latin-dominated Middle Ages."[21] Michael Pragai tells us the following:

> The growing importance of the English Bible was a concomitant of the spreading Reformation, and it is true to say that the Reformation would never have taken hold had the Bible not replaced the Pope as the ultimate spiritual authority. With the Bible as its tool, the Reformation returned to the geographic origins of Christianity in Palestine. It thereby gradually diminished the authority of Rome.[22]

Thus, so it would come to be, that the provision of the Bible in the language of the people would become the greatest spur to the rise of Christian Zionism. The simple provision of the Bible in the native tongue of the people, which gave rise to their incessant reading and familiarization of it, especially the Old Testament, was the greatest soil that yielded a crop of Christian Zionism over time.

THE ENGLISH PROTESTANT ERA

The path that led to the widespread belief in the end-time restoration of the Jews to Israel started with the study of the Bible, first in the original languages, followed by the influence of the newly acquired English translations.[23] When both scholars and laymen alike, for the first time in the history of the church, had the text of Scripture (both Old and New Testaments) more readily available, it led to greater study, a more literal interpretation and a greater awareness of the Israel of the Old Testament. This provided the atmosphere in which a major shift occurred in England (also on the Continent to a lesser degree) from medieval Jew-hatred, which led to the expulsion of all Jews from Britain in 1290, to their invitation under Cromwell to return in 1655. "From such a context and from among this people," notes Douglas Culver, "now growing more and more intimate with things Jewish, the early millenarian protagonists for the restoration of the Jews to their Palestinian homeland arose."[24] However, it would be a tough road to get to the point where belief in a Jewish restoration to their ancient homeland would become so widespread.

It wasn't just any group of English protestants that provided a fertile soil for Jewish Restorationist doctrines, it was out of the English Puritan movement that this belief sprung. "Starting with the Puritan ascendancy," notes Tuchman, "the movement among the English for the return of the Jews to Palestine began."[25] Why the Puritan? Puritans were not just dissenters, they were a Protestant sect that valued the Old Testament to an unprecedented degree in their day. Tuchman tells us:

> They began to feel for the Old Testament a preference that showed itself in all their sentiments and habits. They paid a respect to the Hebrew language that they refused to the language of their Gospels and of the epistles of Paul. They baptized their children by the names not of Christian saints but of Hebrew patriarchs and warriors. They turned the weekly festival by which the church had from primitive times commemorated the resurrection of her Lord, into the Jewish Sabbath. They sought for precedents to guide their ordinary conduct in the books of Judges and Kings.[26]

One of the first Englishman to put forth the view that the Jews should be restored to the land of Israel was a scholar who had taken two degrees from Cambridge named Francis Kett. In 1585 he had published a book entitled *The Glorious and Beautiful Garland of Mans Glorification Containing the Godly Misterie of Heavenly Jerusalem* (one of the shorter titles of the day). While his book primarily dealt with other matters, Kett did have a section in which he mentioned "the notion of Jewish national return to Palestine."[27] This notion, which some think was likely gaining many followers,[28] was deemed heretical to the English establishment of the day and Rev. Kett was quickly burned at the stake on January 14, 1589, for expressing such views about the Jews return to their land, an idea he claimed to have received from reading the Bible.[29] About the same time as Kett, strict Calvinist, Edmund Bunny (1540–1619) taught the Jewish restoration to Palestine in a couple of books: *The Scepter of Ivday* (1584) and *The Coronation of David* (1588).[30]

As the 1600s arrived, a flurry of books advocating Jewish restoration to their land began to appear. Thomas Draxe released in 1608 *The Worldes Resurrection: On the general calling of the Jews, A familiar Commentary upon the eleventh Chapter of Saint Paul to the Romaines, according to the sense of Scripture.* Draxe argued for Israel's restoration based upon his Calvinism and Covenant Theology.[31]

Two great giants of their era were Thomas Brightman (1552–1607), (likely a Postmillennialist) and Premillennialist Joseph Mede (1586–1638) who both wrote boldly of a future restoration of Israel. Brightman's work, *Revelation of the Revelation* appeared in 1609 and told "how the Jews will return from the areas North and East of Palestine to Jerusalem and how the Holy Land and the Jewish Christian church will become the centre of a Christian world."[32] Brightman wrote: "What, shall they return to Jerusalem again? There is nothing more certain; the prophets do everywhere confirm it."[33] Mede's contribution was released in 1627 in Latin [34] and in 1642 in English as *The Key of the Revelation*.[35] The father of English premillennialism was also an ardent advocate of Jewish restoration to their homeland. Momentum was certainly building toward widespread acceptance of English belief in Jewish restoration, but a few bumps in the road still lay ahead.

Giles Fletcher (1549–1611), a fellow at King's College, Cambridge and Queen Elizabeth's ambassador to Russia wrote a work advocating

Restorationism. Fletcher's book, *Israel Redux: or the Restauration of Israel; or the Restauration of Israel exhibited in two short treatises* (shortened title) was published posthumously by the Puritan divine Samuel Lee in 1677.[36] Fletcher cites a letter in his book from 1606 as he argues for the return of the Jews to their land.[37] Fletcher repeatedly taught the "certainty of their return in God's due time."[38]

A key proponent for Israel's future restoration was Henry Finch (1558-1625) who wrote a seminal work on the subject in 1621, called *The World's Resurrection or The Calling of the Jewes. A Present to Judah and the Children of Israel that Ioyned with Him, and to Ioseph (that valiant tribe of Ephraim) and all the House of Israel that Ioyned with Him.*[39] Finch, at the time of the publication of his book was a member of Parliament and the most highly respected legal scholars in England at the time. "The book had been published for a matter only of weeks when the roof caved in on the author's head," notes Culver. "In the persecution which ensued, Finch lost his reputation, his possessions, his health—all precipitated by his belief in Jewish national restoration."[40] "Finch's argument may be considered the first genuine plan for Restoration."[41] Finch taught that the biblical "passages which speak of a return of these people to their own land, their conquest of enemies and their rule of the nations are to be taken literally, not allegorically as of the Church."[42] King James of England was offended by Finch's statement that all nations would become subservient to national Israel at the time of her restoration.[43] Finch and his publisher were quickly arrested when his book was released by the High Commissioner (a creation of King James), and examined.[44] Finch was striped of his status and possessions and then died a few years latter. "The doctrine of the restoration of the Jews continued to be expounded in England, evolving according to the insight of each exponent, and finally playing a role in Christian Zionistic activities in the latter part of the nineteenth and in the first of the twentieth centuries."[45]

Many Puritans of the seventeenth century taught the restoration of the Jews to the Holy Land.[46] One of the greatest Puritan theologians in England was John Owen (1616–1683) who wrote, "The Jews shall be gathered from all parts of the earth where they are scattered, and brought home into their homeland."[47] Peter Toon, speaking of Puritans of this era says:

> Of course, those who expected the conversion of the Jews

> added to Romans 11 other proof-texts from the Old and New Testament. Furthermore, a large proportion of those who took "Israel" in Romans 11:25 ff. to speak of Jews, also taught that there would be a restoration of Jews to their ancient homeland in the Near East either after, or at the same time as, their conversion to Christ.[48]

There was a similar Restorationist movement throughout Europe where the Reformation was strongest, but on a smaller scale. There were a number of Restorationists in Holland during the time of the Puritan movement. Isaac de la Peyrere (1594–1676), who served as the French Ambassador to Denmark, "wrote a book wherein he argued for a restoration of the Jews to Israel without conversion to Christianity."[49] In 1655, Paul Felgenhauever, wrote *Good News for Israel* in which he taught that there would be the "permanent return of the Jews to their own country eternally bestowed upon them by God through the unqualified promise to Abraham, Isaac and Jacob."[50] The Dane, Holger Paulli (1644–1714) "believed wholeheartedly in the Jewish Return to the Holy Land, as a condition for the Second Coming."[51] He even "lobbied the kings of Denmark, England, and France to go and conquer Palestine from the Ottomans in order that the Jews could regain their nation."[52] Frenchman, Marquis de Langallerie (1656–1717), schemed with the Turkish Ambassador in the Hague on a plan defeat the Pope and trade the papal empire for a return of the Jews to the Holy Land. Langallerie was arrested in Hamburg, tried and convicted of high treason and died in prison a year later.[53] Other European Restorationists of the era include: Isaac Vossius, Hugo Grotius, Gerhard John Vossius, David Blondel, Vasover Powel, Joseph Eyre, Edward Whitaker, and Charles Jerran.[54]

James Saddington lists the following seventeenth century English individuals as holding to Restorationist views: John Milton, John Bunyan, Roger Williams, John Sadler and Oliver Cromwell.[55] "The doctrine of the restoration of the Jews continued to be expounded in England, evolving according to the insight of each exponent," concludes Ehle, "and finally playing a role in Christian Zionistic activities in the latter part of the nineteenth and in the first of the twentieth centuries."[56]

COLONIAL AMERICA

Since the American colonies, especially in Puritan New England, were settled primarily by Englishmen who brought with them to the New World many of the same issues and beliefs that were circulating in the motherland, it is not surprising to find many zealous advocates in America for the restoration of the Jews. Perhaps the most influential of the early Puritan ministers in New England was John Cotton, who, following the postmillennialism of Brightman held to the restoration of the Jews to the Holy Land.[57] According to Ehle, in addition to John Cotton (1584–1652), early Restorationists included: John Davenport (1597–1670), William Hooke (1601–1678), John Eliot (1604–1690), Samuel Willard (1640–1707), and Samuel Sewall (1652–1730).[58] Ephraim Huit, a Cambridge trained early minister in Windsor, Connecticut believed that the Jews would be regathered to their homeland in 1650.[59]

One of the standout advocates of the restoration doctrine was Increase Mather (1639–1723), the son of Richard and father of Cotton. Increase Mather wrote over 100 books in his life and was a president of Harvard. His first work was *The Mystery of Israel's Salvation*, which went through about a half dozen revisions during his life.[60] His support of the national restoration of Israel to her land in the future was typical of American Colonial Puritans and was generally widespread. Ehle notes the following:

> The first salient school of thought in American history that advocated a national restoration of the Jews to Palestine was resident in the first native-born generation at the close of the seventeenth century in which Increase Mather played a dominate role. The men who held this view were Puritans, … From that time on the doctrine of restoration may be said to have become endemic to American culture.[61]

"It was Increase Mather's view that this final and greatest reformation of the Christian world would be led by the Jewish people ensuing upon their restoration to the Holy Land."[62]

From the earliest times, American Christianity has always tilted toward support of the restoration of national Israel in the Holy Land. American Christians, when compared with Euro-Asian Christianity has always had a philo-Semitic disposition. Thus, it is not surprising that this tradition continues today, especially in dispensational circles.

EARLY AMERICAN SUPPORT FOR ISRAEL

With a significant number of English speaking Christians during the last 400 years thoroughly saturated with Jewish restoration theology, it should not be surprising that many such Christians in the last two hundred years have risen up to play key roles in the establishment of the modern state of Israel.

It should not be considered strange that President John Quincy Adams expressed his desire that "the Jews again [were] in Judea, an independent Nation, ... once restored to an independent government and no longer persecuted."[63] President Abraham Lincoln in a meeting with Canadian Christian Zionist, Henry W. Monk, in 1863 said, "Restoring the Jews to their homeland is a noble dream shared by many Americans. He (the Jewish chiropodist of the President) has so many times 'put me on my feet' that I would have no objection to giving his countrymen a 'leg up'."[64]

NINETEENTH CENTURY BRITISH RESTORATIONISM

The 1800s marks a high point in British premillennialism and a corresponding apex for Christian Zionism. Many contemporary accounts critical of Christian Zionism focus their emphasis upon J. N. Darby and the rise of dispensationalism as the foundation for British Restorationism. As one examines the record, such is not the case. The real advocates of Christian Zionism in Britain were primarily Anglican premillennialists. By the mid-nineteenth century, about half of all Anglican clergy were evangelical premillennialists. Iain Murray said, "some seven hundred ministers of the Establishment were said to believe that Christ's coming must precede His kingdom upon earth. This was in 1845."[65] Murray went on to add that, "the number almost certainly increased in the latter half of the century."[66] An example of such clergymen would be J. C. Ryle (1816–1900), who wrote a Pre-Millennian Creed.[67] The wave of premillennialism is what produced in Britain a crop of Christian Zionists that led to political activism which culminated in the Balfour Declaration.

Anthony Ashley Cooper (1801–1885), later Lord Shaftesbury, is said by Tuchman to have been "the most influential nonpolitical figure, excepting Darwin, of the Victorian age."[68] As a strong evangelical Anglican, he is said to have based his life upon a literal acceptance of the Bible and was known as the "Evangelical of Evangelicals." Shaftesbury was the greatest influence for social legislation in the nineteenth century. He was led into acceptance of premillennialism by Edward Bickersteth, which then gave rise to his views of Jewish Restorationism.[69] Lord Shaftesbury said concerning his belief in the second coming, that it "has always been a moving principle in my life, for I see everything going on in the world subordinate to this great event."[70] Because of his premillennialism, Shaftesbury became greatly involved as Chairman of the London Society for Promoting Christianity among the Jews.[71] Shaftesbury spearheaded a movement that lead to "the creation by the Church of England of an Anglican bishopric in Jerusalem, with a converted Jew consecrated as its first bishop."[72]

"Oh, pray for the peace of Jerusalem" were the words engraved on a ring that he always wore on his right hand.[73] Since Lord Shaftesbury believed that the Jews would return to their homeland in conjunction with the second advent, he "never had a shadow of a doubt that the Jews *were* to return to their own land. ... It was his daily prayer, his daily hope."[74] In 1840, Shaftsbury was known for coining a slogan that he would often repeat throughout his life, that the Jews were "a country without nation for a nation without a country."[75]

Shaftesbury greatest contribution to the Restoration movement was his attempt to accomplish something in the political realm in order to provoke England to develop a policy in favor of returning the Jews to their homeland. He succeeded in influencing England to adopt that policy, but England failed, at that time to influence the Turks.

In 1838, in an article in the Quarterly Review, Shaftsbury put forth the view that Palestine could become a British colony of Jews that "could provide Britain with cotton, silk, herbs, and olive oil."[76] Next, Shaftsbury "lobbied Lord Palmerston, the Foreign Secretary, using political, financial and economic arguments to convince him to help the Jews return to Palestine. And Palmerston did so. What was originally the religious beliefs of Christian Zionists became official British policy (for political interests) in Palestine and the Middle East by the 1840s."[77] This was primarily the result of Lord Shaftsbury's efforts. However, at the end of the day, Shaftsbury's plan failed, but it succeeded in setting a precedent for putting concrete, political legs on one's religious beliefs. This would yield results at a later time.

Lord Shaftsbury had used his great power of persuasion to sway Henry John Temple Palmerston (1784–1865), to whom he was related by marriage, to the Restorationist position.[78] Palmerston had a distinguished political career serving in government almost the entire time from 1807 till his death in 1865. He served the British government many years as war secretary, foreign minister and was a popular prime minister for about ten years. Even though Shaftsbury influenced Palmerston to hold to the Restorationist position, it appears that it was a deeply held conviction and not one of mere political expediency. While British foreign secretary in 1840, Palmerston wrote the following letter to his ambassador at Constantinople in his attempt to advocate on behalf of the Jews:

> There exists at the present time among the Jews dispersed over Europe, a strong notion that the time is approaching when their nation is to return to Palestine. … It would be of manifest importance to the Sultan to encourage the Jews to return and to settle in Palestine because the wealth which they would bring with them would increase the resources of the Sultan's dominions; and the Jewish people, if returning under the sanction and protection and at the invitation of the Sultan, would be a check upon any future evil designs of Mehemet Ali or his successor. … I have to instruct Your Excellency strongly to recommend [the Turkish government] to hold out every just encouragement to the Jews of Europe to return to Palestine.[79]

Shaftsbury was not the only one lobbying Palmerston during this time. A wave of premillennialism had hit the Scottish resulting in a growing sentiment toward Jewish Restoration. "In 1839 the Church of Scotland sent Andrew Bonar and Robert Murray M'Cheyne, to report on 'the Condition of the Jews in their land.' Their report was widely publicized in Great Britain and it was followed by a 'Memorandum to Protestant Monarchs of Europe for the restoration of the Jews to Palestine.' This memorandum was printed verbatim in the *London Times*, including an advertisement by Lord

Shaftsbury igniting an enthusiastic campaign by the *Times* for restoration of the Jews."[80] "Three hundred and twenty citizens of Carlow, Ireland sent a similar memorandum to Palmerston."[81]

One time governor of Australia, Colonel George Gawler (1796–1869) was one of the most zealous and influential Restorationist, next to Shaftsbury, in the 1840s.[82] "Colonel Gawler was a senior commander at the Battle of Waterloo."[83] When he returned to England in 1841 he became a strong advocate of Jewish settlements in the land of Palestine. Gawler's Restorationism, like most of his day, was sparked by his religious convictions, but he argued for Jewish return to their land upon geopolitical grounds. Gawler stated the following:

> [England] urgently needs the shortest and safest lines of communication. ... Egypt and Syria stand in intimate connection. A foreign hostile power mighty in either would soon endanger British trade ... and it is now for England to set her hand to the renovation of Syria through the only people whose energies will be extensively and permanently in the work—the real children of the soil, the sons of Israel.[84]

Working with Sir Moses Montefiore (a British Jew) Gawler provided an agricultural strategy for Jewish resettlement of the Holy Land. One of these Montefiore-Gawler projects resulted in "the planting of an orange grove near Jaffa, still existent today and known as Tel Aviv's 'Montefiore Quarter.'"[85]

Charles Henry Churchill (1814–1877), an ancestor of Winston Churchill, was a British military officer stationed in Damascus in 1840. "He was a Christian Zionist and he supported the Jews against the non-Zionist Christians of Damascus."[86] It was through his efforts that he helped acquit the Jews accused of the infamous charge of blood libel. Col. Churchill was honored a banquet hosted by a grateful Jewish community where he spoke of the "hour of liberation of Israel ... that was approaching, when the Jewish Nation would once again take its place among the powers of the world."[87] In a letter to Jewish philanthropist Sir Moses Montefiore (1784–1885), dated June 14, 1841, Churchill said,

> I cannot conceal from you my most anxious desire to see your countrymen endeavor once more to resume their existence as a people. I consider the object to be perfectly obtainable. But two things are indispensably necessary: Firstly that the Jews themselves will take up the matter, universally and unanimously. Secondly that the European powers will aid them in their views.[88]

Churchill continued to live in the Middle East and in 1953 wrote *Mount Lebanon* and "predicted that when Palestine ceased to be part of the Ottoman Empire, it would either become an English colony or an independent state."[89]

British General Charles Warren, also known for his archeological work in Jerusalem, served in Syria on behalf of the Palestine Exploration Fund. In 1875 he wrote *The Land of Promise: or Turkey's Guarantee.*[90] Warren proposed that the land be developed with the "avowed intention of gradually introducing the Jews, pure and simple, who would eventually occupy and govern the country." He even speculated that the land could hold "a population of fifteen million."[91]

Laurence Oliphant (1829–1888) was an evangelical "British Protestant, an officer in the British Foreign Service, a writer, world-traveler and an unofficial diplomat."[92] Oliphant was passionate about the Jewish Restoration to their land that came from his intense religious convictions, which "he tried to conceal them behind arguments based on strategy and politics."[93] In 1880 he published a book, *The Land of Gilead*, "proposing Jewish resettlement, under Turkish sovereignty and British protection, of Palestine east of the Jordan."[94] Even then, he foresaw the agricultural potential and the possibilities of developing the resources of the Dead Sea.

> All the fruits of Southern Europe, such as apricots, peaches and plums, here grow to perfection; apples, pears, quinces, thrive well on the more extreme elevation … while the quick-growing Eucalyptus could be planted with advantage on the fertile but treeless plains.
>
> The inclusion of the Dead Sea within its limits would furnish a vast source of wealth, by the *exploitation* of its

> chemical and mineral deposits. ... The Dead Sea is a mine of unexplored wealth, which only needs the application of capital and enterprise to make it a most lucrative property.[95]

There were many other British Restorationists during the nineteenth century that created a momentum that would payoff later in British control of Palestine and the Balfour Declaration. Restorationism found a voice in one of the most popular novelist of the nineteenth century, as George Eliot penned the influential Restorationist novel *Daniel Deronda*.[96] "Among the advocates we may include Lord Lindsay, Lord Shaftsbury, Lord Palmerton, Disraeli, Lord Manchester, Holman Hunt, Sir Charles Warren, Hall Caine and others."[97] Among the nineteenth century British, one observes the "gradual drift from purely religious notion to the political."[98] These two influences, the Bible and the sword (religion and politics), as Tuchman has put it,[99] would merge into a powerful team the lead to the Balfour Declaration and the eventual founding of the Jewish state in the twentieth century.

J. N. DARBY AND RESTORATIONISM

There is no doubt that John Nelson Darby (1800–1882) believed in a future for national Israel, which would make him a Restorationist or Christian Zionist in theory.[100] However, anyone familiar with Darby and the Brethren know that they were not involved politically in any way and their distinctive dispensational views did not penetrate Anglican Evangelicals.[101] Yet, a number of critics of Christian Zionism say that Darby is a major source of Christian Zionism. Donald E. Wagner appears to be the biggest culprit in this matter.[102] "If Brightman was the father of Christian Zionism," declares Wagner, "then Darby was its greatest apostle and missionary, the apostle Paul of the movement."[103] Wagner continues this theme when he says, "Lord Shaftsbury, was convinced of Darby's teachings."[104] Fellow anti-Christian Zionist, Stephen R. Sizer, echoes Wagner's misguided views when he says of Shaftsbury: "He single-handedly translated the theological positions of Brightman, Henry Finch, and John Nelson Darby into a political strategy."[105]

I have never found, within the writings of the specialists on Christian

Zionism, anyone who makes more than a brief mention of Darby.[106] No one includes him among those who could be considered even a quasi-significant Restorationist. In fact, Barbara Tuchman, whose work *Bible and Sword* is considered the most significant and comprehensive treatment of British Christian Zionism does not even mention Darby at all.

When it comes to the alleged influence of Darby upon Lord Shaftsbury, this is most unlikely. One of Shaftsbury's biographers makes it clear that it was Anglican premillennialist, Edward Bickersteth[107] (was not even a futurist, but an historicist) who influenced him toward premillennialism. Battiscombe, speaking about the year 1835, says the following:

> In that year he first met the man who was to be one of the chief influences in his life, and through that man he in all probability first came in contact with a mode of belief which was to be all-important to his view of religion. The man was Edward Bickersteth, a leading Evangelical; the belief was that curiously explicit teaching about the end of the world and the Last Judgment usually known as Millenarianism.[108]

Even though Darby was not really a player in British Restorationism, there is no doubt that his dispensationalism, once imported to the United States would eventually become the staple for current Christian Zionism. "Most dispensationalists were satisfied to be mere observers of the Zionist movement," notes Weber. "They watched and analyzed it." Weber notes that American William Blackstone "was one exception to the general pattern." The fact that Blackstone would become one of the first dispensational activists on behalf of Zionism (after the Civil War), proves the main point that dispensationalist, especially Darby, were generally not active in the Jewish Restoration movement until more recent times. Current realities should not cloud a clear view of the past.

RESTORATIONISTS ON THE CONTINENT

Even though the English-speaking world led the way when it came to Christian Zionism, there were important contributions from continental Europe. While Napoleon's attempt at Jewish Restoration lacked religious motivation,[109] there were many Europeans who were smitten with religious Restorationism. "The Enlightenment in 18th century France and Germany, by its very nature of questioning the past" notes Epstein, "questioned the Jews' status as separated from the rest of society because of religious differences."[110] Such a development made the public, free expression of ideas more common. As a result of the new openness some began advocating the return of the Jews to their homeland. The rise of nationalism was another trend of the day. "Nationalism actually initially had an unusual effect on the restorationist movement: it increased Christian support and decreased Jewish support."[111]

A German Lutheran, C. F. Zimpel, who "described himself as Doctor et Philosopiae, member of the Grand Ducal Saxon Society for Mineralogy and Geognosy at Jena," published pamphlets in the mid-1800s entitled "Israelites in Jerusalem" and "Appeal to all Christendom, as well as to the Jews, for the Liberation of Jerusalem."[112] He addressed a number of geographical issues and warned that if the Jews were not allowed to return to Palestine then it would lead to their persecution and slaughter.[113] Unfortunately Zimpel proved correct on this prediction.

Frenchman, Charles-Joseph Prince de Ligne (1735–1814) advocated Jewish Restorationism. He called upon the Christians of Europe to lobby the Turkish Sultan so that the Jews could return to their homeland. De Ligne's appeal was used by Napoleon in his efforts to establish a Jewish homeland in Palestine. "Among those French Restorationists were theologians and authors, but also, increasingly, politicians."[114] Some of them included Ernest Laharanne, Alexandre Dumas, and Jean-Henri Dunant (1828–1910), who was also the rounder of the International Red Cross.[115]

Restoration proposals were put forth by a number of Europeans in the nineteenth century. A Swiss theologian named Samuel Louis Gaussen who wrote a book advocating a Jewish return to their land in 1844.[116] Italian, Benedetto Musolino (1809–1885) wrote a book, after a visit to the Holy Land, in which he argued "that the restoration of the Jews would allow European culture into the Middle East."[117]

TWENTIETH CENTURY BRITISH CHRISTIAN ZIONISM

Even though the momentum of over three hundred years of British

Restorationism was beginning to fade, there was enough activity to carry through World War I, which saw England finally gain control of the Holy Land. The early 1900s saw some of the most devout Christian Zionist arise and give birth to the Balfour Declaration and the British Mandate for Palestine.

Arthur James Balfour (1848–1930) was born in Scotland and reared in a strong Christian home, which instilled into him a love for the Jews based upon a biblical interest. Balfour, a life-long bachelor, even wrote a book on Christian philosophy and theology.[118] Lord Balfour served much of his life within the highest offices of British government, including Prime Minister. His interest in Jewish Restoration "was Biblical rather than imperial."[119] His sister and biographer said the following:

> Balfour's interest in the Jews and their history was life-long. It originated in the Old Testament training of his mother, and in his Scottish upbringing. As he grew up, his intellectual admiration and sympathy for certain aspects of Jewish philosophy and culture grew also, and the problem of the Jews in the modern world seemed to him of immense importance. He always talked eagerly on this, and I remember in childhood imbibing from him the idea that Christian religion and civilization owes to Judaism an immeasurable debt, shamefully ill repaid.[120]

In 1906, a time in which he had just lost the office of Prime Minister of England, Lord Balfour met Dr. Chaim Weizmann, the foremost proponent of early Zionism next to Theodor Herzel. Balfour's sister said, "Balfour for his part told me often about the impression the conversation made on him." "It was from the talk with Weizmann that I saw that the Jewish form of patriotism was unique," noted Lord Balfour. "Their love for their country refused to be satisfied by the Uganda scheme. It was Weizmann's absolute refusal even to look at it which impressed me."[121]

After many starts and stops, Balfour was finally able to persuade all of the British War Cabinet that the time had come to issue a declaration of British support for Jewish Restoration to their homeland. The declaration is dated November 2, 1917 and was addressed to Lord Rothschild as follows:

> His Majesty's Government view with favour the establishment in Palestine of a national home for the Jewish people, and will use their best endeavors to facilitate the achievement of this object, it being clearly understood that nothing shall be done which may prejudice the civil and religious rights of existing non-Jewish communities in Palestine, or the rights and political status enjoyed by Jews in any other country.[122]

Before the Balfour Declaration was finally issued, much discussion with allies and behind the scene discussion took place. Prime Minister, Lloyd George wanted to make sure that the United States was fully on board before it was issued. President Woodrow Wilson would support it and on October 1918 issued the following statement of acceptance:

> I welcome an opportunity to express … satisfaction … in progress … since the Declaration of Mr. Balfour on … the establishment in Palestine of a National Home for the Jewish People, and his promise that the British Government would use its best endeavors to facilitate the achievement of that object … all America will be deeply moved by the report [on the founding] of the Hebrew University at Jerusalem with the promise that bears of spiritual rebirth.[123]

The impact of the Balfour Declaration was a tremendous event within the Zionist movement. Since Britain was on the verge of controlling Palestine, it provided a great step on the road to the founding of the nation of Israel in 1948. This great declaration was spearheaded, not just by British geo-political concerns, as important as that was within their thinking, but by Christian sympathies that were formed by biblical beliefs. Lord Balfour does not appear to have been moved by his views of eschatology, although it may have been a factor, "but simply exiles who should be given back, in payment of Christianity's 'immeasurable debt,' their homeland."[124]

David Lloyd George (1863–1945) was British Prime Minister (1916–1922) when the Balfour Declaration was issued. Balfour and Lloyd George were both life-long friends. From Wales, Lloyd George was steeped in the Bible in which he was trained as a youth. This clearly predisposed him to view with favor the Zionist movement. Saddington says:

> It was Lloyd George's decision that was primarily responsible for the British launching a large-scale offensive to conquer all of Palestine despite the risks. As a Christian Zionist he was determined to gain control of Palestine without the French to interfere. He also wanted his country to carry out what he regarded as God's work in Palestine.[125]

Lloyd George made a number of statements concerning his biblical upbringing which influenced him throughout his life. "Lloyd George recalled how in his first meeting with Chaim Weizmann in December 1914, place names kept coming into the conversation that were 'more familiar to me than those of the Western front,'" notes Tuchman. "Lord Balfour's biographer says that his interest in Zionism stemmed from his boyhood training in the Old Testament under the guidance of his mother."[126] On another occasion, when speaking about the Balfour Declaration, Lloyd George said:

> It was undoubtedly inspired by natural sympathy, admiration and also by the fact that, as you must remember, we had been trained even more in Hebrew history than in the history of our own country. I could tell you all the kings of Israel. But I doubt whether I could have named half a dozen of the kings of England![127]

Undoubtedly, God put men like Lord Balfour and Lloyd George into powers of position at this crucial time in history to aid the eventual founding of the modern Jewish state. This appears more clearly when one realizes that there were not many men within British government of that era who held the biblically molded views of Christian Zionism, yet, these were the men who were in power at that time. Christian Zionists William Hechler said, "Lloyd George and Arthur Balfour accepted Zionism for religious and humanistic reasons; they saw it as fulfillment of the Biblical prophecies, not just as something suiting British Imperial interests."[128] Tuchman tells us the following:

> Lloyd George's afterthoughts on the motivation of the War Cabinet in issuing the Balfour Declaration have bewitched and bewildered all subsequent accounts of this episode. Unquestionably he doctored the picture. Why he did so is a matter of opinion. My own feeling is that he knew that his own motivation, as well as Balfour's, was in large part a sentimental (that is, a Biblical) one, but he could not admit it. Hew as writing his Memoirs in the 1930's when the Palestine trouble was acute, and he could hardly confess to nostalgia for the Old Testament or to a Christian guilty conscience toward the Jews as reasons for an action that had committed Britain to the painful, expensive, and seemingly insoluble problem of the Mandate. So he made himself believe that the Declaration had been really a reward for Weizmann's acetone process or alternatively, a propagandist gesture to influence American and Bolshevik Jews—an essentially conflicting explanation, neither so simple nor so reasonable as the truth.[129]

Irishman, John Henry Patterson (1867–1947) grew up in a conservative Protestant home in which he was intensely taught the Bible throughout his youth. "His familiarity with the Bible, its stories, laws, geography, prophecies and morals, stood him in good stead when his army superiors chose him to take the Zion Mule Corps."[130] The Zion Mule Corps was a Jewish military unit made up of volunteers from Palestine in the British Army during World War I. Lieutenant Colonel Patterson wrote about his experiences in *With the Judeans in the Palestine Campaign*, which he had published in the 1930s.[131] Patterson's views of Bible prophecy are evident in the following:

> Britain's share towards the fulfillment of prophecy must ... not be forgotten and the names of Mr. Lloyd George and Sir Arthur Balfour, two men who were raised up to deal justly with Israel, will, I feel sure, live for all time in the hearts and affections of the Jewish people. It is owing to the stimulus given by the Balfour Declaration to the soul of Jewry throughout the world that we are now looking upon

> the wonderful spectacle unfolding itself before our eyes, of the people of Israel returning to the Land promised to Abraham and his seed forever. In the ages to come it will always redound to the glory of England that it was through her instrumentality that the Jewish people were enabled to return and establish their National Home in the Promised Land.[132]

As a Christian, Patterson describes the events of his day relating to the Jews as "the fulfillment of prophecy." There were many others from this era who believed similarly that played some kind of role in seeing that the Jews would return to their homeland, but space prohibits their mention.[133]

HERZL'S NUMBER ONE ADVISOR

The modern Jewish founder of Zionism is recognized to have been Theodor Herzl. His earliest and closest advisor just happened to have been the Christian minister William Hechler (1845–1931) who was a zealous Christian Zionist. Rev. Hechler was a pastor who was born in India of German missionary parents. He attended college in Basel, Switzerland,[134] which is where Herzl was living when he first met him. "Hechler, bilingual in English and German from childhood, . . . was like his father, a member of the Church of England."[135] He studied theology in London and then in Tubingen, which was the center of the liberal approach to the Scripture. However, "he was not persuaded by the key arguments of the liberals and retained a distinctly creedal, doctrinal, even literalist theology."[136] This makes sense, since anyone holding to a liberal view of Scripture would not have come to love Israel, as did Hechler.

"Upon recommendation of the British court, he became private tutor to Prince Ludwig, son of Frederick, the Grand Duke of Baden," says Pragai. "At the time he met the Grand Duke's nephew, the future Emperor William II of Germany. After the Prince's premature death, Hechler served in the ministry in England."[137] "At Hechler's behest, the Grand Duke built up a massive library of biblical eschatology, biblical history, and archeology. At the Grand Duke's request, Hechler presented sermons and scholarly papers on these themes before the Court and it's visitors."[138] Hechler was one of the most zealous Christian Zionists of all time. He seemed consumed with the goal of Jewish restoration to their homeland.

In 1882 he had published a book entitled *The Restoration of the Jews to Palestine according to Prophecy.*[139] In 1885, "Hechler was appointed Chaplain to the British Embassy in Vienna."[140] In 1896 Hechler introduces himself to Herzl and thus becomes his most important aid, advisor and advocate. It was said, "William Hechler would prove to be 'not only the first, but the most constant and the most indefatigable of Herzl's followers.'"[141] Hechler's connections in both Germany and England proved helpful to Herzl, as Hechler often arranged meetings for Herzel with the highest officials of each nation. Hechler often told the secular Herzl that what they were doing was "fulfilling prophecy."[142] Merkley tells us that Herzl "grew to trust Hechler more and more. Indeed, frequently, for brief but crucial periods, he virtually entrusted the whole Zionist enterprise to William Hechler, and, though Hechler frequently annoyed and embarrassed him, he never filed him."[143] Herzl said in his diary of Hechler the following:

> Of all the people who have been drawn to me by the 'movement', the Rev Hechler is the finest and most fanciful ... He frequently writes me postcards, for no particular reason, telling me that he hasn't been able to sleep the previous night because Jerusalem came into his mind.[144]

What did Hechler mean when he would say that he and Herzl were helping to fulfill prophecy? We get a glimpse from his writings:

> Every detail of this remarkable Movement is of interest to us ... clergy, who stand as watchmen on the spiritual walls of Zion ...
>
> We are now seeing the stirrings of the bones in Ezechiel's valley: oh! may we soon see the glorious outpourings of spiritual life predicted in Ezechiel 36: The religious element is, according to God's Word, to become the inspiring force, and, I think I can see that it is the religious faith in Zionism, which is now already influencing the whole nation of the Jews. ... What food for reflection to every thoughtful student of the Bible and of history!

> The Jews are beginning to look forward to and believe in the glorious future of their nation when, instead of being a curse, they are once more to become a blessing to all.[145]

Hechler was a true friend and supporter of Herzl and was at his side when he died in 1904. Later Hechler wrote, "I was with him at the beginning of his dreams, and I was with him almost at the last moment of his earthly death."[146] Christian Zionist, William Hechler continued to work hard for the cause that almost solely possessed his mind by trying to convince Gentile Christians of the worthiness of this cause. He died in 1931.

BLACKSTONE AND AMERICAN CHRISTIAN ZIONISM

No doubt, one of the most outstanding examples of a Christian Zionist is that of American William E. Blackstone (1841–1935). Blackstone was born in Adams, New York and reared in a pious Methodist home, where he became a Christian at age 11.[147] When he married he moved to Chicago and became a very successful businessman. Even though he was Methodist, he had become motivated by his dispensational view of Bible prophecy to work for the reestablishment of national Israel.

Blackstone, a tireless, self-taught student of Bible and theology, became very interested in what the Bible had to say about Israel. Like many Christians with similar interests, this lead to attempts to evangelize Jewish people with the gospel. He founded in 1887 the Chicago Hebrew Mission for the evangelization of the Jews. Blackstone wrote the best-selling book *Jesus Is Coming* in 1908, which sold over a million copies in three editions. "Probably no dispensational Bible teacher of his time had a larger popular audience."[148] Concerning the restoration of the Jews to their homeland, Blackstone said in his book:

> But, perhaps, you say: "I don't believe the Israelites are to be restored to Canaan, and Jerusalem rebuilt."
> Dear reader! have you read the declarations of God's word about it? Surely northing is more plainly stated in the Scriptures.[149]

He then proceeds to list almost 14 pages of virtually nothing but

Scriptural citations supporting his belief. Then he concludes:

> We might fill a book with comments upon how Israel shall be restored, but all we have desired to do was to show that it is an incontrovertible fact of prophecy, and that it is intimately connected with our Lord's appearing, and this we trust will have satisfactorily accomplished.[150]

Even though widely known throughout evangelicalism for a number of things, he is best known for his tireless work on behalf of reestablishing the Jewish nation in Israel. Timothy Weber says of Blackstone and dispensationalism the following:

> Most dispensationalists were satisfied to be mere observers of the Zionist movement. They watched and analyzed it. They spoke out in favor of it. But seldom did they become politically involved to promote its goals. There is one exception to the general pattern, however, in the person of William E. Blackstone, one of the most popular dispensational writers of his time.[151]

By 1891, Blackstone the activist had obtained the signatures of 413 prominent Americans and sent this document to President Benjamin Harrison advocating the resettlement of persecuted Jews in Russia to a new homeland in what was then called Palestine.[152] Part of the petition read as follows:

> Why not give Palestine back to them again? According to God's distribution of nation it is their home—an inalienable possession from which they were expelled by force. Under their cultivation it was a remarkably fruitful land, sustaining millions of Israelites, who industriously tilled its hillsides and valleys. They were agriculturists and producers as well as a nation of great commercial importance—the center of civilization and religion.
>
> We believe this is an appropriate time for all nations, and especially the Christian nations of Europe, to show kindness to Israel. A million of exiles, by their terrible

> suffering are piteously appealing to our sympathy, justice, and humanity. Let us now restore to them the land of which they were so cruelly despoiled by our Roman ancestors.[153]

Ehle had the following to say about the signers:

> Among the 413 signers listed by their cities—Chicago, Boston, New York, Philadelphia, Baltimore, and Washington—were the opinion makers of the day: the editors and/or publishers of the leading newspapers and religious periodicals (at least ninety-three newspapers in all), the mayors of Chicago, Boston, New York, Philadelphia, and Baltimore, as well as other officials, leading churchmen and rabbis, outstanding businessmen, and in Washington, Speaker of the House of Representatives, T. B. Reed, Chairman of the House Committee on Foreign Affairs, Robert R. Hitt, and William McKinley, of Ohio, who later became president.[154]

Even though it accomplished little politically, Blackstone's petition was said to have had a galvanizing impact upon Americans as a whole. The petition received widespread coverage in newspapers and generated a great amount of discussion and acceptance. It sparked great interest among the Jews as a whole.[155]

Blackstone later made a similar appeal to President Woodrow Wilson, a Presbyterian minister's son who became a Christian Zionist, which influenced his acceptance of the Balfour Declaration of 1917.[156] It is not surprising that there is today a forest in Israel named the "Blackstone Forest" in his honor. Nor that someone should write, "William E. Blackstone, once dubbed the 'father of Zionism' for his political activities on behalf of the Jews."[157] Like Hechler, Blackstone spent the rest of his life working for his beloved cause until his death in 1935. While he was thrilled with the developments of the Balfour Declaration and the British Mandate after World War I, he basically died disappointed that Israel had not yet become a nation. However, that would indeed take place 13 years later.

HARRY TRUMAN AND RECOGNITION OF ISRAEL

President Harry S. Truman (1884–1972) grew up in Missouri in a devout Christian home. When Harry was born his parents attended a Southern Baptist church which both sets of grandparents help establish in Grandview. "His father, John Anderson Truman was also a strong Baptist. Both his father and mother, Martha, raised him in the conventional Baptist tradition."[158] However, when Harry was six they moved to Independence and they attended the First Presbyterian church at Lexington and Pleasant every Sunday until Harry was 16. When Harry turned 18 and moved to Kansas City, he joined the Baptist church by baptism and remained a Southern Baptist the rest of his life. Truman said, "I'm a Baptist because I think that sect gives the common man the shortest and most direct approach to God."[159]

While growing up, Truman read the Bible through twice by age 12 and two more times by the age of 14. "From Sunday School and his own reading of the Bible, he knew many Biblical passages by heart and could quote many Bible verses at random."[160] Young Harry was an avid reader and remained so throughout his entire life. The Truman family owned a set of *Great Men and Famous Women*, edited by Charles Francis Horne. "According to Truman's daughter, Margaret, the book Truman preferred most after Horne's biographies was the Bible. There is even an indication that Truman considered entering the ministry for a time."[161]

Every indication reveals that Harry and his sister Mary were very active in the church throughout their late teens and early 20s.

What about Truman's Christian beliefs? "Truman had little interest in theological issues, although he had an almost fundamentalist reverence for the Bible."[162] Blending Truman's great interest in history and the Bible, he once stated the following about the United States:

> Divine Providence has played a great part in our history. I have the feeling that God has created us and brought us to our present position of power and strength for some great purpose.
>
> It is not given to us to know fully what that purpose is, but I think we may be sure of one thing, and that is that our country is intended to do all it can, in cooperating

> with other nations to help created peace and preserve peace in the world. It is given to defend the spiritual values—the moral code—against the vast forces of evil that seek to destroy them.[163]

"While premillennial eschatology dominated the Southern Baptist denomination, the church into which Truman was born and to which he returned when he was eighteen," observes Saddington, "Truman never expressed his acceptance of premillennialism. It is even doubtful that he ever adequately understood it."[164] Truman's Christian focus was on the ethics of everyday living and tended to shy away from theological systems. Truman's Christian Zionism was a combination of his attraction to the people of the Bible (the Jews) that grew out of his familiarity of biblical details with humanitarian concern for a persecuted people. "The stories of the Bible," said Truman, "were to me stories about real people, and I felt I knew some of them better than *actual* people I knew."[165] His Christian Zionist beliefs were well developed and deeply rooted long before he became President of the United States. Presidential Counsel Clark Clifford described Truman's

> own reading of ancient history and the Bible made him a supporter of the idea of a Jewish homeland in Palestine, even when others who were sympathetic to the plight of the Jews were talking of sending them to places like Brazil. He did not need to be convinced by Zionists … All in all, he believed that the surviving Jews deserved some place that was historically their own. I remember him talking once about the problem of repatriating displaced persons. "Every one else who's been dragged away from his country has someplace to get back to," he said. "But the Jews have no place to go."[166]

Truman's Christian Zionism came into play during two of the greatest decisions that he would have to make during his Presidency: First, how should the U. S. vote on the partition of Israel, which would result in the creation of the new Jewish state, during the United Nations vote in late November of 1947? Second, should the U. S. diplomatically recognize the newly formed nation when David Ben-Gurion declared the birth of Israel on May 14, 1948?

On both issues, virtually all of Truman's personal advisors, the State Department and the military establishment were opposed to him. Saddington notes:

> Truman's most trusted foreign policy advisers, almost to a man, were dead-set against the establishment of a Jewish state in Palestine. The president faced the formidable front of General Marshall, Under Secretary of State Robert Lovett, Secretary of the Navy James Forrestal, Policy Planning Staff's George Kennan, State Department Counsel Charles Bohlen, and Marshall's successor as secretary, Dean Acheson. Loy Henderson, director of NEA, who arrived at the State Department just three days after FDR's death, also opposed the Zionist aims. William Yale, also at the State Department, said that the creation of a Jewish state in Palestine would be "a major blunder in statesmanship." When Secretary Forrestal reminded the president of the critical need for Saudi Arabian oil in the event of war, Truman said he would handle the situation in light of justice, not oil.[167]

Truman dealt with both issues by applying his "the buck stops here" approach with tough, responsible decisions. "Truman instructed the American delegate at the U. N., Herschel Johnson, to announce U. S.'s endorsement of the UNSCOP partition plan on 11 October 1947."[168] Then, seventeen minutes after David Ben-Gurion's declaration of the new state of Israel, a cable was sent to Israel and a message went to the press from the White House announcing the following:

> This government has been informed that a Jewish State has been proclaimed in Palestine, and recognition has been requested by the provisional government thereof. The United States recognizes the provisional government as the *de facto* authority of the new State of Israel.[169]

Clark Clifford said of President Truman's decisions to favor Israel the following observation:

> As a student of the Bible, he believed in the historic justification for a Jewish homeland, and it was a conviction with him that the Balfour Declaration of 1917 constituted a solemn promise that fulfilled the age-old hope and dream of the Jewish people.[170]

After his presidency, his longtime Jewish friend Eddie Jacobson introduced Truman to a group of professors by saying, "'This is the man who helped create the state of Israel,' but Truman corrected him: 'What do you mean "helped to create"? I am Cyrus. I am Cyrus.'"[171] Truman was comparing himself to Cyrus in the Old Testament who enabled the Jews to return to their land in the sixth century B.C. from their 70-year captivity. Perhaps his response indicates that Truman had indeed found the main reason as to why God's providence placed him into the Presidency at the time in which he arrived. In fact, many who have sifted through the data believe that had Franklin Roosevelt remained President, he would not have made the same decisions as those made by the cussing Baptist from Missouri.[172] It appears to my biblically informed, evangelical mind that God raised-up Harry S. Truman and put him in the White House for the purpose of providing a key human agent through whom He used, as He did Cyrus centuries ago, to restore Israel to her land.

CONCLUSION

God has greatly used many Gentile Christians during the last few hundred years that have prepared the way for Israel's return to their land. God will continue to use believers in the future who believe His prophecies about a national future for His people Israel. Yet, today there are a growing number of voices saying that we are dangerous, heretical, and our influence should be resisted.[173] "The danger isn't going away," declares Gershom Gorenberg. "Not as long as people think they know what God has to do next and where He has to do it, and are terribly impatient for Him to begin."[174] After suggesting elsewhere in his book that dispensational, Christian Zionists could set into motion a self-fulfilling prophecy,[175] Timothy Weber oddly concludes the opposite when he says:

> Since the end of the Six-Day War, then, dispensationalists have increasingly moved from observers to participant-observers. They have acted consistently with their

> convictions about the coming last days in ways that make their prophecies appear to be self-fulfilling. It would be too easy—and completely unwarranted—to conclude that American prophecy believers are responsible for the mess the world is in, that their beliefs have produced the current quagmire in the Middle East. Given the history of the region, the long-standing ethnic and religious hatreds there, and the attempt of many nations, both Western and Arab, to carry out their own purposes in the Holy Land, it is easy to imagine the current impasse even if John Nelson Darby and his views had never existed.[176]

With such a conclusion I have to ask, "Why the fear-mongering?"

As demonstrated in this essay, Christian Zionists have not always had it easy. Nevertheless, like those who have gone before us, we will stand on biblical conviction as we constantly watch for the further outworking of God's historical plan, revolving around His people Israel and His any-moment return. Maranatha!

WHY CHRISTIANS SHOULD SUPPORT ISRAEL

- The Abrahamic Covenant and the promise of the land has never been rescinded.
- The land permanently belongs to the Jewish people.
- The Lord still loves the Jewish people, though they are in unbelief.
- God will not go against His promises.
- The Lord has promised a restoration to the land from the Jews scattered worldwide.
- Israel while in unbelief is still the apple of God's eye.
- God will come against those who come against the Jews and against the land.
- Daniel calls for the righteous to pray for the peace of Jerusalem.
- God is jealous for Zion with a holy jealousy.
- God promises a salvation for Israel "from the land of the east and from the land of the west."
- The return of the Jews is said to happen "in the latter days," and only then will people understand what God is doing!

CHAPTER 6

THE BATTLE FOR JERUSALEM

Dave Hunt

Events transpiring in the Middle East relative to Israel and making today's headlines are not chance occurrences but precise fulfillments of what God through His Hebrew prophets foretold for these "last days." Each day's news adds fresh proof that the biblical God is the one true God and that the Bible alone is His inspired Word to mankind. We see unfolding before us precisely what God said He would cause Israel and the nations around her to experience.

In one of the most awesome and frightening prophecies for the future, God declares, "I will gather all the nations [and He means all] against Jerusalem to battle, and the city will be captured.... Then the LORD will go forth and fight against those nations..." (Zech. 14:1-3). When this will occur we do not know—but as events in the Middle East come to a climax, we may be certain that ultimately a world that is in defiance of God in so many ways, not the least of which is its attitude toward Israel, is headed for the fulfillment of this prophecy.

BUT WHAT ABOUT THE END?

God declared that as the end drew near He would make Jerusalem "a cup that causes reeling to all the peoples around," and that they would all be united against Israel (Zech. 12:2-3). And so it is. Ancient Israel had many independent enemies at various times, but ever since Israel's rebirth in 1948, for the first time in history, all the countries surrounding her are united to destroy her.

It is Islam–not in existence until 1,200 years after this prophecy and 2,000 years after the birth of Israel—that unites these nations (who otherwise would be fighting one another) in the common goal of annihilating Israel. In obedience to Islam, Muslims have pursued that passion fiercely for nearly 60 years.

The dispute is over ownership of Jerusalem and the "promised land" God gave to Abraham and his heirs. The Israelis are Abraham's heirs by descent from him through Isaac and Jacob, whose name God changed to Israel. In opposition, Arabs who call themselves "Palestinians" make the impossible claim of descent both from Abraham through Ishmael and also from the original "Palestinian" inhabitants of that land. But Abraham was from Ur of the Chaldees and Hagar, Ishmael's mother (Sarah's maid), was an Egyptian. Certainly neither Ishmael's mother nor father was a descendant of the "original inhabitants" of Canaan.

In fact, there never was a Palestinian people, nation, government, language, religion, culture, economy or history! This claim by Semitic Arabs of being descendants of a non-Semitic people who allegedly lived for thousands of years in a land called Palestine is a blatant hoax intended to delegitimize the Israelis and claim the land of Israel for themselves. Yet the world accepts this fraud, and all of the peace plans for the Middle East are founded upon it!

Both sides agree that God gave the land of Canaan (which became Israel) to Abraham and to his heirs forever; and that Ishmael was Abraham's firstborn son, whereas Isaac was the second. The custom in Abraham's day, acknowledged in the Torah, gave the firstborn prior claim to the inheritance. The Torah also records the fact that Abraham was satisfied with Ishmael as his sole heir, considered him to be the son God had promised, and didn't even want God to give him another son (Gen. 17:18).

From those facts, the Arab descendants of Ishmael sound like the legitimate heirs. However, there was no such land as "Palestine" in Abraham's day and thus no such people as "Palestinians" from whom any of today's Arabs could claim descent. In fact, Ishmael's descendants settled in the Arabian Peninsula hundreds of miles from the land God gave to Abraham.

God brought Abraham into the "land of Canaan...and the Canaanite [not the "Palestinian"] was then in the land" (Gen. 12:5-6). God gave that land by an everlasting covenant to Abraham, Isaac, and Jacob–not to Ishmael. In obedience to God, Abraham "settled in the land of Canaan" (Gen 13:12). It was then inhabited by Canaanites, "Kenites, Kenizites, Kadmonites, Hittites, Perizzites, Rephaims, Amorites, Girgashites and

Jebusites" (Gen. 12:6; 13:7; 15:18-21; 23:10; etc.). If today's "Palestinian" Arabs are descended from the original inhabitants of the land of Canaan, which ones of those listed above would it be? In fact, no descendants of the original inhabitants of Canaan have survived to this day.

WHAT DOES THE NAME PALESTINE MEAN?

The word "Palestinian" is never found in Scripture. The term "Palestine" is used four times in the King James Version (Exodus 15:14; Isaiah 14:29, 31; Joel 3:4) but never as synonymous with either the land of Canaan or the land of Israel. The Hebrew word is pelensheth and referred to a small region also known as Philistia (Psalms 60:8, 87:4, 108:9), the land of the Pelishtee, or Philistines. It was in the area of the Gaza Strip of today, so named after the Philistine city of Gaza. Their other cities were Ashdod, Gath (home of Goliath), Gerar and Ekron.

Those who currently claim to be Palestinians are Arabs who moved in from surrounding countries to feed off the prosperity of the returning Jews, who had turned desert and malaria-infested swamps (at the cost of many lives) into prosperous farms. Even today the "Palestinians" mostly look to Israel for employment.

Nor can any descendants of Ishmael claim that land. God rejected Abraham's desire for Ishmael to be the son of promise. Rather, he was the product of Sarah's and Abraham's unbelief and conniving. God insisted upon giving a son called Isaac to Abraham by his wife, Sarah – and He did so, naming him as the sole heir, a fact that the Bible makes very clear (Gen. 17:19, 21). Thereafter, God referred to Isaac as Abraham's "only son" (Gen. 22:2).

Biblically, there is no question that God selected Isaac to be the heir to the Promised Land. That fact is stated not only in Genesis 17 but repeatedly throughout both Old and New Testaments. Twelve times the God of the Bible is called "the God of Abraham, the God of Isaac, and the God of Jacob [Israel]"; more than 200 times He calls Himself, or is called, "the God of Israel." Never is He called "the God of Ishmael," much less is He ever called the God of the Arabs or of anyone else. Hear the Word of the Lord: "Remember His covenant forever, the word which He commanded to a thousand generations ... which he made with Abraham, and His oath to Isaac...also confirmed it to Jacob for a statute, to Israel as an everlasting covenant … to you I will give the land of Canaan [for] your inheritance…" (1 Chron. 16:15-18).

Furthermore, God clearly tells Abraham (Gen. 15:13-16) that his heirs to whom the land will be given will be afflicted by another nation for 400 years and only then will they be brought into the Promised Land. It is indisputable history that this slavery happened to the Jews in Egypt, not to the Arabs. There were two reasons for Israel's lengthy enslavement:

> (1) At the time of God's promise to Abraham, the wickedness of the Canaanites was not yet so great as to justify destroying them – but in 400 years it would be.
>
> (2) Isolated in Egypt, the Israelites, as despised slaves, did not intermarry with the Egyptians but became an established ethnic group to be led en masse into the Promised Land – and we know who they are today.

In contrast, the descendants of Ishmael were a nomadic people prone to intermarry with those with whom they traded. The Bible records at least three groups with whom Ishmael's descendants intermarried: the Midianites, to the extent that sometimes the Midianites are called Ishmaelites and sometimes the Ishmaelites are called Midianites (Judg. 8:1,22,12,24); and Esau's Edomite descendants (Gen. 28:9), who had already intermarried with the Hittities (26:34-35). Far from being taken by God into Canaan, they settled in the Arabian Peninsula, where they became known as Arabs.

Although "Jerusalem" is found 811 times in the Bible, it is never mentioned once in the Qur'an, nor are the words "Palestine" or "Canaan." Moreover, the Qur'an agrees with the Bible that the land was given to Israel and possessed by these "chosen people" after their deliverance from Pharaoh at the Red Sea:

> We made a covenant of old with the Children of Israel (Surah 5:70); We brought the Children of Israel across the [Red] sea, and Pharaoh with his hosts pursued them…and we verily did allot unto the Children of Israel a fixed abode (10:91,94); we favored them above all peoples (45:16); [Pharaoh] wished to scare them from the land, but we drowned him and those with him [in the

> Red Sea] all together. And we said unto the Children of Israel … dwell in the land [and] hereafter we shall bring you…out of various nations" (17:103-104); we delivered the Children of Israel … from Pharaoh. … We chose them, purposely, above all creatures (44:30-32); Remember Allah's favor to you … He … gave you what he gave no other of his creatures. O my people, go into the Holy Land which Allah hath ordained for you (95:20-21); etc.

Yet in spite of these clear declarations in the Qur'an, Muslims insist that this land belongs not to the Jews as descendants of Abraham, Isaac, and Jacob, but to the Arabs as descendants of Abraham and Ishmael. Therefore, Israel's very existence and, above all, its "occupation" of Jerusalem, are intolerable insults to Islam. Only by driving the Jews from what the world erroneously calls "Palestine" can Arab/Muslim honor be restored.

How did the word "Palestinian" originate? In A.D. 130, the Romans, who had destroyed Jerusalem 60 years before, rebuilt it as a pagan city with a temple to Jupiter on temple mount. An uprising of the Jews in protest was finally quelled in A.D. 135 at the cost of about 500,000 Jewish lives, with thousands sold into slavery and many thousands driven into exile. To spite the Jews, the Roman conquerors angrily renamed Israel, "Provincia Syria-Palaestina" after the Philistines. From that time, those living there were known as "Palestinians." Who lived there? Jews! It is they who became known as "Palestinians." Yet Bibles by major publishers have maps with such labels as "Palestine Under the Maccabees," or "Palestine in the Time of Christ." Such maps promote a grave error.

In World War II, the British Army had a volunteer brigade called "The Palestinian Brigade." It was made up of Jews; the Arabs were fighting on Hitler's side. There was the Palestinian Post, a Jewish newspaper, and the Palestinian Symphony Orchestra, a Jewish orchestra. In fact, Arabs refused to be called "Palestinians." For example, to the 1946 Anglo-American Committee of Inquiry, Arab historian Philip Hitti declared, "There is no such thing as Palestine in history, absolutely not…"

WHO IS TO BLAME?

In 1956, Ahmed Shukairy testified to the UN Security Council, "It is common knowledge that Palestine is nothing but southern Syria." Eight years later, in 1964, Shukairy, an Egyptian, became the first leader of the Palestine Liberation Organization later headed by Arafat. He is also not a "Palestinian" but was born in Cairo on August 4, 1929. What was the PLO going to "liberate" in 1964? East Jerusalem and the West Bank were held by Jordan, while Egypt held the Gaza Strip. In fact, the PLO was not formed to liberate "Palestinians" but to destroy Israel–and without any of the fundamental causes it now claims.

Always the problems between Israel and "Palestinians" are blamed upon Israel. That despised country alone is castigated—basically for defending itself – while those who make no secret of their determination to destroy her are justified in their terrorism and unprovoked aggression. This is true at the UN, in world media, and even at various religious "peace" conferences.

The "Fifth International Conference of the Sabeel Ecumenical Palestinian Liberation Theology Center," held at Jerusalem, April 14-18, 2004, was typical. It drew more than 600 participants from over 30 countries. Speakers such as Archimandrite Attallah Hanna of the Greek Orthodox Church (outspoken supporter of suicide bombers) trashed the Scriptures, rejecting all of God's promises to Israel. Roman Catholic theologian Michael Prior described the Book of Exodus as "a con job" and Joshua as "the patron saint of ethnic cleansers." The Dean of Te Rau Kahikatea Anglican Theological College in New Zealand, Convener of the Global Anglican Peace and Justice Network, described Christian Zionism (the belief that the land of Israel, as promised by God, belongs to the Jews) as "a manifest evil [an] insidious presence."

Israel is presented at such conferences, as it is at the United Nations and in world media, as the aggressor, a land grabber illegally occupying "Palestinian" land taken from its rightful owners by brute force. As we have seen, those who call themselves "Palestinians" (a name taken from the Philistines, Israel's ancient enemy, a heritage claimed by Arafat), claim to be descended from the original inhabitants of "Palestine." This bold scam, honored as truth, is foundational to world opinion about the Middle East. The Philistines were not a Semitic people. They invaded Canaan across the Mediterranean from Crete and Asia Minor and displaced certain Canaanites, just as they were eventually displaced by Israel under God's judgment. The "Palestinians" of today are Arab Semites and have no ethnic, linguistic or historical relationship to the Philistines.

The truth is suppressed that UN Declaration 181, November 29, 1947, gave Israel only about 18 percent of the land that the League of Nations in its 1922 Declaration of Principles set aside for a Jewish homeland. Unhappy with being given only 82 percent of what didn't belong to them, and demanding it all, six Arab nations attacked the new state of Israel with their regular armies. The invading Arab military high command warned all Arabs and Muslims to get out while they quickly slaughtered the Israeli settlers–then the Arabs who had fled could return to their possessions and take over everything.

To the world's astonishment, the united Arab armies were soundly defeated by poorly armed Jewish settlers, and most of those who heeded the warning and fled were never able to return. War is like that–and it was a war the Arabs started. Arabs who did not flee, but honored Israeli pleas to remain, have, with their descendants, full rights as citizens and comprise about 16 percent of Israeli voters. Some are even members of the Knesset. In contrast, no Jew can set foot in Saudi Arabia or be a citizen even in those Muslim countries that will admit them. Had the Arabs not attacked Israel, they could have been living in peace since 1948 in their "Palestinian" state.

In that 1948-49 war, Jordan took and held East Jerusalem and the so-called West Bank, while Egypt got the Gaza Strip. During the 19 years that they held these territories and used them as launching pads for terrorism, there was never a word from the Arab/Muslim world about a "Palestinian" state. Instead, they put the refugees in camps and have kept them in squalid conditions, refusing to absorb them into normal society. In contrast, tiny Israel integrated about twice as many Jewish refugees (nearly 800,000) who fled at the same time from Muslim countries where, for 1,300 years since the inception of Islam, they had been brutalized and murdered by the thousands in periodic pogroms. With the establishment of a national Jewish homeland, they could flee at last. But in all the sympathy poured out for refugees, it is always the "Palestinians," with no mention of the Jewish refugees, who had to abandon everything and escape with only their lives.

Zechariah's prophecy and its precise fulfillment are all the more remarkable when one considers that the Arab/Muslim nations surrounding Israel have 650 times the land mass (rich in minerals and oil, of which Israel has almost none), 50 times the population, armed forces far outnumbering Israel in men and equipment and the backing of huge oil revenues. Yet in spite of these impossible odds, that miniscule nation has been exactly what God said it would be: "… a torch of fire in a sheaf [to] devour all the people round about …" (12:6). Israel has won every war, against impossible odds.

Zechariah also said that God would make Jerusalem a burdensome stone around the necks of "all the people of the earth." And once again, so it is. Jerusalem is the number-one problem confronting the world. It is no secret that mankind faces the prospect of a nuclear holocaust if this dispute over Jerusalem is not solved peacefully. The united enemies surrounding Israel are feverishly arming themselves to effect at last Hitler's "final solution to the Jewish problem." Israel can deliver from submarines missiles with multiple nuclear warheads and will not allow its citizens to be massacred without using its ultimate weapons. As one more fulfillment of this amazing prophecy, the Israeli Defense Forces (IDF) are the best in the world. Were that not the case, tiny Israel could easily be pushed around and would be a burden to no one, much less to the entire world.

How heavy is this "burdensome stone?" The United Nations has consumed one-third of its time deliberating over Jerusalem and Israel, a small, despised nation with one-thousandth of the earth's population. From 1967 through 1989, out of 865 resolutions in the Security Council and General Assembly, 526 were against Israel. The last anti-Arab vote was 57 years ago in 1947. More than 60,000 individual votes have been cast in the UN condemning Israel.

Yet not once has the UN reprimanded those who have without provocation waged four wars against Israel with the declared intention of annihilating her. Nor have the terrorists ever been condemned by the UN. In November 2003, Israel introduced its first request for a resolution since 1976, asking for a prohibition against Arab terrorists who deliberately target Israeli women and children. Its request was rejected and, instead, the UN adopted a resolution demanding protection of Palestinian children from Israeli aggression. The UN's adamant opposition to Israel and everything it does is in defiance of the God of Israel and His pledge to restore His people to their promised land.

On March 25, 2004, the United States blocked a proposed UN

Security Council condemnation of Israel's targeted killing of Hamas founder and leader Sheikh Ahmed Yassin, because the Council refused to include a condemnation of Hamas terrorist attacks on Israeli civilians. The next month, an Israeli missile also killed Yassin's successor, Abdul-Aziz Rantisi. Again, there was worldwide denunciation of the execution of a mass murderer terrorist leader, but no condemnation for the hundreds of suicide bombers Hamas has trained, equipped and sent into Israel deliberately to kill civilians.

The frequent condemnations of Israel for defending herself, and the refusal to condemn the murderers and their backers who attack her, is a further fulfillment of numerous prophecies foretelling worldwide anti-Semitism. It did not end with Hitler's holocaust. Satan has been attempting to wipe out all Jews since the beginning. If he could have done so before Christ came, he would have won his battle with God by preventing the prophesied Messiah from being born. Even after Christ defeated Satan on the cross, if the Jews could be exterminated today (as Islam requires Muslims to do), there could be no Second Coming of Christ to rule over Israel on the throne of His father David in Jerusalem, God would be proved a liar because of His many promises to preserve Israel, and Satan would have won this world as his own.

Satanic hatred of Jews did not end with Hitler but is growing in intensity, not only in the Muslim world but also in Europe and in America and elsewhere today. However, nowhere is anti-Semitism more clearly and vehemently manifest than in Islam. Every child in the Palestinian Authority's schools reads the textbook, Our Country Palestine. Its title page declares, "There is no alternative to destroying Israel!"

Muhammad said, "The last day will not come until the Muslims confront the Jews, and the Muslims destroy them. In that day Allah will give a voice to the rocks and the trees and they will cry out, 'Muslim, there is a Jew hiding behind me, come and kill him!'" No clearer declaration of Satan's passion could be made. Here we see the true face of Islam, the religion of "peace"!

Immediately after signing the Oslo Accords in 1993, Arafat began to tell Muslim audiences around the world not to accuse him of betraying their sacred cause by making real peace with Israel, but to realize that he was following the example of their prophet, Muhammad. Otherwise, he would have suffered the same fate as Egyptian president Anwar Sadat who visited Jerusalem, signed a peace treaty with Israel, and for that betrayal of Islam was assassinated by the Muslim Brotherhood.

In A.D. 628, Muhammad had signed, with the Quraish of Mecca, a 10-year ceasefire known as the Treaty of Hudaybiyah. Such a hudna is a pretense entered into when Islamic forces are not strong enough to engage the enemy—and exists only to gain a strategic advantage for destroying the enemy. This is the law of war and peace in Islam, which no Muslim leader can abrogate.

Muhammad declared, "Allah has commanded me to fight against all people until all acknowledge there is no god but Allah and Muhammad is his messenger." The entire world is divided into Dar al-Islam (the house of peace) and Dar al-Harb (the house of war) and there is a perpetual Jihad until all mankind are in submission to Islam and Allah. No Muslim leader has the authority to bring an end to the Jihad (holy war) between Islam and the rest of the world. Thus, when Arafat and other Arab leaders speak of "peace," they actually mean a hudna.

President Jimmy Carter persuaded Israel to "give back" the Sinai (though it never belonged to Egypt) and brought Sadat and Israeli Prime Minister Menachim Begin together at the White House to sign a peace treaty between their two countries. Carter, an ecumenist for whom the Book of Mormon or Qur'an is as valid as the Bible, wanted to quote one verse each from the Bible and Qur'an. There are more than 400 such references in the Bible, but Carter's speechwriters searched long and hard in order to find in the Qur'an (which has more than 100 verses about fighting and killing to take over the world for Allah) one verse about "peace." They finally found it: Surah 8:61.

Each of the 114 Surahs (chapters) has a heading. The title of Surah 8 is "Spoils of War." The chapter is about fighting, slaughter, and plunder in the cause of Islam: "Fight them until ... all religion is for Allah ... O Prophet! Exhort the believers to fight ... It is not for any prophet to have captives until he hath made slaughter in the land" (8:39, 65, 67), etc. With great enthusiasm, Carter quoted the lone "peace" verse in the Qur'an, "But if the enemy incline towards peace [i.e., surrenders], do thou also incline towards peace" (8:61). He should have known that the Muslim has an entirely different idea of "peace" from the rest of the world. As Arafat has bluntly said, "Peace for us is the destruction of Israel."

What naivete could cause Carter to imagine "peace" between Islam and Israel? He surely knew of the literally hundreds of pronouncements of destruction upon Israel both in the Qur'an itself and by Muslim leaders. Over BBC radio, May 15, 1948, the day after Israel declared its independence, Azzam Pasha, Secretary-General of the Arab League, had declared, "This will be a war of extermination and momentous massacre which will be spoken of like the Mongolian massacres ..." May 20, 1967, Hafez Assad (at that time Syrian Defense Minister) declared, "The Syrian Army with its finger on the trigger is united. ... The time has come to enter into a battle of annihilation." A week later, President Nasser of Egypt thundered, "Our basic objective will be the destruction of Israel ... We will not accept any coexistence with Israel." On May 30, he announced, "The armies of Egypt, Jordan, Syria and Lebanon are poised on the borders of Israel ... while standing behind us are the armies of Iraq, Algeria, Kuwait, Sudan and the whole Arab nation ... the critical hour has arrived." Iraq's president thundered, "The existence of Israel is an error which must be rectified ... Our goal is clear – to wipe Israel off the map!"

Israel has had to defend itself in four wars (1948, 1956, 1967, 1973) and, after winning each one at great cost in lives, has given back most of the land it has taken in self-defense from an enemy that has sworn never to give up until it has obliterated Israel. Egyptian Foreign Minister Muhammad Salah al-Din declared, "The Arab people will not be embarrassed to declare: We shall not be satisfied except by the final obliteration of Israel." Nasser said, "We demand vengeance, and vengeance is Israel's death." Such pronouncements have continued unabated in spite of Israel's sincere attempts and those of Western leaders to bring "peace" to the Middle East.

Yet the United Nations, European Union, and Western leaders persist in pressuring Israel to make "peace" with an enemy that has sworn to destroy her. A few days after Yasser Arafat's June 8, 2001 "cease-fire" declaration, Sheikh Ibrahim Mahdi declared on Palestinian TV, "Allah willing, this unjust state [of] Israel will be erased...the United States will be erased ... Britain will be erased ... Blessings to whoever waged jihad for the sake of Allah. Blessings to whoever put a belt of explosives on his body or his son's and plunged into the midst of the Jews!"

In spite of such public declarations, which could be cited by the hundreds, the UN (a veritable center for anti-Semitism and anti-Israel propaganda and action) continues to rebuke Israel for defending itself and opposing "peace." Of its members, 21 are Arab nations and 52 Islamic. Israel is not allowed to be a member of UN Commissions, such as The Commission on Human Rights (which always includes terrorist and oppressive governments that deny basic rights to their citizens), etc. Of the UN's 189 members, 188 (including every terrorist member) may take their rotating terms on the Security Council. One nation, Israel, is not allowed to do so, in spite of the fact that it has been a UN member for over 50 years and is the only democracy in the Middle East.

Jerusalem would not be a problem if Israel itself and the nations of the world would acknowledge that the one true God is "the God of Israel" and would submit to His plans for His chosen people. Instead, world political and religious leaders continue to defy God, determined to force their agenda upon Israel. That policy can only lead ultimately to Armageddon and God's judgment upon this world—and it will.

The latest proposal to end the dispute over Jerusalem and the Promised Land is called the "Road Map to Peace." It was first proposed by U.S. President Bush in his June 24, 2002 speech and endorsed by Russian President Putin, the United Nations and European Union. The so-called road to peace, so long in process, and paved with one Arab betrayal after another, would be a joke had it not cost so many lives. Hope is always renewed by another dream, only to be shattered as must be the case when dealing with Islam.

Arafat has never kept one provision of any agreement. Anything he signs is not worth the ink in his signature. In the 10 years before the Oslo Accords, about 200 Israelis were murdered by terrorists; in the 10 years since, more than 1,200 have been killed and some 5,000 wounded. The road map calls for an end to terrorism, and the establishment of an independent "Palestinian" state with recognition of Israel's right to exist, something to which no Muslim can agree without denouncing Islam. The real stickler is Jerusalem, for which the road map offers no solution. No matter what the plan, the world is defying the God of Israel and will be judged accordingly.

FINALLY ...

God said, "The land shall not be sold for ever, for the land is mine"

(Leviticus 25:23). But in exchange for "peace" with an enemy that has sworn its extermination, Israel is continually forced by Western powers to give away ever more of God's land, which He promised to her alone. Israel's actions have not been perfect—and in unbelief she has been willing to give up God's land in exchange for men's promises.

As a people worldwide, the Jews have forsaken God and have been under His judgment. Nevertheless, Scripture says of Israel, "he who touches you, touches the apple of His [God's] eye" (Zech. 2:8).

It is astonishing that anyone would dare to defy the Creator of the Universe, but this is what those who interfere with His plans for Israel have done. Even Christians are rejecting the hundreds of promises God has made to Israel and are trying to apply them to the church. We dare not tamper with God's Word!

God warns the world: "I will gather all the nations … to the valley of Jehoshaphat, then I will enter into judgment with them there on behalf of My people and My inheritance, Israel … [for]they have … divided up My land" (Joel 3:2). The whole basis of the road map (and every other "peace" plan proposed) is to take from Israel the land God gave her. Bush, Putin, the UN and EU ought to tremble! And Christians ought to pray.

THE STRUGGLE FOR THE LAND PROMISED TO ISRAEL	
• The "Promised Land" given to Abraham (Gen. 12; 2000 BC) • Jews enter the land with Moses (1400 BC) • David subdued the land (1000 BC) • David makes Jerusalem capital of Israel (996 BC) • First temple built (960 BC) • Second Jewish temple period (515 BC – AD 70) • Jews revolt against Rome (AD 70, 135) • Muhammad the prophet (AD 570-632) • Muslim conquest (AD 637) • Dome of the Rock built on temple site (AD 691) • Last Muslim rule in Jerusalem (AD 1187-1917)	• Establishment of modern Israel (AD 1948) • Jerusalem divided (AD 1948-1967) • War of Independence (AD 1948) • Six Day War (AD 1967) • Yom Kippur War (AD 1973) • Lebanese Civil War (Ad 1982-1985) • Persian Gulf War (AD 1991) • War on Terrorism (AD 2001- on)

CHAPTER 7

WHO OWNS THE LAND OF ISRAEL?

Tom McCall

Does modern Israel have a right to claim their ancient Biblical land in the face of Palestinian claims today? Should Bible believing Christians support Israel in its claims?

These questions were addressed by Dr. Stanley Ellisen in his 1991 book, *Who Owns The Land*, which was recently republished by Dr. Charles Dyer of Moody Bible Institute.

Dr. Dyer is a Classical Dispensationalist (as are we), who has the unenviable responsibility of attempting to defend the Progressive Dispensationalists whose influence in the classrooms continues to grow at Moody and at Dallas and Talbot Seminaries, and other previously strong Dispensational schools. Progressive Dispensationalism blurs the distinctions between the dispensations, especially the Church Age and the Millennium, and in time develops a viewpoint that downplays Biblical prophecy in general and interest in modern Israel in particular. Previous issues of the *Levitt Lette*r and the book Zola and I wrote, *Battles with the Seminaries*, describe this disastrous theological development. In this chapter, however, we will endeavor to explain the main elements of this new book, which has been revised, updated and republished by Dr. Dyer.

To the credit of both Ellison and Dyer, they very clearly trace the history of the Jewish people in and out of the Land, and God's promise to Israel of ultimate possession and enjoyment of the Promised Land in the time of Messianic fulfillment, the Millennium. They make a very strong case for the inevitability of the blessed future for Israel. If you want to know about the Biblically prophetic future for Israel in the Millennium, this is a good book. Also, the book traces the Palestinian history and issues during the last fifty to one hundred years, and their involvement in various negotiations with Israel and in the devastating terrorist attacks against Israel. If you want a compendium on these issues, this book is also a good reference.

BUT WHAT ABOUT TODAY?

The primary issue, though, is the legitimacy of the current claims of Israel to the Land, and whether or not Christians should support the current nation. We are not living in the Millennium now, and we cannot require Israel to meet Millennial standards today before the Lord has returned to earth! Ellison appeared to be doing that when he originally concluded that we should have an "evenhanded" approach to Israel and the Palestinians. Dyer improves on this by giving some reasons why believers in Christ should support modern Israel, but he seems to be half-hearted and grudging in his argument.

Dyer demonstrates that Israel does not deserve to possess the Land primarily because the Jewish nation has not received Jesus as the Messiah:

> What happens when we put the divine plumb line to the house of Israel claiming the land today? Has it met the biblical conditions for restoration? By most human standards, the Jewish people stand high in regard to moral character. They appear to enjoy a surplus of intelligence, industry, self-sacrifice, high morals, and religious sincerity. Furthermore, they endured the Holocaust. From that crucible they have emerged to command international attention, doing so under constant threat of extinction. They have dramatically demonstrated the truth of the maxim, "Growth comes through struggle."
>
> Measured by the divine standard, however, another picture emerges. Though modern Israel has a human and international right to the land, its people fall far short of covenant obligations. *To put it bluntly, the current generation has no biblical right to possess the covenant land.* The nation has never recognized the Messiah God sent, let alone mourned over his wounding. Though many in Israel admit to Jesus' greatness as a Jewish teacher, most adamantly reject him as Messiah. They see him as but one of several prominent pseudo-messiahs. (Emphasis ours)[1]

Dyer assumes that the only way Israel can have a right to claim the

Land is if they first receive Christ. Yet receiving the Lord Jesus Christ is the end of prophetic developments concerning Israel, not the beginning. The Tribulation has a number of purposes, but one of them is the preparation of Israel for the Second Coming of the Messiah. It is called "The Time of Jacob's Trouble." At the beginning of the Tribulation, Israel will be far from acknowledging Jesus as Messiah, but after the witness of the 144,000 believing Jewish preachers, the Two Witnesses and other means, the remaining nation of Israel will be ready, willing and eager to receive Christ at the end of the Tribulation.

He further emphasizes that, not only does Israel not believe in Christ now, but that the Jewish nation studiously and officially rejects the notion that a Jew can remain a Jew if he is a Christian:

> The State of Israel will allow nearly every deviation from Jewish orthodoxy in its policy of toleration and pluralism. Even Jewish atheists are welcomed as citizens—but not believers in Jesus. Though the Law of Return of 1950 granted citizenship to anyone born Jewish, the Israeli High Court of Justice ruled in 1962 in a case of a man who had been born Jewish but who had converted to Christianity. They decided that "the fundamental conception that 'Jew' and 'Christian' are a contradiction in terms is something which is unreservedly accepted by all." On December 25, 1989, the Israeli Supreme Court ruled that Messianic Jews "cannot claim the right to come to this country as immigrants by virtue of the Law of Return" because those Jews "who believe in Jesus are 'members of a different faith."[2]

It is true that Israel refuses to recognize as Jews those Jewish foreigners who have become Christians and migrated to Israel. This has, in part, to do with the Law of the Return, by which any Jew has a right to a lot of economic and other benefits when they "make aliyah" and return to the Land. The Supreme Court has decided that a Jew who becomes a Christian forfeits his right to those benefits. Nevertheless, a sizable group of Jews living in Israel are believers in the Lord Jesus Christ. Some of them are native born Israeli's, known as Sabras. Dyer ignores this remnant in Israel who are Jewish believers in Christ, which has been estimated to be about 5,000 in number. Out of over five million Israelis, 5,000 is not a majority by any means, but it is significant, and many of them are outspoken and vocal. They are an enigma to the Israeli government, and play a significant role in the spiritual life of the nation.

Dyer concludes by asserting that Israel is a failure and does not meet the qualifications required by the covenant God has with Israel:

> Judged on biblical grounds, the nation today does not pass divine muster as a nation living in covenant obedience to God. The promise to possess the land is directly tied to the nation's response to Messiah. Though its international right to the land can be well defended, Israel's divine right by covenant to possess it today has only sentiment in its favor (emphasis ours).[3]

"Only sentiment" remains as an argument in favor of Israel's biblical claim to the Land, according to Dyer. In other words, the only way Israel can biblically claim the Land is by receiving Christ. Otherwise, they have no claim whatsoever. This is the gloomy conclusion Dyer comes to concerning Israel's current claims to the Land. Following this logic, Israel will have no claim to the Land all during the Tribulation, while they are rebuilding the Temple, being persecuted by the Antichrist, and being tried and prepared to receive Jesus as the Messiah.

BUT WHAT ABOUT THE CHURCH?

The next subject Dyer takes up is the Church's responsibility to Israel in light of what he thinks are dubious biblical claims to the Land under the present circumstances:

> Historically, Israel's right to possess the land in any given generation is conditioned on the nation's obedience to God. Today most of those living in the State of Israel are there in unbelief. Does that mean the church should not support any of Israel's claims to the land? The answer is no, for two reasons.
>
> First, as indicated earlier, God does announce a regathering of the people to the land in unbelief prior to the coming of the Messiah (Ezekiel 37:1-14; Zechariah 12:1—13:1). The current restoration of the State of Israel seems to be a harbinger of God's end-time program. And if that's the case, then God's hand is in the establishment of Israel.

> Second, the Palestinian covenant was established between God and Israel. God, and God alone, has the right to determine the level of blessing or cursing to be meted out to his people. But the Abrahamic covenant does have a component that applies to all the nations. God said, "1 will bless those who bless you, and whoever curses you I will curse" (Genesis 12:3). Even when Israel was under God's judgment, God still held nations accountable for their treatment of the Jewish people. God judged the Assyrians and the Babylonians for mistreating his people (Jeremiah 50:17-19). God also announced he would judge nations based on their treatment of his chosen people (Jeremiah 30:16; Obadiah 15-17). The Abrahamic covenant is still operative, and God still holds nations accountable to seek ways to bless the Jewish people. And one way to do that today is to support Israel's right to their God-given land. [4]

First, Dyer repeats the argument he had previously stated that Israel has failed the covenant requirements with the Lord because they have not believed in the Lord Jesus Christ. This might lead Christians to the conclusion that they should not support Israel's claim to the Land, and many have come to that conclusion, and evangelical support for Israel, especially among Christian leaders, has waned during the past two or three decades. To his credit, Dyer says "No," the fact that Israel has no Biblical claim to the Land does not mean Christians should not support Israel. This is difficult reasoning with a double negative, but it is a decided improvement on the view that Christians should not support Israel. It is a double negative, because it indicates that it is not true that Christians should not support Israel. This is not quite the same as saying Christians should support Israel, but it comes close.

The reasoning Dyer uses is that Israel must be in the Land before the return of the Lord to establish His kingdom. This is a very important point, and one that is ignored by those that are against Christians' supporting Israel. It means that Israel would be fulfilling Biblical prophecy even though coming back to the Land in unbelief, and that God's hand is in the preliminary restoration. How, then can Christians not support what God is doing with His people Israel? Dyer is to be commended for his recognition of this truth, which was apparently not appreciated by Ellisen.

Furthermore, Dyer recognizes that God is sovereign in His plans for

Israel, and it is He alone who determines whether or not He will bless Israel in spite of their disobedience and unbelief. This is known as grace. God is just as gracious to His unbelieving covenant nation Israel as He is to His Church, and to individual believers in Christ. Thus, if God decides to restore Israel to the Land in unbelief, who are we to raise objections, and fail to support Israel in this restoration?

Finally, Dyer says that the Abrahamic covenant is still in effect, and that God has promised to bless those Gentiles who bless Israel, even though the nation is in unbelief. Because of this enduring truth, Dyer (somewhat reluctantly) concludes that one way Christians can bless Israel today is "to support Israel's right to their God-given land." Ellisen, regrettably, did not come to the same conclusion, and Dyer is to be commended again for his recognition of this continuing principle of blessing in the Word of God.

TO SUM UP ...

Having said all of this, the views put forth by Dyer/Ellisen do have some short-comings:

1. *A Simplistic view of God's covenant relationship with Israel.* Dyer states that "Judged on biblical grounds, the nation today does not pass divine muster as a nation living in covenant obedience to God. The promise to possess the land is directly tied to the nation's response to Messiah."[5] There is not just one covenant, there are several. There are the Mosaic Covenant, the Abrahamic Covenant, the Davidic Covenant and the New Covenant. Only one of these, the Mosaic Covenant, is conditioned on obedience from Israel. The other covenants are unconditional, and are based solely on the faithfulness and grace of the Lord toward His covenant People. The New Covenant has to do with Israel's relationship to the Messiah, predicts that the nation would reject Him at His First Coming, but would receive Him at His Second Coming.

The Abrahamic Covenant gives the ownership of the Land, unconditionally, to the descendants of Abraham, Isaac and Jacob. This ownership is irrevocable and forever, as long as this earth stands. Israel does not have to do anything to obtain ownership of the Land. They already have it. However, ownership of the Land is different from possession of the Land.

The Mosaic Covenant spells out how Israel can earn the right to possess the Land which they already own by divine grant. All they have to do is keep the Law of Moses, all 613 commandments. If they do that, God would be obligated to arrange for them to have possession of the Land in abundant blessing. Possession, then, would not be a matter of grace, but of contractual obligation. The problem, of course, is that Israel has never kept the Law to the point where God was obligated to arrange for their possession of the Land. Thus Israel has never deserved the right to possess the Land.

Nevertheless, Israel has possessed the Land in history as a nation for some 1,500 years, even though they were in constant disobedience to the Mosaic Law. How can this be? By God's grace. The Abrahamic, Davidic and New Covenants are grace covenants. When Daniel prays for the return of the Jewish people to the Land to rebuild the Temple at the close of the Babylonian Captivity, his plea to the Lord was not based on Israel's obedience but on God's grace:

> Daniel 9:18 "O my God, incline Thine ear and hear! Open Thine eyes and see our desolations and the city which is called by Thy name; for we are not presenting our supplications before Thee on account of any merits of our own, but on account of Thy great compassion. 19 "O Lord, hear! O Lord, forgive! O Lord, listen and take action! For Thine own sake, O my God, do not delay, because Thy city and Thy people are called by Thy name."

Why should it be any different today? Israel's stunning restoration to the Land in our time has nothing to do with Israel's obedience, but has everything to do with God's faithfulness and grace to His Covenant People. We must have an understanding of all the covenants God has with Israel, especially the grace covenants. After all, where would the Church be if God restricted His blessings and grace based only upon the obedience of believers?

2. *A grudging attitude of support for Israel.* While Dyer finally concludes that Christians should support Israel, it appears to be with a somewhat grudging attitude, as though it were distasteful to support a people who do not accept Jesus as the Messiah. If we can only support a nation which has a majority who believe in Christ and are born-again, how can we support the nationhood of the United States or any other country today?

It seems that the proper attitude for Christians is to rejoice over the current restoration of Israel in unbelief as the most stunning evidence that Christ's return is ever nearer. If the Lord is setting the stage for the events of the Tribulation, then the Rapture of the Church (which must come before the Tribulation) is surely imminent. Furthermore, the day of the Redemption of Israel, when Israel will indeed receive Christ, is drawing ever closer as well.

We should therefore rejoice over the modern state of Israel, back its possession of the Land in every way, support the Israeli believers in Christ, and make pilgrimage trips to Israel to see the wonders of the Land of the Bible. It is a privilege, not a sullen duty, to be living in a time when the Lord is setting the stage for the end time events.

THE JEREMIAH 30 PROPHECY OF THE TRIBULATION "BIRTH PANGS" THAT WILL COME UPON THE WORLD	
The Promise of Israel's Restoration 30:1-4 "I will bring them back to the land" (v.3)	**Israel's Millennial Prosperity 30:18-20** "I will restore the fortunes of Jacob" (v. 18)
Israel's Great Tribulation 30:5-7 "A woman in childbirth … a great day" (vv.6-7)	**Israel's Leader 30:21-22** "A leader (Messiah) shall approach Me" (v. 21)
Israel's Liberation from Bondage 30:8-11 "I am with you to save you" (v. 11)	**God's Final Purposes in the End 30:23-24** "God's final purposes in the latter days" (v. 24)
The Healing of Israel's Wounds 30:12-17 "I will restore you (Israel) to health" (v. 17)	

CHAPTER 8

JEREMIAH 30: BIRTH PANGS, TRIBULATION, AND RESTORATION

Andy Woods

Jeremiah 30 makes enormous contributions to the dispensational view of eschatology. The purpose of this chapter is to highlight some of these contributions by taking the reader through the main sections of chapter 30. First, let us offer some thoughts on the general theme of restoration found in Jeremiah 30. Although there have been a few hints at the nation's eventual restoration earlier in his book (Jer. 3:14-18; 16:14-15; 23:1-8; 24:4-7), up to this point, Jeremiah's prophecies have mostly focused on the imminent judgment that the nation experienced at the hands of the Babylonians. However, Jeremiah 30 begins what many commentators refer to as the "Book of Consolation"[1] found in chapters 30–33, which provides prophecies of national restoration to be fulfilled in the distant future.

Jeremiah was initially commissioned by God to not only "pluck up and to break down" but also to "build and to plant" (Jer. 1:10). His earlier chapters focus upon the first part of this assignment while chapter 30 inaugurates the second part of the assignment.[2] Other commentators have observed that these chapters focus on a second day referred to by Jeremiah. In the early chapters of his book, Jeremiah predicted a day of destruction for the nation (Jer. 5:18; 7:32; 9:25; 19:6), which took place when Judah was taken into Babylonian Captivity in 586 B.C. However, in these latter chapters, a second day of future national restoration is in view (Jer. 30:3, 8, 24; 31:1, 27, 29, 31, 33, 38; 33:14-16).[3]

THE PROMISE OF ISRAEL'S RESTORATION: JEREMIAH 30:1-4

God instructed Jeremiah to record all the divinely spoken words of restoration in a book (Jer. 30:2). The emphasis on "all the words" indicates that Jeremiah was not to omit any divinely communicated detail.[4]

Although the primary purpose of the command to write was no doubt to provide a written prediction of restoration that would serve to encourage the beleaguered exiles after Jerusalem eventually fell,[5] there may have been a secondary purpose as well. Perhaps God wanted the prophecies of restoration recorded in written form in order to counter the tendency of subsequent generations to dismiss His future program for Israel. Paul similarly warned Gentile Christians not to become arrogant on account of Israel's present rejection of her messiah because it was still God's purpose to restore His chosen people (Rom. 11:18-27). Thus, the plain and literal reading of the prophecies of Israel's ultimate restoration found in Jeremiah 30–33 serve as a check against similar Gentile arrogance in any era.

Jeremiah predicted that the promises of restoration would ultimately be accomplished in the very land of Israel that God had given to the Jewish forefathers (Jer. 30:3). Amillennial interpreters and covenant theologians typically understand such a prediction as an eternal heavenly blessing or as finding its fulfillment spiritually in the church, which they consider the New Israel.[6] Such an interpretive maneuver has far more to do with personal philosophy and theological presupposition than it has to do with what the Scripture actually teaches. The land, when read in its normal sense, is an obvious reference to the actual plot of real estate that God unconditionally promised to the physical descendants of Abraham (Gen 15:18-21). Such a prediction will find its literal fulfillment in the millennial reign of Christ rather than mystically or spiritually during the church age.

Many attempt to "preterize" the prophecies found in this chapter by arguing that they were fulfilled in the historic return of the nation from Babylonian Captivity. However, as this presentation will repeatedly point out, preterism is a virtual impossible case to make because the details of this chapter do not fit the known facts of history. For example, Judah alone returned from the Babylonian Captivity and yet Jeremiah 30:3 predicts the restoration of both Judah and Israel.[7] Because such a detail has never been fulfilled in past history it obviously demands a future fulfillment. The unfulfilled details of Jeremiah 30–33 has led Feinberg to conclude, "Jeremiah is contemplating the distant, not near, future of the nation."[8] Those who place these prophecies of future restoration in the same time period as the prophecies regarding the nation's historical destruction forget the principle of prophetic "foreshortening." According to this principle, it is possible to have a series of predictions without always mentioning the lengthy time gaps between the events (Isa. 9:6-7; 61:1-2). Thus, Jeremiah predicted the ancient fall of the nation as well as her ultimate restoration without necessarily mentioning the intervening time period between these events.[9]

ISRAEL'S GREAT TRIBULATION: JEREMIAH 30:5-7

Verses 5-7 provide a description of the coming Great Tribulation period, which is the means that God will use to restore the nation. To portray the terror of the coming Tribulation, Jeremiah analogizes it to men acting as women do when they place their hands on their loins to suppress the pains of childbirth (Jer. 30:6).[10] This birth pangs motif is also used elsewhere in Scripture to depict the same time of great distress preceding the coming of messiah. For example, Isa. 66:7-9 uses birth pangs to describe Israel's sudden millennial birth after the Tribulation.[11] Moreover, Matthew 24:8 employs the identical imagery to describe the time of cataclysmic upheaval leading up to Christ's Second Advent (v. 27). Furthermore, in 1 Thessalonians 5:3, Paul uses labor pains imagery to describe the same horrific period of time that will take the unsaved world off guard.

Verse 7 continues the description of this same time period through the phrase "there is none like it." This phrase draws attention to the uniqueness of the time period. Jesus also calls attention to the uniqueness of the same period when he says, "For then there will be great tribulation, such as has not occurred since the beginning of the world until now, nor ever shall" (Matt. 24:21). Daniel also emphasizes the Tribulation's uniqueness. Daniel 12:1 says, "And there will be a time of distress such as never occurred since there was a nation until that time." Such descriptions of unprecedented terror only harmonize with the future time of unparalleled distress most vividly described in Revelation 6–19 rather than to some past event. Preterist attempts to tie these prophecies in with the adversity that the nation suffered at the hands of the Babylonians in 586 B.C. or the Romans in A.D. 70 are unpersuasive.[12] Although these events brought distress upon the nation, they are simply not unique enough to satisfy the language of Jeremiah 30:7.

Verse 7 continues its description of the coming Tribulation period by labeling it the time of "Jacob's distress." Interestingly, the same Hebrew word translated "distress" in verse 7 is also used in Daniel 12:1 and Zephaniah 1:15 to describe the coming Tribulation. Also, the reference to the patriarch Jacob whose name was later changed to Israel (Gen. 32:28) reminds us that this future time period is specifically focused upon the nation. Although global in scope, the primary purpose of the time period that Jeremiah describes is to bring unparalleled distress upon the nation for the purpose of accomplishing a foreordained result. The last phrase in verse 7 enumerates this foreordained result when it says, "but he will be saved from it." In other words, both spiritual salvation (Rom. 11:25-27) and physical rescue of the nation (Matt. 24:31) will be the ultimate result of the Tribulation period. The future Tribulation will accomplish God's purpose of killing off all Jewish unbelievers except for a remnant (Zech. 13:8) and purifying this remnant in preparation for the Second Advent and the millennial kingdom. Daniel elaborates upon this same time period and foreordained result when he indicates that the purpose of the yet unfulfilled Seventieth Week is to bring about six items in the life of the Daniel's people and city (Dan. 9:24). Because these six items connote restoration and because Daniel's people and city speak of the Jewish nation, the purpose of the Daniel's Seventieth Week is to bring about Israel's restoration.

Understanding the Tribulation period as a process where God takes the nation from unbelief to faith is necessary to counter a developing trend within evangelicalism that contends that God's hand cannot be on the modern state of Israel because she is currently in unbelief.[13] Such a contention is inconsistent with biblical predictions of a twofold national re-gathering. First, Israel will be gathered in unbelief in preparation for the Tribulation period. Numerous passages speak of Israel's initial gathering in unbelief prior to the Tribulation period (Ezek. 20:33-38; 22:17-22; Zeph. 2:1-2). Second, after Israel's conversion in the Tribulation, the nation will call upon Christ (Matt. 23:37-39) and He will subsequently return and rescue her by re-gathering her a second time (Matt. 24:31).[14] Thus, Israel's conversion is simply the end of this prolonged process. According to this pattern, Israel not only has a prophetic program to fulfill after her conversion but she also has a prophetic destiny to complete prior to her conversion. Israel's entrance into a covenant with the antichrist and the erection of the Tribulation temple (Dan. 9:27) are obviously prophecies that she will fulfill while still in unbelief. Thus, any analysis that discounts God's present hand on the Jewish nation simply because Israel is currently in unbelief fails to take into account all of the biblical data.

Furthermore, if faith and obedience are the criteria used to determine whether God's hand is upon modern Israel, then such a standard also forces one to conclude that God's hand was never upon the nation during the 1300 years of biblical history when the nation was in the land. Unbelief and disobedience characterized the nation during this era as well. In sum, the modern state of Israel, even in its present state of unbelief, could very well represent the initial gathering in preparation for the coming Tribulation period. This view is nothing new for traditional dispensational interpreters. Note the following quote by John F. Walvoord as he reflected upon the prophetic significance of the modern state of Israel:

> Of the many peculiar phenomena which characterize the present generation, few events can claim equal significance as far as Biblical prophecy is concerned with that of the return of Israel to their land. It constitutes a preparation for the end of the age, the setting for the coming of the Lord for His church, and the fulfillment of Israel's prophetic destiny.[15]

The description of the Tribulation as found in Jeremiah 30:5-7 also lends support to the pretribulation rapture position. First, if the purpose of the Tribulation focuses upon Israel (v. 7), it is doubtful that the church will be on the earth during this time period. How can the church be present during a time period of such emphasis upon national Israel when the church age is characterized by an obliteration of all national and ethnic distinctions (Rom. 10:12; 1 Cor. 12:13; Gal. 3:28; Eph. 2:11-18)? Furthermore, because God seems to use Israel and the church on a mutually exclusive basis, the church cannot be on the earth during the time period when He is once again specifically at work with national Israel. Perhaps it is for this reason that one notices a conspicuous absence of any references to the church in all Great Tribulation texts.[16] A case in point is the notable absence of the Greek word translated "church" (*ekklēsia*) in Revelation 6–19, which is the body of Scripture most dedicated to vividly describing the coming Tribulation period. Although *ekklēsia* is found 19 times in Revelation 1–3 and once again in chapter 22, the word and is not found a single time in 6–19. The active agents of God during this time period are specifically enumerated as Jews (Rev. 7; 11; 12) rather than members of the church, which is comprised of believers from every ethnicity.

Second, if the Tribulation represents a time of divinely orchestrated distress (v. 7) and anger (v. 24), then the church cannot be present because the church has been promised an exemption from divine wrath (Rom. 5:9; 8:1; 1 Thess. 1:10; 5:9). While the church has not been promised deliverance from ordinary trials (John 16:33), the wrath of man (2 Tim. 3:12), Satan's wrath (Rev 2:10; Eph 6:11-12) or the wrath of the world system (John 15:18-19), the church has been promised deliverance from God's wrath. Mid tribulation and pre wrath rapture schemes typically place the church in some initial part of the tribulation on the grounds that the actual time of divine wrath supposedly does not begin until later on in the Seventieth Week. However, such a dichotomy cannot be defended from Jeremiah 30:5-7, 23-24, which uses the language of divine distress and anger for the entire Tribulation period. Based upon these verses, the church can expect not to be involved in any part of Jacob's trouble.

ISRAEL'S LIBERATION FROM BONDAGE: JEREMIAH 30:8-11

Verses 8-11 describe the political freedom that the nation will experience after her Messiah rescues her. Thus, these verses elaborate upon the salvation that Israel is promised at the end of verse 7. In verse 8, Jeremiah describes this liberation in terms of the breaking off of a yoke from the neck, the tearing off of bonds, and no longer being slaves to strangers. Here, Jeremiah is describing the termination of the curses associated with the Mosaic Covenant. At Sinai, God entered into a conditional covenant with the nation known as the Mosaic Covenant. Part of this covenant involved blessings for obedience (Deut. 28:1-14) and curses for disobedience (Deut. 28:15-68). The curses are depicted as escalating in intensity as Israel persisted in disobedience. These curses would ultimately climax in the form of the nation experiencing oppression at the hands of a foreign power (Deut. 28:49). As a result of these predictions, Israel has routinely experienced foreign oppression throughout her history because of her perpetual disobedience. However, Jeremiah speaks of a time following the nation's conversion when she will obey God. Such obedience will consequently terminate the covenant curses and foreign oppression and instead usher in the covenant blessings.

Jeremiah 30:8 also depicts the conclusion of the "Times of the Gentiles" (Luke 21:24; Rev. 11:1-2). Dispensationalists define the "Times of the Gentiles" as the period of time in between the Babylonian captivity beginning in 586 B.C. and the Second Advent when the nation would experience oppression at the hands of various foreign powers.[17] Chapters 2 and 7 of the book of Daniel describe this period of time. From these chapters it can be ascertained that the various nations that would oppress Israel during the "Times of the Gentiles" would be Babylon, Medo-Persia, Greece, Rome, and revived Rome. However, according to Jeremiah 30:8, when Christ returns He will break the yoke of Gentile oppression and formally terminate the "Times of the Gentiles."

According to verse 9, the nation would no longer serve foreign oppressors but rather would be devoted solely to the service of the Lord and David, who the Lord would enthrone. It is common for interpreters to understand the reference to the resurrected millennial David (Hosea 3:5; Ezek. 34:23; 37:24) as referring to David's greater son Jesus Christ (Luke 1:32, 69; Acts 2:29-30; 13:22-23, 34). However, such an interpretation cannot be supported from Jeremiah 30:9 and constitutes an impermissible reading of the New Testament back into the Old. If Jeremiah wanted David to be taken in a symbolic sense, he would have said so. Fruchtenbaum explains:

> Nothing in the text indicates that *David* is to be taken symbolically. If the prophets wanted to refer to the messiah in connection with David, they used terms such as "Root of Jesse," "Branch of David," "Son of David," or "Seed of David." None of these expressions are used here. The text simply states, *David*. In keeping with literal interpretation, it is best to take the text as it reads, meaning the literal David, who, in his resurrected form, will function as the king over Israel and as a prince in subjection to the King of the world.[18]

Thus, David will be resurrected at the same time as all of the other Old Testament saints (Dan. 12:2; John 5:28-29; Acts 24:15; Rev. 20:4) and rule in submission to Christ during the millennium in a co regency form of government. "While Jesus, the Messiah, will reign over the entire earth, David will be resurrected to reign with Christ as vice regent over the nation of Israel."[19] Regarding the predictions of the millennial David, Walvoord similarly observes, "Though some have attempted to take this prophecy in less than its literal meaning, the clear statement is that David, who is now dead and whose body is in his tomb in Jerusalem (Acts 2:29), will be resurrected."[20]

Putting verses 8-9 together, we learn that the establishment of the Davidic monarchy will follow Israel's conversion and rescue by messiah. This sequence verifies the premillennial chronology of events. The Second Advent of Christ transpires first and is immediately followed by the millennial reign. The reestablishment of the Davidic monarchy in verse 9 also renders implausible the preterist interpretation. According to Kaiser, "These passages cannot refer to the destruction of Jerusalem in A.D. 70, for the Davidic monarchy was not restored after that date and the Jews were not saved out of it, but were killed by the thousands and many were carried away."[21]

In light of these promises, verse 10 admonishes Jacob not to be afraid. The verse then provides more promises of Israel's salvation and pictures her dwelling in ease in her own land. 'The picture of quiet ease is that of sheep lying undisturbed in their pastures…"[22] Interestingly, the nation dwelling at ease in her own land is the very goal of today's world community. The so-called "two state solution" seeks to pacify the aggressiveness of Israel's neighbors by surrendering to them part of Israel's land. It is alleged that such pacification will allow both Israel and her neighbors to live in harmony with one another. Even though the ultimate goal of the "peace process" may be a noble one, verse 10 makes it clear that only Christ's personal intervention will bring this goal to pass. The nation will only dwell at ease in its own land and experience lasting political peace when it comes under the authority of the prince of peace. Human political maneuvering alone will never bring into existence these ideal conditions.

In verse 11, God promises to destroy the very nations that oppressed Israel during the "Times of the Gentiles." This prediction has its roots in God's unconditional promises to Abraham's descendants (Gen. 12:1-3). One of the Abrahamic promises was a protection against anti-Semitism. God promised to bless those who bless Abraham's physical descendants and curse those who cursed Abraham's physical lineage (Gen. 12:3).

Interestingly, every world power that has come against Abraham's descendants is now on the ash heap of history. The Old Testament records how Egypt, Assyria, Babylon and Persia all came against the Jewish nation. Despite the fact that these empires once covered the face of the known world, they no longer exist as world powers. Other examples include Greece, Rome, Britain, and even Hitler's Nazi Germany, which was supposed to last 1,000 years. Those nations that bully Israel or seek her demise would do well to heed the warning of Genesis 12:3 as well as observe this historical pattern.

Verse 11 goes on to draw a contrast "between the fate of God's people and that of their oppressors."[23] Although God will eradicate Israel's enemies, he will only chasten Israel with the intent of humbling her. God's ultimate goal is Israel's restoration rather than her affliction. The affliction is simply the divine means of achieving this goal. He will remember His unconditional covenant (chapter 15) and not destroy Israel completely. Although unbelieving Jews will be destroyed in the Tribulation, God will use this difficult period to preserve and purify a believing remnant (Zech. 13:8).

Verse 11 also describes Israel as being scattered among all the nations. Such a description again renders the preterist interpretation implausible and instead demands a futurist interpretation. While it is common to attempt to connect these verses to the events surrounding the Babylonian Captivity, it must be remembered that during the Babylonian Captivity Israel was incarcerated in one particular geographic locale rather than being dispersed throughout the earth as verse 11 demands. Similarly, when Israel is ultimately gathered she will be collected from all the nations of the earth rather than from one region, as was the case in the return from Babylon. In sum, because the details of verse 11 do not fit the known facts of history, they await a future fulfillment.

THE HEALING OF ISRAEL'S WOUNDS: JEREMIAH 30:12-17

As previously discussed, the ultimate purpose of the Tribulation period is to restore Israel. These verses describe this restoration in terms of the nation being restored to health. However, before the nation can see her need to be healed, she first must understand the seriousness of her present sickness. It is doubtful that any person would submit to invasive surgery unless they are first convinced of the gravity of their illness and consequently the need for such a surgery. The closest New Testament parallel to this concept is found in Romans 1–3. Before Paul discusses salvation, he first emphasizes humanity's fallen condition. Paul's logic is that an understanding of the severity of the spiritual sickness is first necessary in order to give people an incentive to reach out for the divine cure. In a similar way, before predicting Israel's healing, Jeremiah first describes the present sickness of the nation so that she will better appreciate the necessity of a future healing.

Verse 12 describes Israel's present wounds as incurable absent God's miraculous intervention. In verse 13, the prophet uses lawsuit imagery by portraying the nation as a helpless defendant in a lawsuit with no one to plead her case. Jeremiah then switches to the imagery of medicine by speaking of Israel's incurable sores.[24] Israel's lovers had forgotten her (v. 14). The nation's lovers refer to the false gods and alliances that ~~the~~ she had put her hope in. Scripture frequently uses the imagery of adultery and harlotry to depict the idolatry of God's people (James 4:4). False gods have a tendency of deserting us during our greatest time of need. Such was the nation's predicament. "Jeremiah uses the language of an unfaithful wife (Judah) who has deserted her husband (the Lord) and now because she has lived the difficult life of prostitution, is all battered and bruised and has lost her beauty. In this condition, none of those with whom she has been having relations are interested in her."[25] Moreover, Israel's sins had actually put God in the position of becoming her enemy. Israel's persistent rebellion had forced God to continue to pour out upon her the covenant curses, which He was obligated to do under the terms of the Mosaic Covenant. Thus, in Jeremiah 30:15, God asks, "Why do you cry out over your injury?" The nation had no right to complain because it was her own rebellion that created her predicament.

However, in verses 16-17, the prophet's tone begins to change as he begins to describe Israel's healing process. Verse 16 reiterates the fact that Israel's enemies will be destroyed. As previously discussed, such a prediction is simply the outworking of the protection against anti-Semitism provided in the Abrahamic promises (Gen. 12:3). It is staggering to contemplate how many nations and people today are quick to jump on the modern anti-Semitic bandwagon while remaining totally oblivious to the divine repercussions of such activity. Whoever touches Israel touches the very apple of

God's eye (Zech. 2:8). Both biblical and secular history are littered with examples of the demise of nations and individuals who embrace an anti-Semitic philosophy. Modern anti-Semites would do well to take note of these biblical and historical trends. Sadly, Bible prophecy informs us that the nations will not heed such a warning. According to Zechariah 12:3, all nations of the earth will gather against Israel in the Tribulation thus incurring the wrath of God.

The nation's healing is finally described in verse 17. "… very soon God will be the physician of the people of the land of Israel!"[26] Once this process is complete Israel will no longer be called an outcast. On the contrary, she will receive the place of preeminence in the millennial reign. Although some envision Israel as merely one nation among many in the millennium, the Old Testament paints quite a different picture. Once the nation is brought back into fellowship with God, she will be the head and not the tail (Deut. 28:13). The law of the Lord will go forth from Zion. The nations of that time are pictured as streaming to Jerusalem to worship God (Isa. 2:2-3). Those that refuse will receive no rain (Zech. 14:17). During this era, the Gentiles will actually be subservient to Israel (Deut. 15:6; 29:1; Isa. 49:22-23; 61:6-7).[27] Those nations that lorded their authority over Israel during the "Times of the Gentiles" will end up serving Israel during the millennial age. According to the end of Zechariah 14:17, part of the reason for Israel's restoration is the charge of the nations that God had forsaken His people. In order to confound human wisdom, God responds to this taunt by miraculously intervening and restoring His covenant people.

ISRAEL'S MILLENNIAL PROSPERITY: JEREMIAH 30:18-20

Once the nation experiences conversion during the Tribulation period (Zech. 12:10), the covenant curses will be removed and the covenant blessings will be ushered in. Prosperity will burst upon the scene. Verses 18-20 describe the prosperity that Israel will enjoy during this wonderful time period. In contrast to the perpetual dread that the Jew lived with during the "Times of the Gentiles" (Deut. 28:66), the sounds of thanksgiving and merry making will emanate from the millennial Jerusalem (v. 19).

The permanent fixture of the city of Jerusalem will replace the impermanent dwellings of the tents that characterized the Jews throughout their exile.[28] This contrast emphasizes the permanency of Israel's national existence after the Tribulation. Amos 9:15 also comments on the permanence of the millennial Jewish nation when it says, "'I will also plant them on their land, and they will not again be rooted out from their land, which I have given them,' says the Lord your God." In the next chapter, Jeremiah provides a vivid description of the nation's permanence when he says,

> *Thus says the Lord, who gives the sun for light by day, and the fixed order of the moon and the stars for light by night, who stirs up the sea so that its waves roar; the Lord of hosts is His name: 'if this fixed order departs from me,' declares the Lord, 'The offspring of Israel also shall cease from being a nation before me forever.' Thus says the Lord, 'If the heavens above can be measured, and the foundations of the earth searched out below, then I will also cast off all the offspring of Israel for all that they have done,' declares the Lord (Jer. 31:35-37).*

In other words, just as the fixed order of the universe is a permanent reality, so are His promises to His covenant people. Although today some have questioned the legitimacy of the Jewish state, such questions will not persist in the millennial age, as the Lord will permanently settle the nation in the land that He gave to the Jewish forefathers. Although oppressed during the Times of the Gentiles and the Tribulation, the eternal perpetuity of the nation of Israel is all but guaranteed on account of the unconditional promises God made to the Jewish people in the Abrahmic Covenant (Gen. 15). Church age believers can take great comfort in the permanency of God's promises to Israel. God's willingness to keep all of His promises to Abraham's physical descendants proves that He is a covenant keeping God and thus He can be trusted to keep all of His other promises made to church age believers as well.

This same verse goes on to predict the multiplication of the Jewish people in the kingdom age. In past history, Satan saw the multiplication of the Jew as a threat and did everything within his power to thwart it. Satan's ambition has always been to eliminate the Jewish nation. Because messianic prophecies predicted that the messiah would be born from the Jewish nation (Gen. 49:10), Satan attempted to prevent the fulfillment of such predictions by eliminating Israel. Satan was no doubt behind the efforts of the Egyptian leaders to enslave Israel in the early chapters of Exodus as well as Haman's attempt to eradicate that Israel as recorded in the Book of Esther.

Satan pursues a similar pattern in this age as well. Because Bible prophecy predicts that the kingdom will ultimately be established through the Jewish people, Satan has similarly attempted to prevent such a prophecy from coming to pass by eliminating modern Israel. Just as Satan attempted to use the Egyptian pharaohs and Haman in Old Testament times to eradicate the Jew, few doubt that Satan was behind Hitler's Final Solution. Satan continues the same strategy even today through the sentiments of some Middle Eastern leaders that refuse to recognize the state of Israel and seek to drive Israel into the sea. Revelation 12 speaks of the dragon's, or Satan's (Rev. 12:9), perpetual hostility against the woman, who is Israel (v. 1; Gen. 37:9-10). Thus, we can be confident that Satan is the motivating force behind anti-Semitic philosophies and activities throughout history. Because Satan will be bound throughout out the millennial age (Rev. 20:1-3), he will be unable to pursue his historic hostility against the nation. Thus, Jeremiah predicts that the nation will enjoy unhindered multiplication throughout the kingdom era.

Verse 19 also speaks of honor being bestowed to the Jew in the millennium No longer will the nation be deemed insignificant or be blamed for the world's problems but rather will be given the special place of honor that is appropriate for God's covenant people. Verse 20 elaborates upon Israel's millennial prosperity by reiterating the inevitable demise of Israel's oppressors because of the protection against anti-Semitism found in Gen. 12:3. The security of the nation during this time is also reemphasized when verse 20 speaks of Israel's congregation being established before the Lord. Unlike modern Israel that has rejected God's ruling authority through its refusal to acknowledge Christ as savior, millennial Israel will be the beneficiary of the direct rule of God.

Verse 20 also speaks of *their children also shall be as formerly.* Many interpret this phrase as a promise that Israel's children will be just as prosperous during the millennial age as they had been when the nation reached its zenith under the reigns of David and Solomon.[29] Thus, Jeremiah uses the height of the Davidic and Solomonic reigns as a type for future millennial prosperity.

Unfortunately, amillennial commentators often miss this typology and instead contend that the Abrahamic covenant found its complete fulfillment during the height of the prosperity of Solomon's reign. Walvoord explains why such a contention lacks merit:

> Under Solomon, the kingdom of Israel grew to an extent of wealth and recognition never achieved before or after. The extensive wealth and influence of Solomon is portrayed in Scripture (1 Kings 4:1-34; 2 Chron. 9:13-28). "He ruled over all the kings from the river to the land of the Philistines, as far as the border of Egypt" (2 Chron. 9:26). On the basis of this, some amillenarians hold that this fulfilled the promise of the land to Abraham–that is, that Solomon extended his kingdom over the entire area promised in Genesis 15:18-21. A careful reading of the text, however, makes clear that while Solomon put the entire world under his control in the sense that he demanded tribute from these countries, they were not actually incorporated into the state of Israel. This made their defection easy once Solomon died and the power of the kingdom began to decline. The extent to which the promises were fulfilled to Solomon also failed to fulfill the requirement that the land would be possessed forever, for Solomon's' influence was limited to his reign. Further evidence is found for the fact that Solomon's influence reign did not fulfill the Abrahamic covenant in that many later prophecies picture a future fulfillment. In fact, the promise of the land in its ultimate fulfillment fails to find a completion in the entire Old Testament. Hebrews 11 indicates concerning the men of faith, that they looked forward to fulfillment of God's plans and purposes but did not live to see their complete fulfillment.[30]

Thus, the Davidic and Solomonic eras are not fulfillments of the millennial promises but rather serve as mere typology of these future blessings. Jeremiah deliberately picked up upon such typology in order to elaborate upon this future time of millennial blessing.

ISRAEL'S LEADER: JEREMIAH 30:21-22

In order to show who will be responsible for ushering in these millennial blessings, Jeremiah's prophecies now begin to focus upon Israel's future millennial ruler. It is likely that the future leader described in these verses is Jesus Christ. There are at least four reasons for this conclusion.[31] First, verse 21 describes the leader as being *one of them* who *shall come forth from their midst.* In other words, this leader will be Jewish. Such a prediction would have been particularly encouraging to the Jewish nation in the midst of the "Times of the Gentiles" as Israel was being subjugated by one Gentile power after another. Yet during the millennium Jeremiah predicts that the nation will be ruled by one of its own. Jesus certainly fulfills this criterion since he was Jewish (Matt. 1:1; Rom. 9:5).

Second, the leader will have the privilege of approaching God. Thorough the uses of the rhetorical question, *who would dare to risk his life to approach Me?' declares the Lord,* Jeremiah demonstrates the significance of this privilege. In Old Testament times, humans could not approach God. The only exception to this rule was the high priest on the Day of Atonement could approach God only after the appropriate animal sacrifice had been administered. The inapproachability of God had to do with the sin barrier separating sinful man from a holy God. But here Israel's future leader is portrayed as having unlimited access to God. Only sinless Christ could qualify to enjoy such a privilege.

Third, the future leader will enjoy a dual role. He will be both a ruler and a priest. He is referred to as a ruler in verse 21. Verse 21 also refers to him as a priest because the privilege of approaching God was a priestly function. No mere mortal could fulfill both roles. If a king attempted to usurp a priestly function, he was severely penalized. When Saul attempted to usurp the prerogatives of a priest, Samuel told him that his kingdom would not endure (1 Sam. 14). When Uzziah attempted to usurp the prerogatives of a priest, he was smote with leprosy (2 Chron. 26). Because Jeremiah predicts that the ruler will be both king and priest, he must be speaking of Christ rather than a mere man. Only Christ can qualify to fill both roles.

Fourth, Jeremiah 30:22 describes the result of the leader's ministry through the phrase *and you shall be My people, and I will be your God.* This phrase is used several times in the Old Testament to depict the ideal relationship between Israel and God (Lev. 26:12; Deut. 7:6; 26:16-19; Jer.

7:23; 11:4; 24:7; 31:1, 33; Ezek. 11:20; 14:11; 34:30; 36:28; 37:23, 27; Hosea 2:23; Zech. 8:8; 13:9).[32] No mere human being has the capacity to bring about such an ideal condition. Only Christ can bring it about. In sum, the leader's Jewish heritage, unhindered access to God, dual role, and capacity to bring about ideal conditions all strongly argue for a messianic interpretation of Jeremiah 30:21-22. Feinberg observes that even the extra biblical material has embraced this messianic interpretation. He notes, "The Targum, though interpretive, is correct in its rendering 'Messiah shall be revealed to them out of their own midst.'"[33] Jeremiah emphasizes the messiah at this juncture to reiterate that only He will bring the millennial blessings to pass for the nation.

THE ACCOMPLISHMENT OF GOD'S PURPOSES: JEREMIAH 30:23-24

Jeremiah 30 reveals many of God's future purposes. These include the conversion and purification of the Jewish remnant in preparation for the Second Coming and millennium as well as the destruction of Israel's enemies. Verses 23-24 reveal the means that God will use in bringing these purposes to pass. As alluded to earlier in the chapter (v. 7), divine anger and distress to be poured out upon the world during the future Tribulation period will be the means that He will use to accomplish His purposes. Consequently, the tribulation is described as a storm that will suddenly burst upon the head of the wicked (v. 23). God's anger will not be pacified until the intent of His heart is accomplished (v. 24). In other words, God's anger during this terrible time period will be unrelenting until the Jewish remnant bows the knee to the very messiah that they rejected at His first coming and Israel's oppressors have been destroyed.

Jeremiah closes this important chapter with a prediction that the Jew would not understand these prophecies until the latter days. Because the phrase "latter days" is often used in Old Testament contexts that speak of Tribulation and millennial events (Deut. 4:30; Dan. 2:28; 10:14; Jer. 48:47), Jeremiah's use of the expression further confirms that the details of this chapter have never been fulfilled in past history and therefore await a future fulfillment. Although Jeremiah's original audience would not understand his predictions, the Jewish nation living in the predicted time period in the distant future would understand them. In a similar way the prophet

Daniel was told to seal up his prophecies on account of the fact that they were meant to be understood by a future generation rather than his own generation (Dan. 8:26; 12:4, 9).

CONCLUSION

The sweeping prophetic themes found in Jeremiah 30 demand that dispensationalists reconsider its monumental contributions to their eschatological system. This chapter sheds light on Israel's restoration as well as the coming Tribulation as the means that God will use to restore His covenant people. Jeremiah's description of this terrible day also argues for a pretribulational rapture as well as a futuristic interpretation of these prophesied events. Other prophetic themes are evident in this chapter as well such as how and when the "Times of the Gentiles" as well as the curses associated with the Mosaic Covenant will end thus paving the way for Israel's millennial blessings. The chapter also emphasizes the outworking of the protection against anti-Semitism found in Gen. 12:3. Finally, the chapter helps us better understand events taking place in our modern world such as the current re gathering of the Jew in unbelief. In sum, all who take seriously God's future prophetic program would do well to give greater attention to Jeremiah 30.

THE FOUR VIEWS ABOUT GOD AND MAGOG			
There are four main views as to when the prophecy of Gog and Magog (Ezekiel 38-39) is fulfilled. Premillennialists vary in their opinions and can be found to hold all four theories.			
TAKES PLACE BEFORE THE RAPTURE OF THE CHURCH	**TAKES PLACE AT THE VERY BEGINNING OF THE TRIBULATION**	**TAKES PLACE SOMETIME DURING THE TRIBULATION**	**TAKES PLACE AT THE END OF THE TRIBULATION**

CHAPTER 9

WHAT IS "GOG AND MAGOG" IN REGARD TO BIBLICAL PROPHECY?

Manfred Kober

The twentieth century has witnessed the rise and demise of the Soviet Union, a superpower that will yet again reach a prominent position in the end-times. A revived Russia will seek world dominance, as predicted in Ezekiel 38:1-39:24. The emergence of Russia is seen in the context of the physical and spiritual restoration of Israel. Ezekiel 36-37 speaks of the return of Israel to their land from which they will never again be scattered.

Ezekiel prophesies of the physical restoration of Israel when he explains the symbolism of the valley of dry bones in Ezekiel 37:21, "and say unto them, Thus saith the Lord GOD; behold, I will take the children of Israel from among the heathen, whither they be gone, and will gather them on every side, and bring them into their own land:" Ezekiel further foretells the spiritual regeneration of Israel. He writes, "A new heart also will I give you, and a new spirit will I put within you: and I will take away the stony heart out of your flesh, and I will give you an heart of flesh. And I will put my spirit within you, and cause you to walk in my statutes, and ye shall keep my judgments, and do them" (36:26, 27). This restoration and regeneration of Israel are seen as events closely related to the context of the tribulation period.

THE CONFLICTS OF THE END TIMES

Three major geopolitical conflicts are predicted for the tribulation period. In the prophecies of Daniel 2 and Daniel 7 a revived Roman empire is envisioned. A political ruler will arise who will subdue ten nations which were part of the old Roman empire (Dan. 7:23-24). His kingdom will eventually be worldwide, yet he will be destroyed at the Second Advent of Christ (Rev. 13:7; 19:20).

This reign by the Roman ruler cannot extend worldwide until the second phase of the end-time struggle is complete. Russia moves against Israel and is totally decimated, allowing the Roman ruler, also referred to as Antichrist (1 John. 2:18), to extend his reign of terror over the entire earth.

The third geopolitical battle extends over the last three and a half years of the tribulation. This is the campaign of Armageddon, when according to Daniel 11 and Revelation 16, all the armies of the nations will converge on Israel, only to be destroyed at the Second Advent of Christ, who returns to set up His Messianic kingdom.

Many commentators see the invasion of Israel by Gog and Magog as part of the Campaign of Armageddon. The invasion of Gog and Magog would thus correspond to the attack of the king of the north of Daniel 11:40. There are enough differences between these two events, that it is best to see them as separate phases of the end-time drama, setting the stage for Christ's return.

Walvoord says that Gog and Magog "will be distinct, both in its objectives, character and outcome ... The war centering in Armageddon is one which involves all the nations of the world. The Russian war is predominantly Russia with six allies. The Armageddon struggle covers all the Holy Land but the war with Russia is settled on the northern mountains of Israel. Armageddon is the climax of the Great Tribulation, a time of persecution for Israel. Ezekiel 38 describes Israel at peace and in prosperity. For these reasons Ezekiel 38-39 do not fit Armageddon."[1]

THE CHRONOLOGY OF THE BATTLE OF GOG AND MAGOG

At least seven different times have been suggested for the events of the battle, spanning the period from before the rapture through the end of the Millennium.

For example, Tim LaHaye and Jerry Jenkins, in their widely read *Left Behind* series, place the invasion prior to the rapture. They write in the first volume about this pre-tribulational event, "Determined to dominate and occupy the Holy Land, the Russians had launched an attack in the middle of the night ... The attack became known as the Russian Pearl Harbor." Soon thereafter the rapture occurs.[2] Others identify the event with the battle of Gog and Magog, predicted in Revelation 20:7 for the end of the

Millennium. It seems best, however, to see these as two different battles, separated by at least 1,000 years. A good hermeneutical maxim to keep in mind is that similarity does not prove identity. The invasion of Israel in Ezekiel 38-39 ends with a seven-year burial of the dead in a predetermined mass grave. The battle of Revelation 20 is directed against Christ and His church in Jerusalem. The invaders will be consumed by fire, making burial obsolete. The Northern confederacy in Ezekiel is headed by Gog. The rebellion against Christ in Revelation, comprised of a worldwide conspiracy, is spearheaded by Satan.

The similarity in the term "Gog and Magog" in Revelation 20 may be indicative of the fact that the battle of the tribulation period will have become a byword for a massive invasion of Israel in which the invader is totally and supernaturally destroyed. The situation is similar to that of the Battle of Waterloo, a term which is sometimes applied to other battles. One can say that Hitler met his Waterloo at Stalingrad, meaning that he was as completely defeated by the resistance of the Russians and the bitter Russian winter, as Napoleon's forces were when routed by the Duke of Wellington on the fields of Waterloo.

In view of the scenario of end time events, it is best to see the battle of Gog and Magog as taking place toward the end of the first half of the tribulation. Several factors point in that direction.

First, the battle follows the regathering of Israel to the land. The prophecy of Ezekiel 36-37 relates to God's dealings with Israel primarily after the church age which is concluded by the rapture. It is true that there is a partial regathering of Israel today, which began primarily with the establishment of the modern state of Israel in 1948, but its complete fulfillment awaits the tribulation period. Every single Jew on this planet will return to Israel in fulfillment of Ezekiel 39:28, "Then shall they know that I am the LORD their God, which caused them to be led into captivity among the heathen: but I have gathered them unto their own land, and have left none of them any more there." The probable cause of this total return is the vicious worldwide anti-Semitism predicted by Christ for the time immediately after the rapture. Christ warned the Jews in that period, "Ye shall be hated of all nations for my name's sake" (Matt. 24:9).

A second factor indicating the chronology of the battle is the time reference to "latter years" (Ezek. 38:8) and "latter days" (38:16), which are best understood as God's final dealings with His people Israel, prior to Christ's glorious return.

Thirdly, the invasion takes place at the time when Israel is dwelling securely in their land: Ezekiel 38:11 "And thou shalt say, I will go up to the land of unwalled villages; I will go to them that are at rest, that dwell safely, all of them dwelling without walls, and having neither bars nor gates."

This period of security is probably ushered in by a covenant of peace which Antichrist, the Roman ruler, will make with Israel (Dan. 9:26), but which he will break after three and a half years, perhaps because his main opponent, the king of the North, has been destroyed. Russia's divine destruction enables him to be world ruler during the latter half of the tribulation period.

Certainly in its present state Israel does not live safely and securely. Since its establishment as a nation it has been attacked five times by its Arab neighbors, who were, for the most part, armed and encouraged by the Soviet leaders.

The volatile situation in the Middle East forces Israel to be in constant military preparedness. Not just is Israel protecting itself against enemies from without but frequent terror attacks from within. This is why at the time of this writing, after four years of violence, Israel is constructing a 425-mile long barrier between the Palestinian West Bank and Israel proper.

The present conditions seem to preclude a fulfillment of Ezekiel's prophecy before the rapture, though some capable scholars argue otherwise. Fruchtenbaum understands the reference to unwalled villages as "a good description of present-day *kibbutzim* ... Israel is merely living in security, which means 'confidence,' regardless of whether it is during a state of war or peace."[3] He postulates that the actual attack will occur before the tribulation but not necessarily before the rapture.

Visitors to Israel notice that with the present and constant threat of terrorism, especially the *kibbutzim* are protected by barriers. The entire country is one gigantic armed camp. All settlements along the Lebanese border are equipped with air raid shelters. Israel today is in a state of war against the enemies without and terrorists within. After the rapture, Antichrist ratifies his covenant with Israel, making the nation feel secure. It is at this time that Gog and Magog make their move.

THE BATTLE OF GOG AND MAGOG: EZEKIEL 38-39

THE ARMIES: 38:1-3

THE REVELATION:

The message of Ezekiel 38-39 is the last in a series of prophecies given by God to Ezekiel in Babylon and delivered by the prophet the night before the news came of Jerusalem's fall (33:21-22). Like the other messages, the revelation of Ezekiel 38-39 concerns the land of Israel. This final end-time vision concludes with the salvation of the people of God and the glorification of the name of God.

THE RULER:

The prophecy commences with five names, which have led to lengthy discussions and a wide variety of interpretations. God commanded Ezekiel: "Son of man, set thy face against Gog, the land of Magog, the chief prince of Meshech and Tubal, and prophesy against him" (Ezek. 38:2). Gog appears to be the name of a person. The derivation of the name is possibly from a word which means "darkness" or a root word meaning "to be high." Both terms would be descriptive of the northern invader as a high or proud ruler over a kingdom of spiritual darkness. In the Septuagint (the Greek translation of the Hebrew Old Testament), made about 250 B.C., Gog is used as a title for kings, much like the term pharaoh, czar, Kaiser, or Caesar.

THE REALM:

The realm ruled by Gog is Magog. Magog is mentioned in Genesis 10:2 as one of the sons of Japheth, as are Meshech and Tubal: "The sons of Japheth; Gomer, and Magog, and Madai, and Javan, and Tubal, and Meshech, and Tiras."

Magog is identified by the Jewish historian Josephus (*Antiquities* I,123 [vi.1]) as the land of the Scythians, a mountainous region around the Black and Caspian Seas. Commentators are generally in agreement with this first century verdict. The names Meshech and Tubal have been assigned by many Bible students to areas in Russia. Fruchtenbaum, for instance, follows Hal Lindsey,[4] Zola Levitt and Thomas McCall[5] in suggesting that "the tribes of Meshech and Tubal later gave their names to cities that today bear the names of Moscow, the capital, and Tobolsk, a major city in the Urals of Siberia." [6]

While the identity of Meshech and Tubal has not been clearly established, the fact that they, along with Magog and Gog, were Japhethites, is significant.

Pentecost's observations are worth noting: "Ethnologists tell us that the Japhethites, after the flood, migrated from Asia Minor to the north beyond the Caspian and Black Seas . . . in the area of Rosh, that we know today as modern Russia." [7]

Ezekiel's prophecy mentions "the chief prince of Meshech and Tubal" (Ezek. 38:2). The normal meaning of the Hebrew word *rosh* is "head" or "chief," but *Rosh* can also be a proper name with a geographical location or country. Gesenius, the authoritative German lexicographer, has the following entry under *Rosh* in his Hebrew lexicon, "Rosh Ezekiel 38:2,3; 39:1; proper noun of a northern nation, mentioned with Tubal and Meshech; undoubtedly *the Russians,* who are mentioned by Byzantine writers of the tenth century, under the name *Ros.*"[8] It is rare to find lexicographers make such dogmatic statements as does Gesenius, unless they feel they have cogent evidence. Interestingly, Gesenius began work on his lexicon in 1810, at a time when virtually no one saw any prophetic significance in Russia.

The name *Rosh* is rendered as a proper name by the Jerusalem Bible, the New English Bible and the NASV. Yamauchi strongly disagrees with this rendering, saying the identification of *Rosh* with Russia "would be a gross anachronism, for the modern name is based on the name *Rus,* which was brought into the region of Kiev, north of the Black Sea, by the Vikings early in the Middle Ages."[9]

Does the absence of the name *Rosh* in antiquity really prove the absence of such a people? Absence of proof is no proof of absence. Very little is known about the ancient nations and tribes populating the vast expanse of Russia. Then too, why would it be anachronistic for the prophet of God to refer to a yet future nation by name? Could not the same be said of the reference to someone named Cyrus by Isaiah in 700 B. C. (44:28; 45:1), when Cyrus, the temporal deliverer of God's people, did not come on the scene until 150 years later? It is a small thing for a sovereign God to mention persons or places by name long before they feature in fulfilled prophecy. Perhaps the most intensive study of the identity of *Rosh* was done by Jon Ruthven in a 1968 *Bibliotheca Sacra* article, "Ezekiel's Rosh And Russia: A Connection?" Regrettably, this article has received virtually no attention by prophecy scholars, nor is there even a passing reference to his study in *Foes from the Northern Frontier*, which was published 14 years later, in 1982.

Ruthven asks whether the dispensationalist-fundamentalist approach with its facile identification of *Rosh* with Russia has any merit. Rather than identifying the name Rus with a Scandinavian migration in the ninth century, derived from "ruotsi," a Finnish word meaning "oarsman," Ruthven refers to research demonstrating "the name of Rus as coming from one of the Sarmatians, a group of tribes which had gained complete control of the Crimean area (i.e., what is now southern Russia) by 200 B. C., having by this time, gone farther west than the Dnieper River."[10] If Ruthven's research is correct, the appearance of the Rus would be a thousand years earlier than commonly thought.

Ruthven concludes that despite some residual uncertainty on his part, "indications, such as geographical location, ethnography, and the general descriptions of culture, provide us with some confidence that there is a direct connection between the Rosh of Ezekiel and the tribal Rus from which the modern Russia derives its name." [11]

Perhaps an even stronger case can be made for the identification of Gog, the land of Magog, Rosh, Meshech and Tubal with modern Russia with a geographical argument.

Three times Ezekiel refers to the invaders as coming from "the north part" (KJV, Ezek. 38:6, 15; 39:2). The literal rendering of the phrase is "the uttermost parts of the north." Walvoord is correct in his assessment, "The only nation that the description of 'far north' would fit would be Russia which, of course, is immediately to the north of Israel, with Moscow being directly north of Jerusalem." [12]

A line drawn north of Jerusalem on a globe, following the curvature of the earth, will pass directly through the city of Moscow. No other nation qualifies. Generally, when nations are mentioned in relation to Israel, the reference is to countries in the vicinity of Israel. The invaders of Ezekiel 38-39 do not come from Lebanon, Syria, nor even primarily from Turkey but beyond, unquestionably from Russia.

A number of Bible scholars find difficulty projecting Russia into this end-time scenario. With the demise of Communism, the entire Soviet Union collapsed. While it is true that presently Russia seems to be economically bankrupt, her military might is virtually undiminished. America's former Secretary of Defense, Caspar Weinberger, cautions the world: "The many welcome changes in the USSR still do not guarantee that the threat from that quarter has vanished, particularly when we see the size of the Soviet's military and the quality of their weapons and equipment."[13]

After a brief flirt with democracy, Russia is returning to autocracy. The current Russian President, Vladimir Putin, a former KGB officer, is consolidating his power by all but eliminating a free press and, in violation of Russia's constitution, is stifling political opposition. Mikhail Zardov, an independent legislator, ominously predicts, "All these measures mean we are coming back to the U.S.S.R."[14]

THE ARMAMENTS: 38:4

Ezekiel graphically describes the invading army and its weapons: "And I will turn thee back, and put hooks into thy jaws, and I will bring thee forth, and all thine army, horses and horsemen, all of them clothed with all sorts of armour, even a great company with bucklers and shields, all of them handling swords:" (Ezek. 38:4). The invaders come with a dazzling array of horses and horsemen. Ezekiel's description is that of "horses and cavalry, clothed in gorgeous attire all of them lit. clothed in perfection." [15]

The Russian invaders "are not just well dressed but well armed. They will sweep through the land mounted on steeds ... and driving teams of chariots ... armed with defensive (buckler and shield) and offensive weapons (swords) ... The portrait is that of a superbly equipped force, fearfully efficient against unsuspecting targets." [16]

The reference to horsemen and ancient weapons employed in a future tribulation battle has occasioned endless discussion and numerous suggestions. Many expositors have interpreted these weapons in a non-literal way. In a very real sense, this passage is a litmus test of one's hermeneutical procedure. Does one practice consistent literal interpretation even when the passage, though clear in its teaching, seems to go against reason or common sense?

Walvoord opts for a measured literal response: "Some have attempted to explain this terminology by saying that Ezekiel described war in terms that he understood and we have to substitute modern arms. As the account unfolds, additional weapons of bows, arrows, war clubs, and spears are also mentioned (Ezek. 39:9). The fact that later on these weapons are regarded as providing fuel for fire (V. 9) makes it difficult to imagine them as merely figures of speech that could not be used for fuel, and most modern weapons are made of metal rather than wood." [17]

Walvoord suggests a genuine disarmament of the world by that time. Russia would be able to manufacture quickly large quantities of weapons this way for her army.

By way of contrast, Missler sees modern weapons systems referred to by Ezekiel. Horses "may simply be idiomatic for motorized infantry." The bows and arrows "suggest any form of arms … these terms could easily be idiomatic for 'launchers' and 'missiles' … The weapons left over from the battle provide all the energy needs of Israel for seven years. This doesn't sound like conventional weapons, does it? Ezekiel seems to have anticipated our nuclear age 2,500 years ago." [18]

It is common among dispensational commentators to modernize Ezekiel's weapons. Nonetheless, it should be remembered that if God had wanted to refer to modern weapons, He could have used general terminology, disclosing to Ezekiel that the invaders would carry deadly weapons with which they could terrify and destroy everything in their way. This terminology would allow for laser guns, cruise missiles and nuclear weapons. However, Ezekiel makes reference to specific ancient weapons.

An approaching Russian cavalry does not seem as impossible to this writer as it might to some. When the Russian hordes invaded eastern Germany in the spring of 1945, this writer was a witness to their primitive armaments. The Americans had come into our part of Saxony some weeks earlier in tanks, armored personnel carriers, with the most modern instruments of war. A few days later, after they regrettably had withdrawn westward, the Russian army came. Many soldiers arrived in horse-drawn covered wagons, drawn by two diminutive Siberian ponies. Some of their main weapons were threshing flails and pitchforks. True, the Russians had some tanks, trucks and machine guns, but the scene of 1945 is indelibly etched in this writer's mind as he witnessed this barbarian invasion, with soldiers armed with the most primitive of weapons, like the Huns centuries earlier. If this could occur in 1945, why not in 2015, or whenever the invasion will be? Pitchforks, flails, wooden wagons and wagon wheels burn. Kalashnikov rifles are not combustible. Whatever the weapons may be carried by the invaders, they will be a substitute for firewood from the forest.

THE ALLIES: 38:5-6

Russia is accompanied by a confederation of allies: "Persia, Ethiopia, and Libya with them; all of them with shield and helmet: Gomer, and all his bands; the house of Togarmah of the north quarters, and all his bands: and many people with thee" (Ezek. 38:5-6).

Alexander underscores the fact that other armies join Gog from every direction of the compass, "Persia from the east; Cush (Ethiopia/Nubia) from the southwest; and Gomer (probably the ancient Cimmerians) and Beth Togarmah (possibly the ancient Til-garimmu southeast of the Black Sea) … from the north." [19]

Some expositors see Cush (Ethiopia), and its inhabitants, the Kassites, as situated north of Persia and Assyria. *Smith's Dictionary of the Bible* suggests that "the African Cush was named from the older country." [20] The reference to Ethiopia in Ezekiel 38:5 could therefore be to either location.

THE ADVANCE: 38:7-9

THE CHRONOLOGY OF THE INVASION:

The time element of the attack is inferred from the context of Ezekiel 36-37 which points to a situation after the rapture. The reference to the "latter years" (38:8), and "latter days" (38:16), as already noted, relate to God's dealings with Israel in the tribulation period.

THE CONDITION OF ISRAEL:

Two conditions will antedate Gog's attack. First, the land itself will have recovered from "the sword." The expression is a metonym for the carnage of an invading army. Second, the return of Israel from her diaspora will be complete, and she is settled securely in the land.

THE CAMPAIGN OF THE INVADERS:

Like a storm cloud, the vast company of invaders inundates the land with evil design upon the unsuspecting population. This speedy maneuver by a superior mob will leave the population of the land paralyzed.

THE AMBITION: 38:10-13

THE DESIGN OF RUSSIA:

What amazing attraction does tiny Israel hold for the most expansive nation on earth? Why would Russia, roughly the size of North America, invade a nation the size of Vermont, no larger than 65 miles by 120 miles?

Ezekiel discloses three reasons for the Russian invasion.

1) A MALEVOLENT SPIRIT: EZEKIEL 38:10

"Thus saith the Lord GOD; It shall also come to pass, that at the same time shall things come into thy mind, and thou shalt think an evil thought:"

Russia invades because of "an evil thought." Block renders the words of God to Russia thusly, "On that day, ideas will arise in your mind, and you will conceive a wicked scheme." [21] Anti-Semitism propels Russia and her allies toward Israel.

Showers is right on the mark when he notes that Russia is motivated by anti-Semitism: "Before Communism, Russia was notorious for severe persecution of Jews. While Communism held an iron grip on the government of that nation, it suppressed the outward expression of hatred for Jews. Now that Communism has lost that grip at least for a while, anti-Semitism has been allowed to raise its ugly head again. Some members of the Pamyat, a strongly anti-Semitic organization that wants to get rid of all Jews in Russia, blame all of the nation's problems on the Jews. Some have even accused the Jews of being the source of AIDS. As a result of these ominous trends, a mass exodus of Jews from the former Soviet Union has taken place since the early 1990's, with the majority going to Israel." [22] Arguments for the identification of Russia with Gog and Magog converge. To the linguistic and geographical argument can be added the theological argument. There is little doubt that the ruthless antisemitic invader of Israel from the far north is Russia.

2) MATERIAL SPOIL: EZEKIEL 38:11-12

"And thou shalt say, I will go up to the land of unwalled villages; I will go to them that are at rest, that dwell safely, all of them dwelling without walls, and having neither bars nor gates, to take a spoil, and to take a prey; to turn thine hand upon the desolate places that are now inhabited, and upon the people that are gathered out of the nations, which have gotten cattle and goods, that dwell in the midst of the land."

The enemy will be greedy for Israel's wealth and thus embarks on a campaign of conquest and pillage. The returned nation has acquired livestock and possessions. They have made the land productive by irrigating the desert and draining swamp land, thus converting it into productive agricultural soil. Many suggest that the immense mineral wealth of the Dead Sea will attract the invaders. One estimate says that "the Dead Sea holds something like 45 billion tons of valuable chemicals, mainly sodium, chlorine, sulphur, potassium, calcium, magnesium and bromide."[23] Zev Vilnay, in his remarkable guidebook to Israel, itemizes the rich content of the Dead Sea: "The minerals deposited in this sea have been itemized as follows:

22,000,000,000 tons of magnesium chloride
11,000,000,000 tons of sodium chloride
7,000,000,000 tons of calcium chloride

2,000,000,000 tons of potassium chloride
1,000,000,000 tons of magnesium bromide."[24]

Both Jordan and Israel are taking advantage of the riches of the Dead Sea by extracting vast amounts of potash from the Dead Sea, shipped primarily for fertilizer to numerous nations of the world.

Because of its wealth, Israel becomes the cynosure of the Russians. One astute German writer already observed in 1931 that while "all the empires as pictured by Daniel are ravaging wild beasts," none can compare with "the passion on the one hand for mass rule and on the other of pillage and plunder ... manifested by the Russians ... No world power acts like Russia, a veritable steam roller." [25]

3) MILITARY STRATEGY: EZEKIEL 38:12b

An implied third reason for the Russian attack is a strategic one. Israel is in a most central strategic position as the connecting bridge between three continents: Africa to the south, Europe to the west and Asia to the east. Historically, empires who sought control of the Mediterranean world first subjugated the land of Israel. Russia's clever military strategists undoubtedly realize that access to the Mediterranean world and the oil-rich Middle East must entail conquest of Israel. Long before the Bolshevik Revolution of 1917, the Russian czars had designs on the Near East. Some years ago *Newsweek* published a political cartoon from 1890, showing the Russian bear menacingly moving into the Near East (*Newsweek,* January 10, 1977, 23). The Russian bear displayed a voracious appetite for Israel long before there were Communists.

Ezekiel underscores Israel's strategic importance by stating that the regathered and attacked people of Israel will "dwell in the midst of the land" (Ezek. 38:12b). The expression is literally rendered "navel of the earth" or "center of the earth," a concept already stated in 5:5, that God had placed Jerusalem in the middle of the nations. Feinberg cites Rabbinic literature which reflects this concept: "As the navel is set in the centre of the human body, so is the land of Israel the navel of the world ... situated in the centre ... of the world, and Jerusalem in the centre of the land of Israel, and the sanctuary in the centre of Jerusalem, and the holy place in the centre of the sanctuary, and the ark in the centre of the holy place, and the foundation stone before the holy place, because from it the world was founded." [26] (*Midrash Tanhuma Qedoshim* 10)

Visitors to Israel notice a strange two-foot-high stone carving in the main Church of the Holy Sepulchre, built over Calvary. It is in the shape of a human navel and called "The Navel of the Earth." Most likely, Crusaders placed it there to mark the spot where Christ died, as the spiritual center of the earth.

Christian scholars likewise have taken notice of Israel's strategic location. Kurtz observes, "In truth, whether viewed *geographically, politically* or *commercially*, Palestine is the 'umbillicus terrarium" of the ancient world." [27]

THE DISPOSITION OF THE NATIONS

Other nations observe Russia's lightening strike against Israel: "Sheba, and Dedan, and the merchants of Tarshish, with all the young lions thereof, shall say unto thee, Art thou come to take a spoil? hast thou gathered thy company to take a prey? to carry away silver and gold, to take away cattle and goods, to take a great spoil?" (Ezek. 38:13).

God turns His attention to interested parties who profit from trade via the land trade route to the Arabian desert east of Israel (Sheba and Dedan) and the maritime trade route to the west (Spain). These names constitute possibly a merism, that is, an expression of totality, from east to west, involving all the nations involved in Mediterranean commerce.

Their rhetorical questions to Gog's design may either indicate that they fear the Russian rampage, wondering whether they will be the next victims or they evidence their own greed and covetousness, desiring to take advantage of the spoils of war.[28]

6. THE ATTACK: 38:14-16

THE INTELLIGENCE OF GOG: 38:14

Russia takes note of Israel's sense of well-being and security (8, 11). Even in unbelief, God refers to Israel as "my people" and their land as "my land"

(16) and "my mountains" (21). During other periods of unbelief, He calls His wayward nation the "apple of His eye" (Deut. 32:10; Zech. 2:8). An attack on Israel is an attack on Him, as the invader will soon experience, as have numerous nations in antiquity and in recent years. While the invader cleverly takes advantage of Israel's sense of security, based on a covenant with Antichrist, he does not consider Israel's special covenant relationship with God.

THE INVASION BY GOG: 38:15-16

The northern host will sweep down upon the unsuspecting people of God. Ezekiel envisions a mighty army comprised of an innumerable company of horsemen, spilling into Israel with lightning speed. One German writer notes the striking similarities between the ancient Scythians, who devastated the Near East around A. D. 630 and the depiction of their future counterpart by Ezekiel. "The Scythians were such Nordic barbarians full of greed and lust for war; they had likewise immense armies of horsemen, had such superbly protective armour and were dazzling in their consummate skill to handle the bow, just as is attributed here to Gog."[29]

7. THE ANNIHILATION: 38:17-23

THE PREDICTION OF GOG: 38:17

God reminds the approaching armies of what was prophesied "in former days by my servants the prophets of Israel" (17). The absence of any reference to Gog in the other prophets suggests that God is referring to prophecies concerning northern invaders (Jer. 36:1-4; 45:12; Isa. 8:5-8) which prefigure the attack by Gog and Magog, "the mother of all battles."

THE PASSION OF GOD: 38:18-19a

God's emotional reaction to Gog is without parallel in the Old Testament, "My fury shall come up in My face, for in My jealousy and in the fire of My wrath have I spoken." God's hot, fiery anger will be released. God brings Gog against His land and His people. In so doing He manifests

His sovereignty over people whose degeneracy, depravity and godless greed makes them ripe for judgment.

If indeed Gog and his company are the Russians—and overwhelming evidence points in that direction—the emotional outburst of God suggests His wrath at Gog's present intentions, but also His anger over Gog's past iniquities. The deferred destruction of the depraved system known as Communism is about to happen. God has not forgotten the unspeakable crimes perpetrated by the Russian leaders against their own people and those of other nations. The human cost of Communism is enormous. Who can forget the atrocities of Nikita Khrushchev, who starved 9 million Ukrainians in the 1930's by burning their fields? Who can forget the fact that of the 20 million Russians who lost their lives in World War II, 10 million were killed by their own regime? The Russian author Alexander Solzhenitsyn has calculated that at least 60 million Russians were confined to the infamous Gulag Archipelago in the post-World War II era. Some years ago the Free China News Agency reported that between 1949 and 1965, under the Chinese Communist regime, some 65 million Chinese lost their lives.

The unspeakable atrocities of Communism have been detailed in a number of volumes. Six former socialist European scholars, who at last saw the light, wrote an 857-page chronicle of Communist horrors, entitled *The Black Book of Communism—Crimes, Terror, Repression.* After thorough research, they estimate the number of civilian victims of Communism thusly:

U.S.S.R.: 20 million deaths
China: 65 million deaths
Vietnam: 1 million deaths
North Korea: 2 million deaths
Cambodia: 2 million deaths
Eastern Europe: 1 million deaths
Latin America: 150,000 deaths
Africa: 1.7 million deaths
Afghanistan: 1.5 million deaths
The international Communist movement and Communist parties not in power: 10,000 deaths
The total approaches 100 million people killed."[30]

Ezekiel 38-39 is God's answer, in part, to these enormous atrocities. The revelation by Ezekiel has had practical ramification for believers enslaved by this "Evil Empire." During this writer's frequent visits to relatives and friends in Communist East Germany, he made an interesting observation over and over again. As we sat across the kitchen table from each other during family devotions, one could not help but notice that certain sections of their Bibles were well-worn. At two places in the New Testament the edges of the pages displayed frequent wear, namely around John 14 and 1 Thessalonians 4, passages dealing with the any-moment return of Christ. These dear believers lived in daily expectancy of the rapture of the church. Interestingly, the Old Testament passage with the telltale worn pages as evidence of frequent perusal, was Ezekiel 38-39. They found consolation in the truth of the doom of their slave masters and derived comfort from the truth of the rapture.

THE PRELUDE TO THE JUDGMENTS: 38:19b-20a

The long-delayed and well-deserved judgment upon Gog and his company will begin "with a great shaking of all the land of Israel" but its effects will be felt and feared by the birds of the air, animals of the land and fish of the sea, as well as humanity worldwide.

THE PROGRESSION OF THE JUDGMENTS: 38:20b-23

Russia's swift invasion against unsuspecting Israel brings immediate and unparalleled consequences as God directly intervenes for His people and His land by opening the arsenals of heaven to unleash the forces of destruction. Eight specific judgments are cataloged.

1) An earthquake: 38:19-20

"A great shaking in the land of Israel" (19) will be felt by "all the men that are upon the face of the earth" (20), resulting in the overturning of the mountains with the result that "every wall shall fall down to the ground." If the invaders are in Israel at that time, they will be crushed by toppling mountains and collapsing buildings. Believers living today who wish to see the biblical sites of Israel in their present condition should not defer their visit to the Holy Land until the Millennium!

2) Civil war: 38:21
"Every man's sword shall be against his brother." Alexander notes that "Gog's armies and the nations following him would become so confused that they would slay one another in suicidal strife."[31] Three couplets of judgment follow.

3) Pestilence: 38:22

4) Blood: 38:22
Four times in Ezekiel, pestilence and blood are linked (5:17; 14:19; 28:23; 38:22) referring to plagues of all kinds and all manner of diseases leading to sudden death.

Torrents of rain: 38:22
Anyone familiar with Israel knows what havoc and destruction rain can bring. With virtually no topsoil on the mountains of Judah, even an inch of precipitation at higher elevations causes flash floods in the valleys, many times with deadly consequences.

Hail: 38:22
As God brought hailstones upon the Amorites and many died (Josh. 10:10-11), so He will use His lethal judgment upon Gog in the middle of the tribulation period. At the end of the tribulation, hailstones weighing 100 lbs. will decimate much of the human population (Rev. 16:21).

Fire: 38:22

Brimstone: 38:22
Fire and brimstone are paired in Genesis 19:24 as well. Brimstone, or burning sulphur, gives off suffocating fumes. That which destroyed the cities of the plain in 1900 B. C. will be the final judgment upon the end-time invaders.

THE PURPOSE OF THE JUDGMENTS: 38:23

God concludes His announcement of the judgments with a clear statement concerning His purpose. He said, "I will magnify myself … sanctify myself … I will be known." In this climactic drama He is displaying His greatness, His holiness and His person. Put differently, He is glorifying Himself, a theme repeated again at the end of chapter 39.

8. THE AFTERMATH: 39

Commentators are in general agreement that the opening verses of Ezekiel 39 recapitulate the scene described in 38:19-23. One unique opposing view is espoused by Hoehner in the study entitled "The Progression of Events in Ezekiel 38-39." He concludes that "Ezekiel 38-39 is best considered as covering the last half of the tribulation: chapter 38 refers to events in the middle of the tribulation, chapter 39 refers to the end of the tribulation."[32] It seems, however, that the writer is describing, not a second invasion, but the same events from a different perspective, with a different emphasis. Ezekiel enlarges upon chapter 38 to underscore the enormous victory. He does so by emphasizing the numbers of the enemy, shown by the quantity of weapons left behind and the length of time necessary for the burial of the invaders.

Then too, the emphasis in chapter 38 is on God's emotions in light of the attack; in chapter 39 it is on His actions. The narrative moves from the defeat of Gog to the disposal of the enemy and deliverance of Israel. The entire chapter can be summarized by certain key words: the battle (1-8), the burning (9-10), the burials (11-16), the banquet (17-20) and the blessings (21-29).

THE BATTLE: 39:1-8

God's opening declaration against Gog and Magog has puzzled commentators. The King James Version reads, "And I will turn thee back and leave but the sixth part of thee." The NIV translation, based on recent linguistic studies, is preferable, "I will turn you around and drag you along." The unique root word has the meaning of "to lead," "drive" or "drag."

God outlines His strategy with Gog in eight sharp and succinct declarations: (1) Turn Gog around, (2) drive him on, (3) lead him up from the uttermost parts of the north, (4) bring him to the mountains of Israel, (5) knock his bow out of his left hand, (6) force him to drop his arrows from his right hand, (7) deliver his corpse as food for the birds of prey and the beasts of the field, and (8) torch the homelands of Gog and his allies.[33]

The Russian rampage, masterminded by divine design and met by divine defense, demonstrates God's glory, "So will I make My holy name known in the midst of My people Israel" (39:7).

THE BURNING: 39:9-10

The enormity of the battle and extent of the destruction is indicated by the varied nature and vast quantities of weapons gathered by Israel from the vanquished enemy. The weapons will be used for fuel for seven years and include "weapons, both the shields, and the bucklers, the bows and the arrows and the handstaves, and the spears ... so that they shall take no wood out of the field, neither cut down any out of the forest" (9-10).

The catalog of weapons begins with a general word, meaning armor, followed by six specific weapons arranged logically in three pairs: small shields and body shields, bows and arrows, clubs and spears or lances.

It has been mentioned earlier that it is best to understand these as literal weapons, known to ancients and employed again for undisclosed reasons in Gog's attack. Much can happen between now and the day of the invasion which would make modern metallic weapons obsolete.

The weapons will be a substitute for firewood for seven years, or some three and a half years into the Millennium. Those who understand the weapons to be of the modern variety would find it difficult to explain how machine guns, cruise missiles and MIG jet fighters can become substitute fuel for trees for Israeli fireplaces.

THE BURIALS: 39:11-16

With amazing prophetic specificity, God disclosed through Ezekiel some 2600 years ago the location of the burial, the duration of the burial and the people employed for this purpose. The location is, literally, "the valley of those who have passed on, on the east of the sea." Some commentators suggest that the reference is to the Mediterranean Sea and the valley might be that of Megiddo. A more common view is that Ezekiel probably refers to the Dead Sea, which is called "the sea" in Ezekiel 47:8, and contrasted with the Mediterranean Sea as the "Great Sea" in 47:10, 15, 19. The place of burial is renamed the "Valley of Hamon-Gog," that is, the multitude of Gog (39:12). Perhaps the Arnon River valley or some other valley east of the Dead Sea, is in view, so that the polluted land can be purified of alien invaders and their littering corpses (12).

The burial will take seven months, indicating the magnitude of the task, especially when one considers that "not only all the people of the land shall bury them" (13) but also special inspectors are designated to reconnoiter the land for corpses, so that the sextons can dispose of the discovered remains.

Fairbairn has interesting calculations to arrive at the actual number of the invaders:

> The wood of the adversaries' weapons was to serve for fuel to all Israel for seven years! And all Israel were to be employed for seven months in burying the dead! It would be but a very moderate allowance, on the literal supposition, to say that a million of men would thus be engaged, and that on average each would consign two corpses to the tomb in one day; which, for the 180 working days of the seven months, would make an aggregate of 360,000,000 of corpses. Then the putrefaction, the pestilential vapours arising from such masses of slain victims before they were all buried! Who would live at such a time?[34]

Unfortunately, Fairbairn discounts the literal meaning of the text and suggests the material was "written for the amusement of children." To understand the description literally is "to make it take rank with the most extravagant tales of romance, or the most absurd legends of Popery."[35]

Commentators who spiritualize Ezekiel's prophecies and visions are no more able to come to a true understanding of God's special and specific revelation than rationalistic commentators like Fairbairn. Briscoe, for example, expresses an "agnosticism" about the literalness of what Ezekiel revealed. "We have no way of knowing just what the details. . .meant to him. In all honesty, we cannot know exactly what all the details mean to us in our day either. . .When we finally get to heaven. . .Charles Lee Feinberg and Dwight Pentecost ... Hal Lindsey and Carl Keil [will] try to figure out what was wrong with their 'exegesis'."[36]

Ezekiel reveals that a city is located near the valley of mass burial, which he identifies as Hamonah (16). Its name means "horde" and it serves as a perpetual reminder east of the Dead Sea of the proximity of the mass grave of godless Gog and his company.

It is delightful to discern God's effort to underscore the literal nature of prophecy by tying specific prophecies to actual geographical sites. God wishes men to understand that prophetic fulfillment is not in some future ephemeral event but will be realized in time and space. Prophecies are history written in advance and many predictions are closely tied to physical features, especially in Israel. By way of illustration, a sampling of such prophecies might be instructive:

> The rebellion of the nations during the last half of the tribulation in *the valley of Armageddon* (Rev. 16:16).
>
> The refuge of Israel during the same period in *the mountains of Ammon, Moab and Edom* (Dan. 11:41b; Rev. 12:6).
>
> The return of Christ as a climax to the tribulation to *the Mount of Olives* (Zech. 14:4).
>
> The reckoning of Israel after the Second Advent in *Wadi Arabah south of the Dead Sea* (Ezek. 20:35-37; Isa. 63:1).
>
> The reckoning of the Gentiles after the Second Advent in the *valley of Jehoshaphat near Jerusalem* (Matt. 25:31-34; Joel 3:2, 12).

The regeneration of the wilderness after the Second Advent, especially *the desert between Jerusalem and the Dead Sea* (Ezek. 47:9-11).

The rejuvenation of the *Dead Sea* after the Second Advent (Zech. 14:8; Ezek. 47:9-10).

The removal of the mountains resulting in a plain in *central Israel* (Zech. 14:4, 10).

The reign of Christ from His throne in *Jerusalem* (Zeph. 3:14-16; Mic. 4:1-2; Luke 1:32).

THE BANQUET 39:17-20

Ezekiel unfolds a grisly scene as he records God's commands to the birds and beasts of the earth to come to Israel for a banquet hosted by God Himself. The menu includes the "princes of the earth, of rams, of lambs and of goats, of bullocks, all of them fatlings of Bashan" (18). God enjoins the birds and beasts to gorge themselves with the flesh until they are full and to quaff of the blood until they are drunk (19).

Most Bible students believe that these animals are symbolic for the different ranks of the slain (20). Rabbinic literature adds some interesting details why the wicked invaders are consumed by the wild beasts. Speaking to the multitude of Gog, God explains, "Whereas you had no peace among yourself but made peace to march against Me, so I now call upon the birds and the wild animals, which had no peace among themselves, and cause them to have peace with one another, so that they come upon you."[37]

THE BLESSINGS: 39:21-29

The display of God's glory. God's primary purpose of the lengthy account of Ezekiel 39:8-39 is not primarily the depiction of end-time events but a manifestation of Himself to the nations (39:21) and to Israel (39:22) in a display of His greatness (38:23), His holiness (38:23) and His glory (39:13). Above all, Ezekiel 38 and 39 are a demonstration of God's holiness. The passage makes abundantly clear that "God's holiness is not just shown in his saving power but also in his destructive power. . .it is simply that God will sanctify himself through Gog before the nations."[38]

The deliverance of the nations and Israel. In the display of these transcendent qualities of a sovereign God, He shows Himself Who He really is by the destruction of the invader, resulting in the deliverance of the nations and of Israel. The slaughter of the invaders will result in the salvation of numerous people. When the nations of the world see God's righteous judgment upon Gog and Magog, and the deliverance of His people Israel, they are prompted to recognize their own rebellion and will come to Him for salvation. God explains to Israel that because of their iniquity He hid His face from them (39:24) but now with every Jew on earth gathered before Him in the land (28) He says to them, "Neither will I hide my face any more from them: for I have poured out my spirit upon the house of Israel, saith the Lord GOD" (29).

WHAT IS THE MARK OF THE BEAST?	
• "Many attempts have been made to identify the Antichrist based on the meaning of 666. However the number will be understood only by those in the Tribulation." – Mal Couch • "Even [the beast's] symbolic number (666) does not equate perfectly with any historical figure, though both pagan Rome and papal Rome have been suggested." – Ed Hindson • "666 is the combination of civil, religious, and political power satanically inspired." – Walter Scott	• "As to the man whom the number 666 represents, God will give full understanding when it is needed, in those three and a half years of tribulation horror." – William Newell • "It is obvious that there can be many names with the numeral value 666, of course, but only one man can be the Antichrist. … The number 666 is significant in its own right." – Henry Morris • "Probably the simplest explanation [for 666] is best, that the triple six is the number of a man, each digit falling short of the perfect number seven. Six in the Scripture is man's number." – John F. Walvoord

CHAPTER 10

WHAT IS THE MARK OF THE BEAST?

Mark Hitchcock

INTRODUCTION

The church I have the privilege of pastoring is Faith Bible Church in Edmond, Oklahoma. When we were first establishing our street address at our current site, the postal service told us we could choose any number from 500 – 699 North Coltrane. One man in our church suggested that we select the number 666 N. Coltrane as our church address since it would certainly get people's attention and be easy to remember. I have to admit that since I love Bible prophecy so much this suggestion almost tempted me above what I was able. However, my better judgment finally took over, and we settled for the more mundane 600 N. Coltrane.

The number 666, the so-called mark of the beast, may be one of the most intriguing issues in all of Bible prophecy. There has probably been more speculation, sensationalism, and silliness about his issue than any other one I can think of in Bible prophecy.

Revelation 13:16-18 is the key passage on the meaning of 666 or the mark of the beast.

> And he causes all, the small and the great, and the rich and the poor, and the free men and the slaves, to be given a mark on their right hand or on their forehead, and he provides that no one should be able to buy or to sell, except the one who has the mark, either the name of the beast or the number of his name. Here is wisdom. Let him who has understanding calculate the number of the beast, for the number is that of a man; and his number is six hundred and sixty-six.

Let's consider what the Scripture really says about the mark of the beast by answering seven important questions.

Is the Mark of the Beast Past or Future?
What is the Mark of the Beast?
What's the Significance of 666?
Why 666?
What's the Purpose of the Mark?
What Does the Mark Reveal about the Antichrist?
Does Modern Technology Relate to the Mark of the Beast?

IS THE MARK OF THE BEAST PAST OR FUTURE?

When considering the mark of the beast the first issue that must be resolved is the time period of this mark. Has the mark of the beast already been fulfilled or is it something that still lies in the future?

Many scholars, who hold to a preterist (past) view of the book of Revelation, maintain that the mark of the beast was completely fulfilled during the reign of the Roman ruler Nero (A.D. 54-68).[1] They argue that the Greek form "Neron Caesar" written in Hebrew characters is equivalent to 666. They further bolster their argument by pointing out that some ancient Greek manuscripts contain the variant number 616 instead of 666 and that the Latin form "Nero Caesar" is equivalent to 616.[2]

Proponents of the preterist view also point to the fact that the persecution under Nero lasted about 42 months or 1,260 days as mentioned in Revelation 13:5.[3]

However, there are serious difficulties with identifying Nero with the beast out of the sea in Revelation 13.

First, the book of Revelation was written in A.D. 95, after the reign of Nero was already over. Therefore, it can't be a prophecy about him.[4]

Second, preterists Gary DeMar and Kenneth Gentry take the 42 months of the beast's worldwide reign literally, and then turn around and take almost every other number in Revelation symbolically. Why take the forty-two months literally and the others symbolically? There has to be some justification in the text for this inconsistent interpretation.

Third, Nero never fulfilled the numerous clear statements in

Revelation 13. Here are just a few examples:

> The beast will be worshiped by the entire world, "And all who dwell on the earth will worship him, everyone who name has not been written from the foundation of the world in the book of life of the Lamb who has been slain (Rev. 13:8). All classes of humanity will be forced to take sides: "the small and the great, and the rich and the poor, and the free men and the slaves" (Rev. 13:15). Robert Thomas, a noted New Testament scholar, notes that this language "extends to all people of every civic rank, ... all classes ranked according to wealth, ... covers every cultural category, ... The three expressions are a formula for universality."[5]
>
> He will force people to take his mark on their right hand or forehead to engage in any commercial transactions.
>
> An image of the beast will be erected by the false prophet that all the world must worship.
>
> The beast will be slain and come back to life.
>
> The beast in Revelation 13:1-10 will have an associate, the false prophet, who will call down fire from heaven and give breath to the image.

Clearly, none of these things were fulfilled during Nero's reign. Neither Nero, nor any other Roman emperor ever marked the whole world with 666. But all of these prophecies will be fulfilled precisely in the coming Antichrist of the end times.

Fourth, in order for Nero's name to equal 666 you have to use the precise title Neron Ceasar. No other form of his name will work. Moreover, there is an abbreviated form of the name Domitian (the Roman Caesar from A.D. 81-96) that also equals 666.[6]

Fifth, if the relationship of 666 to Nero is so obvious as preterists claim, why did it take almost 1800 years after Nero's death for anyone to make this connection between his name and 666?[7] All of the early church fathers who wrote after the time of Nero adopted a futurist view of the beast out of the sea and the number 666.[8] The first ones to suggest a connection between Nero and 666 were four German scholars in the 1830's.[9]

Revelation 13:17,18 clearly says that the number 666 will be the mark proposed for the right hand or forehead. No one in history, including Nero, has even proposed such a number in anything like tribulation conditions, so past guesses as to his identity can be nullified on this basis. Robert Thomas provides wise guidance in this area.

> The better part of wisdom is to be content that the identification is not yet available, but will be when the future false Christ ascends to his throne. The person to whom 666 applies must have been future to John's time, because John clearly meant the number to be recognizable to someone. If it was not discernible to his generation and those immediately following him—and it was not—the generation to whom it will be discernible must have lain (and still lies) in the future. Past generations have provided many illustrations of this future personage, but all past candidates have proven inadequate as fulfillments.[10]

WHAT IS THE MARK OF THE BEAST?

Having determined that this mark of the beast is future, the next thing we need to do is define the nature of this future mark.

The Bible teaches that during the future tribulation period the false prophet, who is the head of Antichrist's religious propaganda machine, will head up the campaign of the mark of the beast (Rev.13:11-18). Revelation 13:15 makes it clear that the key issue underlying the mark of the beast is "worship of the image of the beast." The mark of the beast is simply a vehicle to force people to declare their allegiance—to the Antichrist or Jesus Christ. All people will be polarized into two camps. It will be impossible to take a position of neutrality or indecision. Scripture is very clear that those who do not receive the mark will be killed (20:4).

All classes of humanity will be forced to take sides: "the small and the great, and the rich and the poor, and the free men and the slaves" (13:15). Scripture is very specific: the false prophet will require a "mark" of loyalty and devotion to the beast and it will be "on their right hand," not the left, "or on their forehead" (13:16).

But what is this "mark"?

We find the word "mark" sprinkled throughout the Bible. For example, it is used many times in Leviticus as a reference to a mark that renders the subject ceremonially unclean, usually related to leprosy. Clearly, in these cases in Leviticus the "mark" is external and visible.

Interestingly, Ezekiel 9:4 uses "mark" similarly to the way it is used in Revelation: "And the Lord said to him, 'Go through the midst of the city, even through the midst of Jerusalem, and put a mark on the foreheads of the men who sigh and groan over all the abominations which are being committed in its midst.'" Here the mark was one of preservation, similar to the way the blood on the doorposts spared those in the Exodus from the death angel. In Ezekiel, the mark is placed visibly on the forehead, which anticipates Revelation's use of the term.

Seven out of the eight instances of the word for "mark" or "sign," (charagma) in the Greek New Testament appear in Revelation and all refer to "the mark of the beast" (Rev. 13:16,17; 14:9,11; 16:2; 19:20; 20:4). The word "mark" in Greek (charagma) means "a mark or stamp engraved, etched, branded, cut, imprinted."[11]

Robert Thomas explains how the word was used in ancient times.

> The mark must be some sort of branding similar to that given soldiers, slaves, and temple devotees in John's day. In Asia Minor, devotees of pagan religions delighted in the display of such a tattoo as an emblem of ownership by a certain god. In Egypt, Ptolemy Philopator I branded Jews, who submitted to registration, with an ivy leaf in recognition of their Dionysian worship (cf. 3 Macc. 2:29). This meaning resembles the long-time practice of carrying signs to advertise religious loyalties (cf. Isa. 44:5) and follows the habit of branding slaves with the name or special mark of their owners (cf. Gal. 6:17). Charagma ("Mark") was a term for the images or names of emperors on Roman coins, so it fittingly could apply to the beast's emblem put on people.[12]

Henry Morris also provides an excellent description of the nature of the mark.

> The nature of the mark is not described, but the basic principle has been established for years in various nations. The social security card, the draft registration card, the practice of stenciling an inked design on the back of the hand, and various other devices are all forerunners of this universal branding. The word itself ("mark") is the Greek charagma. It is used only in Revelation, to refer to the mark of the beast (eight times), plus one time to refer to idols 'graven by art and man's device' (Acts 17:29). The mark is something like an etching or a tattoo which, once inscribed, cannot be removed, providing a permanent (possibly eternal) identification as a follower of the beast and the dragon.

The issue for each person alive during the tribulation will be - Will I swear allegiance to the man who claims to be god? Will I give up ownership of my life to him by taking his mark, or will I bow the knee to the true God and lose my right to buy and sell and even face beheading? (Rev. 20:4).

WHAT IS THE SIGNIFICANCE OF 666?

In the movie *The Omen*, Damien was born on June 6, at 6:00 (666) to symbolize his identification as the coming Antichrist. Almost everyone, including the most biblically illiterate people, have heard something about 666 or the mark of the beast.

As you can imagine, there are several explanations of what 666 means. But I believe the best one is the use of a process called gematria which refers to the numerical indication of names. In gematria, a numerical value is attributed to each of the letters of the alphabet. If you want to find the numerical total of a word or name, you add together the numerical value of each of its letters. Clearly, in Revelation 13 some kind of numerical value for the beast's name is intended since the one with wisdom is to "calculate" or "count" the number.[13] To count the number of a name means simply to add up the numbers attached to all the letters in the name.[14]

Hebrew, Latin, Greek, and English all have numerical values for each letter in the alphabet. For the Hebrew language, each letter in the 22 letter Hebrew alphabet is assigned a numerical value as follows:

1,2,3,4,5,6,7,8,9,10,20,30,40,50,60,70,80,90,100,200,300, and 400.

Revelation 13:16-18 provides five key clues that aid in the interpretation of the mark of the beast that I believe support the idea that gematria is involved. Read Revelation 13:16-18 again and notice the progression of the phrases.

1. The name of the beast
2. The number representing his name
3. The number of the beast
4. The number of a man

The number is 666

When these five clues are followed through their logical progression, the number or mark of the beast is the number of a man who is the Antichrist or final world ruler. This number is the number of the Antichrist's own name.

As prophecy scholar Arnold Fruchtenbaum notes,

> In this passage whatever the personal name of the Antichrist will be, if his name is spelled out in Hebrew characters, the numerical value of his name will be 666. So this is the number that will be put on the worshippers of the Antichrist. Since a number of different calculations can equal 666, it is impossible to figure the name out in advance. But when he does appear, whatever his personal name will be, it will equal 666. Those who are wise (verse 18) at that time will be able to point him out.

When the Antichrist begins to appear on the world scene at the beginning of the tribulation, those who have understanding of God's Word will be able to identify him by the number of his name. The numerical value of his name will be 666.

Many have grossly misused gematria to apply it to the names of modern leaders to see if they could be the Antichrist. It has been applied to Henry Kissinger and Lyndon Johnson, and I have been told that both of their names equal 666. It has also been successfully tried out on JFK,

Gorbachev and Ronald Reagan. Supposedly "Bill Gates III" equals 666. "MS DOS 6.21" equals 666 as does "Windows 95" and "System 7.0."

I received a call from a man recently who told me emphatically that Philip Borbon Carlos, son of Juan Carlos of Spain, is the Antichrist because each of his three names contains six letters.

Phone books are full of names that might add up too 666 if converted to their numerical value. The wisdom of "counting the name" is not to be applied in our day, for that would be jumping the gun. Instead, it is to be applied by believers during the tribulation. All such foolish speculation should be avoided. The Antichrist will not be unveiled until the beginning of the tribulation period or Day of the Lord (2 Thess. 2:2-3). At that time people will be able to identify him because the number of his name will be 666. If you ever do figure out who the Antichrist is, I've got bad news for you, you've been left behind.

> Here is wisdom. Let him who has understanding calculate the number of the beast, for the number is that of a man; and his number is six hundred and sixty six (Rev. 13:18).

WHY 666?

One might ask why the Lord planned for Antichrist's name to equal 666? Many prophecy teachers have pointed out that the triple six refers to man's number, which is the number six or one short of God's perfect number, seven. Remember, man was created on the sixth day. Prophecy scholar John Walvoord writes,

> Though there may be more light cast on it at the time this prophecy is fulfilled, the passage itself declares that this number is 'man's number. In the Book of Revelation, the number '7' is one of the most significant numbers indicating perfection. Accordingly, there are seven seals, seven trumpets, seven bowls of the wrath of God, seven thunders, etc. This beast claims to be God, and if that were the case, he should be 777. This passage, in effect, says, No, you are only 666. You are short of deity even though you

> were originally created in the image and likeness of God. Most of the speculation on the meaning of this number is without profit or theological significance.[15]

M.R. DeHaan, the founder of the Radio Bible Class, also held this position.

> Six is the number of man. Three is the number of divinity. Here is the interpretation. The beast will be a man who claims to be God. Three sixes imply that he is a false god and a deceiver, but he is nevertheless merely a man, regardless of his claims. Seven is the number of divine perfection, and 666 is one numeral short of seven. This man of sin will reach the highest peak of power and wisdom, but he will still be merely a man.[16]

It is interesting to me that the number of the name "Jesus" in Greek is 888, and each of his eight names in the New Testament (Lord, Jesus, Christ, Lord Jesus, Jesus Christ, Christ Jesus, Lord Christ and Lord Jesus Christ) all have numerical values that are multiples of eight.[17] I don't believe this is a coincidence. Jesus is complete perfection, while man, apart from God, is complete, utter failure.

Adam, the first man, was created on the sixth day, while Jesus, the second man, was raised from the dead on Sunday, the "eighth day" of the week (the second first day of the week).

WHAT IS THE PURPOSE OF THE MARK?

The mark of the beast will serve two purposes during the terrible time of the great tribulation. First, as we have already noted, it will serve as a visible indicator of devotion to Antichrist. Antichrist's mark, the numerical value of his name, will be etched or imprinted on the right hand or forehead of those who bow the knee to his iron fist. The mark of the beast will be a Satanic counterfeit of the seal of God on the foreheads of the saints which is the seal of the Holy Spirit (Rev. 7:3).[18]

Second, the mark will be one's ticket or passport for business. It will be required for commercial transaction during the last half of the tribulation (Rev.13:17). This is another clear indication that the mark is literal and visible. After all, how can it serve as a ticket for commercial transactions if it's invisible?

Stop and think about it. This has been the dream of every tyrant down through history—to so totally control his subjects that he alone decides who can buy or sell. When the beast or Antichrist seizes power at the middle of the tribulation, every person on earth will be faced with a monumental decision. Will they take the mark of the beast on their right hand or forehead or will they refuse the mark and face death? Will they take the mark that is required for every private and public transaction, or will they stand firm and say no to Antichrist?

The Antichrist's economic policy will be very simple: take my mark and worship me or starve. But it will be far better to refuse Antichrist and starve or face beheading because in receiving his mark a person will forfeit eternal life. All who take the mark of the beast will face the eternal judgment of God. Taking the mark will seal their everlasting doom.

Revelation 14:9-10 says,

> Then another angel, a third one, followed them, saying with a loud voice, 'If anyone worships the beast and his image, and receives a mark on his forehead or on his hand, he also will drink of the wine of the wrath of God, which is mixed in full strength in the cup of His anger; and he will be tormented with fire and brimstone in the presence of the holy angels and in the presence of the Lamb. 'And the smoke of their torment goes up forever and ever; they have no rest day and night, those who worship the beast and his image, and whoever receives the mark of the name.'

WHAT DOES THE MARK REVEAL ABOUT THE ANTICHRIST?

The Antichrist's mark is significant for at least two reasons. First, his ability to force the whole world to take his mark signifies his worldwide power and authority. Think of the raw power that it will take to make everyone on the earth take this mark or be killed.

Second, the mark allows the Antichrist to get an even stronger stranglehold on the world population. By means of this mark he will control the life of every person on earth. John Walvoord writes:

> There is no doubt that with today's technology, a world ruler, who is in total control, would have the ability to keep a continually updated census of all living persons and know day-by-day precisely which people had pledged their allegiance to him and received the mark and which had not.[19]

DOES MODERN TECHNOLOGY RELATE TO THE MARK OF THE BEAST?

But what exactly will this mark be? What will it look like? What form will it take?

Will it be something as simple as a tattoo? Will it be some kind of ID card? Will it be a chip placed under the skin? In the aftermath of September 11 many have called for some form of national ID card, biometric identification (thumbprint or eyescan), digitizing or scanner technology to be instituted.[20] Many have speculated whether one of these new technologies is the mark of the beast. The mark has been related to Social Security cards, bar code scanners, retina scanners, the new Veri Chip implant technology, and about every other kind of new identification technology that comes along. There have been all kinds of unwarranted speculation on the exact nature of the mark of the beast. As my friend Dr. Harold Willmington says, "There's been a lot of sick, sick, sick about six, six, six."

When it comes to the exact nature of the mark of the beast, the answer is, we really don't know, and we shouldn't waste a lot of time thinking about it. Nothing that we see today is the mark of the beast. We don't know what method Antichrist will adopt to make his mark. The text of Revelation 13:16 clearly indicates that the mark will be placed "on" or "upon" the hand or forehead, not "in" it, that is, on the outside where it can be seen. The Greek preposition epi in this context means "upon."

What we can safely and responsibly say is that the technology is certainly available today to tattoo, brand, or partially embed a visible identifying number or mark on the skin of every person alive to regulate world commerce and control people's lives. While none of the things we see today are the mark of the beast, the rise of these amazing new means of locating, identifying, and controlling people's lives, strikingly foreshadows the scenario depicted in Revelation 13. It's just another indicator that points toward the picture Scripture paints of the end times.

CONCLUSION

Having answered the seven key questions concerning the mark of the beast, here is the summary of the meaning of the mark and the application for our lives today.

1. The mark is future, not past.

2. The mark is a literal, visible brand, mark, or tattoo that will be placed "upon" the right hand or forehead of people during the tribulation.

3. The mark will be given as a sign of devotion to Antichrist and as a passport to engage in commerce.

4. The mark will be the number 666 which will be the numerical value of the Antichrist's name which saints during the tribulation will be able to calculate and use to identify him.

5. Those who take the mark will be eternally doomed.

6. Before the rapture, no one should attempt to identify the Antichrist or his mark – the number 666.

7. While current technology and methods of identifying and locating people strikingly foreshadow Antichrist's ability to control the world, no specific, modern technology should be identified as the mark of the beast.

THE JEWISH TEACHING ABOUT THE ANTICHRIST (ARMILUS)

- In Jewish tradition the Antichrist is called “Armilus,” that could come from the Persian Ahriman, the god of evil.
- Armilus is first mentioned in Jewish literature in the Targum to Isaiah 11:4 where it says the Messiah will slay with His lips the wicked Armilus.
- In the Jewish Midrash, Armilus is actually called “the Antichrist,” who is called “a mysterious satanic king.”
- Armilus will come from Rome and make evil decrees against Israel. The Son of David, the Messiah, will come from Galilee, build the temple and offer sacrifices. He will destroy Armilus and Israel will be safe.
- At one point, Armilus will go to Rome and say “I am your Messiah. I am your god!” He will say to the Jews, “I am your Messiah, your king, and your prince.”
- When the Messiah enters Jerusalem, He will ascend to the house of David and sit there. The Antichrist, Armilus, will gather the world’s armies and go against the Messiah and Israel. Instantly the Messiah will go against Him and bring victory.
- Armilus is the false Messiah. The children of Kedar (the Arab nations) will follow after him!
- The Messiah will slay Armilus. An earthquake will go forth from Zion and the Temple. The flag of the Son of David, the Messiah will be seen. And, the Messiah will destroy God and Magog!

Source: *The Messiah Texts,* Raphael Patai

CHAPTER 11

WHO IS THE ANTICHRIST?

Arnold Fruchtenbaum

This is a study of the coming world dictator who will be the greatest despot of all time. The great dictators of the past; such as, Alexander the Great, Caesar and Adolf Hitler will hardly be comparable to the person of the Antichrist.

To fully understand the person and activities of the Antichrist, he must be viewed within the theme of the "counterfeit son." According to Revelation 13, an "un-holy trinity" is going to be set up in the Great Tribulation. Satan will play the part of the "counterfeit father;" for just as the Father gave all His authority to the Son, so Satan will give all his authority to the Antichrist. The false prophet will play the part of the "counterfeit holy spirit." While the ministry of the Holy Spirit is to call all men to worship the Messiah, the ministry of the false prophet will be to call all men to worship the Antichrist. In every detail, as we shall see in this study, the Antichrist will play the part of a counterfeit son. Once we understand the role he is to play, we can better understand all that the Scriptures say of him.

THE NAMES OF THE ANTICHRIST

The person who is to play the central role in human affairs during the Great Tribulation is given a number of names throughout the Scriptures. These various names, titles or descriptions simply portray the various facets of his character. Taken together, these names portray him as the epitome of evil in the human realm as Satan is the epitome of evil in the angelic realm. The various names are as follows:

The "seed" of Satan—Genesis 3:15
The "little" horn—Daniel 7:8
The king insolent and skilled in intrigue—Daniel 8:23
The prince who is to come—Daniel 9:26
The "desolator"—Daniel 9:27

The "willful" king—Daniel 11:36
The man of lawlessness—II Thessalonians 2:3
The son of destruction—II Thessalonians 2:3
The lawless one—II Thessalonians 2:8
The antichrist—I John 2:22
The beast—Revelation 11:7

The vast majority of prophetic scholars have a single name for this future world dictator—the Antichrist. Although this may not be his most common name in Scripture, it is a well-chosen title. It is a title that will portray his true intent, which is to be "against" Christ. All his other names essentially portray the various facets by which he will attempt to be in opposition to Christ.

However, in this multiplicity of names we should begin to see the nature of the counterfeit son. Just as Jesus has a number of different names, titles and descriptions, so does the Antichrist.

THE ORIGIN OF THE ANTICHRIST

The Antichrist, being the counterfeit son, will have both a natural Origin and a supernatural origin in imitation of the True Son. The natural origin of the True Son is that He was born of a Jewish woman. The supernatural origin was the miraculous virgin conception by means of the overshadowing power of the Holy Spirit. The end product was the God-Man.

HIS NATURAL ORIGIN

As to his natural origin, speculation has centered around his nationality, with the question being whether or not the Antichrist will be a Jew.

THE ANTICHRIST WILL NOT BE A JEW

Those who believe that the Antichrist has to be a Jew do so for several reasons. One reason that is given could be classed as the logical reason. Stated in syllogism, this argument goes as follows:

Major Premise: The Jews will accept the Antichrist as the messiah;
Minor Premise: The Jews will never accept a Gentile as the messiah;
Conclusion: The Antichrist will be a Jew.

The argument is that the Jews will accept him as the messiah. The Scriptures make no such claim. While the Bible teaches that Israel enters into a covenant relationship with the Antichrist, this in no way means that they will accept him as the messiah. Some have stretched this reasoning to say that the Jews would not even enter into a covenant with a Gentile. But none of this is valid, for Jews have often entered into covenant relationships with non-Jews in the past. But this logical reason also fails to view the whole issue. It could be asked another way: how would the Gentiles accept him if he is a Jew? So the logical reason could be used either way, and it is not valid in and of itself. The argument for his Jewishness based on this kind of logic is not valid. It is an argument based on two assumptions, neither of which is able to stand on its own. Furthermore, the final analysis as to whether something is true cannot be based on logic, but must be based on Scripture. The ultimate question is not, "Is it logical?" but, "Is it scriptural?" The assumption necessary for the logical reason cannot be validated by Scripture.

Another reason people often give for the Jewishness of the Antichrist is based on Revelation 7:1-8. Stated as a syllogism, this argument would read as follows:

Major Premise: The tribe from which the Antichrist would come would not be listed among the 144,000;
Minor Premise: Dan is not among the 144,000;
Conclusion: The Antichrist is from the Tribe of Dan.

The folly of such reasoning should be clear to anyone holding to a literal interpretation of Scripture. First of all, it is an argument of conjecture. If the interpreter is at all honest, he would have to admit that he really does not know why Dan is left out of the 144,000. The Bible nowhere spells out why Dan is excluded. If the reason is what the proponent of this view says it is, then it should be explained why an entire tribe is punished because of one man. Furthermore, why is Dan included in the Millennial Israel (Ezek. 48:1) if there is a curse on him? Assuming information where the Bible is silent is a danger to sound hermeneutics. This argument also involves circular reasoning. To repeat the syllogism:

Major Premise:	The tribe from which the Antichrist will come will not be listed among the 144,000;
Minor Premise:	Dan is not among the 144,000;
Conclusion:	The Antichrist is from the Tribe of Dan.

From this syllogism another is developed:

Major Premise	The Antichrist is from the Tribe of Dan;
Minor Premise:	Dan is a Jewish tribe;
Conclusion:	The Antichrist is a Jew.

Or they can be stated another way:

1. The Antichrist is a Jew;
2. The tribe from which the Antichrist would come would not be listed among the 144,000;
3. Dan is not among the 144,000;
4. The Antichrist is from the Tribe of Dan;
5. Dan is a Jewish tribe;
6. The Antichrist is therefore a Jew.

No matter how it is put, this is purely circular reasoning, the truth of which is dependent upon the truth of the presupposition. While circular reasoning is consistent within itself, the consistency does not make it scriptural. The presupposition of circular reasoning has no proof on which to base this doctrine.

The scriptural text used most often for the Jewishness of the Antichrist is found in Daniel 11:37, which in the King James Version reads as follows:

> *Neither shall he regard the God of his fathers, nor the desire of women, nor regard any god: for he shall magnify himself above all.*

The whole argument rests on the phrase, the God of his fathers, which is taken to be clear-cut evidence that the Antichrist is a Jew. It should be pointed out, however, that the argument for the Jewishness of the Antichrist from this verse is based upon the King James Version. But even if it is granted (and it is not) that the King James is the correct translation from the original, the phrase "God of his fathers" need not be used exclusively of the Jews. The phrase "God of his fathers" allows for a wider interpretation. For instance, he could be a person who had Christian parents but rejects their God in this sense. It could refer to a Roman Catholic or a Pagan just as easily as to a Jewish person. The one phrase where the term "Antichrist" is used in I John 2:18-19 refers to those who apostatize from Christianity and not from Judaism.

Ultimately, Bible doctrine should be based on the Hebrew and Greek texts since they are the closest to the original autographs. To base a doctrine on a translation, especially when that translation is known to contain error, is folly. This is exactly the case with the King James rendering of Daniel 11:37. Any student of Hebrew would see from the original text that the correct translation should be: "the gods of his fathers," and not "the God of his fathers." In the whole context, Daniel 11:36-39, the god is used a total of eight times. In the Hebrew text, six of these times it is in the singular and twice in the plural, one of which is the phrase in verse 37. The very fact that the plural form of the word "god" is used in a context where the singular is found in the majority of cases makes this a reference to heathen deities and not a reference to the God of Israel.

Moreover, there is much external evidence to show that this is the correct rendering of the text. The earliest known translation of the Old Testament is the Septuagint (LXX), which is a Greek translation of the Old Testament made about 250 B.C. The LXX has translated the word as "gods," which is in keeping with the Hebrew text. Further evidence that the King James Version is incorrect in its translation here is seen in the fact that almost all other English translations, both from Jewish and non-Jewish sources, have rendered the word for "god" in the plural. Two major Jewish translations, the Jewish Publication Society of America and the Isaac Leeser translation, have rendered the phrase "the gods of his fathers." In Christian translations—such as the American Standard Version, the Revised Standard Version, the Amplified Old Testament, the New American Standard, and the New International Version, among others—have all translated the phrase to read the gods of his fathers. Furthermore, the New Scofield Reference Bible, itself based on the King James Version, has done a great service to scholarship by rendering this passage to read in the plural form. Commentaries based on the Hebrew rather than the English text recognized the correct reading of Daniel 11:37. This is true of the official Orthodox Jewish commentary in the Soncino Commentary on the Old Testament, as well as the prominent Christian commentary in the Kiel and Delitzsch Commentary.

All this evidence shows that Daniel 11:37, the chief argument used by proponents that the Antichrist is to be a Jew, gives no validity to this belief. A doctrine of such magnitude must not be based solely on the King James Version as is this one. It has been shown that even if the King James Version were correct, it would not limit the expression to Jews, but it would be valid for believers as well. However, the truth is that the text is dealing with heathen deities and not with the Jewish Jehovah. If anything, this passage implies that the Antichrist will be a Gentile rather than a Jew.

THE ANTICHRIST WILL BE A GENTILE

It has been shown that the Bible does not teach that the Antichrist is to be a Jew. This raises the question: do the Scriptures plainly teach that the Antichrist is to be a Gentile? The answer is that they do. This is seen to be true from biblical typology, biblical imagery, and the nature of the Times of the Gentiles.

That the Antichrist is to be a Gentile is seen first by looking at biblical typology. The only biblical type of the Antichrist is given in the person of Antiochus Epiphanes, a Gentile. The reason is that the Antichrist himself is to be a Gentile.

Another argument for the Gentile nature of the Antichrist is found in biblical imagery. Whenever the word sea is used symbolically in the Scriptures, especially in the Book of Revelation, it is a symbol of the Gentile nations. Since the Beast in Revelation 13:1-10 arises out of the sea, and since the sea represents the Gentile nations (Rev. 17:15), this points to the Antichrist as being of Gentile origin.

But the key to his Gentile nationality is to be found in the nature of the Times of the Gentiles. It is agreed by most Premillennialists that the Times of the Gentiles does not end until the Second Coming of the Messiah. It is further agreed that the Antichrist is the final ruler of the

Times of the Gentiles. If this is so, how then can a Jew be the last ruler when only the Gentiles can have the pre-eminence? To say that the Antichrist is to be a Jew contradicts the very nature of the Times of the Gentiles. A Jew heading up the final world throne of Gentile power is an impossible postulation. So while arguments from typology and imagery are not strong by themselves, when coupled with the clear scriptural teaching of the nature of the Times of the Gentiles, they can be powerful evidence that the Antichrist is to be a Gentile.

THE ANTICHRIST WILL BE OF ROMAN ORIGIN

But not only does the Bible reveal the fact that the Antichrist is to be a Gentile, it also reveals the very nationality of the Antichrist. The nationality of the Antichrist can be deduced from Daniel 9:26-27:

> *Then after the sixty-two weeks the Messiah will be cut off and have nothing, and the people of the prince who is to come will destroy the city and the sanctuary. And its end will come with a flood; even to the end there will be war; desolations are determined. And he will make a firm covenant with the many for one week, but in the middle of the week he will put a stop to sacrifice and grain offering; and on the wing of abominations will come one who makes desolate, even until a complete destruction, one that is decreed, is poured out on the one who makes desolate.*

The first order of business is to identify the "he" in verse 27 who makes the Seven-Year Covenant with Israel. The rules of Hebrew grammar must be used to determine this. The fact that in the Hebrew text the third masculine singular is used means that one must look for an antecedent. The nearest antecedent is the prince who is to come in verse 26. The "he" of verse 27 is the same as the prince who is to come of verse 26.

The next order of business is to establish the identity of this prince. It is generally recognized that this prince is the Antichrist himself. Daniel used the definite article since he had already spoken of him in chapter seven of his book as the little horn, and again in chapter eight. So then, the prince who is to come is also the he who makes the covenant with Israel, and both have reference to the Antichrist. Verse 26 also states that the prince who is to come is the same nationality as the people who will destroy the city and the Sanctuary. The third step is to establish the nationality of this people, and history has shown that this was accomplished by the Romans in A.D. 70. The obvious conclusion, then, is that the Antichrist is a Gentile of Roman origin.

To summarize the argument of the Gentile Roman origin of the Antichrist, it could be stated as follows:

1. The "he" who makes a covenant and the prince who is to come are one and the same person;
2. They both have reference to the Antichrist;
3. The Antichrist is of the same nationality as the people who destroyed Jerusalem and the Temple;
4. The Romans destroyed Jerusalem and the Temple in A.D. 70;
5. The Antichrist, then, will be of Roman origin.

The conclusion is that the Antichrist will not be a Jew. Most people who believe the contrary merely assume it without giving any reason. Those who present a logical reason—"How will the Jews accept him if he is not a Jew?"—are reminded that the Bible and not logic is the basis for doctrine, including this one. Those who argue from Revelation 7:4-8 are arguing from conjecture and circular reasoning and not from any clear statement from Scripture. Those who argue from Daniel 11:37 are basing doctrine on a faulty translation of the Hebrew text.

Not only has it been concluded negatively that the Antichrist is not a Jew, but it is concluded positively that he is a Gentile, as seen from biblical typology and imagery, along with the very nature of the Times of the Gentiles as presented by the Scriptures. The Bible not only teaches that the Antichrist is a Gentile, but it reveals his exact nationality: a Gentile of Roman origin, as seen by a careful study of Daniel 9:26-27.

HIS SUPERNATURAL ORIGIN

The true son has both a natural origin and a supernatural origin, which became possible by virtue of the virgin conception. Since the Antichrist is to be a counterfeit son, he too will have both a natural and a supernatural origin by means of a counterfeit virgin conception. His supernatural origin is to be found in Genesis 3:15:

> *And I will put enmity between you and the woman, and between your seed and her seed; He shall bruise you on the head, and you shall bruise him on the heel.*

This verse not only contains the first prophecy of the coming of the Messiah, it at the same time gives the first prophecy of the coming of the Antichrist. It should be noted that this verse speaks of enmity in two pairs. First, there is going to be enmity between Satan and the woman. This satanic enmity with woman can be seen to play itself out in the account of Genesis six, where Satan had some of his demons intermarry with human women for the purpose of perverting womankind in an attempt to nullify the first messianic prophecy. This attempt was stopped by means of the worldwide Flood. But second, the verse states that there is going to be enmity between the woman's seed and Satan's seed. The woman's seed is Jesus the Messiah. As God, He was eternally existent; as a Man. He was conceived of the Holy Spirit and born of a virgin. So He was truly both God and Man. The very mention of a seed of a woman goes contrary to the biblical norm, for nationality was always reckoned after the seed of the man. That is why, in all the genealogies of Scripture, only the male names are given with some very rare exceptions.

The reason why the Messiah must be reckoned after the seed of the woman is explained by Isaiah 7:14: the Messiah will be born of a virgin. Since the Messiah will not have a human father, His national origin will have to be reckoned after the woman, since His humanity comes only from her. So the very expression her seed implied a miraculous conception. In reference to Satan's seed, this term, being in the same verse, implies the same thing: that of a supernatural miraculous conception. The enmity against the seed of the woman comes from the seed of Satan.

If the seed of the woman is Messiah, the seed of Satan can only be the Antichrist. From this passage, then, it can be deduced that Satan will counterfeit the virgin conception and will some day impregnate a Roman woman who will give birth to Satan's seed who is going to be the Antichrist. The woman herself may not be a virgin, but the conception of Antichrist will be through the supernatural power of Satan. By this means, the

Antichrist will have a supernatural origin. Another passage dealing with this is II Thessalonians 2:9:

> *that is, the one whose coming is in accord with the activity of Satan, with all power and signs and false wonders*

The Greek word translated "activity" is the word energeo, which means "to energize." His coming, then will be brought about by the energizing of Satan. In other words, the Antichrist comes into being by some supernatural means, and that supernatural means is a counterfeit virgin conception.

Clearly then, the counterfeit son, in imitation of the True Son, will have both a natural origin and a supernatural origin. As to his supernatural origin, his father will be Satan. As to his natural origin, his mother will be a woman of Roman nationality. A time is coming when the situation of Genesis six will be repeated. A fallen angelic being, this time Satan himself, will impregnate a Gentile woman of Roman origin who will then give birth to Satan's son. The end product will be a counterfeit god-man.

THE REVELATION OF THE ANTICHRIST

The identity of the Antichrist is going to be revealed on two occasions. The first revelation will occur before the Tribulation and will be for believers. But the second revelation will occur in the middle of the Tribulation and this revelation is to Israel, which will have been deceived by him. The key passage that speaks of this is found in II Thessalonians 2:1-3:

> *Now we request you, brethren, with regard to the coming of our Lord Jesus Christ, and our gathering together to Him, that you may not be quickly shaken from your composure or be disturbed either by a spirit or a message or a letter as if from us, to the effect that the day of the Lord has come. Let no one in any way deceive you, for it will not come unless the apostasy comes first, and the man of lawlessness is revealed, the son of destruction*

Apparently after Paul left Thessalonica, some false teachers came in teaching a posttribulational doctrine and stating that the believers were now in the Tribulation. The Thessalonians were troubled that the day of the

Lord, the most common title for the Great Tribulation, has come (vv. 1-2).

At this point, Paul said that the Tribulation could not have come yet because two events must precede the Tribulation itself: first, the apostasy of the Church; and second, the revelation of the man of lawlessness, the son of destruction (v. 3). Therefore, revelation of the identity of the Antichrist precedes the Tribulation and is apparently for those who are believers at that time. The Rapture may or may not have already occurred by then since we do not know just how long before the Tribulation when the Rapture will take place. However, there will be a new generation of believers who will have accepted the gospel after the Rapture of the Church. Whoever those believers may be at this time, they will receive a revelation as to the identity of the Antichrist.

This text does not state exactly how this revelation will come, but from other Scriptures we see that it could come because of two things. First of all, it is known from Daniel 9:27 that the Tribulation starts with the signing of a seven-year covenant between Israel and the Antichrist. When this forthcoming covenant is announced, believers may become aware of the identity of the Antichrist. It is also possible that believers will deduce the numerical value of the Antichrist's name, for the numerical value of his name will be 666.

The second revelation to Israel is found later in the II Thessalonians passage, but this too will be studied in a later context under the Abomination of Desolation.

THE ANTICHRIST AND THE START OF THE TRIBULATION

The relationship of the Antichrist to the start of the Tribulation is found in Daniel 9:27:

> *And he will make a firm covenant with the many for one week, but in the middle of the week he will put a stop to sacrifice and grain offering; and on the wing of abominations will come one who makes desolate, even until a complete destruction, one that is decreed, is poured out on the one who makes desolate.*

This verse is part of the famous prophecy of the "Seventy Weeks of

Years" in Daniel 9. The entire context begins in verse 24 and continues through verse 27. The prophecy states that a period of 490 years has been decreed over the people of Israel for the purpose of bringing to completion all history and prophecy (v. 24). During the first sixty-nine weeks or 483 years, Jerusalem was to be rebuilt, but during this period the people of Israel would experience troublesome times (v. 25). At the end of the sixty-ninth week, suddenly a gap enters into the picture, for there is a break of time between the sixty-ninth and seventieth weeks. Between the sixty-ninth and seventieth weeks, three things were to occur: first, the Messiah was to be killed; second, Jerusalem and the Temple were to be destroyed; and third, a long period of desolation would follow.

The first event occurred in the year A.D. 30, followed by the second event in A.D. 70. From the year A.D. 70, the Land lay in desolation and things began to change only when Israel became a state again. However, there is one more week of years to run and this is the seven years of the Great Tribulation. Daniel 9:27 records the single event that will start the last seven years ticking away, when the Antichrist signs a seven-year covenant with Israel, this will mark the beginning of the Tribulation. Therefore, one way that the Antichrist is involved with the beginning of the Tribulation is that the Tribulation cannot begin until he signs that seven-year covenant. As has been shown earlier, believers will already know who he is before this event takes place. A second passage relating the Antichrist to the beginning of the Tribulation is found in Revelation 6:1-2:

> *And I saw when the Lamb broke one of the seven seals, and I heard one of the four living creatures saying as with a voice of thunder, "Come." 2 And I looked, and behold, a white horse, and he who sat on it had a bow; and a crown was given to him; and he went out conquering, and to conquer.*

The one sitting on the white horse who rides forth conquering and to conquer is the Antichrist. He is the first seal of judgment of the "seven-sealed scroll." The seven-sealed scroll is the scroll of the judgments of the Great Tribulation which begin to be poured out on the earth as a result of the signing of the seven-year covenant. The very first seal is that the Antichrist uses the covenant-relationship to begin his movements toward world-wide conquest. He will not attain this goal until the middle of the

Tribulation when he kills three of the ten kings. But his conquerings commence at the beginning of the Tribulation and continue until the middle when three of his ten opponents are killed—at which time the other seven submit to his authority.

Thus the Antichrist's relationship to the start of the Tribulation is seen in two respects: first, he signs the seven-year covenant which begins the Tribulation; and second, he begins a program of world-wide conquest.

THE CHARACTER AND RISE OF THE ANTICHRIST

Because of his supernatural origin as Satan's seed, the Antichrist will always have access to the satanic realm. Ultimately, the counterfeit son will accept what the genuine Son rejected. When Satan offered Yeshua all the kingdoms of the world on the basis that He would worship him just once, Jesus quoted from the Book of Deuteronomy and stated that only One person is to be worshipped, and that is, God Himself. The same offer will be made to the counterfeit son who will accept Satan's offer of the kingdoms. When this temptation is accepted by the Antichrist, it will mark the beginning of his rise to political and religious domination of the world.

The rise to power of the Antichrist is described in several passages. The first passage is found in Daniel 8:23-25:

> *And in the latter period of their rule, when the transgressors have run their course, a king will arise insolent and skilled in intrigue. And his power will be mighty, but not by his own power, and he will destroy to an extraordinary degree and prosper and perform his will; he will destroy mighty men and the holy people. And through his shrewdness he will cause deceit to succeed by his influence; and he will magnify himself in his heart, and he will destroy many while they are at ease. He will even oppose the Prince of princes, but he will be broken without human agency.*

In this passage we are told that "an insolent king" or the Antichrist, will be skilled in intrigue. This is in reference to the world of the occult. The Antichrist then will be involved in the occult and will have the power of the occult behind him. This is further spelled out in the following verse, where it is clearly stated that his power is going to be mighty, but it will not be his own power. In other words, the Antichrist will have access to a tremendous amount of power; yet the power is not his own but that of his father Satan. As a result of this power, he will seek to destroy the Holy People of Israel. Verse 25 states that his basic means of rising to power is through craftiness and deceit. By these means he will lull rulers into a sense of false security and take advantage of it for the purpose of uprooting them.

A second description of the means of his rise to power is found in Daniel 11:36-39:

> *Then the king will do as he pleases, and he will exalt and magnify himself above every god, and will speak monstrous things against the God of gods; and he will prosper until the indignation is finished, for that which is decreed will be done. And he will show no regard for the gods of his fathers or for the desire of women, nor will he show regard for any other god; for he will magnify himself above them all. But instead he will honor a god of fortresses, a god whom his fathers did not know; he will honor him with gold, silver, costly stones, and treasures. And he will take action against the strongest of fortresses with the help of a foreign god; he will give great honor to those who acknowledge him, and he will cause them to rule over the many, and will parcel out land for a price.*

In this passage, Daniel describes the Antichrist as a king who will do as he pleases (v. 36a) characterized by self-exaltation and self-deification (vv. 36b-37). In order to be self-exalted, he will speak monstrous things against the God of gods, deifying himself and magnifying himself above all humanity.

Furthermore, he will be under the total control of Satan (vv. 38-39). The passage states that he will honor a god whom his ancestors on his mother's side never honored: a god of fortresses, who is Satan. Furthermore, with the help of this foreign god, Satan, he will be able to take over the strongest defenses in the world and will appear totally invincible. Those who submit to his authority will be increased and will be given positions of authority in his kingdom.

The above passages primarily deal with the rising power of the

Antichrist on the basis of his contact with the satanic realm. By totally submitting himself to Satan, he is honored with conquests. In his rise to power, Satan will gain absolute political and religious control.

His political control is found in Daniel 7:23-24:

> *Thus he said: 'The fourth beast will be a fourth kingdom on the earth, which will be different from all the other kingdoms, and it will devour the whole earth and tread it down and crush it. As for the ten horns, out of this kingdom ten kings will arise; and another will arise after them, and he will be different from the previous ones and will subdue three kings.*

According to this text, ultimately the Fourth Gentile Empire will take over the entire world and will develop into a one-world government (v. 23). But once it has achieved the status of a one-world government, it will then break down into ten kingdoms ruled by ten men (v. 24a). But while the entire world is in this ten-kingdom division stage, the Antichrist will begin to rise to power and eventually in the middle of the Tribulation, he will kill three of the ten kings (v. 24b).

At that point, all the remaining kings will simply submit to his authority, according to Revelation 17:12-13 and 17:

> *And the ten horns which you saw are ten kings, who have not yet received a kingdom, but they receive authority as kings with the beast for one hour. These have one purpose and they give their power and authority to the beast.*
>
> *For God has put it in their hearts to execute His purpose by having a common purpose, and by giving their kingdom to the beast, until the words of God should be fulfilled.*

With the other seven kings simply submitting to his authority at this point, the Antichrist will gain full political control and become the one-world political ruler.

But in the middle of the Tribulation, he also sets out to become the one-world religious ruler and he accomplishes this in three stages.

The first stage is his destruction of the false religious system of his day known as the Ecclesiastical Babylon. This is recorded in Revelation 17:16:

> *And the ten horns which you saw, and the beast, these will hate the harlot and will make her desolate and naked, and will eat her flesh and will burn her up with fire.*

Throughout the first half of the Tribulation, the religious affairs of the world will be controlled by a one-world super-religious organization which the Bible refers to as Ecclesiastical Babylon. Although she will rule with the support of civil government (Rev. 17:1-5), the political rulers of the world will have no real love for this religious system. After the Antichrist gains political leadership, he will then proceed to destroy the one-world religious system in order to set up his own religious system. But in the first stage of his religious takeover, he must destroy the existing false religious system.

Next he sets out to do away with the true religious system; namely, the born-again believers on the earth in those days. He begins this aspect by moving against the two witnesses in the second stage of his religious takeover. This is found in Revelation 11:7:

> *And when they have finished their testimony, the beast that comes up out of the abyss will make war with them, and overcome them and kill them.*

In the second stage then he will kill the two witnesses who have been troubling the world with their strong preaching.

Having killed what may appear to him as the leaders of the saints of that day, he will then proceed to his third stage in an all-out war against the saints, as recorded in various Scriptures.

One such passage is Daniel 7:25:

> *And he will speak out against the Most High and wear down the saints of the Highest One, and he will intend to make alterations in times and in law; and they will be given into his hand for a time, times, and half a time.*

The Antichrist, being anti-Christ, will seek to wipe out the memory of the true God and his way of doing so is by trying to destroy those who worship Him. So, there will be an all-out war against the saints at this time. Other Scriptures speak of the same point, but they shall be dealt with in a different context.

THE DEATH AND RESURRECTION OF THE ANTICHRIST

Continuing in the role of the counterfeit son, in the middle of the Tribulation comes the death and resurrection of the Antichrist – an imitation of the death and Resurrection of the Messiah. His death takes place in conjunction with his war against the ten kings.

This war is described in Daniel 11:40-45:

> *And at the end time the king of the South will collide with him, and the king of the North will storm against him with chariots, with horsemen, and with many ships; and he will enter countries, overflow them, and pass through. He will also enter the Beautiful Land, and many countries will fall; but these will be rescued out of his hand: Edom, Moab and the foremost of the sons of Ammon. Then he will stretch out his hand against other countries, and the land of Egypt will not escape. But he will gain control over the hidden treasures of gold and silver, and over all the precious things of Egypt; and Libyans and Ethiopians will follow at his heels. But rumors from the East and from the North will disturb him, and he will go forth with great wrath to destroy and annihilate many. And he will pitch the tents of his royal pavilion between the seas and the beautiful Holy Mountain; yet he will come to his end, and no one will help him.*

During his conquests, two major kings are said to stand against him (v. 40); they are the kings of Syria and Egypt. While the Antichrist is conquering, he will take over the Land of Israel although Jordan will escape (v. 41), and from there he will conquer Egypt, Libya, and Ethiopia (vv. 42-43). But then a third, major king, the king of the East from the area of Mesopotamia, will move in against the Antichrist (v. 44), and it is apparently in this battle that he will be killed (v. 45). What happens then is picked up in Revelation 13:1-8:

And he stood on the sand of the seashore. And I saw a beast coming up out of the sea, having ten horns and seven heads, and on his horns were ten diadems, and on his heads were blasphemous names. And the beast which I saw was like a leopard, and his feet were like those of a bear, and his mouth like the mouth of a lion. And the dragon gave him his power and his throne and great authority. And I saw one of his heads as if it had been slain, and his fatal wound was healed. And the whole earth was amazed and followed after the beast; and they worshiped the dragon, because he gave his authority to the beast; and they worshiped the beast, saying, "Who is like the beast, and who is able to wage war with him?" And there was given to him a mouth speaking arrogant words and blasphemies; and authority to act for forty-two months was given to him. And he opened his mouth in blasphemies against God, to blaspheme His name and His tabernacle, that is, those who dwell in heaven. And it was given to him to make war with the saints and to overcome them; and authority over every tribe and people and tongue and nation was given to him. And all who dwell on the earth will worship him, everyone whose name has not been written from the foundation of the world in the book of life of the Lamb who has been slain.

The beast described in Revelation 13:1-2 is the same as the nondescript beast of Daniel 7. Continuing this counterfeit system, Satan, the counterfeit father, will give his authority to the Antichrist, the counterfeit son. This is in imitation of God the Father having given to Jesus all of His authority.

However, the Antichrist will be killed in the war recorded in Daniel 11:40-45 (v. 3a). Then Satan will raise him back to life (v. 3b), even as the Father resurrected the Messiah. Just as the Resurrection of the Messiah helped to prove His deity and caused men to worship Him, the resurrection of the Antichrist will deceive many and the whole world will begin to worship him because of his resurrection (v. 4). He will be allowed to continue his work of blasphemy for 3 1/2 years, the second half of the Tribulation (vv. 5-6).

Verses 1-2 of chapter 13 have been explained earlier, but it is now clear that it is Satan who will resurrect the Antichrist back to life. Many take the phrase, as if it had been slain, to mean that the Antichrist appeared to be dead but was not really. However, the same idiom is used of the Messiah in Revelation 5:6, and there was no question that Messiah died. The idiom, then, refers to a resurrected individual. The person was killed and by all human experience should have remained dead. But suddenly he is very much alive because of resurrection. This idiom must mean here what it means elsewhere: a reference to a resurrected individual. The text clearly goes on to say that his fatal wound was healed, that is, by resurrection.

Some wish to interpret this as a reference to the revival of the Roman Empire, feeling that this would be enough to cause man to worship it. But a revived Roman Empire would not cause man to worship it as God any more than the revival of Poland or Israel did. This kind of thinking is purely imaginary. It is the resurrection of the man Antichrist which creates this worship.

Thus, the Antichrist is the counterfeit son in every respect. There has been a counterfeit multiplicity of names, a counterfeit virgin birth, a counterfeit god-man, and now a counterfeit death and resurrection. A counterfeit second coming to rule the world can be seen as he will move to possess the nations and kingdoms of the world. Satan is playing the part of the counterfeit father in this scenario. For as the True Father gave His authority to the True Son, so the counterfeit father will give his authority to the counterfeit son.

It is at this point that he will have all-out war against the saints as he moves in to take full religious authority in the world (v. 7). However, those who will not believe in Jesus will end up worshipping the Antichrist (v. 8). So in completion of the counterfeit, the Antichrist will claim to be the resurrected god-man and will call all men to worship him. This leads to the Abomination of Desolation to be discussed next.

THE ABOMINATION OF DESOLATION

That which culminates the Antichrist's full religious control of world affairs is what is called in Scripture the Abomination of Desolation. A number of passages deal with this very significant event. The first passage is Daniel 9:27:

> *And he will make a firm covenant with the many for one week, but in the middle of the week he will put a stop to sacrifice and grain offering; and on the wing of abominations will come one who makes desolate, even until a complete destruction, one that is decreed, is poured*

out on the one who makes desolate.

This verse not only speaks of how the Tribulation begins as was discussed earlier, but it also speaks of the breaking of the seven-year covenant between Israel and the Antichrist in the middle of the Tribulation. At this point, there is a cessation of all sacrifices and the Abomination of Desolation occurs. It does not state exactly what the Abomination of Desolation consists of, but it does state that it occurs in the middle of the Tribulation.

Another passage, specifying the length of the Abomination of Desolation, is found in Daniel 12:11:

And from the time that the regular sacrifice is abolished, and the abomination of desolation is set up, there will be 1,290 days.

According to this passage, the Abomination of Desolation will last a total of 1,290 days. This is a full thirty days beyond the end of the Tribulation. So for some inexplicable reason, the Abomination of Desolation is allowed to continue thirty days beyond the end of the Tribulation itself.

At this point Daniel still has not stated exactly what the Abomination of Desolation is, but he has stated two things: first, it starts in the middle of the Tribulation; and second, it continues for thirty days beyond the end of the Tribulation. The third passage that speaks of the Abomination of Desolation is found in Matthew 24:15-16:

Therefore when you see the ABOMINATION OF DESOLATION which was spoken of through Daniel the prophet, standing in the holy place (let the reader understand), then let those who are in Judea flee to the mountains;

When Jesus began to reveal the circumstances of the setting up of the Kingdom in His Olivet Discourse, He provided a warning sign to the Jews who would be living in the middle of the Tribulation. The warning is that whenever they see or hear of the occurrence of the abomination of desolation—just as soon as they learn of it—they are to get out of Israel very quickly. Although it is not stated exactly what the abomination of desolation is, Matthew does say that it will serve as a warning sign to the Jews. So in some way, this will serve as the second revelation of the Antichrist which will be intended to warn Israel. The fourth passage is found in Revelation 11:1-2:

And there was given me a measuring rod like a staff; and someone said, "Rise and measure the temple of God, and the altar, and those who worship in it. And leave out the court which is outside the temple, and do not measure it, for it has been given to the nations; and they will tread under foot the holy city for forty-two months.

Similar to what was already stated in Daniel 9:27, this Revelation passage also states that the normal functioning of the Temple will be stopped, for it will be taken over by the Gentiles who will have control of the Temple area for 3 1/2 years. As in Daniel 9:27, this passage states that the Temple will be given over to Gentiles in the middle of the Tribulation and will be desolated for 3 1/2 years. Again, nothing has been stated as to exactly what the Abomination of Desolation is.

From the Scriptures it can be seen that the Abomination of Desolation involves two key stages.

THE FIRST STAGE

The first stage is recorded in II Thessalonians 2:3-4:

Let no one in any way deceive you, for it will not come unless the apostasy comes first, and the man of lawlessness is revealed, the son of destruction, 4 who opposes and exalts himself above every so-called god or object of worship, so that he takes his seat in the temple of God, displaying himself as being God.

In the first stage of the Abomination of Desolation when the Antichrist takes over the Jewish Temple as prophesied in Daniel 9:27 and Revelation 11:1-2, he will then set up his throne in the Holy of Holies of this Temple and declare himself to be the one true God.

This becomes the first stage of the Abomination of Desolation and also serves as the second revelation of the Antichrist, the one to Israel according to II Thessalonians 2:8-12:

> *And then that lawless one will be revealed whom the Lord will slay with the breath of His mouth and bring to an end by the appearance of His coming; that is, the one whose coming is in accord with the activity of Satan, with all power and signs and false wonders, and with all the deception of wickedness for those who perish, because they did not receive the love of the truth so as to be saved. And for this reason God will send upon them a deluding influence so that they might believe what is false, in order that they all may be judged who did not believe the truth, but took pleasure in wickedness.*

By this very act of the Abomination of Desolation, the Antichrist will be revealed as truly being the lawless one and then Israel can really see with whom they have made a covenant (v. 8). He is one who is totally energized by Satan and is able to do miracles (v. 9) for the purpose of world-wide deception, for he will call all men to worship him (v. 10).

The ones who will be deceived by this are the ones who have already rejected the gospel of Jesus the Messiah. It should be remembered that during the first half of the Tribulation there will be a world-wide preaching of the gospel by 144,000 Jews (Matt. 24:14; Rev. 7). While myriads will accept the gospel, many more will not. Because many will refuse to respond to the preaching of the 144,000 in the first half of the Tribulation, they will be deceived by the Antichrist and begin to worship him during the second half (vv. 11-12). This world-wide worship of the Antichrist will be a direct result of his death and resurrection, as was noted in Revelation 13:1-8.

The first stage of the Abomination of Desolation then is when the Antichrist will take over the Jewish Temple; sit down in the Holy of Holies and declare himself to be the one true God. The fact that this proclamation will come after his own resurrection accompanied by signs, wonders and miracles will deceive the masses of mankind into accepting the deity of the Antichrist.

THE SECOND STAGE

The second stage of the Abomination of Desolation is given in Revelation

13:11-15:

> *And I saw another beast coming up out of the earth; and he had two horns like a lamb, and he spoke as a dragon. And he exercises all the authority of the first beast in his presence. And he makes the earth and those who dwell in it to worship the first beast, whose fatal wound was healed. And he performs great signs, so that he even makes fire come down out of heaven to the earth in the presence of men. And he deceives those who dwell on the earth because of the signs which it was given him to perform in the presence of the beast, telling those who dwell on the earth to make an image to the beast who *had the wound of the sword and has come to life. And there was given to him to give breath to the image of the beast, that the image of the beast might even speak and cause as many as do not worship the image of the beast to be killed.*

The Antichrist will not remain in the Holy of Holies, for his capitol will be in the rebuilt city of Babylon. But at this point, the unholy trinity will be completed with the rise of the false prophet playing the role of the counterfeit holy spirit. The rise of the false prophet will have the same source as that of the false son—namely, Satan (v. 11). Just as the Holy Spirit exercises equal authority with the Son, so the false prophet will exercise equal authority with the Antichrist (v. 12a). Just as the Holy Spirit draws men to worship the Messiah, so the false prophet will call all men to worship the resurrected Antichrist (v. 12b). And just as the initial coming of the Holy Spirit was accompanied by miracles, so the coming of the false prophet will also be accompanied by miracles (v. 13). These signs will continue the work of deception, calling even more men to worship the Antichrist (v. 14a).

Then the Antichrist will initiate the second stage of the Abomination of Desolation (vv. 14b-15). In order to keep the Temple as the center of worship of the Antichrist since he will not remain there, the false prophet will make an image of the Antichrist; this image will be given life and set up in the Holy of Holies of the Jewish Temple. This becomes the second stage of the Abomination of Desolation: the image of the Antichrist "standing" in the Holy of Holies. This is what Yeshua had reference to when He spoke of the abomination of desolation … standing in the holy place (Mat. 24:15). Furthermore, as Daniel 12:11 states, this image will be allowed to remain within the Holy of Holies for a total of 1,290 days—thirty days beyond the close of the Tribulation.

THE MARK OF THE BEAST

In conjunction with the two stages of the Abomination of Desolation, as all men are called to worship the Antichrist, there will be a "counterfeit seal" for those who would own the Antichrist as god. Just as those who are committed to Jesus the Messiah receive the seal of the Holy Spirit, those who will now worship the Antichrist will receive a counterfeit seal. This is recorded in Revelation 13:16-18:

> *And he causes all, the small and the great, and the rich and the poor, and the free men and the slaves, to be given a mark on their right hand, or on their forehead, and he provides that no one should be able to buy or to sell, except the one who has the mark, either the name of the beast or the number of his name. Here is wisdom. Let him who has understanding calculate the number of the beast, for the number is that of a man; and his number is six hundred and sixty-six.*

The place of this mark will be either on the right arm or on the forehead (v. 16). It will be necessary to have it in order to make a living, for that is the means of being able to buy or sell (v. 17). Since only those who have this mark will be allowed to engage in making a living, the pressure will certainly be on for all the people to receive it.

But the mark is more than a mere seal of the Antichrist, for this mark is to be interpreted according to verses 17-18. Four things are stated about the number in this passage and it follows a logical sequence: first, it is the number of the beast; second, the number is that of a man; third, it is the number of his name; and fourth, the number is six hundred and sixty-six. In following through this logical progression, the number of the beast is also the number of a man because the Antichrist will be a man who will head up the final form of the Fourth Gentile Empire and he is portrayed as the beast.

Furthermore, this number is the number of his [very own] name and the numerical value of his name is 666. The point essentially is this; each letter of the Hebrew alphabet has a numerical value. There are 22 letters in the Hebrew alphabet and in the order of numerical value they are as follows: 1, 2, 3, 4, 5, 6, 7, 8, 9, 10, 20, 30, 40, 50, 60, 70, 80, 90, 100, 200, 300, and 400. Whatever the personal name of the Antichrist will be, when it is spelled out in Hebrew characters, its numerical value will be 666.

So the "mark of the beast" will not only be the seal for those who worship him, it will also be the numerical value of the personal name of the Antichrist. And since a number of different combinations can be equivalent to 666, it is impossible to figure the name out in advance. However, when a prominent figure arrives on the horizon, if the numerical value of his name in Hebrew characters is equivalent to 666, then he would certainly be one to watch.

Because believers will not take the mark, life will be extremely difficult for them since they will not be able to engage in making any kind of living. However, there is both a warning and a comfort given regarding this mark of the beast.

This is given in Revelation 14:9-12:

> *And another angel, a third one, followed them, saying with a loud voice, "If anyone worships the beast and his image, and receives a mark on his forehead or upon his hand, he also will drink of the wine of the wrath of God, which is mixed in full strength in the cup of His anger; and he will be tormented with fire and brimstone in the presence of the holy angels and in the presence of the Lamb. "And the smoke of their torment goes up forever and ever; and they have no rest day and night, those who worship the beast and his image, and whoever receives the mark of his name." Here is the perseverance of the saints who keep the commandments of God and their faith in Jesus.*

The clear warning of this angel is that anyone who receives this mark will forfeit any opportunity to be saved in the Tribulation. Until that mark is taken, the opportunity will be there. But once they have accepted this mark, meaning they have owned the Antichrist as their personal god, they will have reached the "point of no return" (vv. 9-11). They will be destined to receive the full judgment of the wrath of God contained in the bowl judgments of Revelation 15-16 and their destiny in the Lake of Fire will be permanently assured. It is this fact that will serve as a point of comfort for the saints living at this time (v. 12). For though they must suffer and maybe even die, this period of world-wide persecution will only be allowed to continue for 31/2 years.

But during this very same period, the bowl judgments will be poured out, especially on those who have the "mark of the beast," according to Revelation 16:1-2:

> *And I heard a loud voice from the temple, saying to the seven angels, "Go and pour out the seven bowls of the wrath of God into the earth." And the first angel went and poured out his bowl into the earth; and it became a loathsome and malignant sore upon the men who had the mark of the beast and who worshiped his image.*

But not only will the persecutors who worship the Antichrist suffer grievously during the second half of the Tribulation, they will also be forever doomed in the Lake of Fire.

THE FALL OF THE ANTICHRIST

The beginnings of his fall occur when the Antichrist gathers all his armies for the Campaign of Armageddon in Revelation 16:12-16:

> *And the sixth angel poured out his bowl upon the great river, the Euphrates; and its water was dried up, that the way might be prepared for the kings from the east. And I saw coming out of the mouth of the dragon and out of the mouth of the beast and out of the mouth of the false prophet, three unclean spirits like frogs; for they are spirits of demons, performing signs, which go out to the kings of the whole world, to gather them together for the war of the great day of God, the Almighty. ("Behold, I am coming like a thief. Blessed is the one who stays awake and keeps his garments, lest he walk about naked and men see his shame.") And they gathered them together to the place which in Hebrew is called HarMagedon.*

The key purpose of this campaign will be to destroy all the Jews—once and for all. This will be a combined effort by the entire unholy trinity but this final effort will also lead to the fall of the Antichrist.

It is in the closing hours of the Campaign of Armageddon that the Messiah will return for His Second Coming and, at this point, the Antichrist will be killed, according to II Thessalonians 2:8:

> *And then that lawless one will be revealed whom the Lord will slay with the breath of His mouth and bring to an end by the appearance of His coming;*

The one who has claimed to be God Almighty and has tried to imitate the true Son, the one who has been able to perform all kinds of miracles, signs and wonders, exercising all the authority in the kingdoms of Satan, will now be quickly dispensed with simply by the breath of the Lord Jesus and, for the second time, the Antichrist will die.

Isaiah describes what happens when the soul of the Antichrist enters Hell once he is slain by the Lord Jesus.

In Isaiah 14:9-11 we read these words:

> *Sheol from beneath is excited over you to meet you when you come; it arouses for you the spirits of the dead, all the leaders of the earth; it raises all the kings of the nations from their thrones. "They will all respond and say to you, 'Even you have been made weak as we, you have become like us. 'Your pomp and the music of your harps Have been brought down to Sheol; maggots are spread out as your bed beneath you, and worms are your covering.*

These verses describe the soul of the Antichrist as it enters into the domains of Hell after he is killed by Yeshua Himself. All those who preceded the Antichrist into Hell suddenly rise in utter astonishment that this great one of the earth—this, the King of Babylon—who had been able to spread fear throughout the entire world, the one who had been so greatly manifested in power and pomp, is suddenly brought down to the same demise! These kings in Sheol rise in utter astonishment that the Antichrist has also suffered the same demise and then suddenly disappear into the shadows of Sheol. The Antichrist finds himself walking on a carpet of worms and his soul is covered with worms.

Later Isaiah describes what happens to the body of the Antichrist still on the earth. In Isaiah 14:16-20 we read:

> *Those who see you will gaze at you, they will ponder over you, saying, 'Is this the man who made the earth tremble, who shook kingdoms, who made the world like a wilderness and overthrew its cities, who did not allow his prisoners to go home?' "All the kings of the nations lie in glory, each in his own tomb. "But you have been cast out of your tomb like a rejected branch, clothed with the slain who are pierced with a sword, who go down to the stones of the pit, like a trampled corpse. "You will not be united with them in burial, because you have ruined your country, you have slain your people. May the offspring of evildoers not be mentioned forever.*

The body of the Antichrist lies trampled upon by the feet of his own fleeing soldiers. Just as the souls in Sheol are astonished that the Antichrist himself had entered Hell, his own soldiers—those who worshipped him as god—also utter statements of surprise that he would so quickly and easily die at the mouth of the Lord Jesus. Suddenly their dashed hopes for the deity of the Antichrist are gone and shattered. As they flee, the body of the Antichrist who claimed to be god is trampled upon by the feet of his own fleeing soldiers.

Isaiah states that the burial will never take place; the body of the Antichrist will never see burial (v. 20). Isaiah does not explain why. At this point there is a little humor on the part of God. The Antichrist has sought to be the counterfeit son and has tried to imitate Him in many ways. He has had the counterfeit virgin birth, counterfeit death and resurrection and counterfeit seal. But now the Lord will allow him to play out his counterfeit role in total. The first Resurrection is the resurrection of all believers (Rev. 20:4-6). However, the Messiah is the first fruits of this first Resurrection, having already been resurrected in advance of all future believers (I Cor. 15:20-23). The second resurrection is the resurrection of all unbelievers (Rev. 20:11-15). Just as the Messiah was the first fruits of the first Resurrection, so the Antichrist will be the first fruits of the second resurrection.

This becomes evident in Revelation 19:19-21:

> *And I saw the beast and the kings of the earth and their armies,*

assembled to make war against Him who sat upon the horse, and against His army. And the beast was seized, and with him the false prophet who performed the signs in his presence, by which he deceived those who had received the mark of the beast and those who worshiped his image; these two were thrown alive into the lake of fire which burns with brimstone. And the rest were killed with the sword which came from the mouth of Him who sat upon the horse, and all the birds were filled with their flesh.

The passage begins by describing the Campaign of Armageddon (v. 19), during which time the Antichrist will be killed according to II Thessalonians 2:8. Then this passage states that the Antichrist, along with the false prophet, will be taken and they will be cast into the Lake of Fire alive. The only way this could be so is if the Antichrist is resurrected after he is killed by the Messiah. So, the Antichrist will be allowed to complete his role of the counterfeit son by becoming the first fruits of the second resurrection. He and the false prophet will have the Lake of Fire all to themselves for the first thousand years of its existence (Rev. 20:10).

With this the career of the Antichrist comes to its end.

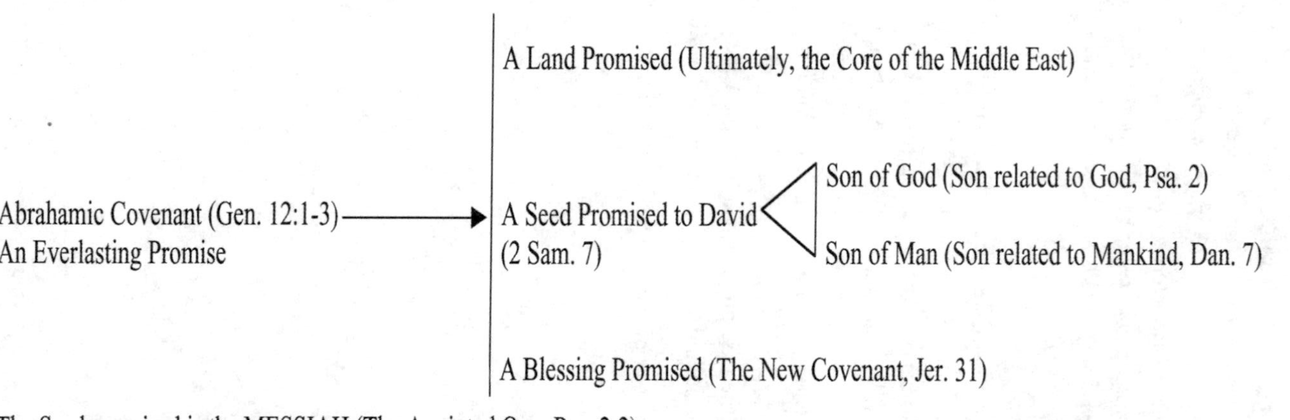
THE ETERNAL COVENANT WITH KING DAVID
Abrahamic Covenant (Gen. 12:1-3)
An Everlasting Promise
A Land Promised (Ultimately, the Core of the Middle East)
A Seed Promised to David
(2 Sam. 7)
Son of God (Son related to God, Psa. 2)
Son of Man (Son related to Mankind, Dan. 7)
A Blessing Promised (The New Covenant, Jer. 31)
The Seed promised is the MESSIAH (The Anointed One, Psa. 2:2)
The Messiah will die to take away sins (Isa. 53; John 1:29)
The Messiah will come forth from the dead (Psa. 16:10; Acts 2:29-36)
The Messiah will return to reign and rule (Isa. 11:1-12; Rev. 19:11-16)

CHAPTER 12

WHAT IS THE DAVIDIC COVENANT?

George Gunn

In the latter 1980s and early 1990s, a few scholars and theologians began to move away from the historical dispensational position (also called "Classical," "Normative" or "Essential" Dispensationalism).[1] They developed an approach to understanding God's program for the Church and Israel that differed significantly from that of historical dispensationalism. They called this new approach "Progressive Dispensationalism." The features that distinguish progressive dispensationalism from historical dispensationalism are: 1) A greater focus on the continuity between the peoples of God of different ages; 2) An insistence that Jesus has already begun (at least to a degree) a fulfillment of the Davidic Covenant; and 3) Adoption of a distinctive hermeneutic called a "complementary hermeneutic."[2]

To many normative dispensationalists, the view that the church is fulfilling the Davidic Covenant blurs the distinction between Israel and the Church. Such a position would significantly weaken the argument for a pretribulational rapture. It must be acknowledged at this time, however, that progressive dispensationalist Craig Blaising affirms a pretribulational rapture position, albeit in relatively weak terms: "This deliverance, or rapture, would appear to coincide with the inception or coming of the Day of the Lord, since that is the focus in 1 Thessalonians 5:2-4."[3] As of this writing, progressive dispensationalists have not written much specifically addressing the issue of the timing of the rapture. To my knowledge, none has claimed a position other than the pretribulational one. However, their theological system moves in the direction of covenant premillennialism, whose adherents have traditionally held to a posttribulational rapture. Only time will tell what the disciples of the first generation of progressive dispensationalists will do with the rapture issue.

Today, progressive dispensationalism is becoming an increasingly popular position among the faculty at many colleges and seminaries that previously held to the historical form of dispensational premillennialism and a pretribulational rapture of the church. Because progressive dispensationalism takes positions that remove some of the strongest arguments in favor of a pretribulational rapture of the church and of a purpose for God's future restoration of Israel, this position has concerned many normative dispensationalists.

SIGNIFICANCE OF THE SERMON

Progressive dispensationalists have argued that at Christ's ascension He started to fulfill the Davidic Covenant by being seated on David's throne. Whether this can actually be seen as a "reigning" seems to be a point of debate among progressive dispensationalists. Darrell Bock frequently uses the terms "rule" or "reign" in reference to Christ's present fulfilling of the Davidic Covenant.[4] Craig Blaising, however, seems to prefer the term "enthronement" as opposed to "rule" or "reign."[5] Nevertheless, Blaising uses terminology that clearly attributes to Christ's present ministry a Davidic "rule" or "reign." For example, he refers to

> the preeminence of His kingdom over all rule and authority on earth as seen in the language in Psalm 89:27: 'I also shall make Him my firstborn, the highest of the kings of the earth' As we have seen, New Testament theology portrays the 'raising up' of Jesus to the Davidic kingship as taking place in His resurrection from the dead. Consequently, Colossians 1:18 declares Him to be the ruler.[6]

Blaising further states, "The Messiah has been raised up, seated (enthroned) at the right hand of God, all things, specifically all rule and authority, have been subjected to Him...."[7] On the other hand, Robert Saucy, while affirming that Christ's present position at God's right hand is essentially an enthronement on the Davidic throne, nevertheless rejects the view that Christ's current status is one of "reigning."[8] But Saucy's position still attributes to the present dispensation a partial fulfillment of the Davidic Covenant, and thus a blurring of the biblical distinction between Israel and the Church.

This is a noteworthy contrast to what dispensationalists have historically held. A significant tenet of dispensationalism has historically been that Christ's Davidic rule will not begin until his second coming when He is seated on the throne of David in Jerusalem during the millennium. In an effort to find support for the progressive dispensationalist's position, Darrell Bock has insisted that Peter, in his Acts 2 sermon, established an exegetical "link" between Psalm 110's "sit" (110:1) and Psalm 132's "set" (or "seat," 132:11), thus placing the seating of Christ on David's throne at the time of the ascension.[9]

The progressive dispensationalists' view has two major problems: It requires a non-literal interpretation of Psalm 110; and it involves a faulty exegesis of Peter's sermon in Acts 2. The interpretation of Psalm 110 has been dealt with in detail elsewhere.[10] Here, I would like to focus attention on the exegesis of Peter's sermon.

SETTING OF THE SERMON

This sermon certainly has significance being the first sermon preached in the church age. However, it must also be recognized that this sermon was preached in the church's infancy and immaturity. F. F. Bruce noted that this sermon has

> marks of [an] early date, such as the hope expressed that 'all the house of Israel', to whom the proclamation is first made, may repent as a nation, that the Messianic Age may be inaugurated at once (cf. ii.36; iii.19 ff.).[11]

Bruce notes further,

> In this and other sermons in the earlier part of Ac. we should observe the absence of the Pauline emphasis on the pre-existence of Jesus, on His unique relation to the Father, on His sin-bearing, on justification (contrast Paul's own words in xiii.39), on the moral and spiritual power of the Resurrection, on the sanctifying influence of the Holy Spirit. What we do find is Christian preaching of an obviously primitive character, against the background of Jewish Messianic expectation.[12]

On the Day of Pentecost, no Gentiles had yet come into the church. In fact, Peter and the other apostles had not yet fully grasped that Jesus' redemptive work would extend in a significant way to the Gentiles. Before the crucifixion, they had thought that Jesus had come to assume the Davidic throne and rule over Israel (Matt. 19:28; 20:21). The crucifixion had dashed those hopes and had left the disciples disappointed and dismayed (Luke 24:21). However, following the resurrection, the disciples' anticipation that Jesus would immediately establish the kingdom was revived (Acts 1:6). It is noteworthy that Jesus did not correct this anticipation. He did not tell them that a long period would precede the establishment of the kingdom. He did not tell them that Jewish involvement in the church would wane or that increasing numbers of Gentiles would come into the church. He said nothing about the middle wall of partition between Jew and Gentile being broken down (Eph. 2:14) so that there would no longer be a Jewish distinctiveness to the way God would work in the world.[13] He only told them that it was not for them to know about the times or the seasons (Acts 1:7). And, though Jesus may have indicated in some of His teachings that there would be some delay (e.g., such parables as that of the minas, Luke 19:11ff, and the story of the widow not to lose heart over the delay, Luke 18), Acts 1 clearly shows that the disciples were not expecting any more delay after the post-resurrection events.

In their early teaching and preaching, the apostles did not comprehend that a lengthy church age reaching out to masses of Gentiles would intervene between the ascension and establishment of the kingdom. Note the difficulty with which Peter was persuaded to take the gospel to the God fearing Gentile Cornelius (Acts 10:9-22). Thus, it is no surprise to see Peter on the Day of Pentecost anticipating Jesus being seated on David's (earthly) throne. This requires neither that Jesus was already so seated, nor that He must be so seated soon. It is only to say that from the perspective of the early Jewish Christians their anticipation was that Jesus would soon be seated on David's throne, reigning from Jerusalem over Israel as Messiah and King.

SUMMARY STATEMENT OF THE SERMON

Those who hold to a literal hermeneutic place a high value on what is known as *authorial intent.* A proper interpretation of Peter's sermon will need to focus on how Peter himself understood his own words. In verse 36, Peter sums up his message in these words: "Therefore, let all the house of Israel know beyond a doubt that God made this Jesus whom you crucified *both Lord and Messiah."* Most English translations use the word "Christ" instead of "Messiah." The English reader needs to remember, however, that the word "Christ" is simply a Greek translation of the Hebrew word "Messiah." The verb "made" is from the Greek *poieo* which, according to the authoritative lexicon by Arndt, Gingrich, Danker, Bauer, in a structure like this (taking a double accusative) takes a meaning like, "Claim that someone is someth[ing]."[14] Thus, Acts 2:36 means, "God has *proclaimed* Him to be both Lord and Messiah."

Later in this chapter, when we consider the structure of the sermon, it will be seen that the words "both Lord and Messiah" refer back to two distinct sections of Peter's sermon. But for now, let us consider the meaning of these two terms and how they relate to each other.

THE *Messiah*

Usually rendered "Christ" in the New Testament, this term means "anointed." Both the Old Testament Hebrew term (*Mashiach* from which we get "Messiah") and the New Testament Greek term (*Christos* from which we get "Christ") mean "anointed." Earlier Christian interpreters frequently explained that the Messiah fulfilled the three anointed offices of the Old Testament – prophet, priest and king.[15] However, of these three, only two (priest and king) can truly be considered as "anointed" offices. The only prophet in the Old Testament supposedly connected with a rite of anointing is Elisha (1Kings 19:16)[16] and even he was not actually anointed, but merely had Elijah's mantle cast over him (1Kings 19:19).

In the first century, the term "Messiah" was understood as denoting the King who will arise in the latter days to fulfill the covenant God had made with David (2 Sam. 7:12-16). There were some, especially the Qumran sect that produced the Dead Sea Scrolls, who held to a belief in two eschatological Messiahs – a kingly Messiah (from David) and a priestly Messiah (from Zadok)[17], but this appears to have been a minority position, based in part on Zechariah's prophecy concerning Joshua (Zech. 6:9-15). It is possible that the brief reign of the Hasmonean priest/kings over Israel (ca. 142 to 63 B.C.) produced a reaction by the majority Israelite population in focusing on the Davidic aspect of Messiah, while minimizing the priestly aspect. "It is … reasonable to suppose that when Aristobulus I and his heirs became kings the Bible-based belief in a Messiah of the dynasty of David was intensified."[18] The idea of the kingly Messiah from the house of David is reflected in the 14th benediction of the Palestinian recension of the Prayer of Eighteen Benedictions,

> In thy great mercy O Yahweh our God, have pity on Israel thy people, and on Jerusalem thy city, and on Zion the habitation of thy glory, and on thy temple, and on thy dwelling, and on the monarchy of the house of David, the Messiah of thy righteousness.[19]

The identification of Jesus as the Davidic Messiah was made from the very earliest of the birth narratives (Luke 1:32-33, 69; 2:11; Matt. 1:1). The earliest New Testament references to Jesus as the "Christ" are intended to identify him as the Davidic Messiah, the One who will rule from the throne of David as the eschatological King. Later, as the Gentile influence became more prominent within the church, references tend to use the term "Christ" not as a descriptive title, but as a name, not necessarily carrying a Davidic implication. Longenecker observes:

> In the twelve instances in Acts where the word "Christ" appears singly (2:31, 36; 3:18; 4:26; 8:5; 9:22; 17:3a; 26:23; and in 3:20; 5:42; 18:5, 28, where "Christ is in apposition to "Jesus" but still "used" singly), it is used as a title – usually articular in form (except here [2:36] and at 3:20) – but not as a name. And in every instance where it appears as a title, it is in an address to a Jewish audience (only 8:5 and 26:23 are possible exceptions, though both the Samaritans and Agrippa II possessed something of a Jewish background and understanding).... Apparently, therefore, the messiahship of Jesus was the distinctive feature of the church's witness within Jewish circles, signifying, as it does, his fulfillment of Israel's hopes and his culmination of God's redemptive purposes.[20]

Thus, in asserting that God has made Jesus to be "Messiah," Peter is affirming the Davidic kingly role of Jesus.

THE *Lord*

The Greek word *Kurios*, translated here "Lord," was the normal word used in the Septuagint to translate the Name of God. Though it *could* be used to refer to concepts other than deity (as in John 4:11, 15, 19), the New Testament regularly does use this term to refer to Jesus' deity (e.g. Rom. 10:9; Phil. 2:10). This was precisely Jesus' point in His encounter with the Pharisees recorded in Matthew 22:41-46 (also in Mark 12:35-37 and Luke 20:41-44).

> *Now while the Pharisees were gathered together, Jesus asked them a question, saying, "What do you think about the Christ, whose son is He?" They said to Him, "The son of David." He said to them, "Then how does David in the Spirit call Him 'Lord,' [Kurios] saying, 'The Lord said to my Lord, 'Sit at My right hand, Until I put Thine enemies beneath Thy feet'"? "If David then calls Him 'Lord,' [Kurios] how is He his son?"*

In quoting from Psalm 110:1, Jesus is attempting to get the Pharisees to understand that the Messiah is more than merely the son of David. In fact, he is nothing less than Yahweh, the God of Israel. Both the New Testament and the Septuagint use the word *Kurios* to translate both occurrences of "Lord" in Psalm 110:1.

With reference to Peter's use of *Kurios* in Acts 2:36 Longenecker says, "The title 'Lord' was also proclaimed christologically in Jewish circles, with evident intent to apply to Jesus all that was said of God in the Old Testament (cf. the Christological use of Isa. 45:23 in Phil 2:10)."[21] Thus, in asserting that God has made Jesus to be "Lord," Peter is affirming the deity of Jesus.

A related question is whether Psalm 110 may be taken as relating to the Davidic Covenant. Jesus' interpretation of the Psalm in the Mark 12 passage is informative. One significant point of Jesus' question to the Pharisees has been lost in most modern translations. The King James Version translates Mark 12:37 as, "David therefore himself calleth him Lord: and whence is he then his son?" The New King James Version and the New International Version, on the other hand, conform the translation to that of the other synoptic gospels ("*how* is he then his son?"),[22] losing the original force of the Greek word *pothen*, unique to Mark's account.[23] Jesus' question to the Scribes, the Jewish interpreters, is, "Whence" ("from where," i.e. from what passage) is the Messiah the son of David? *Pothen* is used here with the sense of "from what source of authority."[24] This usage is illustrated, for example, in Mark 6:1-2. When Jesus came into Nazareth and began to teach the people, they responded with amazement at his teaching and asked the question, "Whence are these things?" (*Pothen touto tauta*); in other words, "What is the source of his authority?" Another example of this usage, though from a different perspective, is seen in Luke 20:7 where Jesus challenges the chief priests, scribes and elders with the question, "The baptism of John: was it from heaven [*ex ouranou*] or from men [*ex anthropou*]?" (verse 4). Realizing their perilous position (verses 5-6), they replied, "We don't know from where [*me eidenai pothen*,]" (v.7). Here *pothen* is clearly the semantic answer to the prepositional phrases with *ek*, denoting the source of authority for John's baptism (viz., "heaven" [=God] or "men").

Mark's version of Jesus' response to the Scribes' teaching about the Messiah being David's Son in 12:35-37 focuses on the source of authority for making such a claim; this is the force of Mark's use of *pothen*. The Scribes appear to have used Psalm 110:1 as a proof text for their point. Jesus does not deny that Messiah is to be a descendent of David's, but he does take issue with the Scribes' interpretation of Psalm 110. We might paraphrase Jesus' response as follows: "You say that Messiah is David's Son? Fine, but on what authority (*pothen*) do you make that assertion? Psalm 110? Impossible! For in that Psalm David addresses Messiah as his Lord, not his son."

The implication is that Jesus knew their literal understanding of Psalm 110 could not allow them to see the Psalm as referring to the Davidic covenant. For them to justify their belief that the Messiah must be a son of David they would have to provide another passage. This passage, on the other hand, promoted something else. Their understanding of the Messiah needed to be expanded to include the Messiah as being more than just a future Davidic King. Jesus says that Psalm 110 puts the Messiah on a plane higher than David or any mere human descendant of his. This Messiah is on an equal footing with Yahweh. His opponents understood well his arguments and because they could not agree with his conclusions nor refute them, they preferred to remain silent.

RELATIONSHIP BETWEEN "LORD" AND "MESSIAH"

1. THE TWO-FOLD CONFESSION

Peter concludes his sermon in verse 36 by claiming that God has made Jesus to be both deity and Davidic Kingly Messiah. This two-fold confession is seen a number of times in the New Testament and appears to be perhaps the earliest Christian confession of faith. According to Matthew 16:16, Peter himself was among the first to recognize this twofold nature of Jesus' identity. At that time, in the region of Caesarea Philippi, Jesus asked His disciples who they thought He was. Peter, receiving information from God the Father, replied: "You are the Messiah, The Son of the Living God."

This two-fold confession acknowledged first, that Jesus was the one sent by God to rule from David's throne ("the Messiah"); and second, that Jesus was no less than deity ("the Son of the Living God"). Though it is possible to view the term "Son" as being synonymous with the term Messiah, based on the use of the term "Son" along with Messianic terms ("anointed" and "king") in Psalm 2, nevertheless, a comparison of the New Testament passages citing the twofold confession appears to connect the term "Son of (the Living) God" with the term "Lord," an affirmation of deity. Note the following New Testament references to this twofold confession:

	Davidic Kingship	Deity
Matthew 16:16	Messiah	Son of the Living God
Matthew 26:63	Messiah	Son of God
Mark 1:1	Messiah	Son of God
John 1:49	King of Israel	Son of God
John 11:27	Messiah	Son of God
John 20:31	Messiah	Son of God
Acts 2:36	Messiah	Lord
Romans 1:3-4	The seed of David	Son of God
1 John 4:15; 5:1	Messiah	Son of God

2. THE GRAMMATICAL CORRELATIVE RELATIONSHIP

Progressive dispensationalists agree that the title "Christ" identifies Jesus as the promised Davidic King.[25] However, they differ from historical dispensationalists by insisting that Jesus began his Davidic reign at the ascension. Darrell Bock explains as follows:

> Peter argues in Acts 2:22-36 that David predicted in Psalm 16 that this descendant would be raised up from the dead, incorruptible, and *in this way*, He would be seated upon His throne (Acts 2:30-31). He then argues that this enthronement has taken place upon the entrance of Jesus into heaven in keeping with the language of Psalm 110:1 that describes the seating of David's son at God's right hand.[26]

There are several problems with this line of reasoning. Under "The Structure of the Sermon" below, I will discuss the problem with the way Bock has tried to link Psalm 110:1 with Psalm 132:11. For now, however, I want to stay with Peter's statement in Acts 2:36 a little longer. Peter joins the two terms "Lord" and "Messiah" in the form of a "both – and" correlative structure. Grammarians refer to the correlative conjunctions as those that occur in pairs to join two items together in a relationship ("both … and," "not only … but also," "not … but," "either … or," "neither … nor," "whether … or," "as … as," etc.). The kind of relationship expressed can emphasize either identity (connective), similarity (comparative) or contrast (adversative). The correlative structure in Acts 2:36 uses the repeated Greek conjunction *kai* before each term. According to the standard New Testament Greek Lexicon by Bauer, Arndt, Gingrich and Danker this correlative relationship typically denotes a contrast, rather than an identity, between the two terms joined: *"not only. . . , but also* … Introducing contrasts: *although. . . yet."*[27] According to Blass, DeBrunner and Funk's Grammar of the Greek New Testament it is used, "to sharpen the distinction between the two..."[28] and may be translated, "'on the one hand … on the other.'"[29] Bock's exegesis does everything it can to link together the seating on David's throne (connected to the title "Messiah") with the seating at God's right hand (connected to the title "Lord"), but the correlative conjunctions used here suggest the idea of contrast, more than connection.[30] Peter could have used a different way of joining the two terms if he had wanted to emphasize their identity more strongly. For example, he could have expressed either an epexegetical or an appositional relationship.[31] Instead, he chose a construction that would emphasize contrast. Though this observation by itself does not absolutely prove Bock's interpretation to be wrong, when taken with observations that will be made about the structure of the sermon itself, it provides important confirmation that Christ's seating on the throne of David is seen *in contrast to* His seating at the right hand of God.

3. THE CHRONOLOGICAL RELATIONSHIP BETWEEN THE TWO SEATINGS

The faithful in Israel had been awaiting the coming of the Messiah for many generations. When John the Baptist began his ministry, he identified Jesus as the Messiah (John 1:24-27), but merely *identifying* Him as Messiah, did not mean that the Davidic reign had begun. In fact, John testified that there would be a period of judgment preceding Messiah's reign, a period of winnowing, separating and burning:

> *As for me, I baptize you with water for repentance, but He who is coming after me is mightier than I, and I am not fit to remove His sandals; He will baptize you with the Holy Spirit and fire. His winnowing fork is in His hand, and He will thoroughly clear His threshing floor; and He will gather His wheat into the barn, but He will burn up the chaff with unquenchable fire (Matt. 3:11-12).*

Frequently referred to as the "Tribulation Period," this time of judgment is identified by the Old Testament prophets as the "Day of the Lord" and, in Daniel, the seventieth "week," which culminates in the arrival of the Messiah to rule from David's throne. Joel 2:30-3:1 sets forth the order of events:

> *I will display wonders in the sky and on the earth, blood, fire and columns of smoke. The sun will be turned into darkness And the moon into blood before the great and awesome day of the LORD comes. And it will come about that whoever calls on the name of the LORD will be delivered; For on Mount Zion and in Jerusalem There will be those who escape, as the LORD has said, even among the survivors whom the LORD calls. For behold, in those days and at that time, when I restore the fortunes of Judah and Jerusalem.*

Malachi very clearly reveals that the messenger introduces a time of judgment that precedes the Messianic rule:

> *Behold, I am going to send My messenger, and he will clear the way before Me. And the Lord, whom you seek, will suddenly come to His temple; and the messenger of the covenant, in whom you delight, behold, He is coming," says the LORD of hosts. "But who can endure the day of His coming? And who can stand when He appears? For He is like a refiner's fire and like fullers' soap. He will sit as a smelter and purifier of silver, and He will purify the sons of Levi and refine them like gold and silver, so that they may present to the LORD offerings in righteousness. Then the offering of Judah and Jerusalem will be pleasing to the LORD as in the days of old and as in former years. Then I will draw near to you for judgment; and I will be a swift witness against the sorcerers and against the adulterers and against those who swear falsely, and against those who oppress the wage earner in his wages, the widow and the orphan, and those who turn aside the alien and do not fear Me," says the LORD of hosts ... "For behold, the day is coming, burning like a furnace; and all the arrogant and every evildoer will be chaff; and the day that is coming will set them ablaze," says the LORD of hosts, "so that it will leave them neither root nor branch. But for you who fear My name, the sun of righteousness will rise with healing in its wings; and you will go forth and skip about like calves from the stall (Mal. 3:1-5; 4:1-2).*

As was the case with John the Baptist, one can identify or proclaim Jesus as Messiah before it is time for Him to reign as Messiah, and this is what Peter does in His sermon. Peter, in affirming that God had proclaimed Jesus both "Lord" and "Messiah," (Acts 2:36) appealed to two Old Testament references: Psalm 132:11-12 and Psalm 110:1. Psalm 132 is Messianic and refers to the seating of David's descendant on his throne. But Psalm 110 is set in the context of the Tribulation Period preceding the Davidic reign (see especially vv. 5-7). The Lord of Psalm 110 is not the Son of David. He is David's Lord (see Matt. 22:41-46). Though we know that it is the same Person, it is nevertheless true that there are two distinct roles in view, and that the role of the judging Lord comes before the role of the reigning Son of David. Peter is saying, "This Jesus, whom you crucified, is both the Lord, who is coming in tribulational judgment, and Messiah, who will then reign on the throne of David."

STRUCTURE OF THE SERMON

Peter's sermon in Acts 2 shows a very definite order and structure. Two features in particular mark out discourse and topic boundaries in the sermon. First, the sermon is divided into 3 sections by the repeated vocatives: v. 14 "Judean Men" (*Andres Ioudaioi*), v. 22 "Israelite Men" (Andres Israelitai), v. 29 "Men, Brothers" (*Andres Adelphoi*). These three sections may be outlined as follows:

I. Verses 14-21, Apologetic for Speaking in Tongues

II. Verses 22-28, Significance of the Death and Resurrection of Jesus

III. Verses 29-36, Identification of Jesus' status

Each of these divisions is artfully introduced by a careful transition from what immediately precedes it.

The first division is introduced by a transition from the crowd's response to the tongues phenomenon (both a question: "What does this mean?" verse 12, and a criticism: "They are full of new wine," verse 13). Peter insists that this is not the effect of wine, but of the Holy Spirit, just as Joel described.

The conclusion of the Joel quote ("Everyone who calls on the name of the Lord will be saved.") introduces the second division, in which Peter clearly lays out the two essential features of the gospel: the death (verses 22-23) and the resurrection (24-28).[32]

The conclusion of the division on the death and resurrection introduces the third division. The quote from Psalm 16:8-11 in the second division raised the question of just who this risen One is in relation to David. As will be seen in the following paragraphs, Peter gives a twofold answer to this question, and then summarizes his conclusion.

The second feature marking discourse boundaries and topic divisions is seen in this third division. The third division is subdivided by the threefold occurrence of the Greek conjunction *oun* which introduces verses 30, 33,

36. The significance of this word here is heightened by the fact that *oun,* a fairly common Greek word in the NT (499x; 61x in Acts), occurs nowhere else in Peter's sermon. This threefold subdivision yields the following refinement to the third part of the outline:

III. Verses 29-36, Identification of Jesus' status

A. Verse 29 – Transition: The risen One is not David himself
B. Verses 30-32 – Resurrection tied to the Davidic promise and reigning
C. Verses 33-35 – Ascension tied to Melchizedekian priesthood and gifting
D. Verses 36 – Conclusion: Jesus is both (Melchizedekian) Lord and (Davidic) Messiah.

In the first subdivision, Peter identifies the risen One as David's descendant Who will be seated on David's throne. To support the idea of David's descendant being seated on the Davidic throne, Peter quotes Psalm 132:11.

In the second subdivision, Peter notes that Jesus was not only raised to the earth so He could sit on David's throne, but He was also exalted to the right hand of God in order to fulfill the role of the Melchizedekian priest who pours out gifts on His people. To support the idea of this Melchizedekian priestly role, Peter quotes Psalm 110:1.

PSALMS 132 AND 110 IN PETER'S SERMON

Darrell Bock insists that Peter, in Acts 2:30, purposely substituted the word *kathizo* for the LXX's *tithemi* (Ps 132:11) in order to establish an exegetical "link" with Psalm 110's *kathou* (cited in Acts 2:34), thus establishing an interpretation for Psalm 110 which sees its fulfillment in terms of the Davidic Covenant. Bock strings together verses and concepts in an amazingly intricate fashion. He argues as follows:

> The crucial linking allusion appears at this point. Peter notes that David was ... the conscious beneficiary of an oath God had made to him that one "of the fruit of his [David's] loins" (KJV) would sit on his throne (Acts 2:30). The key term is *kathisai* (to sit), which is reintroduced in the citation of Psalm 110 (note *kathou,* "sit," in

> v. 34). The allusion in verse 30 is to Psalm 132:11, a psalm which is strongly Israelitish and national in tone (see vv. 12-18). The psalm in turn is a reflection of the promise made to David in 2 Samuel 7, especially verse 12. This 2 Samuel passage is better known as the Davidic covenant. What is crucial is that David's awareness of this covenant promise is immediately linked to his understanding of the resurrection promise in Psalm 16, which in turn is immediately tied to the resurrection proof text of Psalm 110 (vv. 31-35). *Being seated on David's throne is linked to being seated at God's right hand.* In other words, Jesus' resurrection-ascension to God's right hand is put forward by Peter as a fulfillment of the Davidic covenant.... To say that Peter is only interested to argue that Messiah must be raised misses the point of connection in these verses and ignores entirely the allusion to Psalm 132 and the Davidic covenant.[33]

In another publication, where this same basic argument is put forth, Bock elucidates upon his understanding of the hermeneutics at this point.

> One of the ways Jews showed fulfillment of an OT passage was to cite the language in alluding to a second passage, thus linking the two texts conceptually. So by his use of the verb "to sit" (Acts 2:30, 34) Peter links Psalm 132:11 (cited in 2:30) with Psalm 110 (cited in 2:34).[34]

Crucial to Bock's argument is identifying Peter's reason for changing *tithemi* to *kathizo*. He believes he has found the reason in a Jewish method of establishing a link. However, there are some problems with Bock's imagined "link."

First, *kathizo* (Peter's "substitution" in Acts 2:30) and *kathemai*[35] though cognate are in fact different words that are not entirely synonymous. While *kathizo* can be either transitive ("to seat someone") or intransitive ("to sit"), *kathemai* is only intransitive ("to sit"). Had Peter wanted to establish an unquestionable "link" between the two citations by changing the wording of the LXX he could have used the same verb in both citations. Either one of two methods might have been employed for this purpose: (a) He might have phrased verse 30 in such a way as to use *kathemai* (e.g., *poieso auton kathesthai epi ton thronon autou*), or (b) he could have quoted Psalm 110 with a form of *kathizo*, which is frequently done by other NT authors both in quotations and in allusions to Psalm 110:1 (cf. Heb. 1:3; 8:1; 12:2; Mark 12:36 [where the form of *kathizo* is likely the better supported text]; Eph. 1:20; Rev. 3:21). Either of these approaches would have made such a proposed exegetical "link" much more likely, but Peter did not do so. Instead, he used two different words in citing the two texts. In light of this, it is risky at best to insist that Peter is necessarily establishing an exegetical "link" between Psalms 110 and 132.

But even more damaging to Bock's interpretation is the fact that, after all, Peter did not change any wording at all. Bock's explanation of why Peter changed *tithemi* to *kathizo* is more complicated than it needs to be. Peter in fact did not take any terminology out of Psalm 110 to use in his citation from Psalm 132; rather, he merely combined verses 11 and 12 of Psalm 132, where verse 12 refers to David's descendants (ultimately referring to the Messiah). Note carefully the terms used in these two verses:

> Psalm 132:11-12, The LORD has sworn to David, A truth from which He will not turn back; "Of the fruit of your body I will set [Heb. *'asit*, LXX *thesomai* (from *tithemi)*] upon your throne. 12 If your sons will keep My covenant, and My testimony which I will teach them, their sons also shall sit [Heb. *yeshvu*, LXX *kathiountai* (from *kathizo)*] upon your throne forever."

It is in verse 12, which refers to David's descendants who will sit upon David's throne, that the LXX translators used the verb *kathizo*. Peter did not import any words at all from Psalm 110 (which refers to the ascension) into his citation of Psalm 132. He merely combined the wording from verses 11 and 12 of Psalm 132. Psalm 132 looks forward to the seating of the Messiah in the kingdom, but does not make any reference to the ascension.

As an illustration of the ambiguity involved in attempting to read rabbinic interpretive methods into the apostles' OT citations, note that Kilgallen, in his monograph on Peter's sermon, appeals to the exact same rabbinic method as does Bock, only Kilgallen argues for a link between Psalm 110 and Joel 2 in Peter's sermon, based on the repetition of the word "Lord":

> The correct manner of arguing that Jesus is Lord is, as far as the Jewish Peter is concerned before his Jewish audience,

> to find the text which fits properly with the text of Joel; that is, Peter should bring together the text of Joel regarding Lord and another text, using the title Lord, a text which clearly can be associated with Jesus of Nazareth. Peter uses here what is elsewhere a known Rabbinic practice of interpreting one of God's Words (that of Joel) by another text of God's Word.
>
> To argue successfully that Jesus is Lord and thus to be called on for salvation, Peter draws upon the authoritative Old Testament Ps 110: 'The Lord [YHWH] said to my Lord...'[36]

In Peter's sermon, he is simply citing various Old Testament passages to substantiate the points of his message. The citations from Psalms 110 and 132 support *different* points of his message. Peter cites Psalm 132:11-12 in Acts 2:30 in support of Jesus' resurrection, as a part of the subsection in verses 30-32 proving His Davidic messiahship. In verse 33, Peter introduces another subsection with the particle *oun*, describing Jesus' Melchizedekian ministry, supporting it by referring to Psalm 110:1.[37]

CONCLUSION

A major tenet of many progressive dispensationalists is the belief that Jesus began His Davidic reign at the ascension. This position unnecessarily and unscripturally mingles God's program for Israel with God's program for the church and thus weakens the argument for a pretribulational rapture. If proponents of progressive dispensationalism are correct, so be it. Exegesis should determine doctrine, not *vice versa*. If the Davidic reign has already begun, the pretribulational rapture must stand or fall on other arguments. However, a major argument many progressive dispensationalists give in support of Jesus' present Davidic reign suffers from significant problems. This argument comes from an attempted exegesis of Peter's sermon in Acts 2. A close look at the way Peter carefully crafted his sermon, however, has shown that Peter did not signify that Jesus' Davidic reign began at the ascension. Rather, Peter distinguished between two different roles of Jesus: 1) The Davidic reign, made possible by the resurrection, but which will not begin until the second coming; and 2) the Melchizedekian priestly ministry which began at the ascension and will come to completion at the end of the tribulation period, thus ushering in the Davidic reign.

WHAT WILL THE KINGDOM BE LIKE?	
• Characterized by righteousness (Isa. 60:21). • Characterized by obedience (The obedient Son of God shall reign, Heb. 10:9). • Characterized by holiness (Jerusalem shall be holy, Joel 3:17). • Characterized by the work of the Holy Spirit (Ezek. 36:27). • Characterized by peace (Isa. 11:1-9). • Characterized by joy (Isa. 9:3-4). • Characterized by justice (Isa. 9:7).	• Characterized by comfort (Isa. 40:1-2). • Characterized by healing (Isa. 61:1-2). • A unified language (Zeph. 3:9). • Unified worship (Isa. 66:17-23). • Presence of God [in the Messiah] (Ezek. 37:27-28). • Reign of the King (Dan. 7). • David is co-regent (Isa. 55:3-4).

CHAPTER 13

WHEN GOD *RESTORES* THE KINGDOM TO ISRAEL

Mal Couch

One of the greatest misunderstandings in theology is the belief that the church today is the replacement for the prophesied Old Testament Davidic kingdom that is to be set up in Jerusalem by the Messiah. This false claim has dominated Christendom throughout the ages of the church. The implication is that God is through with the Jews, and argues that the church now fulfills those promises made throughout the Old Testament. This misplaced doctrine is given credence by what is called allegorical interpretation. This interpretative approach is wrongly used with the Old Testament prophecies, making the church the kingdom. A literal kingdom, with the Messiah sitting on the throne in the Holy Land, was promised to the Jews through the ancient Hebrew prophets. Allegorical interpretation is used to reinterpret God's plans for Israel. It is given the label *replacement theology*, i.e., the church today has replaced the Jewish people in the Messianic Plan of God!

WHAT DOES THE WORD *KINGDOM* MEAN IN THE BIBLE?

This chapter is dealing with the issue of the earthly Messianic kingdom promised to the people of Israel. God has a universal and a heavenly kingdom reign as testified by the most powerful monarch of history who said, "I Nebuchadnezzar praise and exalt, and honor the King of heaven, for all His works are true and His way just" (Dan. 4:37). Those who belong to the body of Christ today are called "*a* kingdom of priests to His God and Father" (Rev. 1:6). But these *kingdoms* in no way imply that the church presently is that *Messianic kingdom* of Israel. That kingdom is yet future.

WHERE ARE THE PROMISES FOR THE FUTURE MESSIANIC KINGDOM?

The story begins in Genesis. The Jews through their fathers Abraham, Isaac, and Jacob were promised a huge earthly territory that would be more than simply the confines of what is called the Holy Land. The Bible tells us that a covenant was made with father Abraham. The Lord said: "To your descendants I have given this land, from the river of Egypt (a tributary called *Wadi el Arish*, or possibly the Nile river) as far as the great river, the river Euphrates" (Gen. 15:18). This great expanse of land will be someday the outer boundaries of the Messianic kingdom and today includes most of the Arab lands. Have the Jews ever occupied such a vast land? No.

So therefore this prophecy is yet to be fulfilled!

As the Old Testament unfolds, the Lord through what is called *progressive revelation* expands and elaborates on this promise to the faithful descendants of Abraham. What is *progressive* revelation?

> The interpreter must consider progressive revelation. In many prophecies of Scripture, God did not reveal everything at once concerning a specific truth or doctrine. Over years and even centuries, a doctrine may be progressively expanded upon. … Progressive revelation is especially important in gaining a full understanding of eschatology as the prophetic plan unfolds through the Word of God.[1]

Applying this rule one can see the unfolding plan, beginning with Abraham, into other prophecies that are revealed in the Bible. Through the kingly tribe of Judah, and the line of king David (who comes from the tribe of Judah), a promise is given in which through David's son Solomon, the Lord promises: I "will establish his kingdom. … I will establish the throne of his kingdom forever. … And your house [David] and your kingdom shall endure before Me forever; your throne shall be established forever" (2 Sam. 7:12-16). One cannot escape the *forever, eternal* nature of this promise. It has never been rescinded, annulled, changed in configuration, as some claim, though it has been expanded upon, further explained with many additional details. Also, the issue of the kingdom remains as an important future component and feature for the nation of Israel. In other words these

Jewish promises are indeed Jewish and have to do with a national entity and a territorial restoration. When this kingdom and its blessing come, it will affect all of earth's history for a thousand years!

This promise is *spiritual* in nature and implies that the Jews accept the Lord Jesus as their Savior. However this promise is not to be *spiritualized* or *allegorized* away to mean something else than what the plain words imply. In other words, this kingdom promised is not the present *church age*. The church does not take the place of promises made by the prophets of a coming earthly Messianic reign that will bless Israel first, and then the entire world. In that these promises have not come to pass simply means that they are yet to be fulfilled!

Literal kingdom prophecies are mentioned throughout the Old Testament:

> God's Anointed (the Messiah) is the "King" whom God will install "upon Zion (the hill in Jerusalem), [upon] My holy mountain" (Psa. 2:2, 6). He is the Son of God who will shatter the nations and rule over them (vv. 9, 12). God will establish David's Seed forever and He will build up his throne to all generations (89:4). Jesus is the child who is born of David and Solomon and the son given, who will sit "on the throne of David and over his kingdom, to establish it and to uphold it with justice and righteousness" forever (Isa. 9:7). But more, He is deity: He is the Mighty God, Eternal Father, Prince of Peace (v. 6).

The Spirit of the Lord will rest on this One (11:2) and someday all the nations will come to Him who is like a flag or a signal for the peoples of earth (v. 10). He is Israel's leader and ruler who alone can approach God (Jer. 30:21). He is called the Son [who relates to] mankind and who comes up before God the heavenly Father, the Ancient of Days, in glory (Dan. 7:13). This takes place at the dramatic ascension of Christ when He went up from His disciples into glory (Acts 1:10-11). God the Father then bestowed upon Him "dominion, glory and a kingdom, that all the peoples, nations, and men of every language might serve Him. His dominion is an everlasting dominion which will not pass away; and His kingdom is one which will not be destroyed" (v. 14).

WHAT DOES A WORLDWIDE TRIBULATION HAVE TO DO WITH THE KINGDOM?

Anyone who watches current events carefully knows the world is on the brink of a terrible calamity. The Middle East is a near fire storm with no end in sight for peace. The whole world is slowly being dragged into a conflagration like no other. Those who deny the *obvious* about such world affairs are denying what seems so clear, even to those who are spiritually lost and never study what the Bible says about the final days of world history!

The Lord Jesus made a prediction that a terrible tribulation would come in which the Jews would be the central target and would "be hated by all nations on account of My name" (Matt. 24:9). The events that transpire are called the "birth pangs" that fall on the Jewish people (v. 8). But the fact that the Messiah's kingdom is coming will be proclaimed during that terrible time of tribulation to the whole earth, just before "the end comes." Jesus stated it this way: "And this gospel of the kingdom shall be preached in the whole world for a witness to all the nations, and then the end shall come" (v. 14). Jesus, "the Son of Man" (Dan. 7:13) then said, speaking of Himself, that He will come on the clouds of the sky "with power and great glory" (Matt. 24:30). The angels will accompany Him in His radiant appearance and "He will sit on His glorious throne" (25:31). As earth's righteous king He will summon His righteous servants, those who trust in Him for salvation, to "inherit the kingdom prepared for you from the foundation of the world" (v. 34). Those words tell us that the Messianic kingdom as the final chapter of world history was planned in ages past to take place.

THE CURRENT MIDDLE EAST CONFLICT: WHAT DO THE ARABS SAY ABOUT A FUTURE JEWISH KINGDOM?

The Middle East is aflame with the militancy of the Arabic peoples who want to occupy the Holy Land. The Arab mentality states that if Islam has ever occupied a land, a geographic territory, then it forever belongs to Allah! Therefore the Jews can have no claim to *Eratz Israel (the land of Israel).* Though the Jews are returning to the land in unbelief, God will someday open their eyes, they will repent, and Jesus the Messiah will come to establish His 1000 year kingdom reign. Then the people of Israel "will look on [Him] whom they have pierced" (Zech.12:10). Many of the Arab leaders know about such prophecies and will risk the shedding of blood to prevent the arrival of Israel's Messiah and the establishment of a Jewish kingdom.

The concept of a future Jewish Messianic conflict goes back to God's promises to Abraham in Genesis 12-17. The Arabic peoples claim a right to the Holy Land through Abraham's son Ishmael, but the covenant with Abraham made clear that the Lord's promises about the land would come through Abraham's son Isaac and then to his son Jacob, and his twelve sons. Psalm 105:8-11 states:

> *[God] has remembered His covenant forever, the word which He commanded to a thousand generations, the covenant which He made with Abraham, and His oath to Isaac. Then He confirmed it to Jacob for a statute, to Israel as an everlasting covenant, saying, "To you I will give the land of Canaan as the portion of your inheritance."*

"Whether or not Palestinian-Arabs are related to Abraham, who was led of the Lord to Canaan from ~~the~~ Babylon, they claim that they are descendants of the original inhabitants of Canaan—the Canaanites—as well as other ancient peoples who occupied the land *before* the arrival of the Israelites."[2]

DID NOT THE JEWS FORFEIT THE KINGDOM WHEN THEY REJECTED CHRIST?

Though God scattered the Jewish people for their rejection of their king and Savior, the Lord Jesus Christ, the kingdom promises remain. The apostle makes it clear that a "remnant … will be saved" (Rom. 9:27), and "'The Deliverer [the Messiah] will come forth from Zion, He will remove ungodliness from Jacob [the Jewish people]. And this is My covenant with them, when I take away their sins'" (11:26-27). Since the giving of the Abrahamic covenant in Genesis 12 the Jews have been identified as God's earthly chosen people who are still beloved by Him for the sake of the promises made to their ancient fathers, Abraham, Isaac, and Jacob (v. 28).

The prophetic case is made clear: God will someday open the eyes of the Jewish people and they will return to Him and accept the Lord Jesus as their Savior. However they must go through a terrible tribulation period that will engulf the entire world for seven years. Few will be spared both of the Gentiles and the Jews. The vortex of the destruction of the tribulation will be the Middle East where the fuel for such a conflagration is now being stored and waiting for the moment of the outpouring of God's wrath on a sinful and rebellious world (Rev. 6-19).

About the Jews being cast off forever with no kingdom promises, the apostle Paul writes "May it never be!" (v.1). He adds: "God has not rejected His people whom He foreknew [in an intimate relational way]" (v. 2). That would be derogatory to His character as a Sovereign who has made unconditional promises of faithfulness to the Jewish nation. Israel is still "His people"; "theirs" is yet the promises; their rejection is only temporary—until the promises of Israel's future kingdom come to pass. Today God is working to save the Gentiles who believe in Christ. The visible unity of the saved Gentiles is the church, though in many places thousands of Jews also now know Jesus as their Savior! But the fact that we are now in the dispensation of the church does not make null and void the kingdom promises made in the Old Testament. Those promises have never been rescinded.

> But the inclusion of Gentile believers [presently in the church] does not affect the purpose of God with *the nation [of Israel],* nor does the Church displace Israel in the plan of God in relation to the other nations. [God's purposes] are reserved for restored and converted Israel as a nation to bring *the nations* to a knowledge of their glorious Messiah and King, and bring [kingdom] *universal* blessing to the world.[3]

DO SOME *SPIRITUALIZE* THE KINGDOM AND MAKE IT THE CHURCH?

Allegorical interpretation was a full-grown child of the Rationalist movement, though its origins go further back to the pagan teachings of Plato. The church father Origen was a Platonist who converted the whole Bible, the Old and New Testaments alike, into a series of clumsy, varying, and incredible enigmas. "Allegory helped [Origen] to get rid of [the kingdom idea] and [what he called] superstitious literalism."[4]

To spiritualize biblical prophecy is "to take in a spiritual sense,—opposed to literalize." To spiritual Israel, or kingdom, is to replace its obvious, clear meaning, and the meaning intended by the author. Walvoord writes:

> In other words, if Israel should mean something else than Israel, e.g., the church in the New Testament composed largely of Gentiles, this would be spiritualization.[5]

And such *spiritualization* is not biblical, nor is it intellectually honest!

WHAT IS AMILLENNIALISM?

It is the view of Bible prophecy that generally says the church is the kingdom, or that the church has replaced the Jewish hope of a literally earthly kingdom with the Messiah sitting on the throne of David in Jerusalem. To the amillennialist, the *higher* and more *spiritual* view repudiates a physical earthly reign of Christ and substitutes this with a certain kind of spiritual rule. The problem is that all the descriptions in both the Old and New Testaments of the kingdom paint the clear picture of an historical and earthly rule that would dominate the last days of world history as we know it. The *a* before *millennium* is the Greek negative. *A*-millennium then means "no millennium" or earthly "kingdom" for Israel. In fact many amillennialists believe God is through with the Jewish people for their rejection of Christ. Thus the church replaces the idea of a literal kingdom. Amillennialists are usually in the Reformed camp and covenant theological.

> Reformed theologians who follow the amillennial interpretation usually minimize and spiritualize the time of tribulation preceding the second advent, particularly in such passages as Revelation 6-19. Amillenarians often find the tribulation being fulfilled in contemporary events, and interpret Revelation 6-19 as history. While interpreting the second advent literally, they to some extent spiritualize the tribulation. Likewise there is difference in viewpoint on the significance of the second advent itself. The amillenarian holds that it is the event beginning the eternal state while the premillenarian holds

it begins the millennial kingdom on earth.[6]

WHAT IS PRETERISM? HOW DOES IT RELATE TO THE KINGDOM?

A reconstructionist preterist, Kenneth Gentry, describes his view this way:

> The term "preterism" is based on the Latin *preter,* which means "past." Preterism refers to that understanding of certain eschatological passages which holds that *they have already come to fulfillment.*
>
> The preterist approach teaches, for instance, that many of the prophecies of Revelation and the first portion of the Olivet Discourse have already been fulfilled. Matthew 24:1-34 (and parallels) in the Olivet Discourse was fulfilled in the events surrounding the fall of Jerusalem in A.D. 70. In Revelation, most of the prophecies before Revelation 20 find fulfillment in the fall of Jerusalem (A.D. 70).[7]

Preterist Gary DeMar adds,

> A preterist is someone who believes that certain prophecies have been fulfilled, that is, their fulfillment is in the *past.*[8]

While it would not be possible to fully confirm, it seems as if preterists will do anything to deny a distinct literal seven-year tribulation that will engulf the Middle East and the world. They also deny any importance to the fact that the Jews are back in the Holy Land and have reestablished their national entity, and have restored their ancient language of Hebrew. The only mention of the Jews among both the preterists and the amillennialists is that God is through with the Jews, and they point out that more than likely most of the Jewish people will probably not ever trust in Christ as their Savior. Many preterists and amillennialists usually set up a straw man and argue that dispensationalists, and some premillennialists, believe the Jews can be restored and yet do not have to trust in the Lord Jesus. This is in no way what those who are looking for the coming reign of Christ would argue! When the kingdom arrives the Jews will see the Messiah "whom they have pierced; and they will weep bitterly over Him, like the bitter weeping over a first-born" (Zech. 12:10b).

It would seem that many adopt amillennialism or preterism as a reaction against dispensationalists. With a certain scurrilous attitude R. C. Sproul writes:

> The sickness that is epidemic in the evangelical church is the disease of dispensationalism, and more particularly dispensational eschatology [prophecy]. These doctrines not only twist and distort the Scripture but bring the church to near paralysis. The harder we work to build Christ's kingdom, the more we delay it.
>
> Thankfully, God in his mercy has done a great work in waking up many people to their condition. The rapid spread of the doctrine of preterism has been a welcome tonic.[9]

Extreme preterists say the second coming of Christ and the establishment of His kingdom has already occurred at the time of the destruction of the second temple and the city of Jerusalem in 70 A.D.! In evaluating this strange view Ice writes:

> This means there will never be a future second coming, for it has already occurred in A.D. 70. Further, there will be no bodily resurrection of believers, which is said to have occurred in A.D. 70 in conjunction with the second coming. Full preterists believe that we now have been spiritually resurrected and will live forever with spiritual bodies when we die.[10]

WHY IS THERE A DENIAL OF A LITERAL REIGN OF CHRIST BY PRETERISTS?

Some have argued that many interpreters have departed from exegesis of the biblical passages and are arguing from philosophical reasoning rather than textual reasoning. Hermeneutics and interpretation are no longer practiced as a science of understanding the message of Scripture. Exegesis is not linear or chronological in nature but circular in which the interpreter puts his own thoughts and his own agenda into the mix of what a passage from the Bible means. There is confusion with ontology with epistemology. The grammatical-historical approach to interpretation has been the standard for interpreting the Word of God, but now a subjective element and a cultural element has been added as a "weight" and an impediment for the interpreter. The interpreter no longer thinks "biblical" but cultural or with a theological bias in mind.

Ice continues:

> I believe the spirit of our postmodern times, shaped by a dominant mysticism, has led some individuals to become more open to a less literal hermeneutic. This, in turn, has led some exegetical minds to see the supposed shadow of the biblical text instead of the letter, or what is actually written. Today's hermeneutical atmosphere is such that interpretative schemes such as preterism are made to seem feasible, when in the past they were dismissed as too far-fetched. The zeitgeist of our day nudges the mind toward the allegorical and not the literal, the shadow instead of the clear, and the mystical rather than the physical.[11]

There is another reason for a movement to preterism. The philosophical and critical religious climate has brought about doubt and skepticism in the area of hermeneutics. R. C. Sproul, and others who have adopted preterism, admit they were influenced by the doubt and biblical criticism of the likes of Albert Schweitzer, and of the atheist and communist British philosopher Bertrand Russell. These men challenged the words of Christ and assumed that when He said "the kingdom of God is near" (Luke 21:31) that the Lord, only being human, was mistaken about the timing of its arrival. Therefore such men as these re-wrote what Christ was referring to.

To counter the liberal attack, the church must have a wake-up call, repudiate future prophecy, and re-introduce preterism as an interpretative scheme. Sproul, who claims to be a partial preterist, shows how such liberal skepticism molded his views about futurist eschatology. He writes,

> In seminary I was exposed daily to critical theories espoused by my professors regarding the Scripture. What

> stands out in my memory of those days is the heavy emphasis on biblical texts regarding the return of Christ, which were constantly cited as examples of errors in the New Testament and proof that the text had been edited to accommodate the crisis in the early church caused by the so-called parousia-delay of Jesus. In a word, much of the criticism leveled against the trustworthiness of Scripture was linked to questions regarding biblical eschatology.[12]

In other words, Sproul and other preterists like him, use cultural criticisms to determine how to interpret the Word of God! The Scriptures are inspired by the Holy Spirit and stand reliable within themselves. Biblical hermeneutics would not allow such cultural imposition into how we read our Bible.

WHAT DOES JEWISH ORTHODOXY TEACH ABOUT THE *KINGDOM*?

While many of the rabbis fell into mystical teaching, the main stream of orthodoxy took the Old Testament promises with normal and literal meaning. The orthodox believe in the death of the Messiah for the sins of the world, a seven year tribulation, the coming of the Messiah to reign in His kingdom for 1,000 years. They believe in many things about the Messiah and His Davidic kingdom, except the fact that the Lord Jesus is indeed that One!

In the ancient writings of the rabbis can be found the following:

- All will come and fall upon their faces before the Messiah and say: "Let us be servants to You" (*Pesiqta Rabbati, 162a-b).*
- Happy the hour the Messiah was created! Happy the womb from which he issued! Happy the generation whose eyes see Him (*Pesiqta Rabbati, 36)!*
- The Messiah is the stone that smote the image became a great mountain and filled the earth (Dan. 2:35). (*Numbers Rabbi 13:14)*
- All the kings of the earth will prostrate themselves before the Messiah, and all the nations will serve Him (Psa. 72:11). (*Numbers Rabbi 13:14)*

- A Star [the Messiah] shall rise for you [Israel] from Jacob in peace, And no sin shall be found in Him, The scepter of My kingdom will shine forth, He will judge and save all that call upon the Lord (*Testament of Judah 24).*

- The Lord shall raise up a new priest, His Star shall arise in heaven as the Star of a King, He shall be magnified in the world, There shall be peace in all the earth, The heavens shall exult in His days, The glory of the Most High shall pour forth over Him, None shall succeed Him for all generations [He is eternal], By His priesthood the nations shall increase, The just shall rest in Him, He will give the saints the Tree of Life to eat, He will bind up Satan (*Testament of Levi, 18).*

- Once the kingdom of heaven is established over the earth the Messiah's activity will come to an end, and He will then sit as the Son of Man on David's throne in Jerusalem as a visible representative of God in the world of man (*The Messiah Text, 190).*

- The Holy One will reestablish the Sanctuary, and the Shekinah shall return, and He will rebuild the city of Jerusalem, and He will raise her from the dust of the ground, and the exiles of Israel will gather to her (*Zohar 1:134a).*

- Israel will return with the Messiah ... and they will meet together with all of the House of David which will be left from the destruction [the tribulation]. And the Messiah will sit there *(T'fillat Rabbi Shim'on ben Yohai, BhM. 4:124-26).*

- [In the tribulation] they will call [the Antichrist] Armilus. And he will go to Edom [Rome] and say to them: "I am your Messiah, I am your god!" And he will mislead them and they will instantly believe in him, and make him their king. ... And Messiah ben David and Elijah will be revealed, and both will go to Israel who are in the desert [the world]. And Elijah will tell them: "This is the Messiah!" And he will revive their hearts and strengthen their hands. ... And all Israel will know the sound of the shofar and will hear that He has redeemed Israel. (*T'fllat Rabbi Shim'on ben Yohai, BhM. 4:124-26*).[13]

Finally summing up, Jewish historical scholars Avi-Yonah and Baras note:

> In the whole range of literature of Israel, there is no more exalted or nobler picture of the Messiah than the description in the Psalms of Solomon. The Messiah is righteous, holy, and "free of sin," … By the power of the Spirit, He expels the nations from Jerusalem and establishes a great kingdom in Zion that serves as the center of the world. The nations serve the God of Israel and the King Messiah … The ingathering of the exiles (the reunion of the tribes of Israel) is a precondition of the coming of the days of the Messiah. Thus there is a political, national, and territorial aspect to the kingdom of the Messiah. The spiritual aspect, however, remains central.[14]

WHAT COVENANTS ARE FULFILLED IN THE KINGDOM?

The Abrahamic Covenant. The promises in this covenant (first given in Genesis 12:1-3) concerning the land and the seed are fulfilled in the millennial kingdom (Isa. 10:21-22; 19:25). Israel's perpetuity, the nation's place in the land, and their inheritance of blessings are directly related to the prophetic fulfillment of this covenant.

The Davidic Covenant. The promises found in this covenant have to do with the Messiah coming forth from David and someday reigning as the king, reigning on His throne, and restoring the royal house, in the kingdom period (Isa. 11:1-2; 55:3, 11; Jer. 23:5-8; 33:20-26; Ezek. 34:23-25; 37:23-24. Israel's kingdom with David's Son reigning as king is all related to the Davidic covenant.

The Land Covenant. The land promises will be fulfilled in the millennial kingdom (Isa. 11:11-12; 65:9; Ezek. 16:60-63; 36:28-29; 39:28). It is at this time that the Lord Jesus will reign with His full glory and splendor. The nations will come up year by year and worship Him. The prophet Micah paints a graphic picture of how a blissful peace will fall upon the whole earth when the Messiah reigns:

> *And it will come about in the last days that the mountain of the house of the Lord will be established as the chief mountains. It will be raised above the hills, and the peoples will*

stream to it.
And many nations will come and say, "Come and let us go up to the mountain of the Lord and to the house of the God of Jacob, that He may teach us about His ways and that we may walk in His paths."

For from Zion will go forth the law, even the word of the Lord from Jerusalem. And He will judge between many peoples and render decisions for mighty distant nations.
Then they will hammer their swords into plowshares and their spears into pruning hooks; nation will not lift up sword against nation, and never again will they train for war. …
And the Lord will reign [over His people] in Mount Zion from now on and forever (Micah 4)!

Amos also heralds the glories of the coming kingdom when He speaks about the Davidic covenant and its fulfillment. The prophet writes the words of the Lord:

In that day I will raise up the fallen booth of David, and wall up its breaches; I will also raise up its ruins, and rebuild it as in the days of old. …
Also I will restore the captivity of My people Israel, and they will rebuild the ruined cities and live in them.
I will plant [My people] on their land, and they will not again be rooted out from their land which I have given them, says the Lord your God (Amos 9:11-15).

WHAT WILL BRING GLORY TO THE MILLENNIAL KINGDOM?

The kingdom will bring about the complete manifestation of the glory of Jesus Christ. There is a glory concerning His humanity, and a glory in relation to His sovereign dominion over the earth and all of the heavens. There will be a glory concerning His peaceful government in which He, as the Son of David, is given complete power and authority to rule (Isa. 9:6; Psa. 45:4; Isa. 11:4; Psa. 72:4). Then there will be glory in regard to the blessing that will come upon the Holy Land, and even over the entire earth.

In the kingdom the many names of Christ will amplify His person, His glory, and His authority. It is impossible to escape the many names that reflect His deity. His names may be summed up:

Immanuel (God with us) (Isa. 7:14).
The Branch of Jehovah (Isa. 4:2).
Branch of David (Isa. 11:1).
Seed of David (Rom. 1:3).
Jehovah's Servant, the Branch (Zech. 3:8).
Son of Man (Dan. 7:13).
King (Psa. 2).
Son of God (Psa. 2).
Judge (Isa. 11:3-4).
Lawgiver (Isa. 33:22).
Messiah the Prince (Dan. 9:25-26).
Redeemer (Isa. 59:20).
Sun of Righteousness (Mal. 4:2).
The Wall Breaker (Mal. 2:13).
The Shepherd (Isa. 40:10-11).
The Stone (Isa. 28:16; Zech. 3:9).
The Prophet (Deut. 18:15, 18).

IS THE KINGDOM SIMPLY *MATERIAL* OR IS IT ALSO *SPIRITUAL* IN NATURE?

Those who do not believe that all of the descriptions of the earthly kingdom listed in Scripture show an earthly, historical reign of the Messiah, believe the kingdom is only "spiritual" in nature, and in fact is now *allegorically* fulfilled in the church age! "The amillennialist extols his view of the kingdom as a highly 'spiritual' view and minimizes the premillennial concept because it demands the literal and material fulfillment of the earthly blessings."[15] The amillennialist argues the kingdom is a spiritual kingdom, a "spiritualized" kingdom, and a "moral" reign, and he wrongly argues a premillennialist sees it as a "carnal" or "material" only. Such charges fail to differentiate between the issue of the "spiritualizing" of the kingdom into something that it is not, and seeing the kingdom as the spiritual earthly reign of Jesus, the Son of God! However premillennialists teach correctly from Scripture that: "Although emphasizing the multitude of material blessings offered in the millennium, the theocratic kingdom is essentially a spiritual kingdom even though it exists in the realm of the earth."[16] Such an argument is not *made up* by premillennialists, it comes from the normal and literal interpretation of the Word of God!

In the kingdom the nation of Israel will be changed and converted and with a spontaneous response will sound forth an inward righteousness and will praise Jehovah their God. They will no more cry a false legalism of days past (cf. Matt. 5:20). Like the earth bringing forth the flower, "the Lord God will cause righteousness and praise to spring forth before all nations" (Isa. 61:11) so that the Jewish nation and its people will be called trees of righteousness and the planting of the Lord. He alone will be glorified (61:3).

FINALLY: IS IT IMPORTANT TO LOOK FOR THE COMING OF THE MESSIANIC KINGDOM?

If our biblical hermeneutics and interpretation is consistent from Genesis to Revelation, the doctrine of the millennial earthly reign of Christ becomes obvious and constitutes a large part of what the Bible teaches. Therefore to *not* believe in the future millennial kingdom is to outright deny great and numerous passages of the Word of God. It also cuts in half what the Scriptures teach about Jesus Christ. The Lord came the first time to die, and He will come the second time to reign!

At some point along the line, it would seem that such scriptural denial and even clear destruction of intended passages, is virtually heretical. It is not good enough to argue, with poor and limp contextual reasoning, that (1) Jesus reigns as "king" in your heart, or (2) that the church has replaced the literal future kingdom, or (3) that all the verses in the Old Testament were only intended to teach some kind of "spiritualized" rule. Too often those in the Reformed camp only fall back on what the Reformers taught. Unfortunately the Reformers simply mouthed the same eschatological views of the Roman Catholic Church. "The Church *is* the kingdom!"

One would hope and expect better of present-day, sincere teachers of the Word of God. One would wish that their ability to properly interpret Scripture would go beyond the limited abilities and views of the Reformation greats! It is not difficult to understand and even sympathize with the Reformation period. The life and death wars of that period were being fought over soteriology and ecclesiology. But Reformed eschatology is stuck in a time warp in which, if Calvin did not teach it, it must not be true!

In summary from my book *An Introduction to Classical Evangelical Hermeneutics*:

> During Jesus' triumphal entry into Jerusalem, the crowds shouted out Psalm 118:26: "Hosanna! Blessed is He who comes in the name of the Lord! (Mark 11:9). They then added, "Blessed is the coming kingdom of our father David; Hosanna in the highest!" (v.10). Matthew says that the mob in their cheering also called Jesus the Son of David (21:9, 15). Messianic descriptives are also used abundantly in the kingdom parables in Matthew 13. Jesus is called the Son of Man (v. 37), who sows good seed, meaning "the sons of the kingdom" (v. 38). The kingdom belongs to this Son of Man (v. 41), and the righteous will shine as the sun in the "kingdom of the Father" (v. 43). Jesus also called the kingdom "My Father's kingdom" (26:29).
>
> Following Christ's resurrection, He spent forty days "speaking of the things concerning the kingdom of God" (Acts 1:3). The disciples must have been excited about that promised coming reign, because they asked Him, "Lord, is it at this time You are restoring the kingdom to Israel?" (v. 6). They were not seeking a new definition for an explanation about that kingdom. Christ must have confirmed but expanded on information about that kingdom, much of which the disciples already knew. The doctrinal issue about the kingdom must surely have already been settled, because they ask only about the timetable: "Is it at this time You are restoring. …?" Notice, this kingdom is called the "kingdom of Israel." Early on in Jesus' ministry, Nathanael says to Him, "You are the Son of God [a reference to Psalm 2]; You are the King of Israel" (John 1:49-50). These titles are repeated by the crowds at the triumphal entry into Jerusalem: "Hosanna!

Blessed is He who comes in the name of the Lord, even the King of Israel" (12:13).

And when Christ was crucified, Pilate, responding to the mood of some of the Jewish mob, had "King of the Jews" placed as an inscription over the cross (Mark 15:25). A king certainly suggests a kingdom; some mocked Jesus on the cross and cried out, "Let this Christ, the King of Israel, now come down from the cross, so that we may see and believe!" (v. 32). … The only point of reference the Jews would have known is the messianic kingdom and the coming rule of peace that would last for one thousand years. Jesus presented Himself as the king who fulfilled the kingship role for that kingdom. He told neither His disciples nor the crowds that they were mistaken in their perceptions.[17]

PART THREE

GOD'S PRESENT AND FUTURE PROGRAM FOR THE CHURCH

IS THE CHURCH THE "KINGDOM" IN MATTHEW 13?

In Matthew 13:31 the sower is the Son of Man, Jesus, and the seed is the "Word," as the Christian society, the Church. … This parable sets forth the working of the Church of Christ in the world. … The parable is about the kingdom of heaven, i.e., the new order of things which Christ established, describing the Church. Matthew 13:39 deals with the many problems in the history and policy of the Church of Christ.

--John Ellicott *Commentary on the Whole Bible*

The parables of Matthew 13 cannot refer to the coming church age. If they do, then basic hermeneutics would be terribly torn and violated, and the meaning of the text would lose all shape and substance. If the people and the disciples were still hearing with their ears "the kingdom of heaven" and "the kingdom of God," what message were they receiving? They would have heard "Messianic Kingdom" and not Church. Was Jesus just fooling them? Did He sneak in a new message about this new thing, the church, when they did not notice? Is the church what John the Baptist and Christ were proclaiming all along? And were the crowds simply tricked into believing that both were still speaking of the prophesied messianic Davidic Kingdom?

--Mal Couch *Classical Evangelical Hermeneutics*

CHAPTER 14

THE KINGDOM IN MATTHEW 13

Stanley Toussaint

Without a doubt Matthew 13 is a pivotal chapter in the development of the first Gospel in our New Testament. What makes that chapter so critical is the Lord's teaching about the kingdom. It is almost universally agreed the Lord is discussing the present age and its culmination in Matthew 13. Because of this, one's view of the kingdom in this dispensation depends on one's understanding of the parables of the kingdom in Matthew 13. Is Christ telling His disciples the kingdom of heaven will be in some form of existence between His two advents? Is it possible the Lord Jesus is informing His followers about something else than a kingdom in this age? The question before us is, what is the Lord saying about God's kingdom in this age in Matthew 13?

A couple of assumptions are being made in the presentation of this paper. First, the verbal, plenary inspiration of the original manuscripts of the Bible is taken for granted. Along with this, only evangelical and conservative interpretations of the Scriptures will be considered. In other words, critical viewpoints will not be discussed.

A second assumption is the interchangeable use of the terms "kingdom of heaven" and "kingdom of God." It is taken for granted they are practically synonymous. This becomes important because many use Matthew 13 to show unbelievers (tares) are in the kingdom of heaven whereas John 3 says only the saved are in the kingdom of God. Those who say this fail to recognize the Lord's statement in Matthew 18:3 that unless one is converted and becomes like a child he cannot enter the kingdom of heaven. The requirements for entrance into the kingdom of heaven are just as strict as those for entering the kingdom of God. It will be seen even later in this paper that the tares are not in the kingdom of heaven.

RELEVANT BACKGROUND MATERIALS

THE ANNOUNCEMENT OF THE NEARNESS OF THE KINGDOM

This proclamation is made by John the Baptist in 3:2, by the Lord in 4:17, and the disciples in 10:7. In all three cases precisely the same words are used: The kingdom of heaven has drawn near. Contrary to some theologians the kingdom was not said to be here (in the person of Jesus Christ and His power as they claim) but it was in a state of nearness. The kingdom had not yet come.

Significantly, none of those who preached the nearness of the kingdom ever explain it or clarify the meaning of the term. This is very important because all agree the Jews were anticipating the coming of the golden age predicted in the Old Testament. If John or the Lord Jesus or even the disciples had a different interpretation of the term "kingdom," they certainly would have, or at least should have, explained it. No such clarification is found anywhere in the Gospels or Acts.

What is especially significant is John the Baptist's warning about the nearness of the judgment preceding the coming of the kingdom. The axe was already lying at the root of the trees (Matt. 3:10) and God's winnowing fork was already in His hand (Matt. 3:12). Israel knew from the many Old Testament warnings that judgment came before the kingdom (As an illustration see Mal. 3:13; 4:6). John's expectancy of the nearness of this judgment will become important in the interpretation of the parable of the wheat and tares.

In view of the Old Testament promises, the people of Israel's expectations, and the preaching of the kingdom's nearness with no clarifying statements, it is quite clear the term "kingdom" is a noun describing the literal messianic reign of Christ on earth.

ISRAEL'S REJECTION OF JESUS AS MESSIAH

Fairly early in the Lord's ministry His rejection began to be seen. It is broadly hinted at in the Lord's statement in Matthew 8:11-12 in connection with the faith of a Gentile centurion,

> *And I say to you that many shall come from east and west and recline at the table with Abraham, and Isaac and Jacob in the kingdom of heaven; but the sons of the kingdom will be cast out into the outer darkness; in that place there will be weeping and gnashing of teeth.*

By Matthew 11 what is implied in 8:11-12 is clearly stated. In fact, in 11:12 Christ stated the kingdom of heaven had suffered violence ever since it was first announced as being near by John the Baptist. He further stated that violent men seize it. The verb that is used here was used of robbers seizing objects or soldiers grabbing loot and booty. Here it must mean they seize it in the sense of robbing it and keeping it from coming. They were opposing the kingdom. This helps to explain why Jesus in the following verses shows how Israel could not be pleased whether by John or by Himself (cf. 11:16-19). They were like spoiled children.

Matthew 11 goes on to record the Lord's pronouncement of judgment on Israel. Most of His miracles were performed near the Sea of Galilee (11:20). Yet these people refused to repent. Therefore, they were destined for a future judgment worse than Tyre, Sidon and even Sodom (11:22, 24).

Even Christ's gracious invitation to come to Him in the following paragraph (11:25-30) implies the spurning of Him and His message. His followers were to leave the heavy yoke placed upon them by the religious authorities and find rest in Him.

Perhaps the clearest indication of Israel rejecting Jesus as Messiah is seen in their accusing Him of casting out demons by satanic power. The Lord responds by saying they have blasphemed the Holy Spirit and thereby committed the unpardonable sin (Matt. 12:24-32).

The chapter goes on to pronounce judgment on that generation because of their eagerness to see miracles without catching on to the spiritual significance of who Jesus is. In fact the Ninevites and the Queen of the South will stand in judgment against that generation. It was like a person from whom a demon had been cast out only to have the demon return with seven others. (Evidently this describes the revival that had taken place under John and the subsequent rejection of the Lord Jesus).

The context of Matthew 13 is the rejection of Jesus by Israel, particularly by the religious authorities.

THE LORD'S RESPONSE

Matthew 13 is the Lord's response to the opposition. Matthew 13:1 begins "On that day," that is, the day of rejection. His response is in the form of a series of parables given to instruct His disciples about His kingdom and the kingdom program.

Matthew 13 must be approached with some understanding of these three factors—the announcement of the nearness of the kingdom, the rejection by Israel of Jesus as Messiah, and the Lord's recognition of Israel's refusal to accept Him as their Messiah.

THE ARRANGEMENT OF MATTHEW 13

Matthew is famous for the careful arrangement of his Gospel. For instance, in recording the Lord's genealogy he divides the names into three groups of fourteen each; in Matthew 5 the discussion of six Old Testament laws is broken into two groups of three by the adverb again (v. 33); and the nine miracles of chapters 8 and 9 are separated into three's by discussions on discipleship (8:18-22; 9:9-17). One of the clearest illustrations of Matthew's skill in arrangement is his use of the clause, "And it came to pass when Jesus had finished . . ." (cf. 7:28; 11:1; 13:53; 19:1; 26:1). Each time it is used it comes at the end of a discourse implying the words of the Lord are the climax of each section. This means the narrative materials are used by Matthew to serve as a backdrop for the discourses. To Matthew the discourses are the most important element although the works of Christ are crucial to the account.

Matthew 13 is another illustration of material that is very carefully arranged into sections. This clearly has significance not only for meaning but it also makes it easier to remember the contents.

The first division is seen in the clauses "Jesus went out of the house" (13:1) and "[He] went into the house" (13:36). The four parables spoken outside of the house are addressed to the general public (cf. v. 36); the four given in the house were only for the disciples. It seems only the disciples were given the explanations of some of the parables; the multitudes were given no interpretations of any.

It must be observed that although eight parables are presented, only six of them begin with the clause, "The kingdom of heaven is like" or some similar statement (cf. 13:24, 31, 33, 44, 45, 47). The first and last parables have no such introduction. This has some significance. The beginning parable is the story of the sower and the soils and is not a kingdom parable. It is given in the context of explaining why the Lord spoke in parables. All the soils fail to produce fruit except the good soil. The one distinguishing feature of this soil is it represents those who hear and "understand" (v. 23). All heard the word but not all understood; therefore further truth was hidden from them (vv. 11-17), but it was given to the disciples by way of the parables. This is the fruit that is born: more understanding. The first parable then is not a parable of the kingdom, but serves as an introduction to the next seven parables. This helps to explain why the next parable is not given until verse 24. All that precedes is an introduction to what follows.

The last parable is the story of the head of the house who dispenses new and old things from his treasury. This represents the disciples who were to wed old truths found in the Old Testament with the new truths given by Christ in His teachings, especially in the parables of Matthew 13. In a word, it is a concluding parable in which the Lord makes an application to the disciples to teach what they have learned. The first and the last parables are practical in nature. The parable of the sower helps to explain why the Lord speaks in parables and the parable of the householder is a practical application.

This means only the six interior parables give instruction and information about the kingdom in this age. These six become the basis for the discussion that follows.

SOME APPROACHES TO MATTHEW 13:

THE COVENANT/REFORMED/AMILLENNIAL VIEW

These fellow believers teach the kingdom that was announced in Matthew 3, 4, and 10 was a spiritual kingdom. It had arrived in the person and ministry of Jesus. In Matthew 13 Christ simply confirms the spiritual nature of its being. Therefore the kingdom is now and will exist in eternity. In this sense it is "already … not yet."

The problem with this approach begins with their failure to properly understand the meaning of the kingdom as preached by John, the Lord and the disciples. (As was stated earlier it was clearly an earthly, eternal kingdom.)

THE CLASSIC DISPENSATIONAL VIEW AS REPRESENTED BY SCOFIELD

This view, which represents the majority of dispensationalists, holds to a literal earthly kingdom being proclaimed as near by John, the Lord and the disciples. In the face of opposition and because of Israel's rejection, the Lord Jesus in Matthew 13 introduces a new form of the kingdom which is in existence during the church age and the tribulation. This is described as "the kingdom in mystery form."

The primary evidence used to support this interpretation is 13:11, "To you it has been granted to know the mysteries of the kingdom of heaven…" The term "mystery" refers to something previously unrevealed but now revealed. Therefore, there is in existence today a previously unknown form of the kingdom. When Christ returns at the end of the Tribulation He will establish His kingdom on this earth.

It is also claimed the kingdom exists today because 13:41 says the Lord's angel will gather the wicked "out of His kingdom" at the end of the age. Therefore the kingdom must be in existence throughout this dispensation.

The largest problem with this interpretation is the expression "the kingdom in mystery form." 13:11 does not say this. It much more probably means and refers to new truths about the kingdom. This will be discussed more fully later in this paper.

Matthew 13:41 refers to the end of the age when the Lord returns to set up His kingdom. The judgment marks the beginning of His reign (cf. Luke 19:27; Ezek. 20:33-38). This is why the wicked will be gathered out from the Lord's kingdom (cf. Matt. 24:37-41).

A large problem is the change that is given to the expression "kingdom of heaven." If it describes the earthly kingdom in the preceding chapters, how can the meaning be changed in chapter 13? This is a dangerous hermeneutic. What is to keep a person from saying the spiritual form of the kingdom was what the Lord was describing from the beginning and in Matthew 13 He clarifies this point? Or what will prevent one from saying Israel rejected Christ so it has no future kingdom and the only kingdom according to the Gospels is a spiritual one?

THE VIEWPOINT OF PROGRESSIVE DISPENSATIONALISM

A key element to this approach is the "already … not yet" view of the kingdom. It is their position the kingdom arrived with John's pronouncement of its nearness. The Lord Jesus is now sitting on the throne of David. Therefore the kingdom has "already" come. However, the millennial kingdom will come in the future after the Great Tribulation. Thus the kingdom has come but not yet in its final form of the millennium and eternity.

In their approach to Matthew 13 they say they are doing nothing more than building on the same structure that was erected by classic dispensationalism. They claim the present mystery form of the kingdom taught by the latter makes room for their view of the kingdom as being present now. Of course classic dispensationalists would argue the mystery form is a truly different form of the kingdom, whereas progressive dispensationalists say the present form of the kingdom is a prelude to the Davidic kingdom predicted in the Old Testament.

The problem with this view is the belief the promised kingdom arrived with the Lord's ministry. It was not present then, not even in the Lord's powerful miracles. Matthew 12:28, which states, "But if I cast out demons by the Spirit of God, then the kingdom of God has come upon you," is used to support the presence of the kingdom. First, if the kingdom had come, why were the disciples instructed to pray for the coming of the kingdom (6:10)? Furthermore the verb that is used here may be used in the sense of something impending as in 1 Thessalonians 2:16, "hindering us from speaking to the Gentiles so that they may be saved: with the result that they always fill up the measure of their sins. But wrath has come upon them to the utmost." God's wrath will come upon them. The fact of the matter is the vast majority of passages dealing with the kingdom of God or the kingdom of heaven look at it as future, as a place, as something to be seen, etc.

The view of progressive dispensationalism founders on their concept of the kingdom as being "already … not yet."

A CONSISTENT VIEW

This approach holds that the terms "kingdom of heaven" and "kingdom of God" are used consistently with the same meaning throughout the Gospels. That is, they always refer to the promised earthly reign on earth of the Messiah which ultimately goes into eternity.

Several factors support this concept. First, the terms have the same meaning in Matthew 3, 4, 10 and 13. If one changes the meaning in Matthew 13 what is to keep one from making the kingdom totally a spiritual one?

Secondly, Matthew 13 makes good sense if one simply takes 13:11 to say the Lord is revealing new truths about the promised kingdom. "The mysteries of the kingdom" refers to doctrine not previously known. In view of Israel's rejection a whole new age will intervene; this age is not the kingdom but precedes it. This is a totally new teaching and gives good meaning to each of the parables.

The first "kingdom" parable is about the wheat and tares (13:24-30), which is explained in verses 36-43. The mystery or new truth in this parable is the concept of a new age in which good and evil would co-exist before the judgment preceding the kingdom. This age was not predicted in the Old Testament; it is a something new, a mystery. John had taught judgment was near because the kingdom was near. Now the coming of the kingdom was postponed and so was the judgment.

The significance of the second parable, the parable of the mustard seed, (13:31-32) is debated. One possible interpretation is the growth of the number of the heirs of the kingdom. The impression the Lord gives elsewhere is the kingdom will come suddenly, but here there is growth and prosperity in numbers. (The reference to birds in the branches describes outward prosperity {cf. Dan. 4:11-12; Ezek. 17:23}). The believers would grow from a small group to a large number.

The third parable, which is about leaven leavening a lump of dough, is very brief but much discussed (Matt. 13:33). Does the leaven portray what is good or is it evil? In the New Testament leaven consistently illustrates sin. Therefore, it seems best to say the age will end with utter apostasy. The man of sin is predicted in the Old Testament (cf. Dan. 9:27; Zech. 11:15-17, etc.) and it appears sin will be centered in Babylon (5:5-11). The leavening of the whole lump appears to be the new truth; that is, the entire world in this age (except for the elect) will climax in a massive rebellion against God.

The last three parables are addressed to the disciples. They are the hidden treasure (Matt. 13:14), the precious pearl (13:45) and the drag net (13: 47-50). The new truth in the first seems to be the hiddenness of the treasure. The man who finds the treasure is the Lord Jesus. The treasure probably represents the kingdom which was revealed in His ministry, and when He was rejected the kingdom was again hidden. Obviously, the Lord bought the field in which the treasure was hidden. One day it will be revealed. This is implied but it is obvious from the story. Why purchase the field if not to unbury the treasure?

The parable of the pearl is difficult. It is possible the pearl is the redeemed of all ages. The Jews were not the only people of God; there was a group of many nations who would be redeemed by the Lord Jesus. They would be the precious pearl.

The parable of the drag net reinforces the parable of the wheat and tares. At the end of this age there will be a judgment of all who are alive on earth. This assize will take place at the end of this age.

There may well be disagreement over the interpretation of these parables. That does not actually change the purpose of this paper. Its primary intent is to contend the Lord is not describing some form of His kingdom today but is revealing new truths about His kingdom program.

CONCLUSION

It seems best to take the terms "kingdom of heaven" and "kingdom of God" in a consistent sense. The same term that refers to the kingdom that had drawn near in the beginning of Christ's ministry is in view in Matthew 13. This means Christ is not describing a kingdom presently in existence. Instead He is presenting new truths about His kingdom program, truths that had not before been revealed.

AMILLENNIALISTS REPLACE ISRAEL WITH THE CHURCH

- The establishment of the covenant of grace with Abraham marked the beginning of the institutional Church. – Louis Berkhof, *Systematic Theology*
- Whether the Jews have a national restoration to the land of their fathers as the chosen people is not certain. This may be regarded as "the secret things" which belong unto God. – Albert Barnes, *Barnes' Notes*
- Jeremiah's prophecy of the new covenant in Jeremiah 31 receives its Christian application, and Israel becomes the Church, with the promise of perpetual existence. – Albert Barnes, *Barnes' Notes*
- The dispersion [of Israel] yet continues, the reunion will be in the days when Israel shall be gathered into the Church of God. … Ezekiel prefigures the visible Church of Christ. – Albert Barnes, *Barnes' Notes*
- The promise of the kingdom restored to Israel … was fulfilled in the history of Christendom as the true Israel of God. – Albert Barnes, *Barnes' Notes*
- It is not certain that Christ meant in Matthew 24:31 that the regathering of Israel would be literal, but it may mean with certainty that the world would be assembled together as with the Elect. And the word Elect means Christian—the chosen of God. – John Ellicott, *Commentary on the Whole Bible*

CHAPTER 15

THE CHURCH IS NOT ISRAEL

Paul Benware

Any competent realtor will tell that you that the three most important factors in selling property are (1) location, (2) location and (3) location. Any competent theologian will tell you that the three most important factors in arriving at good theology are (1) definition of terms, (2) definition of terms and (3) definition of terms. And so, the way in which the interpreter of Scripture defines the term "Israel" is important. It will have a profound impact on the theological perspective of that person. Furthermore, it will significantly shape that individual's position on many key passages of Scripture. It is, therefore, no small matter how one understands "Israel." If "Israel" is seen as a national, ethnic group of people throughout all of Scripture and the Church is different from that, then certain theological conclusions will be arrived at. But if the Church of Jesus Christ is seen as the "new Israel" that has replaced the nation of Israel, then a very different set of theological positions will be held to.

TWO BASIC VIEWS OF THE CHURCH AND THE NATION OF ISRAEL

There are actually numerous perspectives held by theologians on the relationship of the Church to the nation of Israel. But for the purpose of this brief study the two main positions will be set forth.

THE VIEW OF THE UNIQUENESS OF BOTH ISRAEL AND THE CHURCH

This view believes that Israel is a unique nation chosen by God to fulfill His will and work in this world. Israel is a specific ethnic group, descended from Abraham through Isaac and Jacob, which is united by a covenant relationship with the Lord God. This covenant made with Abraham and his descendants is an everlasting, unconditional covenant and much of it remains to be fulfilled with national Israel. Israel is the only nation that has this relationship and status as is seen by the facts that God calls Israel "My son, My first-born" (Exod. 4:22) and they are seen as an elect people chosen by God Himself. Israel is "a holy people to the LORD your God; the LORD your God has chosen you to be a people for His own possession out of all the peoples who are on the face of the earth" (Deut. 7:6. cf. Deut. 4:37; 14:2; 10:15-16; 26:19).

The election of Israel by God to do His work in the world is a major biblical and theological issue. There are two critically important points that must be understood in relationship to this election of the nation of Israel by God. First, Israel's election does not mean that God abandoned the gentile nations. From the very beginning of God's covenant relationship with Israel, He made it abundantly clear that gentiles were very much part of His care and concern (cf. Gen. 12:3; 26:4; 28:14).

Israel's position as God's elect nation never was intended to isolate the blessings of God to Israel, but rather Israel was to be the channel of God's blessing and salvation to all nations of the earth. Second, Israel's status as an elect nation did not mean that every physical descendent of Abraham would receive spiritual salvation. Jesus and John the Baptist repeatedly warned the Jews of their day that being a physical descendent of Abraham was not a guarantee of entrance into the kingdom of God. There is an important difference between the election of the individual and the national election of Israel.

> In dealing with the concept of election, a distinction must be made between individual election and national election. The former is soteriological and results in the salvation of that individual. This type of election extends to both Jewish and Gentile individuals; and any person who has ever believed, either Jew or Gentile, was the object of God's individual election. However, the concern of Israelology is national election because only Israel is called an elect nation. National election does not guarantee the salvation of every individual within the nation since only individual election can do that.... What national election does guarantee is that God's purpose(s) for choosing the nation will be accomplished and that the elect nation will

always survive as a distinct entity.[1]

Therefore, national Israel is unique because they among the nations are in a covenant relationship with God and they alone were elected by God to be the means by which He would bring salvation, reconciliation and blessing to sinful mankind.

The Church of Jesus Christ, on the other hand, is distinct from national Israel. Because of Israel's disobedience and unbelief related to the Messiah Jesus, they have been temporarily set aside in the plan of God. The Church, which is a new and different entity, has been raised up for an undetermined period of time to do God's will and work in this world. The Church, which is made up of believing Gentiles and believing Jews, came into existence on the day of Pentecost (Acts 2) and will remain on the earth until removed at the Rapture event. When God's purposes for the Church are over, then God will again restore Israel to their original place with the result that salvation will come to the nation and also to multitudes of Gentiles. This restoration will be the result of God's powerful working during the "Seventieth Week of Daniel" (i.e. the tribulation period), which will take place on this earth after the removal of the Church. It must be remembered that the unique place of national Israel and the wonderful purposes of God for all of mankind have co-existed from the beginning. The existence of one does not require the exclusion of the other. Gentile blessing does not require that Israel be set aside.

This view is held by Dispensational Theology but is not exclusive to it. Long before dispensational theology was formulated there were others (including Puritans, Anglicans and Catholics) who made a clear distinction between the Church and national Israel.[2] Evidences for the validity of the position that makes a distinction between the Church and Israel will be set forth later in this chapter.

THE VIEW OF REPLACEMENT THEOLOGY

The view that has dominated the Church since post-apostolic times has been that of *Replacement Theology*. This view holds that Israel's sin and failure caused God to set aside national Israel completely and permanently and replace it with the Church. The promises given to Israel in the Old

Testament have been transferred over to the Church. The view is sometimes called "supersessionism" because national Israel is said to be superseded by the person and work of Christ and the community of believers (i.e. the Church) that came from His work. This is the position of most in Covenant Theology. This perspective is advocated by Wayne Grudem.

> What further statement could be needed in order for us to say with assurance that the church has now become the true Israel of God and will receive all the blessings promised to Israel in the Old Testament.[3]

Louis Berkhof sees the Church as always existing and yet differing from national Israel.

> After the exodus the people of Israel were not only organized into a nation, but were also constituted the Church of God … the whole nation constituted the Church; and the Church was limited to the one nation of Israel, though foreigners could enter it by being incorporated into the nation … The New Testament Church is essentially one with the Church of the old dispensation. As far as their essential nature is concerned, they both consist of true believers, and of true believers only … Yet several important changes resulted from the accomplished work of Jesus Christ. The Church was divorced from the national life of Israel and obtained an independent organization.[4]

William Cox's statement represents the position of *Replacement Theology.*

> The Old Testament records two kinds of promises which God made to national Israel: national promises and spiritual promises … The spiritual promises still are being fulfilled through the church today. Israel's national promises all have been either fulfilled or invalidated because of unbelief.[5]

While there are some variations within this theological viewpoint of

Replacement Theology, there has been an essential unity on the matter of national Israel being set aside by God and being replaced by the Church. The writings of some of the Church fathers (such as Origen and Justin Martyr) as well as Church councils have fostered an anti-Judaic attitude, which has often been seen in *Replacement Theology*.

> However, it is more significant for Christian theology that some anti-Jewish canons were formulated in the context of Councils, such as the Council of Chalcedon (451), which live in the Church's memory as occasions in which orthodoxy was defined. Thus we can speak of a parallel development of Orthodox theology on the one hand and an official anti-Judaic stance on the other.[6]

It should be noted that there has been some modification of the harsher elements of *Replacement* thinking since the re-establishment of Israel as a nation in May, 1948. While the more extreme and hateful attitude towards Israel has been set aside by many and while it has been suggested by some that blessing may yet come to national Israel in the future, these nevertheless remain firmly entrenched in *Replacement Theology.*

Before presenting evidence for the position that the Church and Israel are separate entities in the Scriptures, two observations need to be made about *Replacement Theology.* First and foremost, is its relationship to the New Testament. While it is without question found in church history, is this viewpoint found in the New Testament Scriptures? They would argue that such a view can be deduced from a number of scripture passages. But the following point is important.

> Moreover, in order for *replacement theology* to qualify as a biblical option, passages which *allow* such an interpretation are not enough. There need to be, positively, passages which clearly teach it and, negatively, no passages which actually exclude it.[7]

This insightful statement is accurate because the Old Testament clearly sets national Israel apart as a unique nation elected by God Himself. If there is a change in their status or some sort of transference of their status to another, then somewhere in the New Testament it must be clearly and decisively declared. No such statements exist in the New Testament, but actually the opposite is to be found, especially in Romans 9-11.

Second, the perspective of *replacement theology* was shaped by several factors in the early history of the church and not by a careful study of the scriptures. First, the reality is that it was the Jews who rejected their own Messiah Jesus and were the great antagonists of the early church. This fed an anti-Jewish sentiment in the Church. A second factor in developing this way of thinking was the embracing of Greek thinking and philosophy by many of the early Church fathers. This acceptance of a Greek worldview and the abandonment of a Jewish worldview had a profound affect on their theology. Things physical (such as national Israel and an earthly millennial kingdom) were diminished in importance while things spiritual were elevated. And the allegorical method of interpretation allowed interpreters to take the promises given to national Israel and transfer them to the Church. Origen is considered the father of the allegorical method in the Church, but it must be remembered that he was influenced by the Greeks who employed such methodology.

With these points being stated, it is necessary to look at the Scriptures to see what they do indeed teach about the relationship of the nation of Israel to the Church.

EVIDENCE FOR A DISTINCTION BETWEEN THE CHURCH AND THE NATION OF ISRAEL

Those holding to *replacement theology* put considerable emphasis on the similarities between Israel and the Church. They will point to some similar terms that are used for both, that both have a special relationship with God based on election, that both are to bring the truth of God to the world, as well as other matters.[8] It is clear that there is indeed a certain continuity that exists between Israel and the Church. But some continuity would be expected since the Church is now representing God and His truth in the current age. The Church has been commissioned by Christ to carry the good news of His salvation throughout the world as Israel was once commissioned to do. However, this does not mean that Israel's place as God's elect nation has somehow been cancelled or His promises transferred to another entity. National Israel maintains her key place in God's plans and purposes for this world. The following lines of evidence will support the fact that Israel has not been superceded in her place as God's elect and covenant people.

THE EXISTENCE OF THE UNCONDITIONAL BUT UNFULFILLED BIBLICAL COVENANTS SUPPORTS THE DISTINCTION.

The Old Testament records the indisputable fact that God entered into a covenant relationship with Abraham (Gen. 12:1-3; 13:14-17; 15:1-21; 17:1-27; 18:17-19; 22:15-18) and then personally confirmed it to Abraham's physical descendants Isaac (26:24) and Jacob (28:13-17). The Gentile nations were not specifically parties to the Abrahamic covenant nor were they parties in the three covenants that expanded on the provisions of the Abrahamic covenant; namely, the Land (a.k.a. Palestinian), Davidic and New Covenants. These covenants were made with national Israel.

The essential nature of the Abrahamic covenant (and its three "sub-covenants") is critical in this discussion. The covenant is an *everlasting* covenant (e.g. 13:15; 17:13-19; 1 Chron. 16:16-17; Psa. 105:9-10; Jer. 31:35-36). These and other scripture texts record the declaration of God that this covenant was an everlasting covenant. No time limit was placed on this covenant relationship, which indicates that Israel was to remain a nation forever in this relationship with the Lord their God.

> The Hebrew expression for "everlasting" is *olam,* meaning "in perpetuity." While it might not quite be the equivalent of the infinite term "everlasting," it would certainly mean continuance as long as this present earth should last. It is the strongest expression for eternity of which the Hebrew language is capable. Inasmuch as these promises are reiterated to Isaac and to Jacob and are constantly referred to throughout the Old Testament, the nature of these promises confirms the continuance of Israel as a nation.[9]

The everlasting nature of the Abrahamic covenant means that national Israel must remain in their unique relationship with God as long as the earth and the universe exist. And since we can all testify that the universe still exists and has not yet been destroyed, then we can certainly believe that the nation of Israel has not been removed from their unique place either. This covenant continues to exist because of God's graciousness and faithfulness and not because of Israel's fidelity and obedience. "There may be delays, postponements, and chastisements, but an eternal covenant cannot, if God cannot deny Himself, be abrogated."[10] The failure and disobedience of Israel did not set the covenant promises aside. It is clear that individuals and the nation itself could lose out on the blessings of the covenant (as they did), but those failures did not annul the covenant. In a time of terrible apostasy and judgment of Israel, God spoke through the prophets Jeremiah and Ezekiel. He guaranteed that as long as the sun, moon and stars existed, Israel would continue as "a nation before me forever" (Jer. 31:35-37); and that in spite of Israel's failure and rebellion God would restore them (Ezek. 20). This was not just a truth found in the prophets of the Old Testament but also with the Apostle Paul in the New Testament.

> Moreover the fact that Paul attributes the status of elect nation to Israelites who are "enemies of the gospel" (Rom. 11:28) shows that the continuing elect status of Israel does not depend on her faithfulness, any more than it did in the times of the Hebrew prophets (see Jer. 31:35-37).[11]

The Abrahamic covenant is also an *unconditional covenant*; that is, its fulfillment depends on God alone. When God made the covenant with Abraham it was given without conditions attached to it.[12] When God later reaffirmed the covenant to Isaac and then to Jacob, no conditions were attached to it. Later statements found in Genesis 17, 22 and 26 which seem to add conditions to the covenant really do not do so. These statements were given long after the ratification of the covenant (Genesis 15) and focus on God's intention to bless Abraham in a greater way. This covenant with Abraham, therefore, is both everlasting and unconditional.

Another key part of this discussion is the ratification of the Abrahamic covenant in Genesis 15:7-21. On this occasion, Abraham expressed concern to God about his lack of a future heir, since up to that point no son had been born to him. The Lord assured Abraham that he would indeed have a son. It is said that Abraham believed the Lord's statement on the matter. And then God graciously honored the faith of this man and encouraged him by ratifying the covenant. The ratification ceremony described in Genesis 15 would have been familiar to Abraham and one that he probably had been involved in many times before when he entered into covenant type relationships with other men. This ceremony of ratification made the agreement legally binding. Now in this case, God's promise was, of course, sufficient but He nevertheless sought to encourage Abraham through this familiar ceremony.

Normally when a covenant was ratified by blood, the pieces of the animals were separated so that the parties of the covenant would walk between the pieces together. This obligated both parties to fulfill their part of the agreement. However, in this case, God alone passed between the pieces while Abraham experienced a visionary sleep.

> The significance of that is striking: it means that God swore fidelity to His promises and placed the obligation of their fulfillment on Himself alone ... Clearly the Abrahamic covenant was not conditioned on anything Abraham would or would not do; its fulfillment in all parts depends only on God's doings.[13]
> The promises were unconditional promises, that is, dependent ultimately on God's sovereign determination, as the striking ratification of the covenant indicated (Gen. 15:7-21)...God undertakes to fulfill the conditions Himself, thus guaranteeing by the divine fidelity to His Word and by His power the accomplishment of the covenantal promises.[14]

The Apostle Paul makes a highly significant contribution to this discussion in Galatians 3:15-18. His basic point is that once a covenant is ratified (made legally binding) neither the parties or the provisions of the covenant can be changed. He notes that this is true in all human covenants and it is also true in God's covenant with Abraham (It is worth noting that the unconditional nature of the Abrahamic covenant is emphasized by the Apostle by his use of the word "promise" which he uses nine times in Galatians 3 in reference to this "covenant"). This covenant is made with national Israel and cannot be transferred to another group or nation. The

Church, or Gentiles, cannot take over the promises made to national Israel. Paul says that it simply cannot be done! To change the parties of the covenant would violate the commitment made by God and this is unthinkable. The covenant remains a covenant with national Israel and God's integrity is called into question if He, who committed Himself to its fulfillment, does not do so with Abraham's physical descendants. As noted earlier, Gentiles are not abandoned by God, but clearly through national Israel "all the nations would be blessed."

The covenant commitments by God in the Abrahamic covenant and the three covenants, which emerge out it, remain largely unfulfilled except where individual promises to Abraham and David are involved. Because many of the covenant promises remain unfulfilled and because the covenants are both *everlasting* and *unconditional* in nature, they simply must be fulfilled sometime in the future with national Israel.[15]

Therefore, the existence of the unfulfilled, unconditional and everlasting biblical covenants supports a continuing distinction between the Church of Jesus Christ and the nation of Israel.

THE USE OF THE TERM "ISRAEL" SUPPORTS THE DISTINCTION

The term "Israel" appears frequently in both Old and New Testaments. The Old Testament records over two thousand usages and the New Testament a little over seventy. The word is used throughout the Scriptures to refer to a specific national group. However, those holding to the *Replacement Theology* position believe that the terms "church" and "Israel" are used interchangeably by the writers of Scripture.

> We should not close our eyes to the patent fact that the name "Church" (Heb. *qahal*, rendered *ekkelsia* in the Septuagint) is applied to Israel in the Old Testament repeatedly.[16]
>
> God's people were known in the Old Testament as "Israel." The same people, in the New Testament, are known as "the church." As a matter of scriptural fact, these terms are used interchangeably; the church is referred to as "Israel" (Gal. 6:16) while the Old Testament

remnant is referred to as "the church" (Acts 7:38).[17]

In spite of such an amazing statement, the facts of the New Testament simply do not support this assertion. The writers of the New Testament consistently make a distinction between "Israel" and "church" and do not use the terms synonymously. The term "Israel" is used seventy-three times in the New Testament, and in each occurrence it refers to ethnic Israel, either the nation as a whole or believing Jews within the nation.[18]

Replacement Theology actually uses only three of the "Israel" references to try and establish their case: Romans 9:6; 11:26; Galatians 6:16. The statement in Romans 9:6 is that "they are not all Israel who are descended from Israel." This is used by replacement theologians to demonstrate a larger use of "Israel" to include gentile Christians. But 9:1-5 is unquestionably speaking about ethnic Israel, as those to whom belong many spiritual privileges including the covenants. The failure of the Jews to respond positively to Jesus the Messiah did not, Paul says, thwart the purposes of God. While the majority in Israel rejected God's plan, some in Israel did not. As he does elsewhere in Romans (where he uses "Israel" eleven times in chapters 9-11), Paul is simply acknowledging that within the nation of Israel there are believing Jews and unbelieving Jews. He is simply talking about ethnic Israelites who were Abraham's children both naturally and spiritually and he contrasts them with those in Israel who do not believe. It is not a contrast between unbelieving Jews and the Church, and there is simply not a gentile anywhere in sight. It should be noted, that many replacement theologians agree with this point and, therefore, do not use Romans 9:6 to establish their case.

In 11:26, Paul declares that "all Israel shall be saved." While some holding to the view of *Replacement Theology* believe that "all Israel" includes gentile converts as well as Jewish believers, others in that camp do not. The latter understand that "Israel" in 11:26 is the same as "Israel" in 11:25 where Paul is speaking about the coming salvation of ethnic Israel. This understanding goes along with the whole context of Romans 9-11 where national Israel is the subject. And it should be noted also that the use of "Jacob" in 11:26 gives further strong support for the interpretation that it is national Israel that is being spoken of.

Therefore, of the seventy-three references to "Israel" in the New

Testament, only one, Galatians 6:16, is seen by all replacement theologians as establishing the fact that Israel and the Church are interchangeable terms. At issue is the meaning of Paul's statement, "peace and mercy be upon them, and upon the Israel of God." Replacement theologians base their claim largely on the translation of the word "and" (kai); the word that appears before the term "Israel of God." They set aside the primary meaning of "and" in favor of the secondary meaning of "even." All agree that "them" refers to believing Gentiles. So the verse is said to declare that mercy be upon them (believing Gentiles), *even* upon the Israel of God. This translation essentially equates believing Gentiles with the Israel of God. But this interpretation is weak both grammatically as well as contextually. As Dr. S. Lewis Johnson has observed,

> It is necessary to begin this part of the discussion with a reminder of a basic, but often neglected hermeneutical principle. It is this: in the absence of compelling exegetical and theological considerations, we should avoid the rarer grammatical usages when the common ones make good sense. ... An extremely rare usage has been made to replace the common usage, even in spite of the fact that the common and frequents usage of *and* makes perfectly good sense in Galatians 6:16.[19]

The straightforward rendering of "and" (kai) is to be preferred unless there is significant reasons within the text itself to go with a secondary rendering. None exists in the text or context of Galatians 6:16.

The position of *Replacement Theology* is not only weak grammatically but does not take into consideration the other seventy-two uses of "Israel" in the New Testament. Paul and the other writers use "Israel" to mean ethnic Israel or believing Jews within the nation of Israel. The Church is simply not called Israel or spiritual Israel.

Furthermore, the context of the Book of Galatians does not support the position of *Replacement Theology*. Galatians 6:16 concludes a letter where Paul has been clear that no one is justified by law keeping. Jews and Gentiles alike are saved by faith alone in Jesus Christ alone. Paul warns them not to be persuaded by Judaizers who were attempting to add the law to faith in Christ. After he establishes that both Jews and Gentiles are justified and sanctified by faith alone, he comes to the end of the Galatian letter. And in 6:15-16 he pronounces a blessing on those believing Jews and those believing Gentiles who have come to and remain in that firm conviction. The two groups in the Galatian church were believing Jews and believing Gentiles and these are the ones he is referring to. He is not suddenly focusing on just the believing Gentiles and calling them the Israel of God.

An appeal is often made to the idea that Israel equals the Church because believing Gentiles are called "the seed of Abraham" in 3:29. And indeed they are given that designation. But this does not mean that Gentiles now fulfill the promises given in the covenants to national Israel. The Scriptures actually use the phrase "seed of Abraham" in several different ways. The phrase is used of the natural, physical descendants of Abraham. This could include all those who descend from Abraham, but in the Scriptures the emphasis is on the physical line of Abraham through Isaac and Jacob. The "seed" is also used of those in Israel who are true believers (cf. Rom. 9:8). And it is used of true believers who are not physically descended from Abraham. Gentiles are, therefore, said to be a spiritual seed of Abraham the believer. But having observed this, it must also be noted that the spiritual seed of Abraham is never called "Israel" or used as a synonym for "Israel." And the spiritual seed of Abraham is never said to fulfill the promises given by God in the covenants to the physical seed of Abraham.

> This distinction will explain how the church may be related to the promises of the covenant without being the covenant people in whom the national promises will be fulfilled. Because we are the seed of Abraham spiritually by the new birth, it does not mean we are the physical seed of the patriarch.[20]

Dr. Arnold Fruchtenbaum adds a helpful observation about the matter of "seed."

> What replacement theologians need to prove their case is a statement in Scripture that all believers are the "seed of Jacob." Such teaching would indicate that the church is

> spiritual Israel or that Gentile Christians are spiritual Jews. This is exactly what they do not have. Not all physical descendants of Abraham are Jews, but all physical descendants of Jacob are. The very term *Israel* originated with Jacob and not with Abraham. If there were even one verse that showed that the church is the seed of Jacob, replacement theologians could support one of their key contentions. This they cannot do. They only resort to passages that speak of the seed of Abraham, which, by itself, is insufficient to prove their contention, since the use of "Israel" is more restrictive than the use of "Abraham."[21]

In spite of all attempts to support the idea that it is a "scriptural fact" that Israel and Church are used interchangeably, it simply is not so. Therefore, the use of the term "Israel" in the New Testament supports the idea of maintaining a distinction between the Church of Jesus Christ and the nation of Israel.

THE STARTING POINT OF EACH ENTITY SUPPORTS THE DISTINCTION

The Church and Israel did not begin at the same time and are, therefore, not the same entity. The nation of Israel essentially began when God called Abraham and promised to make a great nation from him. The rest of the Old Testament records the growth, development and existence of that nation. There is really no significant debate on the matter of the starting point of the nation of Israel. It began with Abraham and was formed over the next seven hundred years into a nation with people, law and land. The Church, however, is not found in the Old Testament because it had its beginning on the Day of Pentecost as recorded in Acts 2. The Church began centuries after Israel began.

If the Church began at Pentecost, then it did not begin or exist in the Old Testament. It is worth noting that in Matthew 16:18 the Lord Jesus used the future tense: "*I will* build My Church." He did not say, "I am building My church" or "I have been building My church." The church was something still future in Christ's ministry, which means that it was not in existence during His ministry or in the Old Testament. His apostles would not have understood what He meant by "His church" being built in the future, but the details about the church would be given to them later. In dealing with the matter of the discipline of an individual (18:17), Jesus told them to tell it to the church or assembly. The apostles would have understood that He was speaking of a Jewish assembly. The statement of 18:17 must be understood in light of the previous statement (16:18) of future building of "MY church."

Certain things had to be true before the church could come into existence. First, according to the Apostle Paul, the Church is the "body of Christ" (e.g. Col. 1:18, 24 and Eph. 2:16; 3:6; 5:23, 30). It is clear that the church (the body) could not exist and function without its Head, the Lord Jesus. Jesus did not assume that role until after He had shed His blood on the cross, had been resurrected, and then ascended back into heaven. It was at that time, after those events, that the Father "put all things in subjection under His feet, and gave Him and head over all things to the church, which is His body" (1:22).

Furthermore, the church (the body) could not be formed apart from the baptizing work of the Holy Spirit. This is so because a believer can enter the church, the body of Christ, only by means of Holy Spirit baptism (cf. 1 Cor. 12:13). But this vital ministry of the Spirit did not begin until the Day of Pentecost. Without Spirit baptism no one could enter the body of Christ and, thus, the church could not exist. Not even the Apostles were in the body, but they would experience Spirit baptism shortly after Jesus' ascension. On the day He ascended back into heaven, the Lord Jesus informed His apostles that the baptizing work of the Spirit would begin in the near future (Acts 1:5, 8). Ten days later, on the Day of Pentecost, this and other ministries of the Spirit began. As the Apostle Peter reflected on the Day of Pentecost as the time when this new work of the Spirit began (11:15), he spoke of it as a time of "beginning." Peter's use of "beginning" (*arche*) speaks of a specific point in time when something new commences.[22] This new thing, the church of Jesus Christ, began on the Day of Pentecost.

The Apostle Paul also tells us that the Church's foundation is the apostles and the prophets of the New Testament with Christ being the cornerstone (Eph. 2:20). This suggests two things: first, that the church must have begun in the time of the Apostles if they are the foundation, and second, the Church is not seen being built upon the key Old Testament personalities of Abraham, Isaac, Jacob and David. The Church did not begin in the Old Testament and, therefore, it and Israel are distinct.

THE UNIQUE CHARACTER OF THE CHURCH SUPPORTS THE DISTINCTION

The Church, unlike Israel, is declared to be a "mystery" (Eph. 3:1-12; Col. 1:26-27). In the New Testament a "mystery" is a truth that was not revealed previously in the Old Testament.

> In the N.T. it denotes, not the mysterious...but that which, being outside the range of unassisted natural apprehension, can be made known only by Divine revelation, and is made known in a manner and at a time appointed by God, and to those only who are illumined by His Spirit.[23]

The Apostle Paul is clear that this unknown truth related to the Church was something that was hidden from man and was hidden with God until "now" (the time of the apostles and New Testament prophets). The "mystery" included the facts that believing Jews and believing Gentiles would be united as equals in one body and that Christ Himself would indwell them. While Gentile salvation was seen in the Old Testament, this kind of relationship between Jews and Gentiles, and between God and the believer, was never true in the Old Testament. The church was something new and significantly different from Israel.

The Apostle Paul also declared that the church is "one new man" (Eph. 2:15). He states that based on the death of Christ, reconciliation has taken place between Jews and Gentiles as well as between God and man. The "one new man" is distinct from Israel and it is distinct from the Gentiles. The "one new man" (the church) is *not a continuation of either* but is made up of believing Jews and believing Gentiles. It is something entirely new and points to a very real distinction between the Church and Israel.

SPECIFIC NEW TESTAMENT SCRIPTURES SUPPORT THE DISTINCTION

A number of New Testament scriptures have been mentioned and there are a number that legitimately could be discussed. As was noted earlier, "in order for *replacement theology* to qualify as a biblical option, passages which *allow* such an interpretation are not enough. There need to be, positively, passages which clearly teach it and, negatively, no passages which actually exclude it."[24] *Replacement Theology* does not have any passages that clearly teach that the nation of Israel has been set aside by God and replaced by the Church. But it is faced with Paul's powerful presentation concerning Israel in Romans 9-11, which does not allow for replacement theology. It is beyond the scope of this chapter to deal in detail with the key section in Romans 9-11. Others have done a fine job in demonstrating that the nation of Israel does have a wonderful future and that God fully intends to restore them to a place of prominence as He fulfills His covenant commitments to them.[25]

We simply need to note that the eleven times that Paul uses "Israel" in this section, each time it refers to ethnic Israel, not to Gentiles or the Church. He is talking about his "kinsmen according to the flesh" (9:3). Paul knew that most people in Israel had turned from the Lord, rebelled, and become hardened in self-righteous unbelief. Of course, a believing remnant in Israel had always existed, but the nation as a whole had turned away (Romans 9 and 10). But Romans 11 is clear on this point, that the same people who refused to believe and were temporarily disciplined by God would believe and be received back in the future when the Messiah would return. Using an illustration of an olive tree, Paul states that some of the natural branches of the tree (Israel) were broken off and wild branches (the Gentiles) were grafted in and received life from the "rich root of the olive tree" (the Abrahamic covenant). He then declares that the day is coming when God will graft the natural branches back into the olive tree, which looks ahead to the day of salvation for national Israel—the final fulfillment of the New Covenant. On that day "all Israel will be saved" (11:26).

> It means in usage *Israel as a whole*, not necessarily every individual Israelite (cf. 1 Sam. 7:2-5; 25:1; 1 Kings 12:1; 2 Chron. 12:1-5; Dan. 9:11). The clues to its force are not only the sense of people (Rom. 11:1), but also the nature of the rejection of the Messiah by the nation, a rejection by nation as a whole (the leaders and the great mass of the people, but not every Israelite). This usage, as

> is well-known, is found in rabbinic literature … Thus, Paul affirms that ethnic Israel as a whole will be saved.[26]

The Apostle does not believe that Israel's self-righteousness, unbelief and sin have removed them from God's blessings, but rather that the day is coming when Israel, as a nation, will be brought into the New Covenant, thus fulfilling the Old Testament prophets. Some have said that the phrase "all Israel" is looking at the remnant of Jewish believers that have been saved as a part of the Church over the centuries. But if that were true, then there never was a "breaking off" of the natural branches as the text declares. And there would be no need to graft them back in again, since they have always been part of the olive tree. No, Paul is referring to ethnic Israel and anticipating the day when God will "take away their sins" in light of His "covenant with them" (11:27). Can anything be clearer that this in declaring that national Israel does have a future and has not been replaced or set aside by the Church.

THE EXTERNAL DIFFERENCES SUPPORT THE DISTINCTION

There is general agreement among theologians of all persuasions that there are significant external differences between the Church and Israel. They just do not at all look alike. Replacement theologian Louis Berkhof acknowledges the difference. He states, "In essence Israel constituted the Church of God in the Old Testament, though its external institution differed vastly from that of the Church in the New Testament."[27] He is, of course correct that there are vast differences, and so, we see the nation of Israel having an army, national boundaries, a system of taxation, a priesthood within the nation, animal sacrifices and forms of government (judges, priests and kings) that do not correspond to that which is found in the New Testament Church. One wonders, however, how these two entities can be conceived as being the same or one being the continuation of the other. The external differences support the idea that there is a distinction between the Church and Israel.

THE INTERNAL DIFFERENCES SUPPORT THE DISTINCTION

There are also significant internal differences between the two entities.

First, and of great significance, is the fact that the body of Christ is made up of believers only. There has not, nor will there ever be, an unbeliever in the Church (the body of Christ) since one can only enter through Spirit baptism. This is in stark contrast to Israel where unbelievers were dominant over much of Old Testament history. So Dr. Berkhof's statement is a bit puzzling when he says, "As far as their essential nature is concerned, they both consist of true believers, and of true believers only."[28] It could never be said of Israel, as it can be of the Church, that no unbelievers were in it.

Second, the two entities function under two different covenants. Israel functioned under the Old covenant and the Church has been privileged to be "partakers" of some of the spiritual blessings of the New covenant. (Note: the New Covenant was made with Israel and Judah and must be fulfilled with them). There is a stark contrast between these two covenants as taught in 2 Corinthians 3 and Hebrews 7-10 and the New Covenant is clearly superior to the Old. The new covenant ministry is uniquely a broadened and expanded ministry of the Holy Spirit. The operating principles of the Church are significantly different from that of Israel.

Third, the work of God in Israel was especially carried out by the Levitical priesthood while in the Church it is the anointed, spiritually gifted believer priest that carries out the work of God. The New Testament believer has been given "the ministry of reconciliation" (2 Cor. 5:18-20). A believer in the Old Testament, from the tribe of Asher or Gad, could make no such claim.

Other internal differences exist. But these surely show us that internally the Church and Israel are quite different. The internal differences point to a legitimate distinction to be made between Israel and the Church.

SOME CONCLUDING THOUGHTS

The evidence of the Scriptures is strong and compelling that the Church of Jesus Christ and the nation of Israel are distinct entities in the plan and program of God. The Church is not Israel and Israel has not been set aside or replaced. When the biblical covenants made with the nation of Israel are seen as unconditional and unfulfilled, it is essential that the Lord God fulfills them with Israel, the ones who are the original party in the covenant. When the Scriptures are interpreted literally, one comes to the conclusion that Israel means Israel. And the literal (normal) approach of interpretation also leads one to see that the Church began at a different time that did Israel; that it was a "mystery" and something "new" build on the New Testament Apostles and prophets; and that it is externally and internally different from Israel. Such evidence, along with Romans 9-11, points to the fact that Israel was not abandoned or replaced by God. The Church is important in God's program, but it is not Israel.

WHAT IS A RAPTURE PASSAGE? BELIEVERS "GOING UP" RATHER THAN CHRIST "COMING DOWN" TO REIGN!
[Rapture passages have to do with the believers who are alive being caught up into the presence of the Lord]
• "I will come again and receive you unto Myself; that where I am, there you may be also" (John 14:3). • "We shall not all sleep, but we shall all be changed, in a moment, in the blink of an eye, at the last trumpet; … the dead will be raised imperishable, and we shall be changed" (1 Cor. 15:51-52). • Our citizenship is in heaven, from which also we eagerly wait for a Savior, the Lord Jesus Christ; who will transform the body of our humiliation into conformity with the body of His glory" (Phil. 3:20-21). • "We wait for His Son from heaven … who rescues us from the wrath that is on its way" (1 Thess. 1:10). • "The Lord will descend from heaven … the trumpet of God shall sound … then we who are alive and remain shall be caught up in the clouds to meet the Lord in the air" (4:16-17). • "God has not destined us for wrath but for obtaining deliverance through our Lord Jesus Christ" (5:9). • We look for the blessed hope and the appearing of the glory of our great God and Savior, Christ Jesus" (Titus 2:13).

CHAPTER 16

THE FORGOTTEN RAPTURE PASSAGES: I THESSALONIANS 1:9-10 AND 5:1-11

Mal Couch

WHAT IS THE RAPTURE OF THE CHURCH?

The rapture of the church is the taking home to heaven those who have in this present dispensation trusted the Lord Jesus as their personal Savior. The rapture is about "those in the body of Christ." Jesus comes from heaven and gives, to those saints who are living, a new body for glory. They are "caught up together with [those who are resurrected] in the clouds to meet the Lord in the air" (1 Thess. 4:17).

Tied closely to the rapture of the church, as just mentioned, is the resurrection of "those who have fallen asleep in Jesus" (v. 14). The souls of those who are asleep in Christ are brought back with Him and then united to their new, glorified bodies. These who are thus resurrected instantly join Christ just before those who are changed in their physical bodies. Those changed are then raptured and follow the resurrected into heaven. "For the Lord Himself will descend from heaven with a shout, with the voice of the archangel, and with the trumpet of God; and the dead in Christ shall rise first. Then we who are alive and remain shall be caught up together with them in the clouds to meet the Lord in the air, and thus we shall be with the Lord. Therefore comfort one another with these words" (vv. 16-18).

1 Thessalonians 4 is one of the main passages about the rapture but by no means the only one. There are fifteen or more passages from the Word of God that explain this doctrine. Many of the references mention the teaching in part, but with the plain and full teaching of the Bible on the subject, one has to work hard to deny the implications. However, there are many who try to do just that. They work hard to repudiate the obvious!

Rapture verses have several important and observable characteristics: (1)

The rapture is the going up to meet the Lord in the air in contrast to the Lord coming down to earth to begin His millennial reign. (2) The rapture has to do with the church as His present beloved people, and not Israel as His restored kingdom people. (3) The rapture of the church happens before the tribulation (the wrath, 1:10; 5:9) while His second coming follows after the tribulation. (4) The rapture is something more immediate, i.e., it could take place at any time, while the kingdom follows the seven-year period of tribulation and wrath. (5) The rapture of the believer to heaven requires a change in the body. Paul writes to the Corinthians, "We shall not all sleep [physically die], but we shall all be changed. … The dead will be raised imperishable, and [then] we shall be changed" (1 Cor. 15:51b; see vv. 51-53). And to Philippi he writes of Christ "who will transform the body of our humble state into conformity with the body of His glory" (Phil. 3:21).

Rapture passages have many additional characteristics that should be noted:

- It is about present comfort and anticipation: It is a comfort (1 Thess. 4:18); believers are to "be eagerly expecting" (James 5:7 Greek); and waiting (1 Thess. 1:10).
- It is a going home to glory: It is "our gathering together to Him" (2 Thess. 2:1).
- It is the "blessed hope" (Titus 2:12-13).
- It should create pure living: "Keep the commandment without stain or reproach until the appearing [epiphaneias] of our Lord Jesus Christ" (1 Tim. 6:14).[1]

WHY IS THERE INTEREST IN THE RAPTURE IN OUR TIMES?

Everyone watching world events knows that the Middle East is aflame and about to blow like a powder keg. But putting together all that the Bible has to say about the end-times, the doctrine of the rapture stands out and cannot be ignored. If the present world climate means we are getting close to the tribulation period, the rapture cannot be far away. The rapture doctrine is not about the second coming of Christ to reign, nor the final world judgment. It has to do with the eschatology that closes the church age, i.e., those in Jesus Christ, or the body of Christ! In the last three or four centuries there were Bible scholars who began to see in a primitive and limited way, the doctrine of the rapture.

> The Reformation, Protestant Bible scholars who had greater access to Scripture in the original languages and in translation, began seeing issues related to the Rapture. Joseph Mede (1586-1638), considered the father of English premillennialism, saw a separation between the Rapture and the second coming of the Christ. Others who saw similar threads in the Bible included Thomas Collier, John Gill (1697-1771), Peter Jurieu (1637-1713), and Increase Mather (1639-1723).
>
> With renewed interest in prophecy at the beginning of the nineteenth century, Bible scholars began to look intently at 1 Thessalonians 4:13-18. They noted how the apostle Paul speaks of a resurrection of those who had died in Christ and then writes about those alive being "caught up." Students of prophecy realized that the body of Christ was to go up and meet the Lord in the air. This was distinctly different than saying that Christ would come to earth to reign or judge.[2]

But strangely, it was the plight of the Jewish people over a century ago that caused many scholars and Bible students to look again at the whole issue of Bible prophecy. John Nelson Darby (1800-1882), a Trinity College 1819 graduate who won the prestigious classical gold medallion for scholarship, saw something was missing in the teaching of prophecy in his day. Darby and others began to understand more clearly God's plan for restoring Israel to the holy land.

> Seeing the beginnings of Zionism in their day, they could understand better the Old Testament prophecies that spoke of the literal coming of the Messiah to reign on the throne of David. Other prophetic patterns fell into place, including the idea that the Rapture would take place before the period known as the tribulation.[3]

HOW HAS THE RAPTURE OF THE CHURCH BEEN DESCRIBED?

Some of the most spiritual and Godly of the great Bible scholars of the last several centuries have seen in the Scriptures the rapture of the church. This was mainly among those who were Calvinists who were aware that the place of Israel was being left out in eschatology. They realized they must not come to the Bible with an interpretative agenda. Instead, they simply let the Word of God speak for itself on this issue. When the Bible is taken in its most plain and normal sense, the doctrine of the rapture becomes understandable. But most in the Reformed faith come to the Bible with preconceived notions and refuse to let the plain sense of the Scriptures be heard. In most every case this is why the rapture doctrine is not understood, and in turn, is repudiated. LaHaye writes:

> People with a system of interpretation other than taking the words literally, unless the text clearly indicates otherwise, usually don't want to be confronted with the Scriptures. They could well say the old adage, "Don't confuse me with the facts [Scripture]; my mind is made up." Such people do not want to be confronted with passages that are in conflict with their theological system. … As a general rule, whenever you hear someone preach about Bible prophecy, be sure he uses the two essential keys to understanding Scripture: 1) Interpret the Bible literally (even the prophetic passages of Scripture) unless the context provides good reason to do otherwise. And 2) ask, Does he draw a distinction between Israel and the church?[4]

Rene' Pache (1904-1979) wrote:

> We, therefore, believe that at His return Jesus Christ shall come to take all His true children, all the members of His Body. The Church is one. The Body of Christ forms a whole, and it is inconceivable that some of His members shall groan on earth while the wedding of the Lamb is being celebrated in Heaven. … And since the Rapture can happen in any moment, let us constantly live in the expectation of the Lord, saying to ourselves each day, 'Shall it perhaps be today?'[5]

William Blackstone (1841-1935) said:

> First, let us make a clear distinction between the time of the

Rapture and the time of the Revelation [the second coming of Christ]. The principal thought in regard to the former is that it may happen now. Nothing is given us in Scripture so definite as to form a sign of or date for the Rapture. We are to be always watching and waiting for it, and expecting it at any moment.[6]

J. F. Strombeck (1881-1956) added:

An appalling ignorance of the reason the rapture shall come before the tribulation is found among true believers. Altogether too much is being taken for granted because that view is the prevailing one of the group with which one fellowships, or because certain Bible teachers hold that view. Little, yes, very little, is known of what the Bible teaches. This is one reason, probably the greatest, for the disturbed feeling and why many are willing to exchange the blessed hope of seeing Christ before the tribulation [for other views].[7]

Paul Benware writes:

The Rapture is a supernatural event. The sudden removal of the true church from the world can happen only as a result of the power of God. When the church is removed from this earth, believers will meet Christ in the air, which is one of the facts that distinguishes the Rapture from the second coming of Christ to the earth.[8]

John F. Walvoord (1910-2002) notes:

The scriptural revelation of the translation [rapture] of the saints [in the church age] as presented in major passages of the New Testament lends support to the concept that the church of the present age is a distinct body of believers. The truth revealed concerning the translation is in itself not only a supporting argument for premillennialism as a whole [the fact that Christ comes to establish His kingdom] but by its detail sustains the concept of a pretribulational rapture [the fact that Christ comes for His church before the tribulation begins].[9]

THE PRETRIBULATIONAL RAPTURE OF 1 THESSALONIANS 1:9-10

THE CITY OF THESSALONICA

In the first century the city of Thessalonica was the largest metropolis in Macedonia. Earlier, the city was known as the acting capital of Greece. It was also one of the key trading cities on the Aegean Sea. The city was greatly active in trade with scows plying the shores, carrying fruits and vegetables. Power, wealth, and commerce made Thessalonica an awe inspiring city of 200,000. It was called by some the "Mother of Macedon."

The city had a large active and aggressive Jewish population. They enjoyed the freedom of its cosmopolitan and commercial atmosphere. They were far less susceptible to intimidation and cruelty by the Roman population. The apostle Paul made a point to speak to the Jews in the large synagogue located in the heart of the city. It was here also that the Jews rose up as an organized group to oppose Paul and his message of belief in the Lord Jesus Christ. Acts 17 tells us that the apostle "reasoned" for three Sabbaths (or longer) with an electrifying message of prophecy fulfilled and prophecy yet awaiting fulfillment. Luke in Acts 17:2-4 relates how Paul

> *reasoned with them from the Scriptures, explaining and giving evidence that the Christ had to suffer and rise again from the dead, and saying, "This Jesus whom I am proclaiming to you is the Christ." And some of them were persuaded and joined Paul and Silas, along with a great multitude of the God-fearing Greeks and a number of the leading women.*

The Thessalonian church apparently exploded in numbers. When Timothy returned from a trip to the city he gave to Paul a positive but also a sad report of what was happening to the believers. They were under terrible persecution. The faith of the church there was under fire (1 Thess. 2:14; 3:1-4). The faithful were experiencing criticism against Paul's leadership, probably inspired by Jewish opposition. Nine different Greek words are used in Paul's two letters to this church to describe the torment, persecution, and oppression they were undergoing. More than likely, after Paul wrote his two epistles, many in the city died for their trust in Christ!

CONFUSION ABOUT THE RETURN OF THE LORD

The Thessalonians also were apparently confusing the resurrection and final salvation to be attained at the coming of the Lord (4:13-18). The church experienced too, some consternation in regard to prophetic matters. Many scholars suggest Paul had addressed the doctrine of the rapture and resurrection while with the growing congregation, though many misunderstood what he said and needed reminders. They required more clarification because the concept of the rapture was something new. In fact the rapture doctrine was first introduced in seed form with little explanation by Jesus to His disciples in the Upper Room.

Jesus told His followers, "I go to prepare a place for you. And if I go and prepare a place for you, I will come again, and receive you to Myself; that where I am, there you may be also" (John 14:2b-3). This is a rapture passage because it pictures the Lord returning for the exclusive purpose of taking His own home to heaven. This is not about the earthly kingdom reign or about the final Great White Throne judgment so vividly described in Revelation 20:11-15. Around 56 AD, in 1 Corinthians 15, that was written a few years after Thessalonians (circa. 52), Paul calls the rapture "a mystery," that is, something not before revealed in the Old Testament. He writes, "Behold, I tell you a mystery; we shall not all sleep, but we shall all be changed, in a moment, in the twinkling of an eye, at the last trumpet; for the trumpet will sound, and the dead will be raised imperishable, and we shall all be changed" (vv. 51-52).

To the apostle Paul the rapture doctrine is no small issue. It will be the great rescue of the church before the terrible wrath of God falls on the world. The church, the body of Christ, is not destined for this wrath but for deliverance out from under it. While Christians have experienced much persecution and trials by the world, this persecution from the world is not the tribulation wrath of the end times. The "great tribulation" is the wrath of God upon rebellious humanity and is not to be experienced by the redeemed church saints.

THE CONTEXT OF 1:9-10

In chapter 1, Paul commends the Thessalonians for their "work of faith, labor of love, and steadfastness of hope in Christ" (v. 3). The gospel came powerfully to this people by the Holy Spirit, and many, eagerly and with full conviction, accepted the Lord Jesus as Savior (v. 5). Their faith then became known throughout the Greek regions of Macedonia and Achaia (v. 8). The apostle then says the Christians in these areas

> *report about us what kind of a reception we had with you [the Thessalonians], and how you turned to God from idols to serve a living and true God, and to wait for His Son from heaven, whom He raised from the dead, that is Jesus, who delivers us from the wrath to come (vv. 9-10) (Emphasis added).*

THE MIRACLE OF CONVERSION

We know that the conversion of the Thessalonians was more dramatic because they "turned to God from idols." Their salvation was a miracle and they were divinely chosen of the Lord to respond to the truth. On the human level, however, what was happening within the hearts and minds of these converts that made their response in faith so sudden?[10]

Some Bible scholars note that the "power" of the idols and false religions was wearing down. More and more Greeks were rejecting the impotent human-like gods, but other factors may have also come to play. While the Jews of the city had rejected the gospel with great violent anger, could some of the truth about the One true God of heaven, through the years, have spilled out from the synagogue, and prepared the pagans for the message of Christ? We may never know for sure. For certain, the conversion of these Gentiles was dramatic and apparently sudden, as seen to by the aorist tense of the verb epistrepho, "to turn."[11]

With enthusiasm the Thessalonian Christians began to serve or to be continuously serving (present infinitive) the Lord as a slave or bondservant (v. 9). Before, these Thessalonians, who were lost in their sins, were chained to dead, lifeless pagan idols. In contrast with the idols, God is said to be "a living" (zonti) God. And He is the true or "genuine" (alethinos) God who is "not dead" like the idols from which they turned, but He is alive. He is real as opposed to the phantom and senseless gods of the heathen.

THE PRETRIBULATIONAL RAPTURE OF THE CHURCH

In verse 10 Paul writes that the Thessalonian church was waiting for God's Son from heaven, who delivers us from the wrath to come! This verse introduces the rapture doctrine that the apostle elaborates on more specifically in 4:13-18. Interestingly he says the Thessalonians were said to be serving and to be waiting. Both of these parallel thoughts are grammatically present infinitives. They were "continuously waiting" for God's Son from heaven.

The impact of the verb to be waiting cannot be ignored. It has the idea "to look forward with patience and confidence." It makes clear this church was ready for His return. The thought of that return did not spell terror, for this coming was to rescue (is rescuing) us from the wrath to come (the coming wrath). Note also how they "were waiting" but then Paul says that this coming deliverance was for "us" as well. In other words, all believers in Christ who are living when He comes would be spared and saved from the wrath. It is certain also that Paul is not describing the coming of Jesus to reign on earth on the Davidic throne. This coming would be the taking the believer home to heaven by the rapture. The apostle will develop this "going up" (rather than the "coming down") in 4:13-18!

The "waiting" is for the rapture, the doctrine primarily revealed to Paul (1 Cor. 15:51-54). It was the now expectation of Paul and that generation of believers, and it should also be equally expected by our generation of saints in Christ. The rapture is meant to rescue the believers before the terror of the tribulation begins. Some critics today see this doctrine as escapism, but the Thessalonians did not. They were serving while they were waiting; thus they were doing both. As the old saying, "they were occupying until He comes!"

The who delivers us is a present active participle from ruomai that should be translated the one who is rescuing. Some scholars have translated it as a timeless substantive (that denotes characteristics of the noun), thus, "the Rescuer Jesus," or "Our Deliverer." He is our Savior (Matt. 1:21) true to His name Jesus (meaning Jehovah saves). The prophet Isaiah speaks of the Redeemer who "will come to Zion, and to those who turn from transgression in Jacob." Paul translates from Isaiah 59:20 the "Redeemer" as ho ruomenos meaning Rescuer and applies this to Christ (Rom. 11:26). However, in the context of Isaiah in this case, the reference is to Christ redeeming the nation of Israel when He comes to establish the messianic kingdom.

Ruomai comes from the Classical Greek word eruo but in Koine Greek the e is dropped. In Classical Greek eruo can be translated "drag, draw," implying force or violence as in "drag away the body of a slain hero," or "drag away, rescue friends." With the force of what is called in Greek the middle voice, this could be translated "to draw to one's self, with the specification being from evil or danger. The present participle could have the force of a prophetic future: "The One who will drag us [to Himself]."[12] At the rapture the Lord Jesus will drag the believers away from the impending tribulation and wrath of God.

THE SEVEN-YEAR TRIBULATION PERIOD IS THE WRATH

Paul further writes we are to be delivered "from the wrath to come" (v. 10b). The church is to be rescued from the wrath (orges) that is "coming" or "approaching." Some say Paul is talking about wrath that comes about in the mid part of the tribulation. Some also argue for a pre-wrath rapture. To do this they must say the only wrath mentioned in the tribulation that could fit here is the final or seventh bowl of wrath poured out on the earth, as mentioned in Revelation 16:17-21.

Those who argue this way see the church going through the middle of the tribulation or slightly later. Then believers are raptured to escape the final stages of the tribulation, not the entire tribulation! But this is ludicrous because the wrath of God comes on at the beginning of the tribulation, in fact, the entire period of the tribulation is the wrath of God. John the apostle writes that when the tribulation begins, in Revelation 6, the world begs to be hidden "from the presence of Him who sits on the throne, and from the wrath of the Lamb; for the great day of their wrath has come; and who is able to stand [up under it]" (vv. 16b-17)?

The seven-year period of tribulation is the wrath of Daniel's Seventieth Week that purges Israel and also becomes a judgment upon the world (vv. 12-17). The church, the body of Christ, is rescued by Jesus before that day comes (1 Thess. 5:9). The word wrath is a title description for the period just prior to the setting up of the Messiah's kingdom on earth, when God will afflict earth's inhabitants with an unparalleled series of physical torments because of their rejection of His will. This truth teaches that the Lord Jesus Christ will return to the earth. This rapture doctrine brings about an anticipation and leads the soul to wait for His appearing.[13]

THE WRATH IS ON ITS WAY

The wrath "coming" is a present active participle of erchomai. The wrath is on its way! Some translate this as "the wrath absolutely," or "the wrath absolutely, the Coming!" or "which is already coming." Some critics foolishly say the Thessalonians and others in the early church were tricked by Paul into believing that Christ should absolutely return at that very time. However the time of His appearance is up to the heavenly Father. We are not told the time of the rapture. Some think He returned "spiritually" in A.D. 70 to be with His people in a spiritual and metaphorical way; but this belief does not hold up when tested by all of the Bible passages on the subject.

The hope of the rapture is likened to a couple who has committed to getting married in the future; their union is certain though the date has not been set. The early church had great anticipation, but they certainly had no idea as to when the Lord would come for them. Believers still wait today because they know the "marriage" is certain, but "the when" is not known. The strong emotional desire of those early believers to be taken home to Him in the rapture should be prevalent among us today. In the Greek text in Titus 2:13 Paul puts it this way: "[We are] excitedly expecting continually the joyous prospect, even [the] glorious appearance of our great God, even [our] Savior, Christ Jesus!" (author's translation)

THE PRETRIBULATIONAL RAPTURE OF 1 THESSALONIANS 5:1-11

Paul's great rapture passage is 4:13-18. Here he writes about the resurrection of the church saints ("those who have fallen asleep in Jesus"). The souls of these who have died will be brought back with Jesus when He comes for all the church saints, those who are asleep and those living (v. 14) and they, "the dead in Christ," shall rise first before the living believers are taken up (vv. 15, 17). The raptured church believers, the ones "caught up," will meet those resurrected "in the clouds to meet the Lord in the air, and thus we shall always be with the Lord" (v. 17).

> For those who are resurrected and for those who are raptured, a real body is given. It is impervious to death and will last eternally, and yet it is an actual body. Some of the older commentaries envision the new body to be "spiritualized" or immaterial. But this is not so. Because Christ is a life-giving spirit (1 Cor. 15:45), the new body will be spiritual (v. 46), energized and supported by Christ's resurrected power. "Spiritual" does not mean that this body is an apparition or ghostlike; it will, however, be imperishable and immortal.[14]

THE DAY OF THE LORD

After explaining the rapture to the Thessalonians, Paul says he did not need to remind them about the day of the Lord (the terrible time of the tribulation), "For you yourselves know full well that the day of the Lord will come just like a thief in the night. While they are saying, 'Peace and safety!' then destruction will come upon them suddenly like birth pangs upon a woman with child; and they shall not escape" (5:2-3).

There are several important things to note about these verses:

While the Thessalonians were "uninformed" (4:13) about the rapture, they were not ignorant about the day of the Lord and the seven-year tribulation, for Paul says they well knew about this! (5:2). In all of the Jewish synagogues the day of the Lord was common teaching. The Thessalonians church was well educated on the issues of the day of the Lord, either by Paul, or through the Jewish community. In fact one of the problems of this church was that they thought, by all of the persecution they were experiencing, they could well be in that day. But Paul does not allow for this interpretation. As he explains the day of the Lord he keeps saying "they," the world, will say "peace and safety" just before that sudden destruction comes upon "them" (v. 3). The day of the Lord then would be the wrath Paul will describe in verse 9. The church will escape that wrath by the rapture! The Word of God outlines the horror of the day of the Lord:

> From these Scriptures it is inescapable that the nature or character of this period is that of wrath (Zeph. 1:15, 18; 1 Thess. 1:10; 5:9; Rev. 6:16-17; 11:18; 14:10, 19; 15:1, 7; 16:1, 19), judgment (Rev. 14:7; 15:4; 16:5, 7; 19:2), indignation (Isa. 26:20-21; 34:1-3),

> trial (Rev. 3:10), trouble (Jer. 30:7; Zech. 1:14-15; Dan. 12:1), destruction (Joel 1:15; 1 Thess. 5:3), darkness (Joel 2:2; Amos 5:18; Zeph. 1:14-18), desolation (Dan. 9:27; Zeph. 1:14-15), overturning (Isa. 24:1-4, 19-21), punishment (Isa. 24:20-21). No passage can be found to alleviate to any degree whatsoever the severity of this time that shall come upon the earth.[15]

Paul could be referring to any of the verses above when he speaks of the day of the Lord. Paul continues his argument and ties the cry of the world, "Peace and safety," when the tribulation destruction comes upon them. (The church is not mentioned here because she has been raptured.) This tribulation terror is the "birth pangs" first described in Jeremiah 30:5-6. The day is said "to be great," as a great tribulation, with none like it ever before. It is also called "the time of Jacob's distress (v. 7). Jesus picks up the thoughts of Jeremiah and speaks of the beginning of the tribulation "birth pangs" (Matt. 24:8) and the "great tribulation" that will come like no other day since the beginning of the world (v. 21). Paul also refers to Jeremiah 30:5-6 and the "birth pangs" that come upon a woman with child (1 Thess. 5:3). The church is not in this day of darkness that will overtake the world like a thief (v. 4). Those in the present church age are "sons of light and sons of day. We are not of night nor of darkness" (v. 5).

THE DELIVERANCE FROM THE WRATH

The apostle Paul then writes:

> *For God has not destined us for wrath, but for obtaining salvation through our Lord Jesus Christ (v. 9).*

The for gives the reason for the anticipation of deliverance. Those who trust Christ in this church age are not "assigned" to the wrath "that is on its way" (see 1:10). Destined (tithemi, aorist middle indicative) can mean "to place, position, firmly fix, determine, make something happen." The clause that follows might read, "God has [not] Himself assigned, appointed us for being recipients of His wrath." With the aorist tense and middle voice, the apostle is giving a firm, absolute soteriological promise, the keeping of which will be a sovereign act of the Lord. The promise has no conditions attached. "God, according to His own good will and pleasure has decreed that we shall escape the outpouring of His wrath."

Some hold to what is called "sanctification" rapture. The believers must be "holy" and good enough in order to escape the coming wrath. No one however has decided how good one has to be in order to be raptured! Neither is Paul describing a partial or pre-wrath rapture. The tribulation, the birth pangs, the wrath, is seen as a total entity of terror. Jeremiah, nor Christ, nor the apostle, breaks this period up. It is seen as an entire season of horrors on earth. And certainly Paul in no way says the church must go through any or part of this terrible period!

But what about those who become believers during the seven year-tribulation? Though the blood of Jesus has bought their salvation, they are not technically a part of this present dispensation of the church. They are not called members of the "body of Christ." Their earthly fate will be far different than what believers in Christ now face, that is, the rapture that carries us away from the coming wrath.

What is the difference in regard to believers now suffering tribulations and the sufferings that will come about during the seven-year tribulation? Present troubles are inflicted by the world. In the tribulation believers will suffer persecution, but those trials will produce far more martyrs. In the tribulation God's hand of protection will be removed, so to speak, as if the tribulation saints are specifically called to a life of sacrifice and martyrdom. That whole generation will be living distinctly under the wrath of God being poured out. It is so terrible, no one would survive if it were not stopped (Matt. 24:22). Presently, the church is in the period of grace.

This wrath (*orge*) Paul talks about is dramatically brought forth in Revelation 6 with the breaking of the seal judgments, and is a traumatic time on earth following the rapture of the church. The wrath mentioned here in 1 Thessalonians 5:9 can be no other than the wrath described in Revelation 6 and on.

Paul goes on in 5:9b and writes: "but for obtaining salvation through our Lord Jesus Christ."

Obtaining is the compound noun peripoiesis—*peri* (concerning, about) and poiesis (something made, provided, constructed, created), thus, "concerning [salvation] that has been provided" through our Lord Jesus

Christ. Obtaining is seen "passively" of the adoption of (consisting in) salvation bestowed by God. It must be remembered that salvation is threefold: (1) The believer is saved from the guilt of sin by the death of Christ. (2) He is enabled to overcome sin by the indwelling Holy Spirit. (3) Final delivery from the presence of sin occurs at death or at the rapture.

God's many promises are to all believers whether mature or spiritually carnal, whether spiritually watchful or not. Paul writes in verse 10: "That whether we are awake or asleep, we may live together with Him." All those in Christ will escape the wrath, whether walking in maturity or out of fellowship with the Lord (1:10). Paul is certainly not arguing that a believer should go about living in carnality, nor is he saying a child of the Lord is free to live however he wishes—in fact, he is saying just the opposite! All of our sins have been purged at the cross; our position in Jesus is based on His complete work of redemption. Thus the promise says that, although our experience in Christ may be weak and may need strengthening, every believer should be longing for the return of his Savior. And if the trumpet should sound tomorrow, all who are physically alive, who belong to Him, will join the resurrected in meeting Him in the air![16]

CONCLUSION

Salvation in the future has been completely provided by the finished work of Jesus, and it cannot be cancelled by lack of readiness. Carnality or lack of the same does not affect the issue one way or the other. Paul had to calm the fears of the Thessalonians in order to help them, and to convince them that they would participate in the parousia (the coming) no matter the degree of their preparedness. Every contingency for salvation was met at Christ's work at Calvary. Christians need not fear missing the Lord's return and the rapture, because they are "sons of light and sons of the day" (vv. 4-5). The blessedness of the future resurrection life, or the rapture if He should come today, is certain because of our union with Christ be our faith!

COMPARING THE RAPTURE AND THE SECOND COMING OF CHRIST

THE RAPTURE	THE SECOND COMING
• Christ prepares a place in heaven for the Church	• Christ returns to rule as King on earth
• Christ takes His own to heaven	• Christ's feet touch the Mount of Olives
• The elect of the Church meet the Lord in the air	• The elect of Israel gathered to Jerusalem
• The voice of the archangel is heard	• Many angels sound a great trumpet
• No signs given for His gathering His own	• Many signs given for His coming to rule
• Comforting hope for the future	• Israel will mourn when He comes to rule
• The "lost" will not see His arrival	• The world will see His coming in clouds
• Christ's power is not displayed to the world	• Christ comes with power and glory
• Believers removed from the coming wrath	• Unbelievers face His wrath
• No mention of His coming to rule	• He returns to rule
• Does not battle His enemies	• Does battle with His enemies
• Christ comes as Head of the Church	• Christ comes as "King of Kings"
• No earthly reign takes place	• The 1000 year reign takes place
• The "dead in Christ" are raised	• No mention of "those in Christ"
• Creation is left unchanged	• Creation is changed
• The rapture is called "a mystery"	• The second coming is not called a mystery
• Can happen at any moment	• Happens at the end of the tribulation

CHAPTER 17

THE RAPTURE AND THE RETURN: TWO ASPECTS OF CHRIST'S COMING

Ed Hindson

OVERVIEW

Is there a difference between the rapture and the second coming? Pretribulationists see clear biblical evidence for distinctions between the two events. Most opponents of pretribulationalism do not see these distinctions, even though the author finds overwhelming biblical evidence supporting a pretribulational rapture.

DO BELIEVERS FACE THE TRIBULATION?

And so we can see there will be no rapture for the church! "The pastor thundered as he reached the end of his sermon. "All we can really look forward to is trouble, trouble, and more trouble!"

I sat bemused. It had been a classic defense of the amillennial position on the return of Christ. Like many amillennialists, the pastor, a dear friend, assumed that times of tribulation would continue throughout the church age and intensify toward the end times. Dismissing the idea of a pretribulational rapture (by which the church would escape the Tribulation), he then dismissed the idea of any rapture at all, conveniently throwing 1 Thessalonians 4:13-18 right out the stained-glass windows!

Many who do not believe in a pretribulational rapture falsely assume there will be no rapture at all. This is a complete misconception. If one takes seriously passages like 1 Thessalonians 4: 17 ("We who are alive and remain shall be caught up together with them in the clouds, to meet the Lord in the air"), he or she is forced to conclude that there will be a rapture. The only real debate is over when it will occur.

Arguments raised against the rapture, on the basis that it is difficult to conceive of what it would be like for millions of people to suddenly disappear, are irrelevant. Joking remarks about bumping your head on the ceiling, or false teeth being left behind, or hundreds of car accidents suddenly occurring, are inconsequential in light of the fact that Scripture clearly states that we will be "caught up" (Greek, *harpaz*) into the air.

There will be a rapture! The only serious questions are: 1) When will it occur? and 2) What is its relationship to the return of Christ at the time of His second coming? If it can be proved that the body of believers (the church) will be "caught up" into heaven and that this "gathering together" (Greek, *episunagoges*, ct. 2 Thess. 2: 1) is a separate event from the return of Christ in judgment, the pretribulationist has more than adequately made his case.

As John Feinberg has so convincingly demonstrated, one must first examine the basic passages about the rapture and the return and then look at secondary issues in light of the primary passages.[1] Pretribulationists merely need prove that the dissimilarities between the rapture passages and the return passages are significant enough to indicate that they are separate events.

THE NATURE OF HIS COMING

The New Testament clearly teaches that Jesus Christ will "come again" (John 14:3) and "appear a second time" (Heb. 9:28) for His own. He promised this to His disciples in the upper room. "I go to prepare a place for you," the Lord told His disciples, "and if I go and prepare a place for you, 1 will come again, and receive you to Myself; that where I am, there you may be also" (John 14:2-3).

This is our Lord's first clear indication that He will return specifically and uniquely for His own. There is no reference in John 14 to a return in judgment upon the world. The promise of His return is specifically given to comfort the disciples during the time of His absence. Many believe this is the first clear reference in our Lord's teaching to the rapture of the believers.

In Hebrews 9:28, the writer also has believers in view when he states: "so Christ also, having been offered once to bear the sins of many, shall appear a second time for salvation." Again, the promise of our Lord's return for His own is sounded loud and clear.

At least nine biblical terms are used in the New Testament to describe the return of Christ:

1. *Ho erchomenos.* "The coming one," as in Hebrews 10:37: "For yet in a very little while, He who is coming will come."
2. *Erchomai.* The act of coming. Used often of Christ's return (Matt. 24:30; John 14:3; 2 Thess. 1:10; Jude 14; Rev. 1:7; 22:20).
3. *Katabain.* To "come down" or descend, as in 1 Thessalonians 4:16: "For the Lord Himself will descend from heaven with a shout."
4. *Hek.* Result of one's coming, to have "arrived," as in Revelation 3:3: "I will come like a thief."
5. *Parousia.* Denotes arrival and presence (of a ruler), as in 1 Thessalonians 2:19: "For what is our hope, or joy, or crown of exultation? Is it not even you, in the presence of our Lord Jesus Christ at His coming?"
6. *Apokalupsis.* Meaning to "unveil" or "uncover." Rendered "revelation" in 1 Peter 1:7; 1 Cor. 1:7; and Rev. 1:1. Involves the unveiling of His divine glory.
7. *Phanero.* To be "manifested" (John 21:1), or to "appear" (1 John 3:5): As in 1 John 3:2: "It is not appeared as yet what we shall be. We know that, when He appears, we shall be like Him; because we shall see Him just as He is."
8. *Epiphain.* To "appear" in full light or visibility, (2 Thess. 2:8) and the glory of "that day. . . to all who have loved His appearing" (2 Tim. 4:8).
9. *Hora.* To "see with the eyes," or to "appear" visibly, as in Hebrews 9:28: "shall appear a second time … to those who eagerly await Him."

These terms are often used interchangeably to refer to the rapture or the return of Christ One cannot build a convincing case for the distinction between the two events merely on the basis of the terms themselves.

THE TIME OF HIS COMING

Most evangelicals agree as to the nature of Christ's coming, but there is substantial disagreement about the time. Millard Erickson observes: "The one eschatological doctrine on which orthodox theologians most agree is the second coming of Christ It is indispensable to eschatology. It is the basis of the Christian's hope, the one event which will mark the beginning of the completion of God's plan."[2]

The New Testament picture of our Lord's return emphasizes at least six distinct aspects of the time of His coming. These may be summarized as follows:

1. *Future.* The entire emphasis of the New Testament points to a future return of Christ He promised "I will come again" (John 14:3). The angels promised He would return (Acts 1: 11). The apostles taught the certainty of His future return (Phil. 3:20; Titus 2:13; 2 Pet. 3:3-8; 1 John 3:2-3).

2. *Imminent.* The return of Jesus Christ is always described as potentially imminent or "is near" (Rev. 1:3; 22:10). Every generation of believers is warned to be ready for His coming, as Luke 12:40 states: "You too, be ready; for the Son of Man is coming at an hour that you do not expect." Believers are constantly urged to look for the coming of the Lord (Phil. 3:20; Heb. 9:28; Titus 2:13; 1 Thess. 5:6).

3. *Distant.* From God's perspective, Jesus is coming at any moment. But from the human perspective it has already been nearly 2000 years. Jesus hinted at this in the Olivet discourse in the illustration of the man who traveled into a "far country" (heaven) and was gone "a long time" (Matt. 25:19). Peter also implies this in his prediction that men will begin to scoff at the second coming, after a long period of time (2 Pet. 3:8-9).

4. *Undated.* While the rapture is the next major event on the prophetic calendar, it is undated, as is the glorious appearing of Christ. Jesus said: "But of that day and hour no one knows, not even the angels of heaven" (Matt. 24:36). Later he added: "It is not for you to know times or epochs" (Acts 1:7).

5. *Unexpected.* The mass of humanity will not be looking for Christ when He returns (Matt. 24:50; Luke 21:35). They will be saying "peace and safety," when suddenly caught unprepared by His

return. So unexpected will His return be that, "suddenly like a trap … it will come upon all those who dwell on the face of all the earth" (Luke 21:34-35).

6. *Sudden.* The Bible warns that Jesus will come "like a thief in the night... (and) then destruction" will come upon the unbelieving world (1 Thess. 5:2-3). His return for the bride will occur in a flash: "in a moment, in the twinkling of an eye … for the trumpet will sound, and the dead (believers) will be raised imperishable, and we (living believers) shall be changed" (1 Cor. 15:52).

TWO ASPECTS OF HIS COMING

There are certain similarities between the rapture passages and the second coming passages, since they both refer to future events relating to our Lord's return. But similarity does not mean they are referring to the same event. Pretribulationists believe that there are enough substantial differences between the two aspects of Christ's coming so as to render them as two separate and distinct events.

The distinction between these two phases of the second coming IS substantiated by the contrast between those passages that refer to our Lord's coming for His church and those referring to His coming to judge the unbelieving world. Thomas Ice has provided the following list to identify those distinctions.[3]

Rapture Passages		**Second Coming Passages**	
John 14:1-3	2 Thess. 2:1	Daniel 2:44-45	Acts 1:9-11
Rom. 8:19	1 Tim. 6:14	Daniel 7:9-14	Acts 3:19-21
1 Cor. 1:7-8	2 Tim. 4:1	Daniel 12:1-3	1 Thess. 3:13
1 Cor.15:51-53	Titus 2:13	Zech. 14:1-15	2 Thess. 1:6-10
1 Cor.16:22	Heb. 9:28	Matt. 13:41	2 Thess. 2:8
Phil. 3:20-21	James 5:7-9	Matt. 24:15-31	2 Peter 3:1-14
Col. 3:4	1Peter 1:7.13	Matt. 26:64	Jude 14-15
1 Thess. 1:10	1 John 2:28-3:2	Mark 13:14-27	Rev. 1:7
1 Thess. 2:19	Jude 21	Mark 14:62	Rev. 19:11-20:6
1 Thess. 4:13-18	Rev. 2:25	Luke 21:25-28	Rev. 22:7,12,20
1 Thess. 5:9	Rev. 3:10		
1 Thess. 5:23			

Ice comments that the rapture is characterized in the New Testament as a "translation coming," in which Christ comes for His church, taking her to His Father's house (John 14:3; 1 Thess. 4:15-17; 1 Cor. 15:51-52).[4] Here, He claims her as His bride and the marriage supper of the Lamb begins. Whatever view one holds in regard to our Lord's return, one thing is clear in prophetic Scripture, the marriage occurs in heaven (Rev. 19:7-9) before the triumphal return of Christ with His redeemed church at His side (Rev.19:11-16).

Non-pretribulationists are at a virtual loss to explain how the church got to heaven prior to returning with Christ at the battle of Armageddon. At best, some suggest they are "caught up" after the Tribulation only to return immediately with the Lord. This arrangement, however, leaves little or no time for the wedding!

The return of Christ is a series of events fulfilling all endtime prophecies. These include predictions of His coming for His church and His coming with His church. Pretribulationists divide the return of Christ in two main phases: the rapture of the church and the second coming of Christ. In the first aspect, our Lord comes to take His own (the living and the dead) to be with Him. In the second aspect, He returns with His resurrected and raptured saints to win the battle of Armageddon and to establish His kingdom on earth (Rev. 5:10, "and they will reign upon the earth").

The Bible is filled with detailed predictions about both aspects of Christ's return. Just as the Scripture predicted two aspects of our Lord's first coming (His suffering and His glory), so it predicts two aspects of His second coming. The different aspects of our Lord's return are clearly delineated in the Scripture. The only real issue in the eschatological debate is the time interval between them.

Pretribulationists place the seven-year Tribulation period between the rapture and the return. This allows for the proper fulfillment of Daniel's "seventieth week," and it clearly separates the rapture from the return. Others deal with this issue in the other chapters of this volume. It is my purpose merely to substantiate that there are adequate dissimilarities between the events of the rapture and the event associated with the return.

Rapture	Return
1. Christ comes for His own (John 14:3; 1 Thess. 14:17; 2 Thess. 2:1). 2. He comes in the air (1 Thess.4:17). 3. He claims His bride (1 Thess. 4:16-17). 4. Removal of believers (1 Thess. 4:17). 5. Only His own see Him (1 Thess. 4:13-18). 6. Tribulation begins (2 Thess. 1:6-9) 7. Saved are delivered from wrath (1 Thess. 1:10; 5-9). 8. No signs precede rapture (1 Thess. 5:1-3).	1. Christ comes with His own (1 Thess. 3:13; Jude 14; Rev. 19:14). 2. He comes to the earth (Zech. 14:4; Acts 1:11). 3. He comes with His bride (Rev. 19:6-14). 4. Manifestation of Christ (Mal. 4:2). 5. Every eye shall see Him (Rev. 1:7). 6. Millennial kingdom begins (Rev. 20:1-7) 7. Unsaved experience the wrath of God (Rev. 6:12-17). 8. Signs precede second coming (Luke 21:11,15).

CONTRAST BETWEEN THE RAPTURE AND THE RETURN

IS THE RAPTURE IN THE BIBLE?

The church's hope is the rapture. She awaits the Savior who is coming for His bride. The church may endure persecution, trouble, and difficulty in the meantime. But she is not the object of divine wrath. The church does not await destruction as the world does. Rather, she awaits the coming of her Lord and King. Peter explains that the present world is "reserved for fire, kept for the day of judgment and destruction of ungodly men" (2 Pet. 3:7).

The church is pictured in Scripture as the wife of the Lamb (Rev. 19:7-9). She is not the object of the wrath of the Lamb. He does not beat her up and then marry her! Or marry her, then beat her up! He may discipline her in love. But His ultimate purpose is to present her to the Father as His perfect bride.

The rapture (or "translation") of the church is often paralleled to the "raptures" of Enoch (Gen. 5:24) and Elijah (2 Kings 2: 12). In each case, the individual disappeared or was caught up into heaven. At His ascension, our Lord Himself was "lifted up" into heaven (Acts 1:9). The biblical description of the rapture involves both the resurrection of deceased believers and the transla-tion of living believers into the air to meet the Lord (1 Thess. 4:16-17; 1 Cor. 15:51-52).

The concept of the rapture is expressed in the biblical terms "caught up" (Greek, *harpaz*) and "gathered together" (Greek, *episunagoges*). Hogg and Vine observe that *harpaz* is the same verb used of Paul ("whether in the body, or apart from the body," 2 Cor. 12:2-4 KJV); Philip ("spirit ... caught away Philip," Acts 8:39 KJV); and the man child ("caught up to God," Rev. 12:5 KJV).[6] This explains that *harpaz* conveys the idea of force suddenly exercised and is best rendered "snatch" (John 10:28-29, where Jesus promises that no one can "snatch" His own out of His hand). He alone does the "snatching" at the time of the rapture!

By contrast, *episunagoges* refers to that which results from the "catching up" (*harpaz*). Once caught up into the clouds, we shall be "gathered together" with the Lord. In commenting on 2 Thessalonians 2:1, Hogg and Vine observe: "Here it refers to the 'rapture' of the saints into the air to meet and to be forever with the Lord."[7] The basic meaning is to "assemble together." The raptured church is pictured as the great "assembly" (synagogue) in the sky. Milligan observes:

> The word goes back to the saying of the Lord in Mark 13:27 ("gather together His elect"), and is found elsewhere in the New Testament only in Hebrews 10:25, where it is applied to the ordinary religious assembling of believers as an anticipation of the great assembling at the Lord's coming.[8]

Of course there is a rapture! There can be no valid system of biblical eschatology without a rapture. The church will be "caught up" and "gathered together" with her Lord. The only real debate is over the question of when. Any eschatological system that dismisses the rapture as some hoax has forfeited the essential biblical teaching that Christ will come and snatch away His bride to the great assembly in heaven.

Amillennialists, postmillennialists, and posttribulationists alike must account for the rapture in their eschatological schemes. So away with all talk of debunking the very idea of the rapture. It is taught in these passages of Scripture as clearly as any other doctrine. And any legitimate eschatological system must account for it. There will be a rapture. The question is whether it is separate from the return of Christ or a part of the same event.

ARE THE EVENTS OF THE RETURN DISTINCTLY DIFFERENT?

Those who reject a pretribulational rapture usually argue that the rapture happens simultaneous to the return of Christ.[9] The Lord descends from heaven, "catches up" the church, and then returns to set up His kingdom. In order to make the rapture occur simultaneous to the return, such systems emphasize the similarities between the two: In both Christ comes at the end of the age to bring in the consummation of all things.

However, a simple survey of the second coming passages reveals some significant differences. Unlike the rapture of the saints, several passages refer to our Lord's coming with His saints (1 Thess. 3:13, "at the coming of our Lord Jesus with all His saints"; Jude 14, "Behold, the Lord came with many thou-sands of His holy ones"; Rev. 19:14, "and the armies which are in heaven, clothed in fine linen, white and clean, were following Him on white horses"). Revelation 19:11-16 certainly refers to the church returning with Christ to judge the unbelieving world, overthrow the Antichrist and the false prophet, and to establish the millennial reign of Christ on earth.

Other second coming passages refer to a series of events that find no reference at all in the rapture passages: returning to the earth, splitting the Mount of Olives (Zech. 14:4); punishing the wicked in flaming fiery vengeance (2 Thess. 1:6-9); overthrowing political and ecclesiastical "Babylon" (Rev. 17-18); winning the battle of Armageddon (Rev. 16:16-21); defeating the Antichrist and the false prophet (Rev. 19:19-21); binding Satan in the bottomless pit (Rev. 20:1-3); establishing the reign of the saints upon the earth for a thousand years (Rev. 20:4-10).

All of these events associated with the return of Christ are completely distinct from the promise to rapture and assemble the church in heaven. These distinctions are surely sufficient to warrant viewing them as separate, though related, events. Having established this distinction, pretribulationists have adequate ground for viewing these events as being separated by the Tribulation period.

The church is promised that the coming of the Lord will result in her being "caught up" and "gathered together" unto Him. It is this promise of the rapture, not of the wrath, that is in view in Revelation 3:10, where the Scripture promises, "I also will keep you from [Greek, *ek* 'out of'] the hour of testing, that hour which is about to come upon the whole world." Only a pretribulational rapture makes this promise a reality.

TEN REASONS FOR A PRETRIBULATIONAL RAPTURE

1. Christ promised to keep the church from the Tribulation. In Revelation 3:10, the risen Christ said the church would be kept from (literally, "preserved," or "protected out of") the hour of trial, or divine retribution, that is coming on the whole world.

2. Tribulation judgments are the "wrath of the Lamb." Revelation 6:16 depicts the cataclysmic judgments of the end times as the wrath of Christ. Revelation 19:7-9 depicts the church as the bride of the Lamb. She is not the object of His wrath, which is poured out on an unbelieving world.

3. Jesus told His disciples to pray that they would escape the Tribulation. In Luke 21:36, He said: "But keep on the alert at all times, praying in order that you may have strength to escape all these things that are about to take place." Remember, even Lot was given a chance to escape Sodom before divine judgment fell.

4. His coming in the clouds means the church's deliverance has come. Jesus told His disciples: "Lift up your heads, because your redemption is drawing near" (Luke 21:28). The hope of the church is not in surviving the judgment of tribulation but in escaping it.

5. God will call His ambassadors home before declaring war on the world. In 2 Corinthians 5:20, believers are called "ambassadors for Christ," who appeal to the world to be reconciled to God before it is too late. In biblical times, one's ambassadors were recalled when it was time to make war with the enemy.

6. Moral restraint will disappear when the church is taken home.

Second Thessalonians 2:1-11 warns that after the "coming of our Lord" and "our gathering together to Him," the "man of lawlessness" (Antichrist) will emerge on the world scene. The church's restraining ministry of "salt" and "light" will no longer hold back the tide of evil.

7. The rapture will happen in the "twinkling of an eye." First Corinthians 15:51-52 promises that "in a moment, in the twinkling of an eye . . . the dead will be raised imperishable and we [living at the rapture] shall be changed." This instantaneous disappearance will terminate the church's earthly ministry.

8. The rapture will take place in the air. Unlike the glorious appearing, when Christ descends to earth, splits the Mount of Olives, overthrows Antichrist, and binds Satan, the rapture will occur when we are "caught up together ... to meet the Lord in the air" (1 Thess. 4:17).

9. The woman who suffers persecution during the Tribulation symbolizes Israel This is a very important point. The woman who delivers the male child (Christ) represents the nation of Israel. Israel, not the church brought forth Christ, and He in turn brought forth the church. He is the founder of the church, not its descendant. Therefore, the persecuted "saints" of the Tribulation are Jewish: the remnant of the woman's seed (Rev. 12:1-2,5-6,17).

10. The Marriage of Christ (Lamb) and His bride (church) takes place before the battle of Armageddon. The Bible describes the fall of "Babylon" (kingdom of Antichrist) in Revelation 17-18. But before it tells of Christ's return to conquer the Antichrist, it tells us "the marriage of the Lamb has come, and His bride has made herself ready" (Rev. 19:7-8). This clearly indicates the bride has been taken to heaven earlier, and that she returns with Christ and the host of the "armies which are in heaven, clothed in fine linen, white and clean" (Rev. 19:8,14).

We have clearly seen from the New Testament that the rapture and the second coming are different in nature and therefore separate events. This observation, that there are two future comings, is an important element for determining the timing of the rapture. It is not surprising that non-pretribulationists often ignore these biblical distinctions. A literal interpretation of the passages involved in the two comings is best represented by a pretribulational perspective.

(This chapter originally appeared in *When the Trumpet Sounds*, and is reprinted with the permission of the author and Harvest House Publishers.)

PART FOUR

TO GOD BE THE GLORY!

DISPENSATIONS OF SCRIPTURE				
Innocence Gen. 1:28 – 3:6	Conscience Gen. 4:1 – 8:14	Government Gen. 8:15 – 11:32	Promise Gen. 12:1 – Exod. 18:27	Law Exod. 19:3 – Acts 1:26
Church Acts 2:1 – 2 Thess. 4	[Tribulation Wrath] Rev. 6 – 19:10	Kingdom Rev. 19:11 – 20:9	Eternity Rev. 21:1 – 22:19	

CHAPTER 18

GOD'S OVERALL EARTHLY PLAN

Elmer Towns

God has always dealt with the future. The very first verse in the Bible deals with the future, "In the beginning God created the heavens and the earth" (Gen. 1:1). In eternity past, there was nothing—no throne, no angels, there was not even time and space. There was nothing but God. And God who does not do things aimlessly, had a future purpose for which He created all things, and He had a future plan for the universe and mankind that He created.

God didn't need anything, nevertheless He created the universe for the one thing He couldn't do for Himself. God can't worship Himself. God can affirm His own existence, I AM WHO I AM (Exod. 3:14), but Jesus told us what God really wants, "for such people the Father seeks to be His worshippers" (John 4:23).

The history of the Bible is divided into periods of time; the world calls these epochs, civilizations, or some other term. The Bible calls these dispensations or ages. When Paul described the current Church Age he said, "which in other generations was not made known to the sons of men, as it has now been revealed to His holy apostles and prophets in the Spirit;" (Eph 3:5). As he writes to the new church in Ephesus, he said that for the cause of Christ he is a prisoner for the Gentiles (3:1), and then he adds, "if indeed you have heard of the stewardship of God's grace which was given to me for you;" (3:2). Paul tells us it is his duty to explain these dispensations to the reader.

The word dispensation comes from the Greek word for "manager of the household"; today's terminology would be like a sports manager, i.e., one who manages the daily affairs for another. Scofield says that the dispensation is "a period of time during which man is tested in respect to obedience to some specific revelation to the will of God."[1] Charles Ryrie adds to this definition, "A dispensation includes such ideas of distinctive revelation, testing, failure and judgment."[2]

Accordingly, we are now living in the sixth dispensation of the Church, also called the dispensation of grace or the Holy Spirit. Jesus called it, "The times of the Gentiles" (Luke 21:24). Anyone who is not a Jew is a Gentile, and God is not working primarily with the Jews today, but with the Gentile church.

THE FIRST DISPENSATION – INNOCENCE

In the first dispensation God put Adam in a perfect garden and gave him certain priorities to fulfill for Him in the garden. In love and goodness, God gave Adam everything he needed; but he had certain duties. These were: (1) to replenish the earth with children (Gen. 1:28); (2) to use nature (subdue the earth); i.e., to provide his food, shelter, clothing, etc. (1:28); (3) to have dominion over animal life (1:28); (4) to eat fruit and vegetables (1:29); (5) to work for his sustenance (2:15); and (6) to obey God by abstaining from eating of the tree in the middle of the garden that was prohibited by Him.

This is called the dispensation of innocence because our first parents were to live in innocence, eating every fruit in the garden except the fruit of the tree of the knowledge of good and evil (2:17).

The first dispensation, like all others, ends in failure, Adam deliberately disobeyed God and experienced the knowledge of both good and evil. His transgression ended his broad conscious knowledge of right and wrong. In judgment, Adam was thrown out of the garden (a perfect environment provided by God). Man was not able to obey or please God in a perfect environment and live in innocence. Every dispensation that follows would also demonstrate man's inability to live by God's requirements.

THE SECOND DISPENSATION – CONSCIENCE

The requirements of the second dispensation grew out of the failure of man in the first dispensation. When man sinned in the garden: (1) the serpent, Satan's tool, was cursed and reduced from the beautiful creature to a hated reptile; (2) a prediction was made that Satan would be destroyed with a future head blow (Gen. 3:15); (3) the Seed of the woman would redeem man and destroy Satan (3:15); (4) physical work would be hard and despised, but necessary for life (3:19); (5) nature (Creation) would be cursed and only reluctantly give its fruit for man's necessities (3:17, 18); (6) a woman would have sorrow in childbirth and would be in submission to her husband (3:16); and (7) physical death for the human race (Romans. 5:12).

In this second dispensation of conscience, man would have an inborn conscience that helped determine right and wrong, and man would experientially accumulate a limited knowledge of right and wrong as he applied a knowledgeable conscience to every situation and was given the general responsibility to abstain from all known evil, and the responsibility to perform all noble good.

During the dispensation of conscience, man enjoyed a long physical life, but was not able to follow his conscience. Rather than doing good, "every intent of the thoughts of his heart was only evil continually" (Gen. 6:5). The judgment of the dispensation of the conscience was the flood, "the LORD was sorry that He had made man on the earth, and He was grieved in His heart" (6:6).

THE THIRD DISPENSATION – GOVERNMENT

The story of the flood is well known, and only eight people were left alive. After the flood, God introduced a new covenant to people, i.e., new principles by which they should live. The rainbow was "the sign of the covenant which I am making between Me and you and every living creature that is with you, for all successive generations;" (Gen. 9:12). God no longer allows the conscience of the individual to be the sole basis of human life. Rather, God dealt with corporate mankind as they lived together. In the Noahic Covenant God confirmed certain elements of previous covenants, He told Noah: (1) to subdue the earth and to provide for his necessities (Gen. 7:1); (2) the physical laws of the universe remained ordered (8:12); and God promised, (3) the earth would never have a universal flood (9:15).

The core of the Noahic Covenant was the corporate expression of the judicial taking of life (9:6), which is the ultimate expression of government. All other laws of government that lead up to that judicial decision and find their credibility in the death penalty, i.e., capital punishment.

The three sons of Noah formed three families and were told to go their separate ways, i.e., to inhabit the world. God promised to bless each of the separate families, and implied in their separate blessings was their separate existence as families that were to enlarge into nations.

The test of the dispensation of human government was corporate government of nations or societies, whereby they governed themselves according to God's requirement. The Bible says very little about this dispensation, and how man lived under this test, or how he lived and fulfilled this task. A written history of this dispensation is found in the development of the different sons of Noah, hence Genesis 10:1-32 is only representative of the lengthy but unknown period of time. However, the failure of man to govern himself corporately is well known, i.e., the Tower of Babel, and its following judgment.

Man tried to build a tower unto God, i.e., a ziggurat where a false god was falsely worshipped. "And the LORD came down to see the city and the tower which the sons of men had built" (11:5). God did not like what He saw, "Behold, they are one people, and they all have the same language. And this is what they began to do, and now nothing which they purpose to do will be impossible for them" (11:6).

God judged them by confusing their languages, which implied more than changing their spoken word symbols, it included changing their thought processes, values (dreams), and ethics (judgment of good and evil). "Come, let Us go down and there confuse their language, that they may not understand one another's speech." So the LORD scattered them abroad from there over the face of the whole earth;" (11:7, 8).

THE FOURTH DISPENSATION - PROMISE

When God called Abraham and set him apart, it was a dramatic turning point in history. Up to this point God had dealt with all humanity in different dispensations, now He was going to separate Abraham from the vast river of mankind. God would deal with Abraham and the Jews separately from the Gentiles.

Through Abraham, God promised to bring blessing to the entire world. The Abrahamic Covenant involved: (1) to make out of him a great nation, meaning the Jewish nation would be influential and continue in existence; (2) to bless this nation with financial and spiritual prosperity (Gen. 12:2); (3) to make the name of Abraham universal and enduring; (4) to be a blessing to Abraham (Gal. 3:13, 14); (5) to bless the nations that bless the seed of Abraham; (7) to bless all the families of the earth through Abraham's Seed, the Christ (Gen. 12:3); (8) that God would first show Abraham the land (12:1); then when he obeyed, God promised to give him the land (12:1), hence it is the Promised Land.

Since each dispensation includes a testing, in the fourth dispensation man is tested by his involvement with promises of God. Remember this dispensation relates only to the descendants of Abraham, not all mankind. But the seed of Abraham refused to live by faith in the land, so they migrated to Egypt. The final testing and failure of Israel in this dispensation of promise was when God attempted to bring them out of Egypt into the Promised Land, but they refused in unbelief at Kadesh-Barnea. Israel then wandered forty years in the wilderness.

THE FIFTH DISPENSATION – LAW

The covenant that God gave on Mount Sinai was the Mosaic Covenant as reflected in the giving of the law. Among the many purposes of the law was that it revealed to man that he is a personal sinner before God. During the previous dispensations man was a sinner, even when he did not have knowledge of the law. Paul tells us, "Death reigned from Adam to Moses, even over those who had not sinned in the likeness of the offense of Adam" (Rom. 5:14).

The Mosaic Covenant was not given as a means of life or death (it only revealed death): (1) the law reflected the holiness of a personal God; (2) it instructed them in God's discipline; (3) it reminded them of God's salvation (through its priests and sacrifices); and (4) it was a pedagogue, a schoolmaster, to take them to Christ (Gal. 3:24).

The Mosaic Covenant was expressed in three divisions: (1) the commandments expressing the righteous will of God; (2) the judgments expressing the social life of Israel; and (3) the ordinances directing the religions life of Israel. Jesus called all these "the law" (Matt. 5:17) and they were a "ministry of condemnation" (2 Cor. 3:7-9). No one was ever saved by keeping the law, it was simply God's testing for Israel. The nation's failure to keep the law ended in judgment, as did all other dispensational periods of time.

The fourth dispensation of the Law ended in the cross-judgment of Christ. He perfectly kept the law (Matt. 5:17), then nailed the law to the cross (Col. 2:14), and abolished "in His flesh the enmity, which is, the law of commandments contained in ordinances" (Eph. 2:15). Just as the principles of the previous covenants continue into the next dispensations, so the principles of the law continue past the cross-judgment of Christ. He did not take the law away, only the penalties of the law.

THE SIXTH DISPENSATION – GRACE OR THE CHURCH

This new dispensation is based on the new covenant that God revealed to the world through Abraham (Jer. 31). This new covenant is also called the New Testament. The New Covenant is "better": (1) because it is unconditional, "This is the covenant I will make with the house of Israel" and "I will be their God" (Heb. 8:10); (2) because God guarantees that men will keep its conditions, "I will put My laws into their minds and I will write them upon their hearts" (8:10); (3) because it would extend to all, "for all shall know Me, from the least to the greatest of them" (8:11); (4) because it will completely eradicate sins, "For I will be merciful to their iniquities, and I will remember their sins no more."(8:12) and (5) because it rests upon the sacrifice of Christ, the better Mediator, and assures eternal blessedness for those who accept.

The test of the dispensation of grace is no longer legal obedience to the Law, but rather "what will a person do with Jesus Christ?" A person must accept Jesus Christ as Savior and live by grace. The predicted end to the dispensation of grace happens when the professing church rejects grace living and slides into apostasy. The world is judged by the Tribulation for rejecting Jesus Christ and turning to every type of religion.

We know, of course, that believers must go through "many tribulations [to] enter into the kingdom of God" (Acts 14:22); but there is besides this common experience a future period of tribulation. In Dan. 12:1 it is spoken of as "a time of trouble, such as never was since there was a nation, even to that time;" in Matt. 24:21-29 it is described as a "great tribulation; Luke 21:34-36 refers to it as "that Day," depicted in the preceding part of the chapter; Rev. 3:10 speaks of it as "the hour of trial which shall come upon the whole world, to test those who dwell on the earth;" and in Rev. 7:14 we read of a great multitude who had come "out of the great tribulation." In the Old Testament it is referred to as the "time of Jacob's distress" (Jer. 30:4-7) and the time of God's indignation with the inhabitants of the earth (Isa. 24:17-21; 26:20, 21; 31:1-3; Zech. 14:1-3). That the Tribulation period will come between the two phases of Christ's coming appears from a study of the whole program of the future. Note particularly that Matt. 24:29 declares that it will close with Christ's return in glory, i.e., with His Revelation.[3]

THE SEVENTH DISPENSATION – THE KINGDOM

God first promised a Redeemer-Seed through Eve (Gen. 3:15), then later He narrowed the promise to Shem (9:26), then still narrower to the seed of Abraham (12:3); finally, to the tribe of Judah (49:10).

The Redeemer-Seed is promised to come from the descendants of David in the Davidic Covenant (Ps. 89:20-37). This is an unconditional covenant, based on the nature and promise of God. Remember, God promised to bless the seed of Abraham in the Abrahamic Covenant and God gave His laws in the Mosaic Covenant, and now God establishes His rule over His people in the Davidic Covenant.

The Davidic Covenant has a fourfold promise: (1) that God would establish David's throne (2 Sam. 7:13), i.e., a family line; (2) that God would establish a throne (7:13), i.e., authority from God to rule over His people; (3) that God would establish His kingdom (7:13), i.e., a sphere of rule; and (4) that God would recognize David's reign in perpetuity (7:13).

The seventh and last dispensation is the direct rule of Christ over Israel in the land, and the other nations upon the earth. This seventh dispensation grows out of the apocalyptic judgment at the end of the Church Age, i.e., the Tribulation and battle of Armageddon. Christ rules directly through David and other delegate authorities. Eventually, mankind rebels against God's rule on the earth (Rev. 20:7-9), verifying the truth that man will rebel against God no matter what conditions, and no matter what the test. Therefore, no one in the future will ever be able to challenge the righteousness of God concerning His test and judgment. Man fails under every conceivable kind of conditions and government, and in every dispensation God's righteousness is vindicated.

This dispensational approach provides the believer a biblical orientation to history. It is important to understand that God has a purpose for placing man on this earth (for worship and praise) and that in every age and dispensation God expected man to worship Him and live in accordance with His will and keep the conditions for that dispensation.

In this present Church dispensation, we do not live under the Mosaic dispensation of Law, rather we are now under the commands called the Law of Christ (1 Cor. 9:21; Gal. 6:2). Our current responsibilities are combined from previous ages and continue to give us a complete biblical framework for understanding God and how we can please Him; yet in this dispensation of grace and the church, we must handle "accurately the word of truth" (2 Tim. 2:15) and live according to God's expectations (2 Cor. 2:15).

NOTES

Chapter 1 – Globalism and the New World Order

[1]"The Moscow Connection: Gorbachev and Bush," Newsweek, 17 Sept. 1990.

[2]United Nations Conference on Environment and Development (UNCED) or Earth Summit, June 1992.

[3]ICPD Programme of Action, Interactive Population Center, United Nations Population Fund.

[4]"Gendered Habitat," United Nations Human Settlements Programme, UN-Habitat.

[5]Maurice Strong quoted in Earth in Focus (1992) No. 2, UNCED, 2.

[6]Ashley Montague, lecture at Anaheim, California, 9 Nov. 1970, quoted in Vince Nesbitt, Humanistic Moral and Values Education, N.S.W. 2066 Australia, 5.

[7]Paul Brandwein, The Social Sciences (New York: Harcourt Brace, 1970), T10.

[8]Buckminster Fuller quoted in William Bowen, Globalism: America's Demise (Shreveport, LA: Huntington House, 1984), 20.

[9]Dr. Pierce, addressing teachers in Denver, Colorado in 1973, quoted in "Education to Remold the Child," Parent and Child Advocates, Rt. 4, Watertown, Wisconsin 53094, 30.

Chapter 2 – The New Interpretation of Bible Prophecy

[1]See "An Interview: Dr. John F. Walvoord Looks at Dallas Seminary," Dallas Connection 1/3 (Winter 1994): 4.

[2]Grand Rapids, Kregel, 2002.

[3]Forward to The Eclipse of the Reformation in the Evangelical Church, eds. Gary L. W. Johnson and R. Fowler White (Phillipsburg, NJ: Presbyterian and Reformed, 2001), xix.

[4]Iain H. Murray, Evangelicalism Divided: A Record of Crucial Change in the Years 1950 to 2000 (Edinburgh: Banner of Truth, 2000), 51.

[5]Ibid., 185.

[6]Alan Rifkin, also entitled "Jesus with a Genius Grant," Los Angeles Times Magazine (November 23, 2003): 22-25, 38-40.

[7]Ibid., 24.

[8]Stuart Silverstein and Andy Olsen, "Evangelical Colleges Make Marks in a Secular World," Los Angeles Times (November 30, 2003): A1.

[9]Teresa Watanabe, "Evangelical Seminary Reaches Out to Muslims," Los Angeles

Times (December 6, 2003): B1, B13.

[10]Ibid.

[11]Jay Tolson, webpage: <www.usnews.com/usnews/issue/031208/misc/8evangelicals.htm>.

[12]Ibid. [emphasis added]

[13]Andreas J. Köstenberger, "Editorial," JETS 47/1 (March 2004), 2.

[14]See Thomas, Evangelical Hermeneutics 23-24, 26, 28, for the eight definitions and their sources.

[15]Ibid., 27-31.

[16]Some time in the early 1980s a major evangelical publisher's representative responded negatively to my suggestion of a new work on grammatical-historical principles because of a shift in evangelical hermeneutics. In personal conversation a little later, a prominent OT scholar divulged a similar experience when he was told by a major evangelical publisher that his proposed work on hermeneutics would not sell because it did not represent the recent hermeneutical trend among evangelicals.

[17]M. S. Terry, Biblical Hermeneutics: A Treatise on the Interpretation of the Old and New Testaments (1885; reprint, Grand Rapids: Zondervan, 1947), 205.

[18]G. R. Osborne, Hermeneutical Spiral: A comprehensive Introduction to Biblical Interpretation (Downers Grove, Ill.: InterVarsity, 1991), 88-89.

[19]Ibid., 89.

[20]Craig A. Blaising and Darrell L. Bock, Progressive Dispensationalism (Wheaton, Ill.: Victor, 1993), 35-36. [emphasis added]

[21]In a public dialogue between Robert Saucy, the father of PD, and myself in 2001, I represented dispensationalism and he represented PD. I spent my whole allotted time on the subject of hermeneutics, but his only mention of the subject came when he disclaimed responsibility for what some of his PD "children" were advocating regarding a change in hermeneutics being at the root of PD.

22D. E. Aune, The New Testament in Its Literary Environment (Philadelphia: Westminster, 1987), 13.

[23]Blomberg, "New Testament Genre Criticism for the 1990s," Themelios 15/2 (January-February 1990):45.

[24]D. E. Aune, "The Form and Function of the Proclamations to the Seven Churches (Revelation 2–3)," NTS 36/2 (Apr 1990):183.

[25]James L. Blevins, "The Genre of Revelation," RevExp 77/3 (Summer 1980): 393-408.

[26]David E. Aune, "The Apocalypse of John and the Problem of Genre," Semeia 36 (1986): 66.

[27]Aune, "The Apocalypse" 67-91. As for terminology, a distinction between "apoc-

alypses" (as literature), "apocalyptic eschatology" (as a world view), and "apocalypticism" (as a socio-religious movement) appears to have wide acceptance among specialists in this area of study (Theodore N. Swanson, "The Apolyptic Scriptures," J.Dharma 8 [July 1982]: 314; James C. VanderKam, "Recent Studies in Apocalyptic," Word and World 4 [Winter 1984]: 71-72; Aune, "The Apocalypse" 67), though acceptance is by no means universal (VanderKam, "Recent Studies" 73; Adela Yarbro Collins, "Reading the Book of Revelation in the Twentieth Century," Int 40/3 [July 1986]: 235-38). The purpose of this study is not to advance proposed distinctions in definition, but to comment on the literary result. The socio-religious movement that produced the Apocalypse is the one begun by Jesus and continued by the apostles, not the apocalyptic spirit that developed among the Jews following the abuses of Antiochus Epiphanes (contra Swanson, "Apocalyptic Scriptures" 321-27). Within this framework apocalyptic eschatology cannot be distinguished from prophetic eschatology as, for example, being more pessimistic (contra ibid., 314-17). The outlook of the two is no different. The brief evaluation here elaborates on the literary factors of Revelation as compared to other "apocalypses."

[28]Aune, "The Apocalypse," 86-91.

[29]David E. Aune, Prophecy in Early Christianity and the Ancient Mediterranean Word (Grand Rapids: Eerdmans, 1983), 108; idem, The New Testament 226-27.

[30]Robert H. Mounce, The Book of Revelation, NIC (Grand Rapids: Eerdmans, 1977) 19-23; Paul J. Achtemeier, "An Apocalyptic Shift in Early Christian Tradition: Reflections on Some Canonical Evidence," CBQ 45/2 (Apr 1983): 232. Ladd is too narrow in his statement that "the central element in apocalyptic is the glorious second coming of Jesus Christ, who will raise the dead, judge persons and usher in the glories of the Age to Come" (George E. Ladd, "New Testament Apocalyptic," RevExp 78/2 [Spring 1981]: 205).

[31]Leon Morris, The Revelation of St. John, TNTC (Grand Rapids: Eerdmans, 1969) 23-25; Mounce, Revelation 23-25; Blevins, "Genre" 393; Lowell J. Satre, "Interpreting the Book of Revelation," WW 4/1 (Winter 1984): 60-61.

[32]Paul Feine, Johannes Behm, and Werner Georg Kümmel, Introduction to the New Testament, trans., A. J. Mattill, Jr. (Nashville: Abingdon, 1966) 324; Morris, Revelation 23.

[33]David Hellholm, "The Problem of Apocalyptic Genre and the Apocalypse of John," Society of Biblical Literature 1982 Seminar Papers, ed. Kent Harold Richards (Chico, CA: Scholars Press, 1982), 164-65.

[34]Craig A. Blaising, "Premillennialism," in Three Views on the Millennium and Beyond, ed. Darrell L. Bock [Grand Rapids: Zondervan, 1999] 209 n. 72.

[35]Robert L. Thomas, Revelation 1–7: An Exegetical Commentary, ed. Kenneth Barker (Chicago: Moody, 1992), 25.

[36]Ibid.

[37]Ibid., 29. Blaising exemplifies an all-too-often tendency of recent evangelical scholars in practicing superficial scholarship. They attain their scholarly reputations because of agreements with nonevangelical scholars, not because of the thoroughness of their research. Unfortunately, they often do not check the claims of their nonevangelical counterparts. Rather, they slavishly copy their conclusions.

[38]K. L. Gentry, Jr., "A Preterist View of Revelation," Four Views on the Book of Revelation, ed. C. M. Pate (:Grand Rapids: Zondervan, 1998) [38]. [emphasis in the original]

[39]E.g., David Chilton, The Days of Vengeance (Fort Worth, Tex.: Dominion, 1987), 63-64.

[40]Gentry, "Preterist View," 38.

41M. C. Tenney, Interpreting Revelation (Grand Rapids: Eerdmans, 1957), 143.

[42]R. H. Mounce, The Book of Revelation, NICNT (1977), 43.

[43]S. Hamstra, Jr., "An Idealist View of Revelation," in Four Views on the Book of Revelation, 96-97.

[44]Theological Educatin Fund, Ministry in Context: The Third Mandate Programme of the Theological Education Fund (1970-77) (Bromiley, Kent, U.K.: New Life, 1972); cf. G. Fackre, "Evangelical Hermeneutics," Int 43/2 (April 1989):128.

[45]See chapters 4, 7, and 14 of Thomas, Evangelical Hermeneutics, for more discussion of contextualization.

[46]W. C. Kaiser, Jr., "Legitimate Hermeneutics," in Inerrancy (Grand Rapids: Zondervan, 1979), 122; N. L. Geisler, "Does Purpose Determine Meaning?" WTJ 51/1 (spring 1989):153-55.

[47]Blomberg, "Genre Criticism," 46.

[48]G. K. Beale, The Book of Revelation: A Commentary on the Greek Text (Grand Rapids: Eerdmans, 1999), 48.

[49]H. S. Kvanig, "The Relevance of the Biblical Visions of the End Time," Horizons in Biblical Theology 11/1 (June 1989): 49-50.

[50]For documentation on these four, see Thomas, Evangelical Hermeneutics, 332-33, 347.

[51]Leland Ryken, Words of Life: A Literary Introduction to the New Testament (Grand Rapids: Baker, 1987), 144-45.

[52]C. M. Pate, "A Progressive Dispensationalism View of Revelation," in Four Views on the Book of Revelation, 173-75.

[53]Triumph of the Lamb: A Commentary on Revelation. Phillipsburg, N.J.: P & R, 2001.
[54]For a full discussion of "the seven spirits," see Thomas, Revelation 1–7, 66-68.
[55]M. S. Terry, Biblical Hermeneutics: A Treatise on the Interpretation of the Old and New Testaments (1885; reprint, Grand Rapids: Zondervan, 1947), 595.
[56]E.g., C. A. Blaising and D. L. Bock, "Dispensationalism, Israel and the Church: Assessment and Dialogue," in Dispensationalism, Israel, and the Church: The Search for Definition (Grand Rapids: Zondervan, 1992), 380; idem, Progressive Dispensationalism, 58-61.
[57]Blaising and Bock, Progressive Dispensationalism, 59.
[58]D. McCartney and C. Clayton, Let the Reader Understand: A Guide to Interpreting and Applying the Bible (Wheaton: Victor, 1944), 65.
[59]Terry, Biblical Hermeneutics, 231. [emphasis in the original]
[60]D. L. Bock, "The Son of David and the Saints' Task: The Hermeneutics of Initial Fulfillment," BSac 150/600 (October-December 1993):445.
[61]Ibid., 445 n. 9. Blaising and Bock elsewhere call the three levels of reading the historical-exegetical, the biblical-theological, and the canonical-systematic (Progressive Dispensationalism 100-101).
[62]Bock, "The Son of David," 447.
[63]Ibid.
[64]D. L. Bock, "Current Messianic Activity and Old Testament Davidic Promise: Dispensationalism, Hermeneutics, and New Testament Fulfillment," Trinity Journal 15 NS (1994):71; cf. Blaising and Bock, Progressive Dispensationalism, 64.
[65]Blaising and Bock, Progressive Dispensationalism, 29-30.
[66]Bernard Ramm, Protestant Biblical Interpretation: A Textbook of Hermeneutics, 3d rev. ed. (Grand Rapids: Baker, 1970), 113.
[67]Blaising and Bock, "Dispensationalism, Israel and the Church," 392-93.
[68]Blaising and Bock, Progressive Dispensationalism, 68.
[69]Bock, "Current Messianic Activity," 71.
[70]Ibid.
[71]Terry, Biblical Hermeneutics, 583.
[72]E.g., McCartney and Clayton, Let the Reader Understand, 162, 164; W. W. Klein, C. L. Blomberg, and R. L. Hubbard Jr., Introduction to Biblical Interpretation (Dallas: Word, 1993), 139, 145-50; Moisés Silva in a work coauthored with Walter C. Kaiser Jr., An Introduction to Biblical Hermeneutics: The Search for Meaning (Grand Rapids: Zondervan, 1994), 267.
[73]Blaising and Bock, Progressive Dispensationalism, 64.
[74]Ibid.; cf. also ibid., 65-68.

[75]Bock elsewhere denies that this practice amounts to sensus plenior or spiritualizing interpretation, choosing to refer to it as "pattern" fulfillment or typological-prophetic fulfillment ("Current Messianic Activity," 69; cf. Blaising and Bock, Progressive Dispensationalism, 102-4). Whatever name one applies to the practice, it still violates the strict standards of a consistent grammatical-historical interpretation.

[76]Blaising and Bock, Progressive Dispensationalsim, 93-96.

[77]C. Marvin Pate, A Progesssive Dispensationalism View of Revelation," in Four Views on the Book of Revelation, ed. C. Marvin Pate (Grand Rapids: Zondervan, 1998), 160.

[78]R. L. Saucy, The Case for Progressive Dispensationalsim: The Interface Between Dispensational and Non-Dispensational Theology (Grand Rapids: Zondervan, 1993), 49.

[79]Ibid., 71.

[80]Ibid., 206.

[81]Kenneth L. Gentry, Jr., Before Jerusalem Fell: Dating the Book of Revelation (Tyler, Tex.: Institute for Christian Ecomomics, 1989), 5 n. 12, 336-37.

[82]Gentry, Before Jerusalem Fell, 162-63.

[83]Ibid., 163-64, 310-16.

[84]Ibid., 223-224, 233.

[85]Ibid., 250-53.

[86]Ibid., 234.

[87]Ibid., 254-55.

[88]Ibid., 336.

[89]Ibid., 121-23; Chilton, Days of Vengeance 64.

[90]Chilton, Days of Vengeance 64; Gentry, Before Jerusalem Fell, 131-32.

[91]Gentry, Before Jerusalem Fell, 123-27.

[92]Ibid., 127.

[93]Ibid., 144.

[94]Ibid., 143, 144.

[95]Ibid., 127-28.

[96]Cf. W. Lee, "The Revelation of St. John," in The Holy Bible, ed. F. C. Cook (London: John Murray, 1881), 4:502; J. P. M. Sweet, Revelation (Philadelphia: Westminster Pelican, 1979), 67; G. V. Caird, A Commentary on the Revelation of St. John the Divine, HNTC (New York: Harper and Row, 1966), 18; J. Moffatt, "The Revelation of St. John the Divine," in The Expositor's Greek Testament, ed. W. R. Nicoll (Grand Rapids: Eerdmans, n.d.), 5:339-40; J. B. Smith, A Revelation of Jesus Christ (Scottdale, Pa.: Herald, 1961), 44.

[97]A. F. Johnson, "Revelation," in EBC (1981), 12:423.
[98]Gentry, Before Jersualem Fell, 143 n. 27.
[99]For a fuller discussion of this issue, see Thomas, Revelation 1–7, 78-79.
[100]Gentry, Before Jerusalem Fell 128-29; Chilton, Days of Vengeance, 66.
[101]Gentry, Before Jerusalem Fell, 143.
[102]Ibid., 144.
[103]Ibid., 144-45.
[104]Ibid., 144.
[105]Ibid., 146.
[106]Ibid., 149-51.
[107]Ibid., 151-52.
[108]Ibid., 159-64.
[109]Lee, "Revelation of St. John" 4:744; Johnson, "Revelation," 12:558.
[110]G. E. Ladd, A Commentary on the Revelation of John (Grand Rapids: Eerdmans, 1972), 227.
[111]M. Kiddle, The Revelation of St. John (New York: Harper, 1940), 349.
[112]Gentry, Before Jerusalem Fell, 240-41 n. 26.
[113]Ibid.
[114]Ibid., 165-69.
[115]Ibid., 169-74.
[116]Ibid., 174-75.
[117]Ibid.
[118]Ibid., 169-70.
[119]Ibid., 174.
[120]See the chapter on "The Principle of Single Meaning," in Thomas, Evangelical Hermeneutics 141-64, for further elaboration on the importance of single meaning. Widespread neglect and violation of this principle has characterized recent evangelical studies on hermeneutics.
[121]"Behold, I am laying in Zion a stone, a tested stone, a costly cornerstone for the foundation, firmly placed. He who believes in it will not be disturbed."
[122]"The stone which the builders rejected has become the chief corner stone."
[123]Jesus said to them, "Did you never read in the Scriptures, 'The stone which the builders rejected, this became the chief corner stone; this came about from the Lord, and it is marvelous in our eyes'"?
[124]"I gave My back to those who strike Me, and My cheeks to those who pluck out the beard; I did not cover My face from humiliation and spitting."
[125]"Then they spat in His face and beat Him with their fists; and others slapped Him … after having Jesus scourged, he delivered Him to be crucified … And they

spat on Him, and took the reed and began to beat Him on the head."

[126]But He looked at them and said, "What then is this that is written, 'The stone which the builders rejected, this became the chief corner stone'? Everyone who falls on that stone will be broken to pieces; but on whomever it falls, it will scatter him like dust."

[127]"Then He shall become a sanctuary; but to both the houses of Israel, a stone to strike and a rock to stumble over, and a snare and a trap for the inhabitants of Jerusalem. And many will stumble over them, then they will fall and be broken; they will even be snared and caught."

[128]"But there will be no more gloom for her who was in anguish; in earlier times He treated the land of Zebulun and the land of Naphtali with contempt, but later on He shall make it glorious, by the way of the sea, on the other side of Jordan, Galilee of the Gentiles. The people who walk in darkness will see a great light; those who live in a dark land, the light will shine on them."

[129]Now when He heard that John had been taken into custody, He withdrew into Galilee; and leaving Nazareth, He came and settled in Capernaum, which is by the sea, in the region of Zebulun and Naphtali. This was to fulfill what was spoken through Isaiah the prophet, saying, "The land of Zebulun and the land of Naphtali, by the way of the sea, beyond the Jordan, Galilee of the Gentiles–"the people who were sitting in darkness saw a great light,and to those who were sitting in the land and shadow of death, upon them a light dawned."

[130]"Indeed, He will speak to this people through stammering lips and a foreign tongue. ..."

[131]"Brethren, do not be children in your thinking; yet in evil be babes, but in your thinking be mature. In the Law it is written, 'By men of strange tongues and by the lips of strangers I will speak to this people, and even so they will not listen to me,' says the Lord. So then tongues are for a sign, not to those who believe, but to unbelievers; but prophecy is for a sign, not to unbelievers, but to those who believe."

[132]"I will also make You a light of the nations so that My salvation may reach to the end of the earth."

[133]"For thus the Lord has commanded us, 'I have placed you as a light for the Gentiles, that you should bring salvation to the end of the earth.'"

[134]Further examples of both literal and nonliteral uses of the NT's use of the OT may be found in Thomas, Evangelical Hermeneutics, 243-51.

[135]E.g., D. E. Aune, Prophecy in Early Christianity and the Ancient Mediterranean World (Grand Rapids: Eerdmans, 1983) 252; D. Hill, New Testament Prophecy (Atlanta: John Knox, 1979) 91.

[136]Cf. Thomas, Revelation 1–7 26 n. 70; idem, Understanding Spiritual Gifts, rev. ed. (Grand Rapids: Kregel, 1999), 33-34, 58-661, 133-72.

Chapter 3 – The Rediscovery of the Jewish Perspective of the Bible

[1]Voicing a Jewish perspective of the Bible, especially the Old Testament, is not the same enterprise as modern readings from various perspectives such as feminist, homosexual, and political theologies. Such approaches are reader oriented. What is in view here is not any notion of reader response but recognition of the very character of the text, one written mostly by Jews and mostly for Jews, although not exclusively so. It is also not an attempt to read the rabbinic tradition, which is frequently and decidedly non-literal, into the Bible. It is, however, an honest attempt to deal with the text as it is in itself within the history of its own writing without any later accretions from extra-biblical thought.

[2]Oswald T. Allis, Prophecy and the Church (Phillipsburg, NJ: Presbyterian and Reformed Publishing Co., 1945), 244.

[3]Arnold G. Fruchtenbaum, Israelology: The Missing Link of Systematic Theology (Tustin, CA: Ariel Ministries, 1989) and "Doctrine of Israelology" in Dictionary of Premillennial Theology, Edited by Mal Couch (Grand Rapids: Kregel, 1996), 197-203.

[4]Louis Berkhof, The History of Christian Doctrine, Reprint ed., (Grand Rapids: Baker Book House, 1975), 262.

[5]Philip Schaff, History of the Christian Church, Reprint ed., (n. p.: AP & A, n.d.), 2:275.

[6]Ibid.; Schaff shows his lack of sympathy for chiliasm in general when he characterizes Jewish chiliasm with an Origen-like depiction: "The Jewish chiliasm rested on a carnal misapprehension of the Messianic kingdom, a literal interpretation of prophetic figures, and an overestimate of the importance of the Jewish people and the holy city as the center of that kingdom."

[7]Ronald E. Diprose, Israel in the Development of Christian Thought (Rome, Italy: Istituto Biblico Evangelico Italiano, 2000), 164.

[8]Ibid., 161-64.

[9]One can see precursors to dispensationalism in the early Church Fathers, although there is no developed dispensationalism as was to be systematized in modern times. See Larry Crutchfield, "The Blessed Hope and the Tribulation in the Apostolic Fathers" in When the Trumpet Sounds, Edited by Thomas Ice and Timothy Demy (Eugene, OR: Harvest House, 1995), 85-103). However, these precursors appeared in a context that was growing more hostile to the Jewish perspective of the Bible as our ongoing discussion demonstrates.

[10]Ibid., 164.

[11]Rodney Peterson, "Continuity and Discontinuity: The Debate Throughout Church History" in Continuity and Discontinuity: Perspectives on the Relationship Between the Old and New Testaments, Edited by John S. Feinberg (Westchester, IL: Crossway, 1988), 19.

[12]Diprose, Israel in the Development of Christian Thought, 155.

[13]Peterson, "Continuity and Discontinuity: The Debate Throughout Church History," 19.

[14]Origen's well-known approach was a three-fold use of Scripture. The first layer was the literal or historical sense of a passage. This was good for those who were babes in Christ. Critics of Origen have sometimes overstated his position as one that rejected this sense. It is not that he rejected it; it is that there were other more important interpretations added to passages. The second layer was the moral sense of a passage, which comes close to our understanding of application. The third and highest sense of a text was the spiritual or allegorical sense in which the mature believer could discern in a mystical way the deeper meaning of text, which was not evident in a purely textual way.

[15]Schaff said that "Origen opposed chiliasm as a Jewish dream" (History of the Christian Church, 2:276).

[16]Origen, Principles, II.XI.2.

[17]It is hard to know whether Origen misunderstood the chiliasts of his day or if some of them actually taught this particular doctrine. Certainly many modern dispensationalists believe that there will marriage and childbearing in the millennial phase of God's coming kingdom based upon passages like Isaiah 65. However, few if any would believe that those who marry and have children in the millennium will have resurrected glorified bodies.

[18]Again, it is impossible to know for sure whether Origen is responding to clearly held arguments by chiliasts, is giving a caricature of them, or merely misunderstands them on this point.

[19]Ibid.

[20]Ibid.; The passage is Luke 19:11-27, especially verse 19.

[21]Ibid.

[22]Diprose, Israel in the Development of Christian Thought, 93-94, 164-74. Diprose comments: "Augustine's Tract Against the Jews was one of the most influential anti-Judaic writings emanating from the centuries following Origen. Because of the almost canonical status enjoyed by Augustine's writings during medieval Church history, the dominant form of the anti-Jewish polemic during this period is commonly called 'Augustinian'. In this tradition, replacement theology and the con-

sequent normativity of Jewish subservience to Christians were understood to be certain" (94).

[23]Martin Luther, Table Talk No. 335 recorded by Veit Dietrich, Summer or Fall, 1532, Luther's Works, Vol. 54 Edited and Translated by Theodore G. Tappert, General Editing by Helmut T. Lehmann, (Philadelphia: Fortress Press, n.d.), 46-47.

[24]For helpful resources on the Anabaptists, see Harold S. Bender, Conrad Grebel (Scottsdale, PA: Herald Press, 1950); Torstein Bergsten, Balthasar Hubmaier: Anabaptist Theologian and Martyr, translated by Irwin Barnes and William Estep (Valley Forge, PA: Judson Press, 1978); Claus Peter Clasen, Anabaptism: A Social History, 1525-1618 (Ithaca, NY: Cornell University Press, 1972); William Estep, The Anabaptist Story: An Introduction to Sixteenth-Century Anabaptism, (Grand Rapids, MI: Eerdmans, 1996 [3rd ed.]); Leland Harder, ed., The Sources of Swiss Anabaptism: The Grebel Letters and Related Documents (Scottsdale, PA: Herald Press, 1985); Hans J. Hillerbrand, ed., Radical Tendencies in the Reformation: Divergent Perspectives (Kirksville, Missouri: Sixteenth Century Journal Publishers, 1988); Cornelius Krahn, Dutch Anabaptism: Origin, Spread, Life and Thought 1450-1600 (The Hague: Martinus Nijhoff, 1968); Franklin H. Littell, The Anabaptist View of the Church: A Study in the Origins of Sectarian Protestantism (Boston: Starr King Press, 1958); John Allen Moore, Anabaptist Portraits (Scottsdale, PA: Herald Press, 1984); Werner O. Packull, Mysticism and the Early South German-Austrian Anabaptist Movement 1525-1531 (Scottsdale, PA: Herald Press, 1977); C. Arnold Snyder, Anabaptist History and Theology: An Introduction, (Kitchener, Ontario: Pandaro Press, 1995); C. Arnold Snyder, The Life and Thought of Michael Sattler (Scottsdale, PA: Herald Press, 1984); Henry C. Vedder, Balthasar Hübmaier: The Leader of the Anabaptists (reprint ed., New York: AMS Press, 1971); J. Denny Weaver, Becoming Anabaptist: The Origin and Significance of Sixteenth-Century Anabaptism (Scottsdale, PA: Herald Press, 1987); John H. Yoder, ed., The Legacy of Michael Sattler (Scottsdale, PA: Herald Press, 1973).

[25]All of the references to Whitby's statements are taken from chapter two of his treatise.

[26]For examples of this premillennial historicism, see Le Roy Edwin Froom, The Prophetic Faith of Our Fathers: The Historical Development of Prophetic Interpretation, Vol. III (Washington, D.C.: Review and Herald, 1946).

[27]For helpful resources on the eschatology of Wesley, see John Wesley, Explanatory Notes on the New Testament, (New York: Carlton & Porter); Stanley Ayling, John Wesley, (New York: Collins, 1979); Kenneth O. Brown, "John Wesley--Post or

Premillennialism?" Methodist History 28 (October 1989); William M. Greathouse, "John Wesley's View of the Last Things" in The Second Coming: A Wesleyan Approach to the Doctrine of Last Things, edited by H. Ray Dunning, (Kansas City, Missouri: Beacon Hill Press of Kansas City, 1995); Le Roy Edwin Froom, The Prophetic Faith of Our Fathers, Volume III, (Washington, D. C.: Review and Herald, 1946).

[28] John Bengel, Gnomon of the New Testament, edited and translated by Charlton T. Lewis (New York: Sheldon, 1862), 832.

[29]John Wesley, Explanatory Notes on the New Testament, 724.

[30]Ibid., 676.

[31]Ibid., 697-702.

[32]Ibid., 732.

[33]H. de Goltz, Genève Religieus au Dix-Neuvième Siécle (Genève: Henri George, 1862), 452. See also Michael D. Stallard, The Early Twentieth-Century Dispensationalism of Arno C. Gaebelein, (Lewiston, NY: Edwin Mellen Press, 2002), 65-66. I have chosen Guers for primary focus because of the clarity of his methodological statements and to foster more interest in unknown persons like him from the dispensational tradition in the hopes that others might join the historical search.

[34]Guers makes mention of Benjamin Newton in the Preface to The Future of Israel (see next note) as one whose works he had read with qualified profit. In addition, while mentioning both Newton and Darby as literalists who had some influence, he is careful to add that literal interpretation existed before Newton and Darby and that he first heard of that approach to prophecy from other Anglican evangelicals in 1829 or 1830. He does not name these other teachers he had encountered. See Émile Guers, Le Littéralisme dans la Prophétie: Lettres a M. Le Pasteur F. Bertholet-Bridel (Genève: Émile Beroud, 1862), 4. I am indebted to Timothy Stunt for the existence of this resource so that I could find a copy and review Guers' statement.

[35]Émile Guers, Israël aux Derniers Jours De L'Économie Actuelle ou Essai Sur La Restauration Prochaine De Ce Peuple, Suivi D'Un Fragment Sur Le Millénarisme (Genève: Émile Beroud, 1856). An English translation was produced in 1862. The short title Future of Israel will be used in future references with pagination from the English edition.

[36]Ibid., 24, 197-201.

[37]Ibid., 16-37. Guers' first two principles of interpretation (literalism and a distinction between Israel and the Church) were codified as part of the essence of dispensationalism by Charles Ryrie over one hundred years later (Dispensationalism Today, [Chicago: Moody, 1965], 43-47). For a discussion of this similarity and its

implications, see Mike Stallard, "Emile Guers: An Early Darbyite Response to Irvingism and a Precursor to Charles Ryrie," The Conservative Theological Journal 1 (April 1997): 31-46.

[38]Guers, Future of Israel, 35-36.

[39]Ibid., 36.

[40]Ibid., 36. Guers' criticism brings to mind recent directions in much evangelical and even some dispensational thought concerning the metaphorical nature of language in general and prophecy in particular (see Brent Sandy, Plowshares and Pruning Hook [Downers Grove, IL: InterVarsity Press, 2002], 58-74). Guers' concern is the overuse of metaphor, figurative language, or allegory to dismantle the straightforward meaning of the text.

[41]Ibid.

[42]One can surmise that Guers believes similarly about the New Testament. It must be interpreted literally. He never, to my knowledge, uses the term the Jewish sense relative to the New Testament although his approach would allow such a designation for passages that relate to the promises of Israel's future (e.g., Rom. 9-11; Rev. 12).

[43]Arno C. Gaebelein, Half a Century: The Autobiography of a Servant (New York: Publication Office "Our Hope," 1930), 5-6. Also, see Stallard, The Early Twentieth-Century Dispensationalism of Arno C. Gaebelein, 18.

[44]Gaebelein, Half a Century, 18-19.

[45]Arno C. Gaebelein, "Jewish Eschatology," Our Hope 5 (July 1898): 10.

[46]Ibid., 10-11.

[47]Arno C. Gaebelein, The Harmony of the Prophetic Word (New York: Fleming H. Revell Co., 1907), 118-19.

[48]Arno C. Gaebelein, Will There Be a Millennium? (New York: Publication Office "Our Hope," 1943), 36.

[49]Of course, the primary way that Israel blesses the world is through the first advent of Jesus to die for the sins of the world. However, His second coming is equally important and is often described in Scripture in terms of the national recovery of Israel. It is this Jewish perspective that should not be lost.

Chapter 4 – The Jewish Longing for the Messiah

[1]Raphael Patai, The Messiah Texts (Detroit: Wayne State University Press, 1979), x1iii.

[2]Jacob Neusner, ed., Judaisms and Their Messiahs at the Turn of the Christian Era (Cambridge: Cambridge University Press, 1987), 10.

[3]Ezek. 21:27.

[4]Arthur W. Kac, The Messianic Hope (Ann Arbor: Baker, 1975), 19.

[5]Ibid., 19-20.

[6]Genesis R. 98:13.

[7]Babylonian Talmud, Sanhedrin 98b.

[8]Kac, 20.

[9]Craig A Evans, "Messianism," in Craig A. Evans and Stanley E. Porter, eds., Dictionary of New Testament Background : A Compendium of Contemporary Biblical Scholarship, electronic edition (Downers Grove: InterVarsity Press, 2000).

[10]Maimonides, Mishnah Torah, Hilkhot Melakhim Umilchamoteihem (Laws of Kings), chp. 11.

[11]Philo, The Works of Philo: Complete and Unabridged (Peabody: Hendrickson, 1996), The Special Laws, I 65.

[12]Arnold Fruchtenbaum, Messianic Christology (Tustin: Ariel, 1998), 34.

[13]Michael L. Brown, Answering Jewish Objections to Jesus, vol. 2 (Grand Rapids: Baker, 2000), 46.

[14]Craig A Evans, "Messianism," in Evans and Porter, electronic edition.

[15]Rabbi Don Yitzchak Abarbanel, quoted in Fruchtenbaum, 124.

[16]The Zohar, quoted in Fruchtenbaum, 124-125.

[17]Babylonian Talmud, Sanhedrin 98b.

[18]Patai, 165-166.

[19]1 Enoch 48:4-6 as quoted in Patai, 18.

[20]1 Enoch 62:7-8 as quoted in Patai, 19.

[21]Mishnah Torah, Hilkhot Melakhim Umilchamoteihem (Laws of Kings), chp. 11.

[22]Talmud, Sanhedrin 98a, as quoted in Fruchtenbaum, 66.

[23]Talmud, Succah 52a, as quoted in Fruchtenbaum, 72

[24]Fruchtenbaum, 80.

[25]Jacob Neusner, ed., Judaisms and Their Messiahs at the Turn of the Christian Era (Cambridge: Cambridge University Press, 1987), 275.

[26]Emet ve-Emunah: Statement of Principles of Conservative Judaism.

[27]Jack Riemer, "Will the Rebbe Return?," Moment, (web edition archives, 2002).

[28]Jonathan Mahler, "Waiting for the Messiah of Eastern Parkway -- Lubavitch Rebbe Schneerson" New York Times, (Sept. 21, 2003).

Chapter 5 – History of Christian Zionism

[1]Jane Lampman, "Mixing prophecy and politics," Christian Science Monitor (July 7, 2004), Internet edition accessed July 14, 2004.

[2]Timothy P. Weber, On The Road to Armageddon: How Evangelical Became

Israel's Best Friend (Grand Rapids: Baker Academic, 2004).

[3]Weber, Armageddon, 249–68.

[4]"Major US Christian Denomination Backs Divestment From Israel," Arutz Sheva, Israel National News.com, July 16, 2004. Internet edition.

[5]Donald E. Wagner, Anxious for Armageddon: A Call to Partnership for Middle Eastern and Western Christians (Scottsdale, PA: Herald Press, 1995). Grace Halsell, Forcing God's Hand: Why Millions Pray for a Quick Rapture—and Destruction of Planet Earth (Washington, DC: Crossroads International Publishing, 1999). Stephen R. Sizer, "Dispensational Approaches to the Land," in The Land of Promise: Biblical, Theological and Contemporary Perspectives, ed. Philip Johnston & Peter Walker (Downers Grove, IL: InterVarsity Press, 2000). Stephen R. Sizer, Christian Zionists: On the Road to Armageddon (Colorado Springs, CO: Presence Ministries International, 2004).

[6]Irenaeus, Against Heresies: Book V, Chapter 30, Paragraph 4.

[7]Carl F. Ehle, Jr., "Prolegomena to Christian Zionism in America: The Views of Increase Mather and William E. Blackstone Concerning the Doctrine of the Restoration of Israel," Ph.D. Dissertation at New York University, 1977, 31.

[8]R. Kendall Soulen, The God of Israel and Christian Theology (Minneapolis: Fortress Press, 1996), 35.

[9]Peter Richardson, Israel In The Apostolic Church (Cambridge: At The University Press, 1969), 2. Richardson contends: "In spite of the many attributes, characteristics, prerogatives of the latter which are applied to the former, the Church is not called Israel in the NT. The continuity between Israel and the Church is partial; and the discontinuity between Israel B.C. and its continuation A.D. is partial," 7.

[10]Soulen, God of Israel, 50. Soulen adds: "In addition to narrowing the thematic focus of the Hebrew Scriptures to the problem of sin and redemption, the standard model also foreshortens the Hebrew Scriptures into a temporal sense. As perceived through the lens of the standard model, the Hebrew Scriptures do not relate a story that extends indefinitely into the future," 53.

[11]Jeffrey S. Siker, Disinheriting The Jews: Abraham in Early Christian Controversy (Louisville, KY: Westminster/John Knox Press, 1991), 194.

[12]Ehle, "Prolegomena," 32.

[13]Robert E. Lerner, "Millennialism," in John J. Collins, Bernard McGinn, and Stephen J. Stein, editors, The Encyclopedia of Apocalypticism, 3 Vols. (New York: Continuum, 2000), Vol. 2, 356.

[14]Marjorie Reeves, The Influence of Prophecy in the Later Middle Ages (London: Oxford University Press, 1969), 14.

[15]Reeves, Influence of Prophecy, 6, f.n. 2.

[16]Reeves, Influence of Prophecy, 382.

[17]Reeves, Influence of Prophecy, 304.

[18]Ehle, "Prolegomena," 41–42.

[19]Lerner, "Millennialism," 353.

[20]James A. Saddington, "Prophecy and Politics: A History of Christian Zionism in the Anglo–American Experience, 1800–1948," PhD Dissertation at Bowling Green State University, 1996, 32.

[21]Barbara W. Tuchman, Bible and Sword: England and Palestine from the Bronze Age to Balfour (New York: Ballantine Press, 1956), 93.

[22]Michael J. Pragai, Faith and Fulfillment: Christians and the Return to the Promised Land (London: Vallentine, Mitchell, 1985), 10

[23]See Douglas J. Culver, Albion and Ariel: British Puritanism and the Birth of Political Zionism (New York: Peter Lang, 1995), 51–70.

[24]Culver, Albion and Ariel, 60.

[25]Tuchman, Bible and Sword, 122.

[26]Tuchman, Bible and Sword, 125.

[27]Culver, Albion and Ariel, 73.

[28]Culver, Albion and Ariel, 73.

[29]Culver, Albion and Ariel, 71-73; Ehle, "Prolegomena," 47–48.

[30]Lawrence J. Epstein, Zion's Call: Christian Contributions to the Origins and Development of Israel (Lanham, MD: University Press of America, 1984), 7

[31]Culver, Albion and Ariel, 75–78; Ehle, "Prolegomena," 49.

[32]Peter Toon, "The Latter-Day Glory," in Toon, editor, Puritans, the Millennium and the Future of Israel: Puritan Eschatology 1600 to 1660 (Cambridge: James Clarke & Co., 1970), 30.

[33]Malcolm Hedding, "Christian Zionism," essay on the website of the International Christian Embassy Jerusalem, February 18, 2001, 4.

[34]Culver, Albion and Ariel, pp. 79–82; Ehle, "Prolegomena," 53–56.

[35]Robert G. Clouse, "The Rebirth of Millenarianism," in Toon, Puritans, 56.

[36]Culver, Albion and Ariel, 89–93; Ehle, "Prolegomena," 51–52.

[37]Culver, Albion and Ariel, 94.

[38]Cited in Culver, Albion and Ariel, 93.

[39]Culver, Albion and Ariel, 101.

[40]Culver, Albion and Ariel, 101.

[41]Epstein, Zion's Call, 8.

[42]Toon, "The Latter-Day Glory," 32.

[43]Culver, Albion and Ariel, 102-03.

[44]Culver, Albion and Ariel, 116-17.

[45]Ehle, "Prolegomena," 61.

[46]Culver provides the most detailed information concerning the seventeenth century British Puritan development of Restorationism in Albion and Ariel. Tuchman's Bible and Sword also provides deep insight into this movement.

[47]Martha Lou Farmer, "They Believed the Scriptures–The Story of Christian Zionism," Bridges For Peace website, May 21, 2004, 2; see also Ehle, "Prolegomena," 79.

[48]Toon, "Conclusion," in Toon, Puritans, 126.

[49]Hedding, "Christian Zionism," 4.

[50]Grace Halsell, Prophecy and Politics: Militant Evangelists on the Road to Nuclear War (Westport, CT: Lawrence Hill & Company, 1986), 35.

[51]Pragai, Faith and Fulfillment, 15.

[52]Saddington, "Prophecy and Politics," 38.

[53]Epstein, Zion's Call, 14.

[54]Saddington, "Prophecy and Politics," 38.

[55]Saddington, "Prophecy and Politics," 34–38.

[56]Ehle, "Prolegomena," 61.

[57]Ehle, "Prolegomena," 66; Toon, "The Latter-Day Glory," 34–36.

[58]Ehle, "Prolegomena," 67.

[59]Le Roy Froom, The Prophetic Faith of Our Fathers: The Historical Development of Prophetic Interpretation, 4 Vols. (Washington, D.C.: Review and Herald, 1950), Vol. III, 60, 66.

[60]Ehle, "Prolegomena," 67, 80.

[61]Ehle, "Prolegomena," abstract.

[62]Ehle, "Prolegomena," 186.

[63]Pragai, Faith and Fulfillment, 49.

[64]Farmer, "They Believed," 4.

[65]Iain Murray, The Puritan Hope: Revival and the Interpretation of Prophecy (Edinburgh: Banner of Truth, 1971), 197. See also Froom, Prophetic Faith, Vol. III, 706 and Grayson Carter, Anglican Evangelicals: Protestant Secessions From The Via Media, c. 1800–1850 (New York: Oxford University Press, 2001), 155, 157.

[66]Murray, Puritan Hope, 197.

[67]J. C. Ryle, Are You Ready For The End of Time? (Guernsey, Scotland: Guernsey Press [1867] 2001), 8–10.

[68]Tuchman, Bible and Sword, 176.

[69]Georgina Battiscombe, Shaftesbury, a biography of the Seventh Earl: 1801–1885 (London: Constable, 1974), 100-03.

[70]Tuchman, Bible and Sword, 178.

[71]Battiscombe, Shaftesbury, 103.

[72]Tuchman, Bible and Sword, 202.

[73]Pragai, Faith and Fulfillment, 45.

[74]Tuchman, Bible and Sword, 178.

[75]Wagner, Anxious for Armageddon, 92.

[76]Saddington, "Prophecy and Politics," 62.

[77]Saddington, "Prophecy and Politics," 62.

[78]Battiscombe, Shaftesbury, 119–20.

[79]Tuchman, Bible and Sword, 175.

[80]Ami Isseroff, "British Support for Jewish Restoration," (www.mideastweb.org, 2003), 1.

[81]Epstein, Zion's Call, 35.

[82]Epstein, Zion's Call, 37.

[83]Pragai, Faith and Fulfillment, 22.

[84]Tuchman, Bible and Sword, 216–17.

[85]Pragai, Faith and Fulfillment, 23.

[86]Saddington, "Prophecy and Politics," 62–63.

[87]Pragai, Faith and Fulfillment, 48.

[88]Tuchman, Bible and Sword, 209.

[89]Saddington, "Prophecy and Politics," 63.

[90]Saddington, "Prophecy and Politics," 63.

[91]Pragai, Faith and Fulfillment, 70.

[92]Pragai, Faith and Fulfillment, 53.

[93]Tuchman, Bible and Sword, 270.

[94]Tuchman, Bible and Sword, 272.

[95]Pragai, Faith and Fulfillment, 55.

[96]See Epstein, Zion's Call, 48–50; Pragai, Faith and Fulfillment, 23; Tuchman, Bible and Sword, 236–40.

[97]Isseroff, "British Support," 1.

[98]Epstein, Zion's Call, 26.

[99]Hence the title of her book, Bible and Sword, Tuchman said, "The origins of Britain's role in the restoration of Israel, which is the subject of the following pages, are to be found in two motives, religious and political." xiii.

[100]For an overview of Darby's teachings on this matter see Weber, Armageddon, 20–23.

[101]See Carter, Anglican Evangelicals, 195–248.

[102]Donald E. Wagner, Anxious for Armageddon (Scottdale, PA: Herald Press,

1995).

[103]Wagner, Armageddon, 89.

[104]Wagner, Armageddon, 91.

[105]Stephen R. Sizer, Christian Zionists: On the Road to Armageddon (Colorado Springs: Presence Ministries International, 2004), 14

[106]Pragai, Faith and Fulfillment, 20; Epstein, Zion's Call, 39; Saddington, "Prophecy and Politics," 64–65; Ehle, "Prolegomena," 231–32.

[107]Bickersteth wrote a number of books on prophecy including The Restoration of the Jews to Their Own Land, in Connection with Their Future Conversion and the Final Blessedness of Our Earth, 2nd edition (London: L. Seeley, 1841).

[108]Battiscombe, Shaftesbury, 99. Carter makes the same observation, Anglican Evangelicals, 157.

[109]For an account of Napoleon's Restoration efforts see Tuchman, Bible and Sword, 147–174.

[110]Epstein, Zion's Call, 16.

[111]Epstein, Zion's Call, 17.

[112]Pragai, Faith and Fulfillment, 49–50.

[113]Pragai, Faith and Fulfillment, 51.

[114]Epstein, Zion's Call, 40.

[115]Epstein, Zion's Call, 41; see also Pragai, Faith and Fulfillment, 75–77.

[116]Epstein, Zion's Call, 40.

[117]Epstein, Zion's Call, 40.

[118]Arthur James Balfour, The Foundations of Belief Being Notes Introductory to the Study of Theology (London: Longmans, Green, and Co., 1895).

[119]Tuchman, Bible and Sword, 311.

[120]Blanche E. C. Dugdale, Arthur James Balfour: First Earl of Balfour, 1848–1906 (New York: G. P. Putnam's Sons, 1937), 324.

[121]Dugdale, Balfour, 325.

[122]Photocopy in Encyclopaedia Judaica, 17 vols. (Jerusalem: Keter Publishing House, n.d.), vol. 4, 132.

[123]Cited by Pragai, Faith and Fulfillment, 123.

[124]Tuchman, Bible and Sword, 312.

[125]Saddington, "Prophecy and Politics," 176–77.

[126]Tuchman, Bible and Sword, 83.

[127]Pragai, Faith and Fulfillment, 87.

[128]Pragai, Faith and Fulfillment, 271.

[129]Tuchman, Bible and Sword, 337.

[130]Pragai, Faith and Fulfillment, 80.

[131]Pragai, Faith and Fulfillment, 80.

[132]Pragai, Faith and Fulfillment, 88.

[133]For more detail about these individuals see Pragai, Faith and Fulfillment; Tuchman, Bible and Sword; Epstein, Zion's Call; Paul C. Merkley, The Politics of Christian Zionism: 1891–1948 (London, Frank Cass, 1998); Saddington, "Prophecy and Politics;" Bruce R. Crew, "A Structural Framework For British Geo-Political Perceptions Toward Land as Sacred Place: Christian Zionism and the Palestine Question, 1917–39," (Ph.D. Dissertation, The University of Wisconsin-Milwaukee, 1995).

[134]Merkley, Politics of Christian Zionism, 11.

[135]Merkley, Politics of Christian Zionism, 11.

[136]Merkley, Politics of Christian Zionism, 12.

[137]Pragai, Faith and Fulfillment, 58.

[138]Merkley, Politics of Christian Zionism, 12.

[139]Merkley, Politics of Christian Zionism, 3.

[140]Pragai, Faith and Fulfillment, 59.

[141]Merkley, Politics of Christian Zionism, 25.

[142]Merkley, Politics of Christian Zionism, 17.

[143]Merkley, Politics of Christian Zionism, 23.

[144]Merkley, Politics of Christian Zionism, 23.

[145]Pragai, Faith and Fulfillment, 60–61.

[146]Cited by Saddington, "Prophecy and Politics," 128.

[147]Weber, Road to Armageddon, 102.

[148]Weber, Road to Armageddon, 103.

[149]William E. Blackstone, Jesus Is Coming, 3rd edition (New York: Fleming H. Revell, 1932), 162.

[150]Blackstone, Jesus Is Coming, 176.

[151]Weber, Road to Armageddon, 102.

[152]Ehle, "Prolegomena," 240–44.

[153]Ehle, "Prolegomena," 241–42.

[154]Ehle, "Prolegomena," 242–43.

[155]Ehle, "Prolegomena," 243.

[156]Ehle, "Prolegomena," 290-93.

[157]Ehle, "Prolegomena," abstract. This fact is recognized by Benjamin Netanyahu in his book, A Place Among The nations: Israel and the World (New York: Bantam, 1993), 16–17.

[158]Saddington, "Prophecy and Politics," 362.

[159]Merkley, Politics of Christian Zionism, 160.

[160]Saddington, "Prophecy and Politics," 363.

[161]Saddington, "Prophecy and Politics," 363.

[162]Merkley, Politics of Christian Zionism, 161.

[163]Merkley, Politics of Christian Zionism, 162–63.

[164]Saddington, "Prophecy and Politics," 364.

[165]Merkley, Politics of Christian Zionism, 159.

[166]Cited in Saddington, "Prophecy and Politics," 372–73.

[167]Saddington, "Prophecy and Politics," 436.

[168]Saddington, "Prophecy and Politics," 448.

[169]Merkley, Politics of Christian Zionism, 190.

[170]Cited in Saddington, "Prophecy and Politics," 464.

[171]Merkley, Politics of Christian Zionism, 191.

[172]See Saddington, "Prophecy and Politics," 347–54; Merkley, Politics of Christian Zionism, 149–54; John Goodall Snetsinger, "Truman and The Creation of Israel," (Ph.D. dissertation, Stanford University, 1969); Earl Dean Huff, "Zionist Influences Upon U. S. Foreign Policy: A Study of American Policy Toward The Middle East From The Time of The Struggle For Israel to The Sinai Conflict," (Ph.D. dissertation, University of Idaho, 1971).

[173]James Solheim, "Jerusalem conference calls Christian Zionism a 'heresy,'" in Episcopal News Service, April 28, 2004, accessed on the internet.

[174]Gershom Gorenberg, The End of Days: Fundamentalism and The Struggle for The Temple Mount (New York: The Free Press, 2000), 232.

[175]Weber, Armageddon, 249–68.

[176]Weber, Armageddon, 266.

Chapter 7 – Who Owns the Land of Israel?

[1]Stanley Ellison, and Charles Dyer, Who Owns The Land, (Wheaton: Tyndale, 1991), get info, 136.

[2]Ibid. 137.

[3]Ibid.

[4]Ibid. 137-38.

[5]137.

Chapter 8 – Jeremiah 30: Birth Pangs, Tribulation and Restoration

[1]Charles Feinberg, "Jeremiah," in Isaiah-Jeremiah, ed. Frank E. Gaebelein and Richard P. Polcyn, The Expositor's Bible Commentary. 12 vols. (Grand Rapids: Zondervan, 1986), 6:558; Merill F. Unger, Unger's Commentary on the Old Testament (Chattanooga, TN: AMG, 2002), 1416.

[2]Irving Jensen, Jeremiah and Lamentations, Everyman's Bible Commentary series (Chicago: Moody, 1966), 85.

[3]Charles H. Dyer, "Jeremiah," in Bible Knowledge Commentary, ed. John F. Walvoord and Roy B. Zuck (Colorado Springs, CO: Chariot Victor Publishing, 1983), 1167; Charles Dyer and Gene Merrill, Old Testament Explorer, Swindoll Leadership Library, ed. Charles R. Swindoll and Roy B. Zuck (Nashville: Word Publishing, 2001), 617.

[4]Mal Couch, "Jeremiah 30-A Warning to the Palestinians and the Gentiles!," Conservative Theological Journal 7, no. 21 (August 2003):137.

[5]Dyer, "Jeremiah," 1167.

[6]For an example of such a hermeneutic, see Derek Kidner, The Message of Jeremiah, The Bible Speaks Today Series (Downers Grove, Ill: Inter-Varsity Press, 1987), 103, 105.

[7]Dyer, "Jeremiah," 1168.

[8]Feinberg, "Jeremiah," 559.

[9]Dyer, "Jeremiah," 1167-68.

[10]Unger, Unger's Commentary on the Old Testament, 1417.

[11]Ibid.

[12]Feinberg, "Jeremiah," 560.

[13]John Piper, "Land Divine?" World, May 11 2002.

[14]Arnold Fruchtenbaum, Footsteps of the Messiah, rev ed. (Tustin, CA: Ariel Ministries, 2003), 99-104.

[15]John F. Walvoord, Israel in Prophecy (Grand Rapids: Zondervan, 1962), 26.

[16]John F. Walvoord, The Rapture Question, rev. ed. (Grand Rapids: Zondervan, 1979), 41.

[17]J. Dwight Pentecost, Things to Come: A Study in Biblical Eschatology (Findley, OH: Dunham Publishing Company, 1958), 315.

[18]Fruchtenbaum, Footsteps of the Messiah, 403.

[19]Tim LaHaye, ed., Tim LaHaye Prophecy Study Bible (Chattanooga, TN: AMG Publishers, 2001), 875.

[20]John F. Walvoord, Every Prophecy of the Bible (Colorado Springs: Chariot Victor Publishing, 1999), 187.

[21]Walter Kaiser, "Evidence from Jeremiah," in A Case for Premillennialism: A New Consensus, ed. Donald Campbell and Jeffrey Townsend (Chicago: Moody Press, 1992), 112.

[22]Feinberg, "Jeremiah," 561.

[23]Ibid.

[24]Ibid., 562.

[25]LaHaye, ed., Tim LaHaye Prophecy Study Bible, 876.

[26]Couch, "Jeremiah 30-A Warning to the Palestinians and the Gentiles!" 138.

[27]Fruchtenbaum, Footsteps of the Messiah, 406-7.

[28]Unger, Unger's Commentary on the Old Testament, 1418.

[29]Feinberg, "Jeremiah," 564; Unger, Unger's Commentary on the Old Testament, 1419.

[30]John F. Walvoord, Major Bible Prophecies (Grand Rapids: Zondervan, 1991), 82.

[31]Feinberg, "Jeremiah," 564; Unger, Unger's Commentary on the Old Testament, 1419.

[32]Dyer, "Jeremiah," 1169.

[33]Feinberg, "Jeremiah," 564.

Chapter 9 – What is "Gog and Magog" in Regard to Bible Prophecy?

[1] John F. Walvoord, *The Prophecy Knowledge Handbook* (Wheaton: Victor Books, 1994), 190.

[2] Tim LaHaye and Jerry B. Jenkins, *Left Behind* (Wheaton: Tyndale Publishers, 1995), 10-11, 16.

[3] Arnold G. Fruchtenbaum, *Footsteps of the Messiah* (Tustin, CA: Ariel Ministries, 2003), 117.

[4] Hal Lindsey, *The Late Great Planet Earth* (Grand Rapids: Zondervan, 1970), 65.

[5] Thomas S. McCall and Zola Levitt, *The Coming Russian Invasion* (Chicago: Moody Press, 1974), 26.

[6] Ibid., 107.

[7] J. Dwight Pentecost, *Prophecy for Today* (Grand Rapids: Zondervan, 1963), 107-108.

[8] *Gesenius' Hebrew and Chaldee Lexicon to the Old Testament Scriptures*, translated by Samuel Pridaux Tregelles (Grand Rapids: Eerdmans, n.d.), 752 (emphasis in the original).

[9] Edwin Yamauchi, *Foes from the Northern Frontier* (Grand Rapids: Baker, 1982), 20.

[10] Jon Ruthven, "Ezekiel's Rosh And Russia: A Connection?" *Bibliotheca Sacra*, October 1968, 125:500, 329.

[11] Ibid., 332.

[12] Walvoord, Ibid., 192.

[13] Caspar Weinberger, "Atlantic Overture," *National Review*, (Oct. 1, 1990, 42:19), 30.

[14] Steven Lee Myers, "Putin strengthens his political grip," *International Herald Tribune*, September 14, 2004, 1.

[15] G. A. Cooke, *A Critical and Exegetical Commentary on the Book of Ezekiel* (New York: Scribner's, 1937), Vol. 2, 410.

[16] Daniel I. Block, *The New International Commentary on the Old Testament. The Book of Ezekiel* (Grand Rapids: Eerdmans, 1998), II, 439.

[17] John F. Walvoord, *Major Bible Prophecies* (Grand Rapids: Zondervan, 1991), 331.

[18]Chuck Missler, *The Magog Invasion* (Palos Verdes, CA: Western Front Ltd., 1995), 174-175.

[19]Frank E. Gaebelein, gen. ed., *The Expositor's Bible Commentary*, 12 Vols. (Grand Rapids: Zondervan, 1986), 6:931.

[20]William Smith, ed., *Dr. William Smith's Dictionary of the Bible*, (New York: Hurd and Houghton, 1871) I:519.

[21]Block, Ibid., 445.

[22] Renald Showers, "Gog and Magog," *Dictionary of Premillennial Theology* (Grand Rapids: Kregel, 1996), 124-125.

[23]Gordon Gaskill, "The Dead Sea Isn't Dead Anymore," *The Reader's Digest* July 1966, 89:531, 158.

[24] Zev Vilnay, *The Guide to Israel* (Jerusalem: "Hamaker" Press, 1973), 320.

[25]Konrad Bussemer, "Was Sagt das Prophetische Wort über Russland?" *Bibel und Gemeinde*, 1981-1, 56 (translation by the writer).

[26]Charles Lee Feinberg, *The Prophecy of Ezekiel* (Chicago: Moody Press, 1969), 223.

[27]J. H. Kurtz, *History of the Old Covenant*, (Edinburgh: T. and T. Clark, 1859), I, 147 (italics in the original).

[28] Block, Ibid., 448-449.

[29]Conrad von Orelli, "Gog and Magog," *Realencyclopädie für protestantische Theologie und Kirche* (Leipzig: J. C. Hinrichs'sche Buchhandlung, 1899), 6:761(translation by the writer).

[30]Stéphane Courtois, Nicolas Werth, Jean-Louis Panné, Andrzej Paczkowski, Karel Barto?ek, Jean-Louis Margolin, *The Black Book of Communism—Crimes, Terror, Repression* (Cambridge: Harvard University Press, 1990), 4.

[31]Gaebelein, Ibid., 434.

[32]Charles H. Dyer and Roy B. Zuck, eds., *Integrity of Heart, Skillfulness of Hands* (Grand Rapids: Baker, 1994), 91.

[33]Block, Ibid., 461.

[34]Patrick Fairbairn, *The Exposition of Ezekiel*, (Minneapolis: Klock & Klock,

1851), 421.

[35]Ibid.

[36]Stuart Briscoe, *All Things Weird and Wonderful*, (Wheaton: Victor, 1977), 163-164.

[37]Hermann Strack and Paul Billerbeck, *Kommentar zum Neuen Testament aus Talmud und Midrasch* (München: C. H. Beck'sche Verlagsbuchhandlung, 1965) III, 839 (translation by the writer).

[38]Ka Laung Weng, "Profanation/Sanctification and the Past, Present and Future in the Book of Ezekiel," *Journal for the Study of the Old Testament*, December 2003, 28:2, 230.

Chapter 10 – What is the Mark of the Beast?

[1]Gary DeMar, *End Times Fiction* (Nashville, TN: Thomas Nelson Publishers, 2001), 142-45; Kenneth Gentry, *The Beast of Revelation* (Tyler, TX: Institute for Christian Economics, 1989).

[2]Gentry, 35. O. Ruhle says that the 616 variant was an attempt to link Gaius Caesar (Caligula) to the beast out of the sea in Revelation 13. The numerical value of his name in Greek equals 616. Gerhard Kittel, ed. *The Theological Dictionary of the New Testament*, trans. Geoffrey W. Bromiley, vol. 1 (Grand Rapids, MI: Wm. B. Eerdmans Publishing Company, 1964), 462-63.

[3]Gentry, 53-4.

[4]For a thorough discussion of the date of Revelation, see, Mark Hitchcock, "The Stake in the Heart: The A.D. 95 Date of Revelation," in *The End Times Controversy* (Eugene, OR: Harvest House Publishers, 2003), 123-50

[5]Robert L. Thomas, *Revelation 8—22: An Exegetical Commentary* (Chicago: Moody Press, 1995), 179-80.

[6]David E. Aune, *Revelation 6—16*, Word Biblical Commentary, gen. ed. Bruce M. Metzger vol. 52B (Nashville, TN: Thomas Nelson Publishers, 1998), 771.

[7]For a complete refutation of the view that Nero is the beast of Revelation 13, see, Andy Woods, "Revelation 13 and the First Beast, in *The End Times Controversy* (Eugene, OR: Harvest House Publishers, 2003), 237-50.

[8]Irenaeus who wrote in the late 2nd century suggested three names for the total 666: Evanthas, Lateinos, and Teitan (*Against Heresies* 5.30.3). But he never suggested Nero.

[9]Simon J. Kistemaker, *Exposition of the Book of Revelation*, New Testament Commentary (Grand Rapids, MI: Baker Books, 2001), 395.

[10]Thomas, 185.

[11]BAGD, 876.

[12]Thomas, 181.

[13]Henry Morris, *Revelation Record* (Wheaton: Tyndale House Publishers, 1983), 252.

[14]Hal Harless, "666: The Beast and His Mark in Revelation 13," *The Conservative Theological Journal* 7 22 (December 2003): 342-46

[15]Morris, 255.

[16]Arnold G. Fruchtenbaum, *The Footsteps of the Messiah*, rev. ed. (Tustin, CA: Ariel Publications, 2003) 255.

[17]Ibid.

[18]John F. Walvoord. *The Prophecy Knowledge Handbook* (Wheaton, IL: SP Publications, 1990), 587.

[19]M. R. DeHaan, *Studies in Revelation* (Grand Rapids: Zondervan, 1946; reprint, Grand Rapids: Kregel Publications, 1998), 189.

[20] Morris, 256.

[21]Ibid.

[22]The word used for the seal of God on the foreheads of the saints in Revelation 7:3 is the Greek word *sphragizo* which is used of the invisible seal of the Holy Spirit in the New Testament (2 Corinthians 1:22; Ephesians 1:13; 4:30). The word mark (*charagma*), on the other hand, refers to a visible mark, imprint, or etching. Therefore, while God's mark on His saints will be invisible, the beast's mark will be visible.

[23]John F. Walvoord, *Prophecy: 14 Essential Keys to Understanding the Final Drama* (Nashville: Thomas Nelson Publishers, 1993), 125.

[24]Steven Levy, "Playing the ID Card," *Newsweek* (May 13, 2002), 44-6.

Chapter 12 – What is the Davidic Covenant

[1]On Nov. 20, 1986, the Dispensational Study Group met at the annual meeting of the Evangelical Theological Society in Atlanta Georgia. Apparently an outgrowth of a previous informal meeting of about two dozen dispensationalists held at Talbot Theological Seminary in 1985 (Grace Theological Journal 10:2, Fall 1989, p.123) the group has continued to meet in conjunction with the annual ETS meeting. It was from the meetings of the Dispensational Study Group that progressive dispensationalism began to have its first wide spread appeal. Some of the early progressive dispensationalist scholars included Darrell Bock, Craig Blaising and Robert Saucy.

[2]For an analysis of progressive dispensationalist hermeneutics, see Robert Thomas, "A Critique of Progressive Dispensational Hermeneutics" in *When the Trumpet Sounds,* Thomas Ice and Timothy Demy, edd. (Eugene, OR: Harvest

House Publishers, 1995) 413-425.

[3]Craig Blaising, "The Kingdom of God in the New Testament" in *Progressive Dispensationalism,* Craig A. Blaising and Darrell Bock (Wheaton: Victor Books, 1993) 264.

[4]Darrell L. Bock, "The Reign of the Lord Christ" in *Dispensationalism, Israel and the Church,* C.A. Blaising and D. L. Bock, edd. (Grand Rapids: Zondervan, 1992) 37-67.

[5]See his chapters in *Progressive Dispensationalism,* Craig A. Blaising and Darrell Bock (Wheaton: Victor Books, 1993).

[6]*Progressive Dispensationalism,* 178-79.

[7]*Progressive Dispensationalism,* 259.

[8]Robert L. Saucy *The Case for Progressive Dispensationalism* (Grand Rapids: Zondervan Publishing House, 1993) 72-73, 75.

[9]Bock, "The Reign of the Lord Christ" 49. Darrell L. Bock, "Evidence From Acts" in *A Case for Premillennialism,* D.K. Campbell and J.L. Townsend edd. (Chicago: Moody Press, 1992) 194.

[10]See the paper I coauthored with Jerry Neuman at http://www.shasta.edu/articles/ggunn/psalm110-article-dispensationalism.htm. In this paper, we argue that Ps 110 does not have the Davidic Covenant in view. Rather, it is a description of Christ's ministry during the Tribulation Period as a holy war king/priest who is like Melchizedek. In this role, Christ awaits the triumphal outcome of the holy war conflict of the Tribulation Period. Only after the triumph does his role change from that of Melchizedekian king/priest to that of Davidic king. See also G. Gunn and J. Neuman, "Psalm 110" in *Dictionary of Premillennial Theology,* ed. Mal Couch (Grand Rapids: Kregel Publications, 1996) 326-329.

[11]F. F. Bruce, *The Acts of the Apostles: The Greek Text With Introduction and Commentary* (Grand Rapids: Eerdmans Publishing Company, 1951) 19.

[12]Bruce, *Acts of the Apostles: The Greek Text* 96.

[13]I suppose that if Jesus had revealed all this to His very Jewish disciples, they would never have gotten very excited about proclaiming the gospel in the first place!

[14]W. Arndt, F. W. Gingrich, F. W. Danker, & W. Bauer, *A Greek-English Lexicon of the New Testament and Other Early Christian Literature* (Chicago: University of Chicago Press, 1979) *poieo* I.1.b.i, page 681.

[15]For example, Joseph Addison Alexander, *The Gospel According to Matthew,* (Grand Rapids: Baker, 1980 [reprint of orig. 1860 ed., Charles Scribner and Co.]) 435.

[16]The poetic reference in 1Chr 16:22 is to the Patriarchs: Abraham, Isaac and Jacob.

[17]*Theological Dictionary of the New Testament.* Vol. 9, edd. G. Kittel, G. W. Bromiley & G. Friedrich. (Grand Rapids: Eerdmans, 1964-c1976) 512.

[18]D. Flusser, *Society and Religion in the Second Temple Period,* edd. Michael Avi-Yonah and Zvi Baras (Jerusalem: Masada Publishing Ltd., 1977) 30.

[19]*Theological Dictionary of the New Testament.* Vol. 9, 521.

[20]Richard N. Longenecker, *The Acts of the Apostles* in "The Expositor's Bible Commentary" Vol. 9 (Grand Rapids: Zondervan Publishing House, 1981) 281.

[21]Longenecker, 281.

[22]The NASB has "in what sense."

[23]Compare the Vulgate, *unde* "from where, whence; from whom, from which." Both Mt 22:45 and Lk 20:44 have the Greek *pos* "how?"

[24]Cf. Arndt, Gingrich, Danker, Bauer, s.v. *pothen*, 2; H. Alford, Alford's Greek Testament, 7th edition (Grand Rapids: Guardian Press, 1874) I, 403.

[25]Darrell Bock, *Progressive Dispensationalism,* (Wheaton: Victor Books, 1993) 176-77.

[26]Bock, *Progressive Dispensationalism,* 177.

[27]W. Arndt, F. W. Gingrich, F. W. Danker, & W. Bauer, *A Greek-English Lexicon of the New Testament and Other Early Christian Literature* (Chicago: University of Chicago Press, 1979) *kai* I.6, page 393.

[28]F. Blass, A. Debrunner, *A Greek Grammar of the New Testament and Other Early Christian Literature*_(Chicago: University of Chicago Press, 1961) §444.3.

[29]F. Blass, A. Debrunner, §444.3.

[30]John Kilgallen in his monograph on Peter's sermon also argues for a strong distinction between the terms "Lord" and "Messiah," John J. Kilgallen, "'With many other words' (Acts 2,40): Theological Assumptions in Peter's Pentecost Speech" *Biblica* 83 (Rome: Pontifical Biblical Institute, 2002), 75-76.

[31]See, e.g., "epexegetical *kai"* in Blass, Debrunner, §444.9, or the ascensive use of *kai* in Dan Wallace, *Greek Grammar Beyond the Basics* (Grand Rapids: Zondervan Publishing House, 1996) 670-671.

[32]For the twofold nature of the NT gospel message, see 1Co 15:3-8, *Death,* vv. 3-4a; *Resurrection,* vv. 4b-8. The death is proved by the burial; the resurrection is proved by the sightings. See also 2Co 5:15; 1Th 4:14; etc.

[33]Darrell L. Bock, "The Reign of the Lord Christ," 49, emphasis his.

[34]Darrell L. Bock, "Evidence From Acts" 194.

[35]The aor. impv. *kathou* is used in both the LXX of Ps 109:1 (= 110:1 Heb. and Eng. texts) and Peter's quotation in Ac 2:34.

[36]Kilgallen, 76.

[37]This second subsection is also resumptive of verses 14-21 and addresses the

question of the tongues phenomenon. For resumptive use of *oun* cf. BAGD s.v. *oun* 2.b.; BDF §451(1). Peter's point is that these gifts are poured out from on high because Jesus has assumed authority as the Melchizedekian King/Priest (Cf. Eph 4:7-10).

Chapter 13 – When God *Restores* the Kingdom to Israel

[1]Mal Couch, gen. ed., *An Introduction to Classical Evangelical Hermeneutics* (Grand Rapids: Kregel, 2000), 64.

[2]Randall Price, *Unholy War* (Eugene, OR: Harvest House, 2001), 151.

[3]David Baron, *Israel in the Plan of God* (Grand Rapids: Kregel, 1983), 283.

[4]John F. Walvoord, *The Millennial Kingdom* (Findlay, OH: Dunham Publishing, 1959), 64.

[5]Ibid.

[6]Ibid., 109.

[7]Kenneth L. Gentry, Jr. *He Shall Have Dominion: A Postmillennial Eschatology* (Tyler, TX: Institute for Christian Economics, 1992), 159.

[8]Gary DeMar, *Last Days Madness: Obsession of the Modern Church* (Powder Springs, GA: American Vision, 1999), 8.

[9]R. C. Sproul, Jr., "Forward" in Seraiah, *End of All Things*, 9.

[10]Tim LaHaye and Thomas Ice, *The End Times Controversy* (Eugene, OR: Harvest House, 2003), 23.

[11]Ibid., 65.

[12]R. C. Sproul, *The Last Days According to Jesus* (Grand Rapids: Baker, 1998), 14-15.

[13]Raphael Patai, *The Messiah Texts* (Detroit, MI: Wayne State University Press, 1979), quoted from.

[14]Michael Avi-Yonah and Zvi Baras, *Society and Religion in the Second Temple Period* (Jerusalem: Massada Publishing, 1977), 171.

[15]J. Dwight Pentecost, *Things to Come* (Grand Rapids: Zondervan, 1964), 481.

[16]Ibid., 482.

[17]Mal Couch, gen. ed., *An Introduction to Classical Evangelical Hermeneutics*, 298-99.

Chapter 15 – The Church is Not Israel

[1]Arnold G. Fruchtenbaum, "Israel and the Church", *Issues in Dispensationalism* (Chicago: Moody, 1994) ed. Willis and Master, 114.

[2]Ronald E. Diprose, *Israel in the Development of Christian Thought* (Rome:

Istituto Biblico Evangelico Italiano, 2000), 3.

[3]Wayne Grudem, *Systematic Theology* (Grand Rapids: Inter-Varsity, 1994), 863.

[4]Louis Berkhof, *Systematic Theology* (London: Banner of Truth Trust, 1941), 570-571.

[5]William Cox, *Amillennialism Today* (Phillipsburg: Presbyterian and Reformed, 1980), 37.

[6]Diprose, 102.

[7]Ibid., 70.

[8]Grudem, 859-863; Berkhof, 571-572.

[9]John F. Walvoord, *Israel in Prophecy*, (Grand Rapids: Zondervan, 1988), 48.

[10]Charles C. Ryrie, *The Basis of the Premillennial Faith,* (New York: Loizeaux Bros., 1958), 53.

[11]Diprose, 71.

[12]If there was an implied condition that Abraham had to leave his land and go to Canaan, then that was clearly fulfilled. We can only speculate what God would have done if Abraham had chosen to stay in Haran or in Ur. We suggest that God still would have fulfilled His covenant though Abraham would have lost out on personal blessing that always comes with obedience.

[13]Charles C. Ryrie, *Basic Theology* (Wheaton: Victor, 1988), 454-455.

[14]S. Lewis Johnson, "Evidences from Romans 9-11," in *A Case for Premillennialism* (Chicago: Moody, 1992), 220.

[15]For a fuller discussion of the Biblical covenants, both their provisions and fulfillment, see my book *Understanding End Times Prophecy* (Chicago: Moody, 1995) as well as Arnold Fruchtenbaum, *Israelology: The Missing Link in Systematic Theology* (Tustin: Ariel Ministries, 1992).

[16]Berkhof, 571.

[17]Cox, 46.

[18]Fruchtenbaum, 118-120.

[19]S. Lewis Johnson, "Paul and the 'Israel of God': An Exegetical and Eschatological Case-Study" in *Essays in Honor of J. Dwight Pentecost* (Chicago: Moody, 1986), 183.

[20]J. Dwight Pentecost, *Things to Come* (Grand Rapids: Dunham, 1964), 88.

[21]Fruchtenbaum, 126-127.

[22]Gerhard Delling, "arche," *Theological Dictionary of the New Testament,* eds. Bromiley and Friedrich, (Grand Rapids: Eerdmans, 1992), 81.

[23]W.E. Vine, *Expository Dictionary of New Testament Words* (London: Oliphants, 1963), 3:97.

[24]Diprose, 70.

[25]Several helpful discussions can be found in S. Lewis Johnson's study of Romans 9-11 in *A Case for Premillennialism* (Chicago: Moody, 1992), and several sections in Arnold Fruchtenbaum's work *Israelology: The Missing Link in Systematic Theology* (Tustin: Ariel Ministries, 1993).

[26]S.L. Johnson, 215.

[27]Berkhof, 572.

[28]Berkhof, 571.

Chapter 16 – The Forgotten Rapture Passages: I Thessalonians 1:9-10 and 5:1-11

[1]Mal Couch, *An Exegesis of the Rapture Passages* (Ft. Worth, TX: Tyndale Seminary).

[2]Mal Couch, gen. ed., *The Fundamentals for the Twenty-First Century* (Grand Rapids: Kregel, 2000), 521-22.

[3]Ibid., 522.

[4]Tim LaHaye, *The Rapture* (Eugene, OR: Harvest House, 2002), 243-44.

[5]Rene' Pache, *The Return of Jesus Christ* (Chicago: Moody, 1955), 134-35.

[6]William E. Blackstone, *Jesus is Coming* (Grand Rapids: Kregel, 1989), 209.

[7]J. F. Strombeck, *First the Rapture* (Grand Rapids: Kregel, 1992), 13.

[8]Paul N. Benware, *Understanding End Times Prophecy* (Chicago: Moody, 1995), 160.

[9]John F. Walvoord, *The Rapture Question* (Grand Rapids: Zondervan, 1979), 33.

[10]Mal Couch, *The Hope of Christ's Return* [Thessalonian commentary] (Chattanooga, TN: AMG, 2001), 57.

[11]Ibid., 58.

[12]Ibid., 59.

[13]Ibid., 60.

[14]Ibid., 128.

[15]J. Dwight Pentecost, *Things to Come* (Findlay, OH: Dunham, 1961), 235.

[16]Couch, *The Hope of Christ's Return*, 143.

Chapter 17 – The Rapture and the Return: Two Aspects of Christ's Coming

[1]John Feinberg. "Arguing for the Rapture: Who Must Prove What and How?" paper presented to the Pre-Trib Research Center; quoted by Thomas Ice, in "Why the Rapture and the Second Coming are Distinct Events," *Pre-Trib Answers to Post-Trib Questions* (Aug.-Sept. 1994), 2.

[2]Millard Erickson, *Christian Theology* (Grand Rapids: Baker Book House,

1985), 1186.

[3]Thomas Ice, "Why the Rapture and Second Coming are Distinct Events," in *Pre-Trib Answers to Post-Trib Questions* (Aug.-Sept. 1994), 2.

[4]Ibid., 3.

[5]Cf. Robert Gundry, *The Church and the Tribulation* (Grand Rapids: Zondervan, 1973), 85-86.

[6]C.F. Hogg and W.E. Vine, *The Epistles to the Thessalonians* (London: Exeter Press, 1929), 144.

[7]Ibid., 242.

[8]George Milligan, *St. Paul's Epistles to the Thessalonians* (Old Tappan, NY: Revell, 1908), vol.2, 96. Cf. also A.T. Robertson, *Word Pictures in the New Testament* (Grand Rapids: Baker, 1931 reprint), vol. IV. 47. He also notes that it refers to the rapture in 2 Thess. 2:1.

[9]Cf. W.S. LaSor, *The Truth About Armageddon* (Grand Rapids: Baker Book House, 1982), 120-134; and G.E. Ladd, *The Blessed Hope* (Grand Rapids: Eerdmans, 1956), 71-104.

[10]These may be found in an expanded version in Edward Hindson, *End Times & the New World Order* (Wheaton: Victor Books, 1991), 164-67.

Chapter 18 – God's Overall Earthly Plan

[1]*The Scofield Reference Bible*, 1917, 5.

[2]Charles Caldwell Ryrie, *Dispensationalism Today* (Chicago: Moody Press, 1979), 31.

[3]Henry Clarence Thiessen, *Lectures in Systematic Theology* (Grand Rapids: Wm. B. Eerdmans Publishing Company, 1951), 464.